In Service of
Emergent India

The "Guerrilla"—of indian wars—

In Service of Emergent India

A CALL TO HONOR

Jaswant Singh

Foreword by Strobe Talbott

INDIANA UNIVERSITY PRESS
Bloomington and Indianapolis

This book is a publication of

Indiana University Press
601 North Morton Street
Bloomington, IN 47404-3797 USA

http://iupress.indiana.edu

Telephone orders   800-842-6796
Fax orders   812-855-7931
Orders by e-mail   iuporder@indiana.edu

An earlier version of this work was published by the author in 2006 in India as *A Call to Honour.*

© 2007 by Jaswant Singh

Manufactured in the United States of America

Library of Congress Cataloging-in-Publication Data

Singh, Jaswant, date
 In service of emergent India : a call to honor / Jaswant Singh ; foreword by Strobe Talbott.
  p. cm.
 Previously published in India as: Call to honour. 2006.
 Includes index.
 ISBN 978-0-253-34936-1 (cloth)
 1. India—Foreign relations—1984– 2. India—Politics and government—1977– I. Singh, Jaswant, Call to honour. II. Title. III. Title: Call to honor.
 DS480.853.S579 2006
 327.540092—dc22
 [B]
                               2007005241

1 2 3 4 5 12 11 10 09 08 07

Book design: Alcorn Publication Design

सो सब तव प्रताप रघुराई ।
नाथ न कछुः मोरि प्रभुताई ।।

तुलसीकृत रामचरित मानस
सुन्दर काण्ड

(A free translation)
All your radiance, only that, no more, Raghurai*
Not mine, no, not mine.

(*Descendant of Raghu)

"רתמא לע רדסח לע דובכ ןת רמשל יכ ונל אל הוהי ונל אל"

"non nobis Domine non nobis sed nomini tuo da gloriam"

Not unto us O LORD, not unto us but unto thy name,
give glory for thy mercy and for thy truth's sake

[Psalm 115:1]

In Him I have put my trust and to Him I turn penitently

Sura Hud Verse 88 (11.88)

Contents

Illustrations follow page 264

Foreword
by Strobe Talbott

This book deserves international attention because of what it tells us about the author's country, his time in its leadership, and the man himself. Jaswant Singh is a remarkable figure in the annals of diplomacy—someone of exceptional intellect, integrity, erudition, breadth of experience, and force of personality.

It is not just a cliché but an important fact of our era that India is "the world's largest democracy." It is on its way to becoming the world's largest country as well, since its population, already over 1.1 billion, will, in the coming decades, surpass that of its neighbor China.

Moreover, as the title of this book asserts, India is indeed "emergent." Not very long ago, it was a big country with big problems and a big chip on its shoulder. Its statist economy was largely closed to the world, and it prided itself on its prominent place in the Nonaligned Movement, an anachronism after the end of the Cold War. India's relationship with the United States was frequently described as one of "estrangement."

That changed in the 1990s, first with the opening of the economy (thanks largely to the reformist policies of the then finance minister, now prime minister Manmohan Singh) and then with the adoption of a more assertive foreign and defense policy. A defining moment came in May of 1998, when India—to the surprise and acute displeasure of the United States and much of the rest of the world—conducted a nuclear weapons test in the desert of Rajasthan, blasting its way into a club from which it had previously been excluded. That club consisted of the five countries that also happened to be permanent members of the United Nations Security Council. India was putting the world on notice that it intended to be not just a regional power but a global power as well.

Jaswant Singh was, at that time, an influential figure in the BJP, the principal party in the National Democratic Alliance, which governed India for six years, from 1998 to 2004. It was during that period that I came to know him. President Bill Clinton and Prime Minister Atal Bihari Vajpayee assigned us the task of engaging in a "dialogue" that was intended to manage our governments' disagreement over India's decision to test while improving the overall relationship. These goals were obviously in some tension with each other.

When we began, Mr. Singh was Mr. Vajpayee's deputy on the powerful Planning Commission and his principal spokesman on foreign policy (the prime minister himself retained the title and portfolio of minister of external affairs). Over a period of two and a half years—during which I was deputy secretary of state and Mr. Singh held (sometimes simultaneously) the portfolios of minister of foreign affairs, finance, and defense— we met fourteen times at ten locations in seven countries on three continents. Those encounters added up to the most intense and prolonged set of exchanges ever between American and Indian officials at a level higher than ambassadors. We were, in effect, sherpas who prepared the way for the breakthrough summit that President Clinton had with Prime Minister Vajpayee in New Delhi in March 2000.

We were less successful in advancing the cause of nuclear nonproliferation. We might have made more progress had it not been for domestic setbacks and pressures in both our countries—an argument I have made in my own account of the dialogue.*

Insofar as our dialogue made a contribution to the U.S.-Indian relationship, it was largely because of Jaswant Singh's ability to advocate and defend his government's position while instilling in me and other American officials a high degree of trust and respect. That brings me to another word in the subtitle of this book: "honor." Even though our dealings were marked by profound and often irreconcilable differences, I found his conduct to be, without exception, honorable. When he told me what he thought he could accomplish or deliver, I believed him. When he explained why something he had thought possible turned out not to be, I believed him. Having been a student of diplomacy throughout my career and a practitioner for eight years, I found him, in this regard, to be a rarity.

I also found him to be someone of unusual intellectual breadth and depth. Disagreeing with him was (as he liked to put it) *not* a disagreeable experience. It was, moreover, often an edifying one for me. I came to understand much that I had not known about Indian history and the lingering effect of British rule; the complexity of Indian society, culture, and religion; the ins and outs of Indian politics; and, crucially, Indians' adamancy about their sovereignty.

Engaging India: Diplomacy, Democracy and the Bomb (Washington, D.C.: Brookings Institution Press, 2004).

Mr. Singh and I spent considerable time talking about Hindutva, a vision of national identity associated with his party. He and other spokesmen for the BJP object when Indian and foreign political observers describe its program as "Hindu nationalist." The concept, they say, is cultural rather than religious, and the term should be understood to embrace Muslims and followers of other faiths. The fact remains, however, that the BJP has included—and not just on its fringes—sectarian zealots who have been implicated in incidents of communal violence. The party evolved from the political wing of the RSS, an organization that rejected root and branch Mohandas Gandhi's concept of nationhood based on diversity as a virtue of Indian society and inclusiveness as a necessity of Indian politics. I listened carefully to Mr. Singh's explanation of what he called the "civilizational" nature of his party's ideology and, as he saw it, his country's sense of its role in the world. I did so not just because of the sophistication of his argument, but because I knew that he had publicly—and with a bluntness that showed real political courage—deplored the RSS-backed and often RSS-instigated practice of tearing down mosques and burning churches. ("I believe," he had said, "that this country cannot be constructed through demolitions.")

Partly because of his outspokenness as an internationalist who believed that globalization could work to India's advantage and as a moderate on domestic policy, he was regarded with some suspicion by the more extreme elements associated with his party. I bore this fact in mind when he had difficulty in Parliament, in the council of the governing alliance, and in the arena of public opinion.

Another quality manifest in this book is Mr. Singh's facility with words. The reader will miss the full effect of his personal style, but there is a hint of it in the photographs that accompany the text. He carries himself like the soldier he once was. His ramrod posture gives him an air of severity. He speaks in a sonorous baritone and measured, often rather complex sentences. Yet what many commentators and interlocutors, myself included, have often called Mr. Singh's "elegance" still comes through on the printed page.

So do his pride and patriotism, not just as an Indian but as a Rajput. Readers will fully understand what that word means when they finish this book.

Mr. Singh was born in the desert village of Jasol in Rajasthan, about 100 miles southwest of Pokhran, where the underground explosion of a thermonuclear device made the earth shake in 1998. The early autobiographical sections remind me of "magical realism," only in nonfiction form.

I mean this comment as high praise. Mr. Singh's recollections of growing up in Rajasthan re-create the spirit of wonder that he felt as a child and that infuses the rich culture of the region. Coming from someone else, his language might sometimes border on grandiloquence ("I sensed that I was being chiseled into a certain shape by that great Stonemason above, daily being honed"). But bearing, as it does, the imprint of his panache and originality of mind, it has instead the ring of eloquence and authenticity.

I thought that I knew him reasonably well, but I felt that I knew him—and India—better after reading this book. I learned much, for example, from his recollection of traditional beliefs in the relationship between the calendar and nature, his explanation of the rituals of village and barracks life and why they have such meaning to those who follow them. He tells these and other stories with a combination of wry humor, affection, and irony, with an eye for the telling small touches (such as the privy behind the family home for his grandmother's use only). His treatment of Partition—an often-told tale, but one that cannot be told too often, given its importance in the history of the subcontinent and its enduring lesson for those contemplating partition as a solution to other countries' problems—is especially powerful.

One of the most moving chapters in this book is Mr. Singh's description of his role in ending the hijacking of an Indian civilian jetliner in Afghanistan in December 1999. He was much criticized at the time—unfairly so, in my view. I remember from my dealings with him the anguish he felt in making the hard choice of doing a deal with terrorists to save innocents. That anguish is still with him, and it comes through in these pages. What is new and important for an American audience is his description of how this hijacking appears to have been a dress rehearsal for the attacks on the United States of September 11, 2001.

The chapters on Mr. Singh's public life provide, in addition to an authoritative perspective on a number of important events, a consistently high quality of insight into the worldview, mindset, strategic calculations, and domestic-political backdrop of Indian policymaking and diplomacy. These aspects of the book will make it all the more valuable to students and teachers of international relations in general and to those who want better to understand a crucial period in—that word again—India's *emergence* as a more activist and self-confident player on the world stage.

Like any such work, Mr. Singh's book is a chapter in an ongoing story. The government of which he was an important and constructive part, like the American administration that I worked for, passed into history. Mr. Vajpayee's and Mr. Clinton's successors, Manmohan Singh and George W. Bush, solidified the U.S.-Indian relationship with an agreement granting India virtually all the rights of full membership in the nuclear club while leaving unanswered the question of what these two great, no-longer-estranged democracies were going to do together to avert the danger of a new wave of nuclear proliferation. In that sense, as in others, the dialogue Mr. Singh and I conducted represents unfinished business. Or, to put the point more optimistically, what we started nine years ago is a work in progress, awaiting statesmanship in the future that I can only hope, on the Indian side, will approximate the standard set by Jaswant Singh.

Preface: Prelude to Honor

Time and distance, we are told, add perspective to our vision. Writing about events soon after their occurrence doubtless adds the flavor of immediacy to description, but often at the cost of objectivity. There is an obverse to this: if such writing is delayed beyond a certain point, then a haze descends, memory becomes obscured, recollection turns opaque, and the account loses definition. Where exactly does this "balancing point" lie? That determination is important, for if judged correctly, the writing pulsates with the feel of the immediate; if delayed, it turns into a plod. But there are no universal criteria; it is an entirely subjective variable. I have judged that "balancing point" as well as I could in sharing these thoughts: not entirely as a memoir, and not as an autobiography, either. This book is both, and it is an analysis, too. In that sense—and if I may be permitted to say so myself—*In Service of Emergent India* is a distinctive genre.

In May 2004, the BJP-led National Democratic Alliance government narrowly lost the Indian parliamentary election. Consequently, we demitted office after having held it for six years. Those years were, in all respects and by all accounts, extraordinarily challenging. Domestically, they were path-breaking: we demonstrated an effective and well-coordinated functioning of the first successful coalition government in Delhi. Internationally, India's foreign policy was then steered through extremely treacherous and uncharted waters. We proved ourselves equal to the aftermath of the Pokhran nuclear tests of May 1998. This was a period of transition, of the transformation of India's external policies, a reordering of its priorities, a reorientation of its vision, and above all a reassertion of India's global centrality. It was a testing period, a demanding period, a greatly exhilarating period. This was the period that sounded the call—a call that had to be honored.

Several foundations were laid in the NDA years. The path we charted then continues to steer the defense, foreign, and economic policies of the successor government. In terms of national well-being, it was no mean achievement to reach the GDP growth figures that were attained—and this in spite of a number of adverse factors: one devastating earthquake (2001); two catastrophic cyclones (1999 and 2000); the worst drought in thirty years (2002–2003); Gulf War II and an oil crisis (2003); one conflict (Kargil, 1999) and one standoff (2001–2002); continual cross-border terrorist actions (e.g., Parliament, Delhi—2001; and Kaluchak Camp—May 2002); and above all, the U.S.-led sanctions after our nuclear tests (1998). Despite all these, for the NDA government to achieve economic progress, reform, judicious liberalization, and the transformation of India's infrastructure (telecom, infotech, village roads, expansion of highways); to contain inflation; to restore the foreign exchange reserves to health (to more than $125 billion); and to then hand over the national economy to a successor government with GDP growth at 8.4 percent was an accomplishment that deserves recounting. Almost as an afterthought, does anybody now remember the Y2K scare? The world was supposed to come to a halt at midnight on December 31, 1999. All those "worst-case scenarios" now lie forgotten; for those of us in the NDA government, they were all in a day's work.

Is this what *In Service of Emergent India* is about? Is the book a kind of hagiography of that period from 1998 to 2004? No, it is not. Neither is it simply a tabulated narration of events. I share my experiences, but of only a part of my journey through that period, for a full account would fill many volumes. In these days of attention spans no longer than a web page, no one has time for that. Besides, it is impossible to narrate the entirety of the overwhelming avalanche of events that transformed India's external image, politically and economically, as well as—and above all—its self-image. The cautious, tentative India of March 1998 had by May 2004 become a self-confident, resurgent India. Its voice was being heard once again. This was the call, a call that had to be answered, especially in that charged atmosphere of May 1998. And answer we did. The team was led by the sagacious, discerning, imperturbable, and severely open-minded and humane Atal Behari Vajpayee, "Atalji" to us all. He headed a government democratic to the core: as no other government, no cabinet, had been in independent India's annals.

Because I am the author of this book, and because my principal responsibilities in the NDA government period spanned the "D, E, and F of the governance of India"—the ministries of Defence, External Affairs, and Finance, in itself a true honor—my account will naturally be heavily weighted in favor of foreign policy and of the challenges posed to our security. And though economic security is the very first security, the bulwark, really, of all our policy platforms, it does not find the same space in this narrative. Why? Because that is so much more difficult to recount, and because narrative accounts of economic policy management have far less "sex appeal" for the reader. Bimal Jalan, governor of the Reserve Bank of India for many of those years and now a colleague in Parliament, has ceaselessly reminded me, wisely and accurately, that without "healthy balances in the tiller of the RBI's reserves," and in the absence of the innate resilience of India's entrepreneurial, financial, and commercial genius, where would we have been then? For that matter, where would we be today?

For the management of India's foreign policy in that period, the central challenge was transformation, addressing the call of the times; that was the "call to honor." How could we turn it down? Foreign policy is not just the sum of crisis-management techniques—although, clearly, multiple and ever-mounting challenges are almost always the signposts of such management. This narrative is in part an account of that journey, that seemingly endless journey in which I served as a caravaneer for some years. Ours was a process of rerouting—from the unrealistic idealism of a past that was long gone to the needed realism of a new, demanding, and impatient age; between the fixities of handed-down wisdom and the needed dualism of our times. This call had to be honored.

We were met by that extremely complex conundrum of our times: the paradox of the WMD, the "weapon of mass destruction." (What an ominous and grim nomenclature.) It confronted us with a singular challenge: to break this nuclear apartheid. How could we assert equal and legitimate security for all, as a given verity, a birthright of all nation-states, and yet do so in belief, in conduct, and in a voice of reassuring moderation? How could we reduce the centrality, the currency, and the symbolism of such weapons even while acquiring them ourselves? We needed to expose the long-running double standards of the global nuclear regime, and yet, in the process, to join it, to share those privileges, and thus to become partners in a double standard—but to still be able to stand apart from it all. How? This was, and remains, a conceptual and philosophical challenge of great profundity; only India could and can address it. This I believed in, and still do—implicitly. And thus this, too, was a call that had to be honored.

It is in all of these things that the genesis of *In Service of Emergent India* lies, but this is not yet all. For this book is—at least in part, and without being an autobiography or a subjective memoir or a personal and personalized history of contemporary India or merely a recollection of my six years in office—also an analysis of those times, of those multiple challenges and the origins of the challenges. Why did India face them? Why then, and not earlier or later? Perhaps it was because we in the NDA broke the mold: we stood for and represented *change*. Beginning with the Pokhran nuclear tests, my country, the NDA government, and I personally found ourselves navigating decidedly stormy diplomatic seas—explaining the logic of India's nuclear program to an initially suspicious world, and ultimately bringing that world as close to India's view as circumstances permitted. Assessing the challenges and using the opportunities thrown up at us by the most monstrous acts of terrorism in those years—whether in New York or in New Delhi—and steering India's external relationship away from those perilous shoals of the Cold War, into the vast and overwhelming ocean that is the twenty-first century: that really was our task. That was, and remains, a call to honor: how could it not be answered?

At the simplest level, this book is an account of how I went about my job—my actions and responses, my conversations and negotiations with a host of interlocutors, my thoughts and feelings as those momentous events unfolded, as they unwrapped themselves. Yet, to understand what I did and why, it is necessary to understand the influences that shaped me, that contributed to my becoming, at least in part, what I am. These were the sources of my conduct—instinctual, individual, institutional, and, in the ultimate reckoning, national. My early life and my country's recent history are not mere background noise here; they have been the clarion call since I first embarked upon my ministerial journey. That truly was a call to honor.

I cannot end without a word about the subtitle of the book. Discerning readers will no doubt recognize it as an adaptation of the title of a volume of Charles de Gaulle's memoirs. Other than being a perfectly apposite term, *A Call to Honor* is also a silent tribute to one of my heroes. As a military man with a strong sense of national duty, de Gaulle moved almost naturally into public life. I like to believe that there are similarities between us that help me to identify with him. This title is, in that sense, an homage to his immortality.

Everything that I write here is obviously my own responsibility, and mine alone; how could it be anyone else's? After all, these are *my* views. Not everything that I write will be agreed with, but that is inevitable. This book is not a party document—I have written it as an individual author. Thus I alone am accountable, no one else, for the views, opinions, and analyses expressed here. For mistakes and errors of judgment, expression, or otherwise, too, I am solely responsible.

Acknowledgments

In Service of Emergent India: A Call to Honor could not have been written without the generous assistance of many friends, well-wishers, and colleagues in India, the UK, and the U.S. It is simply not practical to list all.

To Ayesha Jalal, Sunil Khilnani, and Roderick MacFarquhar, I extend my gratitude for the readiness and the generosity with which they let me quote from their works.

To Matthew Rudolph, thank you for so willingly undertaking a review of the book and offering so many valuable suggestions.

I also remain very grateful to Lloyd and Susanne Rudolph for selflessly giving so much of their time in guiding me through the many intricacies of publishing a book in the U.S.

To Mr. R. K. Laxman, I remain deeply indebted for his great generosity in gifting me with the originals of his cartoons, then so warmly inscribing them, and also for consenting to my using some of them in this book.

It was Professor Sumit Ganguly of Indiana University who first proposed, then with conviction and persistence continued to reason, that I must offer the script of *In Service of Emergent India: A Call to Honor* to Indiana University Press (IUP)—to them alone and to no one else. It is to him, therefore, that I owe this debt, and I acknowledge it fully and with gratitude.

Thereafter, the staff at IUP took this book in hand and expertly completed their assessments. Without them, and their professional competence, this book would not be in the global market today.

My gratitude to Rebecca Tolen, who with calm and composed efficiency, patience, and attention saw the book through a variety of IUP requirements. It is to her persistence that I attribute the present cover, too.

I owe a special thanks to Pamela Rude for designing the book so imaginatively and effectively.

My gratitude, above all, to Jane Lyle, who with rare dedication, professionalism, and sympathy painstakingly copy-edited my manuscript in great detail, correcting, suggesting, "Americanizing" it for a U.S. audience, and she did all this repeatedly, until now, when the book finally emerges as *In Service of Emergent India: A Call to Honor.*

Thank you all at Indiana University Press.

My team labored hard. They put up with the many eccentricities of my working style, the uncivil hours that I keep, and they tolerated my unending and impatient demands for corrections, revisions, alterations, and those endless repeats of the script. The team was ably strung together by Ashwini Channan and his principal aides; Natarajan Swaminathan, Anjan Bhowmick (secretarial and stenographic assistance), and Vikas Thotada (technical support) gave him admirable support. Without them, this book would not be where it is today. Raghvendra Singh went through the manuscript on several occasions, provided valuable suggestions, labored in preparing the index, and helped in refining the notes.

To Lord Chris Patten of Barnes and Sir Vidya Naipaul, my lasting gratitude for their generous and greatly encouraging endorsement of this book.

It is not possible to adequately express my sense of gratitude to Strobe Talbott. I unhesitatingly acknowledge the great debt that I owe him. He and I set off in search of what we called "a way to the village"—the achievement of good relations between our two countries, the U.S. and India. With great understanding, patience, courtesy, and transparent integrity, he addressed this responsibility. We started the journey as the respective interlocutors of our two nations, then engaged in great contention. My salutations to Strobe that he converted that contention into cooperation. And he further indebts me by so generously writing the foreword to this edition. Thank you, Strobe.

Illustration Credits

Except as noted below, all illustrations are from the personal collection of Jaswant Singh. Grateful acknowledgment is made to the following for permission to reprint images:

Press Information Bureau, Government of India (figures 9, 10)
Army Headquarters, Indian Army (figures 14–25)
Times of India and R. K. Laxman (figures 45–47)
Hindustan Times (figure 48)
India Today (figure 49)

Abbreviations

ASEAN	Association of South East Asian Nations
BJP	Bharatiya Janata Party
CTBT	Comprehensive Test Ban Treaty
DGMO	Director General of Military Operations
FMCT	Fissile Material Cut-off Treaty
G-8	Group of Eight
ISI	Inter-Services Intelligence
MEA	Ministry of External Affairs
MP	Member of Parliament
NDA	National Democratic Alliance
NEFA	North East Frontier Agency
NPT	Nuclear Non-Proliferation Treaty
P-5	Permanent 5
SAARC	South Asian Association for Regional Cooperation
WMD	Weapons of Mass Destruction

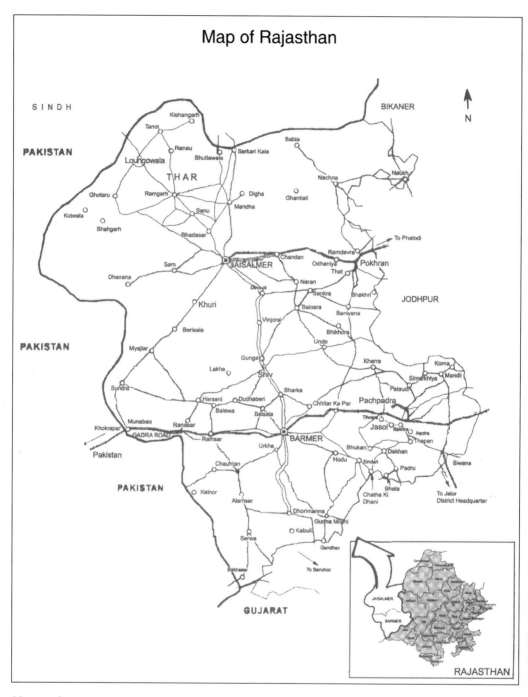

Map of Rajasthan

N

SINDH

PAKISTAN

BIKANER

Kishangarh

Tanot

Babla

Ranau

Loungowala

Bhuttewala

Sarkari Kala

Nachna

Naukh

THAR

Ghotaru

Ramgarh

Digha

Ghantiali

Kotwala

Sanu

Mandha

Shahgarh

Bhadasar

To Phalodi

Sam

Chandan

Ramdevra

JAISALMER

Odhaniya

Pokhran

That

Dhanana

Neran

Deval

JODHPUR

Khuri

Sankra

Bhakhri

Baiosra

Baniyana

Berisala

Vinjorai

Bhikhora

Myajlar

Undo

Gunga

Kharra

Korna

Lakha

Simarkhiya

Mandli

Shiv

Pataudi

Sundra

Bharka

Harsani

Dudhaberi

Pachpadra

Balewa

Chhitar Ka Par

Khokrapar

Munabao

Baisala

Tilwara

Jasol

Ransar

Balotra

Asotra

GADRA ROAD

Ramsar

BARMER

Bhukan

Thapan

Pakistan

Urkha

Dakhan

Chauhtan

Hodu

Sindari

Padru

Siwana

PAKISTAN

Kelnor

Bhata

Alamsar

Chatha Ki
Dhani

To Jalor
District Headquarter

Dhorimanna

Serwa

Gudha Malani

Kabuli

Bakhasar

Gandhav

To Sanchor

GUJARAT

JAISALMER

BARMER

RAJASTHAN

Not to scale.

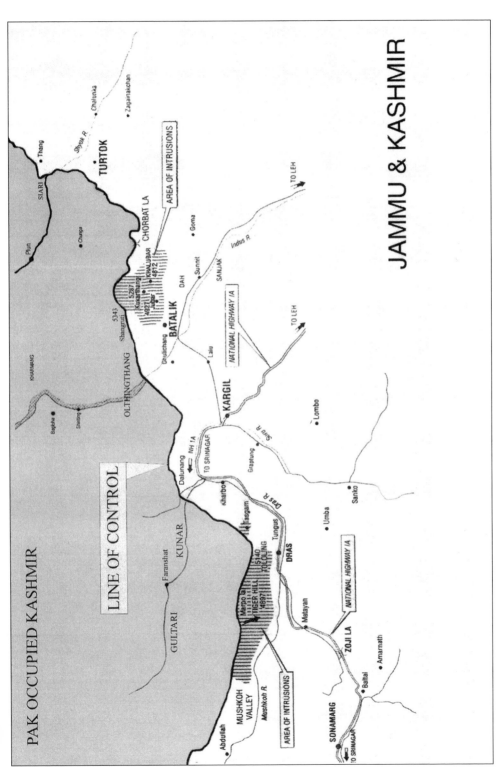

Line of Control between Pak-Occupied Kashmir and Jammu. Not to scale.

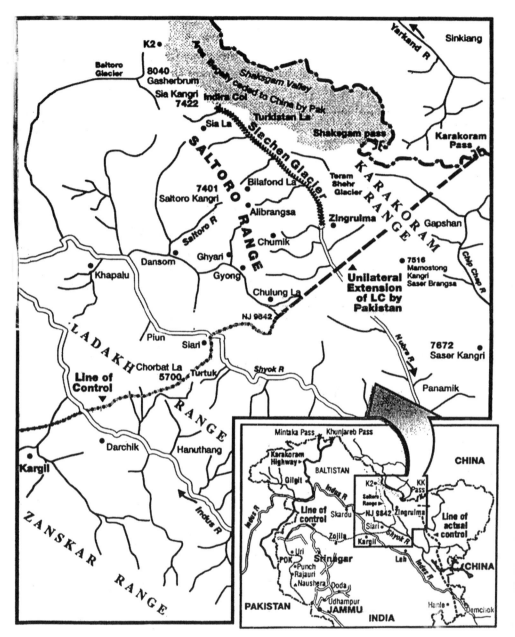

Siachen Glacier and Saltoro Range. Not to scale.

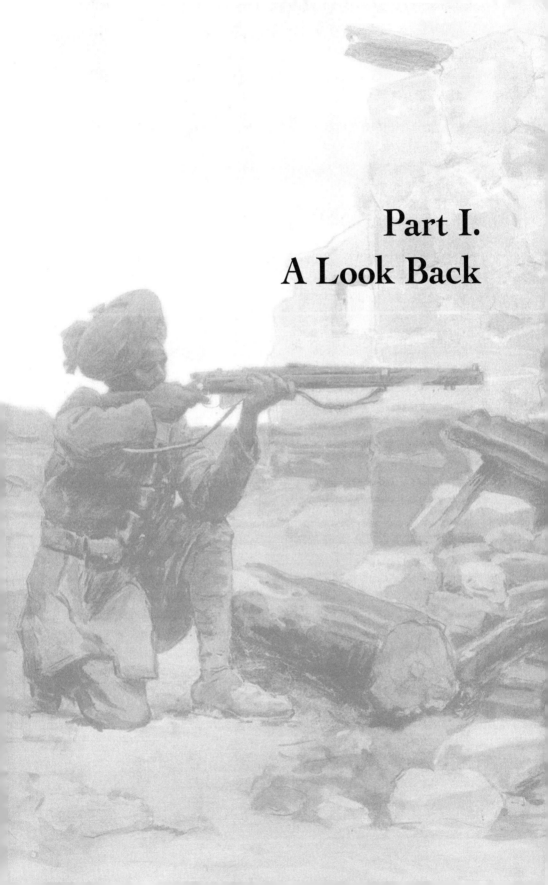

Part I.
A Look Back

1

Memories of a Sunlit Land

When I was stuck at the very start by that immobilizing query—where do I begin?—I found greatly reassuring a reference to Pascal's admission that he too faced similar difficulties. I sought shelter then in memory, letting it wander free. But is it merely an occasional glimpse of the past, this memory? Or is it more a spatial re-creation of past events that reappear randomly but in all their vivid, unfragmented entirety? Memory, this depthless pool into which life keeps pouring endlessly, until the stream itself dries up—is this "drying up" in death an event of such ultimate finality that from this "black hole," this "shunya," this limitless void of "non-being," there is no returning, ever? And if in recollecting past events we travel back in time, why then can we not go forward, too?

I often reflected thus upon life and death and the universe, perhaps hearing echoes of some earlier preconscious as I slept in the open, next to my mother. I did not think in exactly those words—of course not—but I know that even infants think, that thought precedes language; indeed, thought is the modulator of language, its employer. On some clear nights, the starlit sky would descend until it was almost close enough to touch, and so densely packed with stars as I have not again seen. "Am I but a speck in this great dome of the firmament?" I would wonder. Lying awake, looking skyward, as my mother breathed softly and gently in sleep, I watched the slow pirouette of the stars, as the reassuringly constant "Saptarishi" carried their celestial hoe across the heavens.[1] To till which field of creation? Why is only the Pole Star fixed, and not the others? Did these questions arise then, or are they today's embroidery on yesterday's memory? A bit of both, perhaps; the language is today's, the memory certainly yesterday's.

I was born in 1938, in Jasol, a village that lies directly west of and more than 100 kilometers from present-day Jodhpur. It is the principal village of a large tract known by the traditional name of Mallani, now also called

---

1. The Saptarishi are the seven brightest stars in the constellation Ursa Major ("the Great Bear"); in North America they are collectively known as the Big Dipper.

Barmer District. India's westernmost district, it adjoins Sindh in Pakistan. My paternal grandfather, Zorawar Singhji, was the Rawal Sahib of Jasol.[2] He is succinctly, even if somewhat colorlessly, described in the district gazetteers of that period in this fashion: "Rawal Zorawar Singhjee of Jasol, Marwar, was born in Samvat 1938.[3] He is the head of the Mallani Jagirdars and represents the senior line of the Rathores. In the words of Major C. K. M. Walter, Resident of Jodhpur state, 'Mallani justly claims the cradle of the Rathore Race in the West.'" Rawal, as a title, is older than other titles in India and is not limited to the feudal establishment alone. On visiting Jasol, some friends of the Maharajah of Jodhpur from his Oxford days inquired of my uncle, Rawal Amar Singhji, who had by then succeeded and inherited the title, as to what Rawal meant. He reflected for a bit, being of an extremely judicial mind, and replied with characteristic succinctness: "It is partly regal, partly ecclesiastical." And that is what the title is, for it is used only in parts of West Rajasthan as a hereditary title, denoting the heads of certain large estates, some of which are larger than princely states in the rest of India. In South India it is used to denote the heads of "maths" in large temples.[4]

Rawal Zorawar Singh was the head of the Mallani Jagirdars, there being only four others, all cadet branches. Jasol actually covered the entire stretch of desert lying between Sindh and Kutch; it was not a dependency of the state of Jodhpur. On the contrary, Jasol is the home of the senior branch of the ancient and valiant warrior clan known as the Rathores, for it was the younger brother who (as is still the custom), receiving a very small inheritance, branched off and created or carved out his own domain. Thus was created Jodhpur, and in turn Bikaner, and so on, so many others: what was one later became several.

The second but equally integral part of my identity is Khuri, a village some distance away from Jaisalmer, which was then an independent state, adjoining Sindh, which was in British India, and Bhawalpur, which is now part of Pakistan. Back then, Jaisalmer had no rail, road, or any other connections with the rest of the world. The ruler at the time frowned upon all such conveniences as "ruinous modernity." Khuri is my maternal home, my mother's village. Her father, my maternal grandfather, was Thakur

2. The suffix "-ji" (also spelled "-jee") is added to names to denote respect.
3. That was his birth year according to the Vikram Samvat calendar. The Gregorian equivalent is 1881. The method for converting exact dates between the two calendars is complex; the difference is a bit more than fifty-seven years.
4. "Maths" means roughly "Hindu monastery." The monks are religious, but it is not entirely accurate to describe them as living in a monastery.

Mool Singhji. This village lies about fifty kilometers west of Jaisalmer, and of course had no access road.

In Jasol, we lived in the "House." And here I mean more than just a dwelling, a structure; our House encompassed our family line, our family name. It had been built by time, not by any one person. It was a construct of episodes, for it had grown with events, absorbing them as it evolved. But this continual evolution had a central identity, though not any central architectural design, and around that central identity various sections had been added to the House. Some that were of earlier vintage grew tired and were hardly lived in; some that had been neglected felt abandoned and over time simply collapsed. The House, by its sheer continuity, began to epitomize the authority of age and ancientness. In that lay the essence of its identity, its acceptance by all. Yet it never got fully built, for the House is accompanied by a belief: that "the sound of a stonemason's hammer and chisel must always be heard in the House." In reality, what that counsel meant was: "Keep building, keep moving, keep growing—always." As my grandfather, in any case, had also always advised, "If an animal doesn't move, how will it graze?"

What was transferred to us, even as fledglings, was this sense of the prestige and standing of the House when we arrived, as we grew up in its shadow, and when we moved out to get on with our lives—without, however, ever bidding goodbye to the House. For it had become a part of us, our first identity, permanently urging: "Keep moving, keep building." And wherever we went, one single injunction accompanied us, as a task and a responsibility: "It is the name of this House—remember!"

No other detailed code, and no elaborate do's or don'ts, accompanied that injunction, for it had said it all. The task, the code, and the path to be taken were clear; if thereafter one did not instinctively grasp the essence, then it could not be taught anyway. We filled in the details individually, to meet a contingency, a responsibility, or a challenge that this stream of life always brought forth. Through all this, those early injunctive words always echoed: "Honor, Courage, Loyalty, Faith." Very hesitantly do I even write these now, for in today's cynical world, they sound contrived. Our world now mocks such notions, and yet it is this code that once, not so long ago, was the standard. The wealth of our name was the sum total of our wealth, and if, heaven forbid, we ever lost that, then we lost "izzat": respect, regard, honor, reputation. And what is left after izzat is gone?

But I have to come to specifics, not dwell on these horary messages. It was in this House in Jasol that I was born. According to the Gregorian calendar, the year of my birth was 1938. At home, however, at the direction of my grandfather, the year was recorded by the family pundit and astrologer—as all records and activities were then—in the calendar that is our standard, the Vikram Samvat. I know this because the subsequent conversion of that date to the Gregorian equivalent, for filling out various forms, certificates, entrance to school, and so on, required a "modernization" of sorts. That "janam kundli" (birth chart) became a reference point. The manuscript—an attractively calligraphed scroll containing diagrams, calculations, and determinations that I found totally incomprehensible—was rolled into a tube, then tied with auspicious Moli thread, and left in the care of my mother. It was taken out annually, and after due ritual and observances, the learned man known as a punditji would read the "varsh-phal," that year's predictions. But all of that I learned much later. This fragment of memory surfaced even as I wrote, not in any sequence of events, but more like a collage, clamoring to exit from that closet of the past to reemerge as memory.

From that period of my life, I have no memory of my father; nothing comes back at all. For one thing, in accordance with convention and etiquette, fathers never acknowledged the presence of their sons in public. Daughters, perhaps—but sons? That was forbidden. It was an unforgivable breach for a father to publicly display affection, tenderness, caring, or any other such feeling toward a male child; he would be seen as rearing a weakling. For another thing, my father was a soldier. He carried the commission of the Jodhpur State Forces and served in the Jodhpur Lancers. War was imminent—so I understood many years later—and Father went, I was informed, first to Basra in Iraq, and subsequently to other theaters of the Second World War. The first time I met him, having been told by my mother in advance to expect him, was when he returned to the village—around 1946, I think. But he had to leave again very soon thereafter.

In consequence, my paternal and maternal grandfathers brought me up—with great but undemonstrative love and care. It was they who taught me speech and deportment; about horses and camels and animals and birds of the desert, migratory and resident; about guns and rifles and swords; about the meaning of duty, task, responsibility, and appropriate conduct; about our land and history; and about the sky and the wind and the signals that nature is always sending. My grandfathers belonged to a different century altogether; they did not grasp what was suddenly happening in the twentieth. After all, their world had always had a certain completeness, a self-assured certitude. That was all disappearing now, in front of their very eyes, with bewildering speed. For the first time in their lives, they were unable to influence events, let alone alter them. So they imparted all that they had inherited, all that they had learned while grow-ing up in the previous century, to the three of us—my two cousins and I, the youngest. It was this trio who lived and grew up in the village. But I had a bonus: I had a maternal grandfather who had decided that I must fully imbibe the code of the desert.

The House I was born and grew up in gave the appearance of being glued to the side of a hill, about halfway up the slope, overlooking the village sprawled haphazardly below. The nearest railway station is some distance away. Between the village and the railway station is a river, Luni by name. The Luni is not a perennially flowing river, so its dry, sandy bed lies there quietly most of the time. When it does decide to flow—which may not be every monsoon, and may not happen during the full four months of the rainy season—it is an eccentric, unpredictable, and self-willed thing, not possessed of much charm. Collecting the overflow of several nullahs and desert streams from its catchment area, the Luni then meanders through the desert, emptying out in the Rann of Kutch. The Hindi word "luni" means "salt-bitter," so the river's name is entirely appropriate; it does not contain saltwater when it flows, but the region's subsoil water is so bitter that not even camels will drink from it.

Although I was born in Jasol, I live now in a tiny hamlet nearby. This hamlet, little more than a cluster of huts, was established after we left the House, in accordance with the unyielding dictates of primogeniture, which still governed inheritance back then. I spent my years from infancy to childhood in Jasol, and thereafter in the hamlet, spending half of the year in my "nanihal," my mother's home village of Khuri. Khuri was a dream desert village then, a fair distance away from Jaisalmer, toward Sindh. In Khuri, I lived with my maternal grandfather.

Khuri was everything that people find picturesque in a desert village—towering sand dunes; thatched huts with unmatched shades of ocher and unique yellows adorning their walls; camels and color; arrestingly beau-tiful women and stalwart men; and haunting desert music. But it was also where searing heat of unimaginable ferocity visited us every year, as did great, darkly menacing sandstorms that blanked out the sun, with the wind howling in vengeful anger. Why do I say that it "was" rather than "is" a dream village? Because of the development that brought a road and later a railway station to Jaisalmer. Admittedly that is some distance away from Khuri, but now there is even a seasonal airport adjacent to Jaisalmer.

In Jasol, the section of the House where I was born and lived the early years of my life has now collapsed. Many years after I left, I tried to learn which room I was born in. I was shown an airless room in one corner of the zenana, the separate women's quarters where the village midwife had attended to my mother. Eventually, this part of the House must simply have given up; it was, after all, the oldest part of the zenana, once my grandmother's "zenani-deodhi"—her personal domain. This entire wing of the zenana was enclosed by a high wall, more for privacy than protection, for none dared enter there uninvited. This area was strictly for women and children; only some of the male servants had entry.

At the entrance to this old wing were a few steps, then a doorway of exquisitely carved sandstone, with two ancient brass-studded wooden doors that creaked and groaned when moved, as if in agonizing pain. Inevitably, those doors became the objects of play and torture for all the children in the zenana—and their numbers, God be praised, abounded. The children would attempt to swing the doors, which would groan complainingly in response, evoking shouts from the courtyard inside asking them not to— but when (and where?) have children ever obeyed instantly? Persistence was rewarded with a cuff or two, followed by some howling and some cry- ing—but after a while, it was "torture the doors" again!

Just inside was a kind of waiting area—a covered verandah with a privy in one corner, which was for my grandmother's use only. Then there was another arched doorway, through which you entered the zenana proper. A large courtyard was open to the skies, full of light and air, enclosed by a row of open kitchens to one side, and some pantries and rooms opposite. (Alas! I never did go inside.) Directly opposite the entrance was a large room, frescoed with wall paintings, and some more strong rooms inside. This was my grandmother's preserve. I was among the very few allowed in there, at any time of the day or night.

On one side of this courtyard there was a stone staircase with no rail- ings. It led to the roof, around which ran a low wall and then a covered verandah, and beyond that was a large, open room without doors and then another room with doors, a privy nearby—and a balcony, again with exquisite sandstone carving. This balcony opened out to a corner of the village, and then to the desert that lay beyond—an unimpeded view all the way to the horizon. These were my mother's apartments, the most beautiful part of the House. My father was away most of the time, and in any event men were not to be in the zenana during the daylight hours; their place was in the "mardana"—the male section. Most of the year we slept on the roof; and when cold weather came, we moved to the room with the balcony. All this has left me with an indelible sense of space, an enduring need to live in openness, but also an ease and comfort in being by myself, on my own. My mother, her maids, and I were the only occupants of this space; but when the House was full to capacity, so too was the zenana.

We lived with the rhythms of nature, our routines directed by the demands of sunrise and sunset, the seasons with their various changes (and we have eight seasons), and the changing hues of weather. I do not remember that our daily routines were ever driven by watches and clocks. The eldest of my three cousins was married when I was about five; he brought a bashful young wife back with him who instantly adopted me, more to assuage her own homesickness, I think. Among the items in her dowry was an antique wall clock. It came as a novelty, really, and when hung—it is still there—it became an object of curiosity. Much later, it was from that ancient piece that I first learned how to tell time.

Time we measured differently, for we had altogether a different yardstick. Our calendar (the "Panchang," literally "five limbs") informed us of the months; nature divided the year in accordance with the movement of the sun. Seasons, in consequence, were born of the "dakshinardh" (the winter equinox) and the "uttarardh" (the summer equinox), those great oscillations, south or north, of the earth. Days lengthened or shortened; summer heralded the arrival of searing heat and burning winds, and in their wake came the majesty of the monsoon, however sparse and for however short a time it was with us. Then the earth cooled, and all of nature seemed to slow down. Most bewilderingly, it simultaneously went into a frenzy of reproduction. It first absorbed all those great downpours, then sprouted from within all the myriad seeds of life that had lain dormant. The desert literally bloomed overnight, turning lush green in a very short time. With the abundant grazing, all the cattle, the cows and the calves, the bullocks and the bulls (though curiously, I do not remember any buffalo in the village, or even nearby), took on a satiated look. With bulging bellies came long, ruminant afternoons of contentment; all nature then multiplied. The month of "Ashwin" ("Asoj" in our dialect) brought the first hint of change. From high in the sky would float echoes of the first calls of the migratory demoiselle cranes, and just a few days later the honks of the grey lag or the bar-head geese, their fascinating arrowhead flights and altering formations presaging the arrival of winter: of crackling cold, plentiful game, sand and imperial grouse, male camels in rut frothing lustfully at the mouth and becoming uncontrollable out of frustration; bareback rides on a pony assigned to me in the sandy bed of the Luni, learning to fall, to get up, to fall again, and to get back up and once more vault onto the back of my dear, dear childhood friend, the dun pony. "Sit up, sit up, sit front, sit forward on your 'langot' [crotch], not on your buttocks like a sack of flour" were among my earliest lessons in horsemanship—all from a wonderful natural horseman whom my grandfather had assigned to the job. How astonishing that in today's classifications, he would be termed as belonging to a scheduled tribe! With us, however, he was part of the family. For us—in fact, for most others of my age in the village—he was "Bhaitloji Ba": the first seven letters imperfectly spell his name in English, "ji" is the suffix of respect, and "Ba" is used for father or an elder of a father's status. He played the drums as no one else could; slinging the large drum called a dhol up around his neck and cocking his turbaned head at a rakish angle, he would play with no other accompaniment, but with such abandon that the maids could not resist swaying to the beat, involuntarily, irresistibly.

He was my first riding instructor. Entirely innocent of letters, or of any acquired theory about "forward seat," he had no sense of anything mechanical; he had never even sat in a railway train. But every day he took a stallion, bareback and on a watering snaffle, with three or four mares in tow on their stall ropes, to the village well for watering—all so tame when he handled them.

I remember, too, the first time I was sent by my grandfather down the hill to the "bagur," the all-purpose "grass and animal depot" where hay, fodder, and grain were stored, where cattle were herded in the evening, and where horses stood tethered in their stalls. In this spacious animal yard, I watched as a goat was killed for that day's meat. When I returned, my grandfather inquired of my escort whether I had cried, and asked the same of me. I did not grasp why at the time; only later, much later, did I realize that he was getting me accustomed to the sight of blood. He was really interested in whether that had upset me.

I cannot now recollect the order in which the sounds of early morning announced the arrival of a new day. It might have started with the noise of sweeping and cleaning. Or of yogurt being churned in giant clay pots, the rhythm of it almost a lullaby in that drowsy half-light of early dawn. The churning had to be done in the cool of dawn or the butter would not set.

The pounding of spices in a mortar was also heard, for spices had to be fresh, so they were crushed, ground, and prepared daily. Besides, each dish needed an altogether different combination of spices, their prickly fragrance mingling with the incense of dawn prayers. Wheat for flour was ground in the afternoons; the stone grinders were rotated by hand, producing yet again a soporific, siesta sound. The camels carrying water would arrive before daybreak, and an announcement was made by the carrier from just outside the zenani-deodhi gates. An untidy scrum of maids then always appeared, for missing this early morning delivery meant waiting at least another hour, the time it took for the cameleer to go back to the sweet water well in the river bed, fill the "pakhals"—capacious leather pouches that were slung on both sides of the camel's back and carefully balanced so that they would not slide off (a tedious job, as each bucketful had to be yanked up by hand)—then take a breather, a conversational smoke, and perhaps even a detour home, before returning. Fresh milk from the bagur also arrived then, the herdsman carrying a large urn on his turbaned head as well as milk containers in his hands.

Dust particles danced on the slanting rays of the early morning sun as I lay in bed and gloried in the luxury of the day that stretched ahead. A whole day! What an unending infinity that is in childhood! Time has altogether a different dimension then, a measure that is its own. As life advances, this measure loses its generosity, shrinks in experience, passes so rapidly—perhaps because by then, watches and clocks begin to devour time by the microsecond, and that too insatiably.

On those great, endless afternoons when heat rose from the earth in waves, when shade was scarce and drowsy, even the great House and its ceaseless bustle paused. The maids left their work, lay down, gossiped, yawned, and napped. Mother would sleepily admonish me to lie down, not to do any of those endless numbers of things that children must not do. In the overpowering silence of those afternoons, sometimes the only sound was the wind that soughed through the bush and endlessly across the sand, rippling its surface in ridges and troughs. The pigeons were wide awake, though, strutting and gurgling amorously in the eaves, upon roof corners, and on the ledges, the males ceaselessly trying their luck with reluctant and uncooperative females. I would sit in the balcony and watch and listen and see the shadows shift until the afternoon heat eased, the sun rode lower in the sky, and the first of the traders arrived—the bangle sellers, the village goldsmith, the "gandhi" selling perfume—to tempt the women in the zenana. On one such afternoon, my earlobes were pierced; I cannot recall by whom. I have no recollection of any pain, either, but soon after that, like the others, I was adorned with tiny ear studs.

Dusk would arrive with more milk and water deliveries, and then the hour came for the lighting of evening lamps. The convenience of hurricane lanterns had arrived by then; all were lit at one spot, for economy in fuel use, I suppose. The lantern carrier, clutching several in each hand, would emerge in the gathering dark and greet everyone for the evening, sharing a salutation in the name of a saintly forefather of mine. Ancestors are a natural part of our veneration, and though not in the pantheon of gods, they have always been included in our devotions. For a half-hour or so after that, we observed a mandatory period of evening silence, the "maun." For the children this was agony; we found it nearly impossible to sit silently and pray and meditate every evening, compulsorily. And every evening at that hour, the entire House would fall reverentially silent, as its inhabitants all observed that half-hour of quietude. I do not know if memory plays tricks, but no sound broke the silence until the light had faded from the sky, lanterns cast pools of dark shadow, and stars dotted the heavens again. The ending of maun was announced with a handclap from someone senior, and then a loud greeting to all, again in the name of my saintly forefather.

Now and then, a storyteller would be present at night, among the many who visited Grandfather. He received our folk at all hours—from waking to sleeping, whenever he could, he always met callers, and he heard all petitioners personally. After the evening meal had concluded, the lamps were dimmed, and the storyteller would be asked to relate the tale of this or that hero. We had heard them all before, but every telling was a new experience, as he then narrated, fascinatingly but also unendingly, tales of such great bravery and incredible feats that everyone listened spellbound. My grandfather contentedly bubbled smoke from his last hookah of the day before retiring to bed. I was required to vocalize my appreciation and not doze off, for as the storyteller cautioned at the beginning of a tale, "Just as soldiers need drums in war for inspiration, so does a storyteller require the encouragement of continuous approval." Despite such strict instructions, my efforts to stay awake and follow the story were always futile.

Friday mornings were eventful, and always fascinating to watch. They were reserved unvaryingly for the barber, and if Grandfather was required to travel, then his barber would go, too. Early in the morning, Grandfather would begin to restlessly pace the airy verandah of his living quarters. Friday was the day of his weekly head-shave and massage. A unique and exotic mix was prepared for this massage. The ingredients included a cooling paste containing a special clay from Multan called "multani mitti"; this was combined with fragrant sandalwood paste, and then—the most important step—just the right quantity of opium dissolved in water was added and mixed thoroughly with the rest of the paste. The barber had a privileged position, for only he had the honor of trimming Grandfather's beard and moustache; the connotation otherwise of cutting these symbols of personal pride is altogether different. This was the day on which Grandfather got the "fix" to which he was habituated: his weekly dose of opium through this soothing head massage. Any delay in the barber's arrival would make him irritable: "Where is he? Can he not even walk up the hill on time?" All this was accompanied by loud, jaw-stretching yawns and a constant refrain of complaints. When the barber finally came, Grandfather would sit in a shady corner of that great verandah, his view stretching to the horizon, and after the trim and the head-shave would follow that first liberal application of the exotic paste on his shaven head. And then, miraculously—to me, at least—all his irritation would instantly evaporate. This head massage went on and on, soothingly, almost hypnotically, for what seemed to us children endless hours, but it did serve its true purpose: the slow absorption through Grandfather's skin of his weekly dose of opium—one time a week without fail, but never twice, and only in this fashion, never taken orally.[5] The astute and the knowing in the village would then spring into action; this was the right time to conduct business with Grandfather, to ask him for favors, for it was only on such occasions that they found him dreamily relaxed, even indulgent, and at his most generous. I witnessed this on most Fridays, but never questioned him about it, for I found it so much a part of the fixed order of things. I myself never even thought of trying opium, it simply never occurred to me.

In this tranquil, ordered manner, days became months and then years. I was sent to my first school—in the village itself, run in a part of the house that belonged to my first teacher, Balu Ramji. A balding, portly man, he taught me the Devanagar script, the alphabet of the Hindi language, and rudimentary arithmetic, including tables that he had me learn by rote, again in Hindi. But he taught so effectively that I remember them still, even complex ones involving multiplication with halves such as $2\frac{1}{2} \times 7$— well, some of them, at least! There were no notebooks in that school, only slate and chalk; and there was no homework, of course—we didn't know

5. The desert region of Rajasthan is known for its traditional use of raw opium. People medicate themselves with opium to treat a variety of health problems, and it is also used for ceremonial purposes.

the word. I walked to school and walked back. Now and then I received an allowance of one pie. (Rupees, annas, pice, and pie—that was the currency then. 1 rupee = 16 annas; 1 anna = 4 pice; 1 pice = 3 pies, therefore, 1 rupee = 192 pies—got it?) This coin was of the lowest possible denomination; yet I would soak it overnight in whey, then polish it with wood ash till the copper in it gleamed like new. This one pie then got me nineteen lemon drops in our village shop—not twenty or eighteen, but exactly nineteen, counted accurately as they were given out. Those tiny, delicious droplets of something lemony left my hand sticky for a whole day—but they lasted that whole day, too.

We walked wherever we had to go. When we went to the great animal fair at Tilwara, some distance from the village, we rode either in bullock carts or on camel or horseback. My grandfather occasionally ordered his car out, but most of the time it was parked in a tin-roofed garage in the bagur. His chauffeur, a turbaned, bewhiskered member of his personal staff, was supercilious about his distinctive position: he dealt not with animals, like everyone else in the village, but with a machine! He was brisk and sharp with the three of us: "Don't touch the car!" We loathed him, and the car, too, for it made us sick whenever we were made to ride in it with Grandfather. It was a Chevrolet, with heavy doors and leather seats, the insides always suffocating (to us, at least) and always reeking of gasoline fumes. No wonder the chauffeur discouraged us! The car was used very infrequently; there were no paved roads back then, just rutted or sandy tracks. And in the whole of Mallani (Barmer District today), there were only two automobiles. (There were a few buses, though—not in Jasol but in Barmer, through which we passed annually on our way to Khuri.)

A single-track meter gauge railway line connected us in the north to Sindh. This same railway then looped southward, traveling to Jodhpur, branching off en route to Ahmedabad and then to distant Bombay. The company that ran these trains was Jodhpur Railways; their efficiency and reliability and the courtesy of their staff were legendary. The trains chugged past twice in twenty-four hours—one at around 2 AM, when it headed for Karachi, hooting forlornly in the silent and empty dark of the surrounding desert. The other, if I remember right, came through around midday on its way to Jodhpur, and then on to Bombay.

My grandfather's apartments were on the top floor of the House, with a long, open verandah running the entire length of that floor. The view from that verandah was always stunning, no matter the time of day or the season of the year. In one corner of the verandah, Grandfather cleaned his dentures every morning with monotonous repetitive motions, listening simultaneously to petitions, reports, news from surrounding villages, and complaints, while also giving instructions and issuing his "rulings." Well above where this daily ritual was performed, on the roof of the verandah, stood a device with a pulley and rope. This apparatus, which was shaped like a ship's yardarm, extended well beyond the wall of the House. This was our meat storage device. From it a full hare could be suspended, or even the haunch of a deer, but no more; and so suspended, the meat dried in the scorching sun, the burning desert winds aiding the process. In another corner of that verandah lay a heap of orange peels, collected daily, for those oranges came all the way from Jodhpur and were only for Grandfather's consumption: "Why do you keep these peels?" I asked him once. "To brew," he answered.

How this was done, by what process, I neither knew nor understood. But there was no mistaking or missing the day the vats were opened, for whenever that time came, word would be sent out to neighboring villages. The House would begin to fill up the evening before, often even earlier. The kitchens in the House worked endlessly then; the maids were overworked and became flustered and quarrelsome. Just one camel fetching water would not suffice, and often three or four of them would work all through the daylight hours. My grandmother was not fond of this annual event. She held that there were always too many guests, and they always overworked the maids and servants.

The actual opening of the vats was a ritual, too. It had to be done at an astrologically determined auspicious hour, and when that hour arrived, Grandfather would signal his assent. Only the eldest of the "kalal," the wine dealers whose family had worked with ours for generations, was entitled to do it. When the vats, sealed with layer upon layer of clay-hardened impermeable cloth, were opened, the whole House would suddenly be filled with the fragrance of oranges, or of other exotica such as "kesar-kasturi," a liqueur so named because the ingredients included saffron (kesar) and musk (kasturi). The first drink from each vat was presented as an offering to Goddess Durga, in the temple to her that lay in a section of the House. Only then would Grandfather take sampling sips from each of the vats—not in a glass or in unseemly gulps, but in a silver vessel with a fluted neck through which he sucked a small amount of these fiery double- and triple-distilled brews. Only then was that year's brew distributed—never liberally, but just the right amount. The balance was then bottled in ceramic jars, labeled, and stored for aging or for use later in the year.

At least once a year, my mother, her maids and attendants, and I took a trip to Khuri. Sometimes a private carriage was attached to the train that took us to Barmer, after which we traveled, but always by some different means, on to Khuri. Between the maids and their children (but with no male attendants), more people always piled in than were authorized. No ticket checker ever dared question that, though, for my mother traveled in strict privacy within the screened enclosure known as a purdah; no male could enter her compartment even to check our tickets, and the carriage was guarded by those deputed for the purpose by my grandfather. This journey was always a great adventure, especially for me. At Barmer we detrained, again in special privacy, and thereafter went overland to Khuri. This normally took us two days and one night, for along with my mother, there were many women and children who also had to be attended to.

There was no road between Barmer and Jaisalmer then. My mother traveled in a specially canopied cart—a chariot, it was called—pulled by bullocks. Several other bullock carts, camels, and some horsemen completed our caravan. For the maids, particularly the younger ones, this was freedom from the confines of the zenana and enforced purdah. They rejoiced at this freedom until tired out by song and laughter and merriment. As we neared Khuri, my mother's escort would invariably fire several joyful fusillades into the air, sending the village dogs into paroxysms of hysterical barking and greeting, all in one; the children then running, yelling incoherent greetings; the maids, free now of all restraint, rushing madly on ahead—for Khuri was their home, Jasol the confines of "in-law-dom." My mother, flushed with joy, could barely contain herself. As soon as she reached the bosom of her birth family, she could shed all responsibility and become a young girl again. All this I saw and observed, and it has all remained indelibly imprinted on the plates of my memory, for nothing like that exists anymore. That world has gone; it had to, for it was already living on borrowed time.

My maternal grandfather, Thakur Mool Singhji of Khuri, was altogether a different personality. "Thakur" is a formal title for a "jargirdar," the head of a "jagir," a feudal domain of lands and villages. In West Rajasthan, jagirs were all either inherited legacies or conquests. The name used for the latter is "moondkatai jagir," meaning a fiefdom acquired through feats of valor; hence the assertion heard so often in my childhood: "My forefathers gave their lives for this—it is nobody's gift!" "Moondkatai jagirs" in old Rajputana were set distinctly apart, having a very different status in the social hierarchy than, say, jagirs that had been rewarded to someone for service to a maharajah. In addition, jagirdars were different in every respect from the "zamindars" of the old United Provinces, Bihar, or Bengal (where they were called "zamindari"). Part of a system for collecting land revenue, zamindars were originally introduced by the Mughals, albeit in a very different form then, and the system was later modified and reintroduced by Warren Hastings, the governor-general of India from 1773 to 1784, under whom the hereditary holdings became permanent land settlements. These zamindars were British appointees. They had no roots in the land assigned to them for collecting land revenue on behalf of the East India Company, and therefore they became rapacious exploiters and extortionists of the populace.

A jagirdar, on the other hand, was of the soil, from it; he was a man of the people, one of them, and he cared for the land and the people as part of his "dharma," and vitally for self-preservation, too. Jagirdars were at the opposite end of the social spectrum from zamindars.

But then Khuri was so different, too, the difference from Jasol being not at all in the value systems, customs, and norms, but in the environs, in the ambience. Khuri was all desert; in comparison, Jasol was much more densely populated. Here our houses were mostly huts, with only a very few structures consisting partly of stone masonry. The nearest railway station was not "across the river," it was more than 150 kilometers away. There were no automobiles until you got to Jaisalmer, where the ruling maharawal might have had one or two. In Khuri, nature reigned supreme; man was not subservient but most definitely subsidiary.

My maternal grandfather, known to everyone as Moolji, must have been crafted by nature itself. A tall, imposing presence, he was large-boned, with a full beard and a gruff voice—an exemplar of desert manhood, epitomizing the values of this harsh, hard, desiccated, incomparably beautiful land. As a young man, I was told, he had once accompanied the Maharawal of Jaisalmer to Bundi, on the eastern border of the Rajputana of those days. His strikingly tall frame, full jet-black beard, and confident demeanor attracted a lot of attention. After all, he was part of a wedding party. The size of his wrists, his hosts insisted, must be measured, for they were as big as some men's forearms. Years later, when his beard had turned gray and he was already a grandfather, I asked him about this. He looked at me wonderingly, and then at his own wrist, turning it around, and said laughingly, "They are a funny lot, those easterners. Who ever thought of measuring wrists?"

My mother was his only daughter, and he doted on her, caring for her as for nothing else in the world. I was her only son at the time—her flesh, and therefore his blood. He took me under his wing. I can scarcely describe that careful nurturing; there is so much that I owe him. He was not well-lettered, in the strictest sense, but he epitomized learning. He was not educated in a formal sense, yet he was highly educated, cultured so as to embody the values and traditions of the desert: above all, freedom, an unbending spirit, self-esteem without pride, and a clear sense that there is a thin line between self-confidence and arrogance that is often not visible. And he taught me morality and integrity: "Don't give your word lightly, Jasu, but if you have given it, then never, ever go back on it." "Remember, the best favor that you can do for somebody is to forget the favor that you did; don't ever remind the beneficiary of it. But if you receive a favor, never forget it." It is not as if he sat me down and delivered this lecture in a single tutorial; this is a distillate of many, many conversations.

Sometimes he took me to see his cattle (he owned large herds of them), as well as his camels and herds of sheep, but the cattle always had to be where there was grazing available. We lived and slept in the open at those times, and on moonlit nights he would ask me and some of the children of the herdsmen (the rabaris) to wrestle in the sand, play kabbadi till late, then drink milk straight from a cow. On one occasion, we went out early to collect some venison. Spotting a herd of the Indian gazelle called chinkara, he reined in the camel that we were riding, lightly resting his rifle on my shoulder, for I was in front, occupying the more comfortable of the seats. As he took aim and pulled the trigger, the camel shifted its weight slightly, from one foot to another. An animal had fallen, that much I could see, but he let out a curse: "I have committed a grave sin, an unforgivable sin. . . ." He raced the camel toward the fallen animal. With one fluid motion, he yanked the camel to a crouch, jumped off, rushed to the fallen chinkara, took out his knife, and slit open the stomach. "Look, Jasu, I have killed a female, a doe, and she was carrying a fawn—what a great sin!" In his blood-soaked hands lay the lifeless body of a tiny, birdlike fawn. He had realized even as he fired that a great wrong had been committed—a female had been shot.

Khuri is closer to Sindh than to Jodhpur, and in myriad ways. Now, of course, Sindh is part of Pakistan. Earlier, when it was "British India" and we were not, fugitives from that alien legal system and its petty harassments often sought temporary shelter with my grandfather. He never declined, never turned anyone back, not even those wanted for "murder" in British Sindh. No one was ever sent away; his code and his sense of honor did not permit it. Besides, as he often shared with me, but always in no more than a sentence or two, these "murders" were not cold-blooded killings; they were invariably the outcome of the settling of some old debt: a family feud, or revenge for an earlier wrong. It is for this reason that he was sought out by a variety of petitioners and disputants—Hindus and Muslims, from far and wide—to judge, to arbitrate, to rule on even family quarrels and inheritance disputes. The verdict he arrived at—and it often took him a very long time to do so—no one then disputed.

The area around Khuri has long been home to a large Muslim population. They found no reason persuasive enough to make them leave when "Partition" came, and overnight what had been Sindh became Pakistan. Our relatives across that imaginary line in the sand, the "border," had become foreigners while we slept, needing passports and visas to be with us—their own kin! The land itself had not changed, but what in living memory, and history, had never been alien territory suddenly was labeled so. We were divided by time, by circumstance, and by events and forces way beyond my grandfather's world. For him and for us, the Muslims of this land were just as much our kin as were Hindus. As a measure of mutual accommodation, these subscribers to the faith of Islam had, centuries earlier, given up eating beef or killing cows; and the Hindus, not because of any prohibitory law but in the traditional give-and-take of a desert society, had stopped hunting wild boar, which is a favorite sport and food among such desert-dwelling tribes. Did we also not revere each other's saints—pir, fakir, and darvesh, the annual mela at Ramdevra, also known as "Ramsa Pir," being one of many examples?[6]

This is not an autobiography; it is but a sketch of that time when so many earthshaking events occurred, almost at the same time, and in such rapid synchrony that scarcely anyone could keep pace, certainly not in Jasol or Khuri. My childhood rapidly receded; circumstances simply gulped down that joy-suffused dawn of time, and the very measure of time then changed, forever. No longer did I measure it by the great cycles of nature and live in harmony with the seasons. Seconds and minutes and daily timetables and calendars took over. Where we had earlier created events, then crafted time around them, the order was now reversed; it was time that now dictated all action. I sensed that I was being chiseled into a

---

6. "Peer" or "pir," "fakir," and "darvesh" all denote a wandering religious mendicant who lives on alms given by the pious. A mela is a gathering, congregation, or fair—for example, a religious fair or an agricultural fair. The mela at Ramdevra is held in memory of Baba Ramdev, also known as Ramsa Pir, a fifteenth-century saint whose miraculous powers continue to inspire strong faith beyond Rajasthan. He is venerated by both Hindus and Muslims.

certain shape by that great Stonemason above, daily being honed. But for what? I was not to know until quite a bit later.

In Jasol, my paternal grandfather perhaps sensed this change well before others did. He was, as we all were, too far from the centers of decision-making. We influenced nobody, and no decisions, either. This was galling, even for the growing child that I was. Grandfather, with the sense and wisdom of centuries—for this family, our clan, he often reminded us, had come to Kher (near Jasol, the first seat of our clan) in AD 1028 and had lived there ever since—pulled in all his sensibilities and closed the hatches of his perceptions and faculties, as if he were drawing down shutters and extinguishing the lamps, one by one. In that exquisitely appointed room full of incomparable antiquities, the light was finally going out, and with it time, too. Grandfather did exactly what Mool Singhji had done in Khuri: he recognized the coming change and prepared for it. Jasol, governed for centuries by the rules of primogeniture, had to follow the same path.

The war had ended. They had set off an "atomic bomb," we came to learn in the village. "What is this bomb?" we wondered open-mouthed. A rumor began to float: "The Congress will rule now." Congress? What Congress? Who is this Congress? Have the "Angrez" (the English) gone? Who sits in Delhi? Where are the maharajahs? The air was thick with anxiety, with unanswered queries. My father returned, dressed differently from everyone else in the village, impatient about the "slowness of things here." Grandfather summoned his three sons and informed them of his intentions: "I want to effect the separation before this change attacks us, before I die. Otherwise," he said without a trace of sentimentality or rancor, "you will end up quarreling among yourselves." He paid no heed to the protestations that followed; he listened to no contrary views. He enfeoffed his two younger sons with a settlement that was just enough, not a hair's breadth of emotion more or less.

We established a new settlement then, a tiny hamlet of a few huts some miles away from Jasol, but within walking distance. I left the House, but the House did not leave me; that could never happen. When I went to pay my respects to my grandfather, he held me close for a long time—he was never a sentimental man—then held me at arm's length, looked intently at me, and said: "Go, go and earn a name. Tell Delhi what a great wrong they have done."

My uncle named the hamlet Anandpur—literally the abode of happiness. That is where I spent the next phase of my life, well into my commissioned service in the Army. From the time I was a child until much later,

I cleared fields, built fences, and tilled land with a plow pulled by bullocks; I sat on a Persian wheel and drew water from a well to irrigate a tiny patch of land, for where is "irrigation"—indeed, what is "irrigation"—in a desert? My hands grew calloused, and my feet grew inured to thorns. There was, however, never a sense that anything was wrong in this work with the land. Such was the natural order of things, and that was how it had to be. The new has always to be created, constructed, achieved through endeavor, not served on a platter. These were invaluable lessons. Had not Grandfather always enjoined, "Move; if an animal doesn't move, how will it graze?" And we were a range-fed lot, not stall-fed city cattle.

Father thought, correctly, that I was growing up too wild. He was with his unit most of the time in any case. To a boarding school, Mayo College, I therefore had to go. I knew no English, not a word of this alien language; I had never eaten with a knife and a fork; I had never so much as set eyes on an Englishman, a white man. Yet 1947 was rapidly drawing closer; there was little time to lose.

Things were changing so rapidly that it was difficult to keep pace with the terrifying velocity of the age. It affected Jasol much more than it did Khuri, for in a very real sense, my paternal grandfather, Zorawar Singhji, represented the central core of an ancient tribal order of the desert. With him, in his House, lived the essence of almost a thousand years of his clan's history and tradition. Not so in Khuri—yes, it was deeper in the desert, but it was always more freewheeling, and therefore not so confined; it was freer in spirit and conduct, too. In a sense, adjusting to the new was so much easier there.

The war had ended, and the British, we were told, had gone. Our neighboring Sindh was now Pakistan, and we were "free" (of what, I often wondered) and "independent" (but that we had always been). Moreover, we were now a part of India—although from Jasol, my country had always been the same: Hindustan it was, and so it remained. Whenever I asked my grandfather about it, he would merely give me a long and perhaps somewhat sad look and then answer: "You will understand well enough in time. And when you go to Delhi, tell them what a great wrong they have done. You do not make things by breaking them." (He pronounced it "Dilli," not "Delhi"; and he remained absolutely convinced, to his last, that I would one day go to "Dilli.")

He had begun to age, suddenly and very rapidly, his frame almost shrinking. Always a very proud man, he began to withdraw into himself more and more. I was devotedly attached to him and would head straight to him, to Jasol, when school closed in Ajmer. By then, my parents had moved to Jodhpur, but I never felt comfortable there, never at home. After all, that was *not* "home"; it was only where we had "shifted to."

The House was winding down, falling silent. My grandmother was no more; the zenani-deodhi was now empty, and very few maids remained. My grandfather's ordered life was also changing. The great stables at the House were thinning, gradually emptying. His daily ride had stopped. This was too dispiriting, actually shattering, for him, but he never voiced it. He told me during one of my school vacations: "Why spend so much time in Jasol now? Go out into the world; keep moving. It is 'Dilli' that you have to reach one day. You will get there someday, I know, and when you do, tell them what great wrongs they have committed against our 'ryot.'"[7] This "them," he knew and I understood without being explained, was that system, the "order" that had brought about this "disorder." "Why uproot millions and millions and millions and leave them homeless, to have so many killed . . . What wisdom, what statecraft is this? What is the reason for this division of our land? Is this the Independence that 'Dilli' wanted?" he often wondered aloud. His lands, his jagir, the great estates he had inherited from his father, all were to be "taken away," abolished. Silently, unprotesting, he saw this happen, detached, as if entirely separated from the event. His three sons paid him a formal visit one day. "You must file a claim for compensation, for a just recovery of dues against this acquisition," they pleaded. He sat silent for a very long time, then raised his head and responded in a flat, unemotional voice: "Compensation? Compensation for what? For my lands? What a strange idea! Never in my life have I traded land and cows for money; they are part of my dharma. My duty and obligations. Now you, my sons, say that I should take money for that land?" After another long pause, he spoke again: "Compensation? You say I should claim compensation for this jagir? How strange again! Tell me how to place a monetary value on the thousand years of history that sit behind this jagir. How do I ask to be compensated for history?"

Of course, he never did ask, the only one of his kind not to do so. With obstinate, unbending pride, he slowly let this ancient legacy merge into the dark shadows of time, or perhaps into that "depthless pool of memory."

I was sent to a boarding school in Ajmer, called Mayo College. It was named for an Irish nobleman, Richard Southwell Bourke, the Earl of Mayo, who was viceroy of India between 1869 and 1872 and was fatally stabbed by a prisoner in the Andaman Cellular Jail. It was one of several schools that

---

7. Tenant farmers or peasants.

were established in Rajputana to "civilize" and educate the sons of rough nobility of the region, with the goal of turning us into some semblance of English gentlemen. Mayo College strove to inculcate us with virtues such as "fortitude, temperance, justice, and benevolence," as "splendidly exemplified" by Lord Mayo in his own life—or so, at least, we were told.

At first I hated the school, with a secret, silent loathing. Until then, I had grown up in wide open spaces, as free as the desert wind, unconfined, unconstrained; I was extremely touchy—needlessly, I now think in retrospect—about inconsequential trivia such as not knowing how to write or speak English well enough, and not understanding how to use knives and forks when I ate. ("Why? What is wrong with using one's hand?" I continued to argue for years.) I had, and still have, an extremely heightened sense of privacy, characteristic of inhabitants of free, open spaces. When, upon our leaving the House, my uncle established Anandpur, my grandfather asked with some irritation: "Why on earth are you setting up house on that lifeless patch? Only sand grouse feed there, on stone pebbles!" The reply, "So that we can be near enough to visit you regularly," further irritated him. "Harrumph," he grumbled. "Well . . . I find it suffocating. I can hardly breathe—you are so close, it's as if you were sitting on my head!" We were actually a good four or five kilometers from the village, but I knew exactly what he meant, how and why he felt confined by that kind of closeness.

Dormitory living was hell for me. I never really got used to it. I found it unclean to share bathrooms; at first I couldn't understand this business of moving one's bowels while sitting as if in a chair. Such strange, alien ways, I thought. Because even such inconsequential trivia troubled me greatly, I took to creating my own space—in time, if not physically. I awoke very early, well before anyone else, and I went to bed at inconveniently (for others) early hours, too. By 4 AM or even earlier, while everyone else was still sleeping, I would be up. This habit stood me in good stead when I was a cadet, as well as later when I was a commissioned officer. Those additional two or two and a half hours, until the rest of the world awakened, became my private time, unencroached upon, reserved for me only, to roam freely in and do exactly what I wanted. I never did shed this habit, and now, of course, it is a faithful companion that will not leave me.

I also became conscious of the relative absence from my upbringing of the English language and ways. The language came, of course—eventually, but at first very slowly, like water rising gradually in an open well of the desert, and then suddenly like a desert flood, filling all those empty cavities of my brain that were reserved for knowledge of languages but which till then had lain hollow and empty. Another oddity was how other boys used money. In this respect, I was always a total outsider. I did eventually adjust to their anglicized ways, but I continued to find their habits absurd. When it came to money, I remained acutely conscious and sensitive.

Our lineage was long, so embarrassingly old that it had become almost archaic. And because we so deliberately, generation after generation, had led secluded lives, withdrawn, content in and with our own wildernesses, the more recently arrived upstarts became decidedly uncomfortable whenever we arrived. They could hardly be blamed, for with our discomfiting eccentricities, our rough and knobbly ways, it was as if a country bumpkin had suddenly arrived in hobnailed boots in their midst, in the pretended elegance of their bogus salons, ruining the faux patina of their wooden floors. We definitely were not and had never been "money rich"; we had vast spreads of land, yes, but all that empty space in the desert would not be sold—and it was the kind of wealth that money could never have bought. Besides, there was just no space in my upbringing for indulging myself in money. Neither of my grandfathers was a miser, of course, but they were renowned for their thrift. My grandmothers dotingly gave me whatever I wanted—but again not money, for what use could I possibly have had for money? They took care of what I needed. In consequence, I never really learned the proper handling of personal money; I did not acquire a proprietary, modern-day sense of it—earning, saving, investing, the typical routine.

Thus, when other boys at school spoke of "pocket money" or "shopping," I was bewildered. Why go shopping and spend just for the sake of spending? It seemed foolish. In the village, we bought only necessities, and when something had to be purchased, it was done by those assigned the task; besides, merchandise from shops always came to the House. I did not learn these different ways until I had been away from Jasol for many years.

I was greatly embarrassed by my lack of knowledge of, and fluency in, the English language. But I was too proud to admit it or to ask for help, so I decided to learn English on my own. However, I didn't know how or where to start. All my schooling till then had been in the village, and all of it in Hindi, along with perhaps some Sanskrit. But of English there was absolutely nothing, not even a mention, for even my dear and rotund teacher Balu Ramji knew not a word of the language. It was then that I stumbled upon the device of reading: reading anything that I could lay my hands on, copying sentences in a notebook, articulating words to myself in the dark of those very early mornings. During my first school vacations, I practiced with one of my cousins as the judge; much older than I, he was in a different school, and was much more proficient in the language. In fact, he liked mimicking the English, for in Dehradun, where he went to school, there were many more of them. Hearing me pronounce an English word or attempt a sentence made him laugh uproariously, mockingly, as only brothers can. I hated him for it, for being so "typically Jasol" by not wasting time in sympathy. This sentiment called "sympathy" just did not exist in Jasol back then. Does it now? I wonder.

Then somehow, suddenly and almost miraculously, a door opened. I began to absorb whole sentences, and English-language books opened their secret wonders to me. I entered a very new world. The more I read (and I was reading anything and everything), the more I learned, and the more I therefore wanted to read. In fact, during vacations, which were always spent in the hamlet, I would often sit reading in the gathering dark of evening. We had, blissfully, no electric light. I read mostly by the tiny, trembling glow of an earthen lamp; that lamp truly gave me light. "You will ruin your eyes," my mother always remonstrated, but never to any avail. That, I think, is also when I first began to experiment with expressing my thoughts in this new language—hesitantly, searching for the right tone, the correct sequence, learning to string words together in a way that would release the music of thought, the language and that united voice in harmony. (I had always been able to express myself on paper in Hindi, but at home our language of daily use was, and still is, Marwari.)

It was at school, too, that I found that other boys had things I had never known of, let alone possessed. After a while, I drove all these things out of my mind—not because they were unattainable; they were more like unwanted extras. I had always lived inside the "minimum-need index"— carrying the least possible weight in the "rucksack of my life," and only as heavy a load as would rest easily on my own shoulders, so that no one else would be troubled. I didn't own a watch; I had never really needed one in the village. All the other boys had watches of their own, but I could not, would not, ask my parents for one; in consequence, I learned to do without one, and still managed to be punctual. At school it was easy to be on time, but that I managed to do without what was considered an essential piece of equipment even during my rigorous four years of training at military academies still fills me with amazement. I was not punished even once, not for lateness, certainly. Only those who have gone through such academies will know why I consider this a remarkable feat, if I may say so myself. So, too, with the ownership of a bicycle; distances at Mayo College are generous, but while everyone else bicycled, I jogged or ambled along on foot. It was only after being commissioned in the Army that I purchased my first watch and my first bicycle.

Empire-related books abounded in the school library. I plunged headlong into that genre, haphazardly, unguided, finding my own way through the dense maze. Vicarious thrills of adventure such as westerns and mysteries soon got left behind. I spent time with *Tess* (Hardy) and *Emma* (Austen); I strode over the heath darkly (*Wuthering Heights* and Heathcliff). Then there were D. H. Lawrence, Faulkner, Hemingway, Mark Twain, and an early introduction to Joyce; Whitman's *Leaves of Grass* became a companion. I traveled vicariously, from Central Asia to the frozen wastes of the South Pole. I was struck by William Sleeman's account of the murderous highway robbers known as "Thugs"; his voice sounded authentic, I had heard it, I could tell. The Russians arrived—even their names were fascinating: Turgenev, Tolstoy, Lermontov, Chekhov. Gorky I found too stolid and forced, but Dostoyevsky's *The Brothers Karamazov*—imagine! With Anna, I fell immediately, irretrievably, everlastingly (I thought) in love—the sheer music of it, the sound of her stay laces "hissing" as they were undone in desperate haste. I did not even know what a stay was, or what a woman would do with one; I was but a precocious thirteen. I have written not a word about so many others, or about the Hindi authors Munshi Prem Chand, Agyeya and Sarat Chandra Chattopadhaya, and the now almost forgotten Chandra Dhar Sharma "Guleri" and *Usne Kaha Tha* (*So She Had Said*):

> "Teri kudmai ho gayi?" ("Are you engaged?")
> The girl: "Dhat!" ("Get away!")
> "Lehna paani pila de." ("Give me some water to drink.")

I can still remember those moving lines after more than fifty years!

It was at the end of 1953 when I left school. I was still fifteen, and had sat for my Senior Cambridge School Certificate Examination. Our answer sheets went all the way to England to be judged, or so we were told. The school, in that final year, had made me a prefect—or was it called a monitor then? As a parting gift, I suppose, I was also awarded the President's Medal for the best all-round merit. This pleasantly surprised me. Perhaps it was also my childhood's final and parting gift.

My school days were over. No longer a totally outdoor-loving (and -living) boy, I had turned into an almost adult personality, totally immersed in books. Schooling at Mayo had done what education is meant to do: it led me out, opened many new vistas, gave form and some direction to my constant search. I began to grasp at least the outlines of what was happening all around me, within the country and in the larger world as well.

There was an aspect, entirely outside the school curriculum, that occupied a lot of my thinking space. If Pakistan had to be, was it because "Muslims" wanted a different "home"? Or was it to separate our landholdings, as in a family division? Or was it another "country" that they wanted? "Country," "state," and "nation": these words demanded that I understand them more clearly. I was beginning, however, to see some faint rays of light above the horizon of my own future.

Why did Mohammed Ali Jinnah do what he did? Why did Gandhi, Nehru, Patel, and all those other champions of our Independence agree to let tens of millions of humans be uprooted from their homes and forced elsewhere, with hundreds of thousands killed? What if they had asked all of us in Khuri to move? We lived but a short distance from the Sindh border, after all. My grandfather and all my other relatives, forced to move? Out of Khuri? The very thought paralyzed my senses. Suddenly I began to grasp what that terrible word "refugee" meant, how much pain and sorrow and loss and hurt this single word contained.

And Islam—what is Islam? I began to read, to search, to look for it. I knew very little about this faith then. In both Jasol and Khuri, Muslims lived with us, as our own folk; we saw no difference, felt none. Yes, they had another way of praying and worshipping, but that was their choice, nothing more. Our clothes, our dress, our language—all were so alike. Besides, both of my grandfathers were almost venerated by the Muslims who knew them—the one in Jasol with such great respect, the one in Khuri with such abounding affection and trust. The former was a bit distant—he was a Rawalji, after all—but the latter was totally "theirs," day or night, in joy and in sorrow, a shoulder to lean on, a hand to accept punishments from, however severe, but often an encouraging clap on the back.

I was born in very conservative, traditional circumstances; thus I understood early the essence of belief, although faith came much later. The temple in Mayo College is a place of such abounding light and openness that it was always a sheer joy to go and pray there—twice a day, morning and evening, as per school orders respectfully wearing a turban. Muslim students went to a mosque on the school premises itself. It was in the Mayo temple that I received my first formal "education" about my religion. "What is it?" I would often ask of the venerable punditji; addressed by all as "Gurudev," he led the prayers and gave us Sanskrit lessons. "You are a 'Sanatani Kshatriya,'" he always answered. "What of this name 'Hindu'?" "That is wrong," he always replied. "It is a misnomer; your dharma·is 'Sanatana Dharma.'"[8] Still confused, I added "Hindu—Hinduism" to my list of reading subjects.

I longed to travel, to move, to be away, for in Grandfather's words I was "now free," with "no reins" to hold me back; it was time to "go out to those great, unending pastures of the globe." I could at last graze where I wanted to, at will. "Go," he had said when I went to meet him after my Senior Cambridge Exams. But could I? From these dreams of the wide world, I was shaken awake with a sudden jolt. After Mayo College, my father sought to know: "What do you want to do now?" Quite hesitantly, for we were not entirely free with one another—we never had been, and sadly never became so—I ventured to voice my dream: "I want to go to a foreign university—Oxford, Sorbonne, Heidelberg—whichever grants me suitable admission." Those great names: their resonance still echoes against the now-closed walls of my dreams.

I remember that conversation well. It was an evening, if memory serves, in the monsoon season of 1953, and we were on one of the roofs of the new house that he had built for himself in Jodhpur, a rather ritzy, art-decoish residence, as was the fashion and style then. This finally was my parents' home, and they loved it; no longer did they need to live in the dominating shadow of Jasol. For me, Jasol is permanence; this house remained simply what it is: a townhouse in Jodhpur for occasional living.

Was I unreasonable and unfeeling to have said then what I did? I was aware, though only vaguely and with a child's characteristic unconcern, that our family had suffered yet another financial blow—although what exactly it was, I did not know. In response, my father looked at me even as I was voicing my dream. A lengthy silence followed, and then he shook his head in negation: "No, you cannot; we do not have the money."

"Well, that's that, isn't it?" I said to myself. And without informing anyone, or seeking anyone's consent, that very month, following the lead of my elder cousin Hanut—he was many years ahead of me—I filled in the forms for admission to what was then called the Joint Services Wing,

---

8. A Kshatriya is a member of the Hindu military caste. "Sanatana Dharma," which translates as "eternal teachings, universal truth," is a set of holistic principles for expressing the spiritual essence of life. "Hinduism" is a more recent term.

a tri-service (Army, Navy, Air Force) academy that put cadets through their preliminary training before they were sent off for further grounding in the service-specific academy of their choice.[9] That was in 1953; I was barely fifteen and had only a hazy notion of what I was seeking admission to. Was it "admission" or was it an escape that I sought? That I might not succeed, that I might be found not suitable or physically fit, that I might fail the medical examination, did not even occur to me. It was thus that I was selected for training. Life had taken a turn.

First Steps in Soldiering

On a cold and wet January morning in 1954, with a freezing wind adding to my discomfort, I found myself on the Dehradun railway platform. A posse of uniformed men rather brusquely inquired whether I was a trainee cadet. "Come on, then, quit loitering, move your stumps!" I was about to be broken in again! I was used to the saddle and reins, not to a whip and spurs, nor to the harsh words of the military: "Come on, cadet, jump! Or do you want to go back to your darling mama on the same train that brought you here? Stop shuffling around like a constipated camel. Come on, pick up your bags, and quickly. Hey, coolie! What do you mean, coolie? You are the coolie now, and permanently. So you think you are already an officer, do you! I will take that 'officer' out of you! From now on, you will not walk; you will do everything on the double. Come on, get on with it! Tighten your f——g arsehole and run, you bloody specimen of a cadet!"

I was in the hands of the Indian Army of 1954, just some six years of Independence old. The Army vowed to "teach" me, to "break" me—"or else I will go back to f——g Dublin!" roared Regimental Sergeant Major Ayeling of the Irish Guards, a shining example of British soldiery who was on temporary assignment to India as a drill instructor and a "breaker-in-chief" of raw, unbroken cadets. We were in his care now. (Why are British NCOs and ORs so foul-mouthed? Their Indian counterparts are not, and they do their jobs equally efficiently. This thought came back to me as I wrote this.)

I cannot remember now my predominant first reaction to such deliberate affronts and gratuitous insults. Retaliate physically? I could hardly

---

9. Hanut Singh, who retired as a lieutenant general from the Indian Army, has had an illustrious and distinguished career. He commanded the Poona Horse during the 1971 Indo-Pakistan War at the Shakargarh Bulge and was awarded the Maha Veer Chakra, the second-highest gallantry award in India. Second Lieutenant Arun Khetrapal, a subaltern in his regiment, won the highest gallantry award in India, the Param Veer Chakra. Such was the distinction achieved by the Poona Horse regiment that the Pakistan Army called it "Fakre Hind"—"the Pride of India."

match the British military's wealth of insulting profanity. Shout back in response or complain? This I rejected instantly as too cowardly. Resign? No! From what? I can't be defeated. Do not be cowed, obviously, yes; stay cool, be yourself, and continue to do whatever is required, but in your own way; or ignore all this and do not let it get to you. How does one ignore something like that, or get through it unaffected? It is amazing how rapidly all this passed, even as I plotted my revengeful response!

Dehradun in the early 1950s was the unspoiled end of a branch-line kind of a small town, a haven for pensioners, and home to boarding schools of certain ersatz modernity, two military academies (later only one), and a truly outstanding establishment, the Forest Research Institute of India. This institute was appropriately located, for in those years, at least, Dehradun was surrounded by lush, dense forests and a great wealth of wild animals and bird life. For a cadet, it was bliss to take an evening's quiet walk in the institute's massive, park-like compound.

The Joint Services Wing (JSW) was housed in temporary wooden barracks, hastily built at the beginning of World War II to house Italian and German "internees." The facility was separated from Dehradun proper; we were in what is still called "Clement Town." It lay well to the east of the main township. But this township was not "clement" at all—not where we lived and trained as cadets. True, it was incomparably clement if you ventured just a little farther east. Back then, the forest came up almost to the makeshift barracks, and a small mountain stream called Tons gurgled over a pebbled bed all year round, becoming a roaring, raging, foaming torrent during the monsoon season. This and the library of the JSW were discovered by a friend and fellow cadet, someone who, like me, was sick of the constant yelling and noise. We sought escape from it whenever possible.

Technically, there was little I found difficult in my military training. It was all so clearly exaggerated, needlessly loud and overbearing, and especially condensed, so as to break us in quickly. And for most cadets, that breaking-in was permanent. As I tried to cope with the daily assault on my sensibilities, and upon my incurably free spirit, this understanding helped me arrive at just the right response: "I must preserve myself and not sink into the anonymity of totally submissive obedience. For this, technical excellence in the 'externals' of what is being imparted as training is all that is needed." That bought me privacy; it saved my self-respect and my spirit, too. Was this perhaps the true aim of all the bullying and baiting— to inculcate qualities of individuality, initiative, the ability to think and act on one's own? I doubt it. The system is designed to develop conformity, not individuality; unthinking obedience, not questioning assent.

I gained a lot from military training—infinitely more than what it took from me. What I had to give was conformity and obedience; even a pretense sufficed. In return, I got self-control, a sense of regulating time, and much greater self-discipline. Vigorous physical training, on top of the outdoors life and upbringing I had already experienced, became a kind of fixed deposit of value, of habit, of exercising the body daily. A certain military directness replaced the rounded courtesies of village dialect. I had been raised with horses, almost *on* horses, and yet I became much more proficient when the method and polish of Army equitation was added to that basic grounding. What earlier I had only sometimes watched my father and other relatives do in Jodhpur—play polo—I now got an opportunity to do myself. Indeed, I became fairly proficient at it, and also at other equestrian events, some requiring skill and expertise—including eventing, show jumping, and, most demanding of all, dressage. There were others, such as the fast-paced sport of tent pegging, that were far more dramatic and thrilling for spectators to witness but required no more expertise than the ability to simply stay in the saddle.

Here, too, fortuitous circumstance played its part. I had always had a streak of defiance and daredevilry, stubbornly attempting the seemingly impossible, the things that others would not touch. I suppose this was born of being the youngest of the three cousins who lived and grew up together in the House. The JSW was emphatic about physical training—and drill parade, too, but for us that was more of an additionality; in contrast to the Army, life in the Air Force and the Navy did not actually depend on bashing the drill square. There were classes on various academic subjects, but they were largely pro forma. For cadets rushing from one physical to another, academic classes functioned more as a breather, an interlude of rest, best used for a refreshing snooze. Some cadets, I was told, had so perfected this art that they could actually sleep with their eyes open. Boxing was compulsory and competitive; my long nose was such an easy and obvious target for my adversaries that they needed only to repeatedly punch it to get me to lose my temper, which then made me lose what little skill I had at this "sport." Riding, too, was compulsory. This was dreaded so deeply by some that they preferred to risk disciplinary action rather than attend this class. My rural upbringing and ease with horses—riding, grooming, feeding, watering, and stabling them—put me in a far more comfortable position.

That was not entirely the case that morning, however. "The commandant is coming to watch the riding class," we were told by our worried-looking instructors. "So what," I thought to myself. This was still the first term, and the beginning of it at that, and I was new and still "unbroken." We were ordered to mount, wheel, and trot to a jumping lane nearby. Volunteers were then invited to go through the jumping lane without stirrups or reins. My companion cadets were by then ashen-faced, sitting rigidly frozen on their mounts. I had never even seen a jumping lane, despite having lived with and ridden horses all my life. I might have crossed a low bush or a fence now and then, but I had never made any formal effort to jump over obstacles. Before that thought could breed hesitation, I volunteered. I walked my horse to the entrance of the lane, crossed the stirrups, knotted the reins, and let the by now impatient horse go. It galloped excitedly all the way through, not veering, jinking, or refusing a single jump. And I did not fall off, not even at the end of the lane, where my mount, as any self-respecting horse would do, gave a joyful buck or two of abandoned freedom. Major General E. Habibullah, the commandant, was impressed enough to call me over. This led subsequently to polo, to equestrian sports, to participation in competitive events, and to a lifelong companionship with horses. Where but in a horse is it possible to find "nobility without pride, friendship without envy, or beauty without vanity?" asked the British poet Ronald Duncan so aptly in *Ode to the Horse.* "He serves without servility, has fought without enmity. There is nothing so powerful, nothing less violent; nothing as quick, nothing more patient."

General Habibullah thereafter virtually adopted me. An outstanding patriot, he had opted to stay in India, his home, declining several invitations to join the members of his family who had chosen to live in Pakistan. A man of eclectic learning, opinions, and preferences, he was quintessentially a representative of the great and prosperous culture of Awadh. In one of those bewildering quirks of life that are impossible to explain, many years later, in 1982, we were both guests at the golden jubilee celebrations of the Indian Military Academy (IMA). By then, I had left the Army and was already a member of Parliament. I was, as per protocol, asked to sit in front, and he a row behind. Greatly embarrassed, I promptly declined. His reprimand was immediate and sharp: "Don't be such an obstinate fool, Jaswant, just as you were at the academy. Can you not understand how happy and proud it makes me to see my student, my own cadet, sitting ahead of me? I am being recognized, too, not you alone." A few years later, I found Begum Habibullah in Parliament. We sat at opposite ends, though. She never ceased to treat me as her husband's student, his cadet, and thus as her own kin, complaining that whenever it came to making a choice, "Why does he always prefer you, and even your politics to mine?" But all this was still several decades away, and whatever dreams and aspirations I might have had for my life, at the time I was still a first-term cadet in the JSW—as low as a human being can go in the military hierarchy.

There was so much else that I got from the JSW, the most treasured and lasting being the entry of Western classical music into my life. It was an accidental arrival, ordinarily so improbable. A type of hazing known as "ragging" was de rigueur for all new arrivals, and in the JSW in those years, it was fierce, indescribably tyrannical, and deeply humiliating. Under the guise of "We will make a man out of you" or "This is to toughen you up," every effort was made to break the spirit, particularly of spirited new entrants. I am still not sure—and I obviously was not sure then—what it was that made my "seniors" unfailingly pick on me. The more they yelled at me, the more rigid I became. I did whatever I was ordered to, however illegal the order, but I did it at my own pace. "Of three things never be ashamed or even embarrassed, Jasu," my grandfathers had often cautioned: "labor, no matter how hard, no matter how long, and no matter how menial; old clothes, no matter how worn; and old parents and relatives, no matter how dependent." So I took what they gave at whatever time of the day or night. I "executed" all their orders, "obeyed" all their commands, but all at my own pace. Fury broke them, eventually.

The barracks that were our living quarters stood in rows. They were rather run down, but they were laid out in straight lines like a drill square. Pebbles were not to be found "loitering in a disorderly manner," but must always be in their assigned place on the gravel path. I was often punished for the waywardness of those pebbles: "Why is this pebble not on the path, you bloody man?" Why indeed! One evening, to escape this senseless indignity, Suraj, a fellow first-termer, invited me to accompany him to the Wing Library. "I didn't know they even had one," I responded. "There is more; you will find out when we get there." This "library" was housed in the barracks, just as we were, but it occupied two barracks, which were divided with plywood planks into separate rooms, marked "Books," "Reading Room," "Store," "No Entry," and so on. In Army parlance, a "No Entry" sign is often there merely to hide disorder beyond it. When we spotted this notice, we of course had to go in. Inside we found stacks and stacks of 78 rpm records, some new, most with their covers unbroken; and also many gramophones, again stored one on top of the other, and all of the hand-wound variety that now are highly sought after by collectors. It was there, on those scratchy 78s, that I first heard Western classical music. With time, it was to become a constant companion. I discovered other treasures in this library as well: Romain Roland's *Jean Christophe,* Thomas Mann's *Buddenbrooks,* Joyce and his *Portrait of the Artist as a Young Man.* I immersed myself in this incomparable world of Western classical music, and of the glory and beauty of the written word, too. These were my own discoveries. I traveled here all alone, with neither a map nor any guide, with no prior knowledge, no background. I have cited just three books and three authors, for I think those works typify the struggle and search of a young man. That search was constant but it was all internal, and I could successfully keep it within myself for one very good and helpful reason: the schedule and pace of military training left hardly any time for free play in the mind. If you gave yourself up, it would suck you down, instantly. I don't know what I did, or even how, but I met the demands of the system, I think with competence but without submission. That rather dilapidated barracks and the books and music that lived there saved me. Thanks to them, I was able to lead a "double life" during the entire four years of my military training at three different academies: a "military life" externally and an "internal life" of the spirit, of a constant search for myself, for self-expression.

Those JSW–Clement Town days were short-lived. After only a year, we were all shifted south, to Khadakvasla, near Poona, where the new National Defence Academy was being built for exactly the same purpose and tasks as the JSW. This move was made even before all the buildings of the new academy were ready. Clement Town and its JSW had a "makeshift," temporary feel; the Defence Academy at Khadakvasla looked more solid, even though it was still rather unsettled and incomplete. The routine of training was much the same, but the land, climate, and countryside were very different. Khadakvasla had one great advantage: each of us got a room to ourselves. Privacy at last; the sheer bliss and luxury of this benefit is fully appreciated only after enforced community living! A fellow cadet from those days met me recently, and reminded me about many details. "You secretly kept a radio then, Jaswant." And suddenly I remembered: yes, I did. The radio actually belonged to a fellow cadet from Malay (it was not Malaysia then), but as we were forbidden to keep one, he lent it to me, and I used it to surreptitiously listen to Western classical broadcasts.

Back then, even All India Radio had a lunchtime classical music program. "Also, you hung a notice on your doorknob such as only you would. It said something like: 'Do not enter! Certainly not without knocking, but knock only if you must.'"

I rode a lot more in Khadakvasla. I joined the Poona Hunt, a wholly inappropriate sport for our climes. I may well have been among the first to ride from Khadakvasla to the top of Sinhgarh Fort and back in a day. Because the academy gave me this unique facility, I acquired some basic knowledge of three languages: Persian, French, and Russian. This was imprudently handled, for my hunger for instant knowledge was much larger than the time I had to absorb and retain it. I wish I had stuck to just one language, but even now I would have difficulty deciding which to choose.

It was at the National Defence Academy that I made my first acquaintance with the great musical traditions of the Maharashtra region, and the genius of its singers. It was also there that I first saw Jawaharlal Nehru; he was a guest of the academy. The academy gave me a chance to shake Marshal Zhukov's hand (or was that later, at the IMA? Events overlap in memory), and also to meet the famous duo of Khrushchev and Bulganin. General Habibullah chose me to hold the umbrella over Iran's Queen Soraya when she visited. We waited for her on the steps of the imposing main building; I was somewhat behind and to the side of the general. Her car was driving up when I opened the large and colorful umbrella, exactly as I had been instructed to. A sudden gust, an unexpected updraft of wind, caught me by surprise, and the umbrella struggled to fly off. I held on to it, but by then I was somewhat unbalanced. The general was looking at me with some concern. Came another sharp gust, and the umbrella turned inside out. The car was now about twenty feet away. The general wasn't sure whether to be angry, irritated, or amused: "Jaswant! You bloody fool, didn't you even learn how to open an umbrella in that blasted desert of yours?" "Yes, Sir," was all that I could say. I somehow managed to get the umbrella fixed just as Queen Soraya stepped out of her car. I held it over her, just right, as I had been taught to. By now, the general was smiling; the queen, though, looked immensely sad to me, and therefore even lovelier than I had imagined her to be.

The term at the Defence Academy was ending. The cadets were going their separate ways: those who had opted for the Army were heading back to Dehradun, to the IMA at Premnagar. The Navy and Air Force cadets were going to their respective academies. When the passing out parade, an impressive ceremony akin to graduation but of the military variety, was but some hours away, life, as it is wont to do, delivered a sharp rap on my knuckles. On the eve of the parade, I suggested to some friends who were also due to graduate the next morning that we have a great feast of collective rule-breaking. After some initial hesitation came curiosity: "How? What should we do?" I must have been seized by some form of madness; how else could I possibly have suggested what I did? The others all followed instantly. At around midnight, there we were, six defiant cadets, riding three to a bicycle, wearing shorts and vests with our skin exposed to the mosquitoes, swilling merrily out of the bottles of beer we carried so jauntily, puffing cigarettes even though none of us actually smoked. To top it all off, we were singing lustily but discordantly, belting out some kind of ribald nonsense at the top of our lungs. We were in violation of: lights-out rules; bicycle-riding rules; malaria-prevention rules; rules against alcohol consumption, smoking, and disorderly behavior in a public place; and that catchall "conduct unbecoming to an officer and a gentleman"! What followed was inevitable. In the midst of all this defiant merriment arrived our collective nemesis.

We were caught in the blinding headlights of a car. Like wild animals encountered during a night drive, we instantly froze into the silence of apprehensive confusion. One of the most dreaded and tyrannical of the instructors, best known by his nickname, the "Hun," stepped out of the car. Why now? What on earth is this king of the killjoys doing here? Such thoughts went through my mind even as I stood stiffly silent at attention. After a tongue-lashing, six hangdog cadets trudged back to their quarters. What was going to happen to us? Withdrawal from the academy (a kinder word for expulsion), or relegation to a lower term, which meant six additional months of this grind? I pretended to be unconcerned. I was the originator of this mad scheme, after all, so how could I be deflated? Or, outwardly, even worried? Yet three worries haunted me all that sleepless night: How can I face everyone back in Jasol? What will I do and where will I go if I am expelled? What will this do to our name?

The next morning we were summoned to the commandant's office before the passing out parade. For cadets, the commandant's office is the holy of holies. Ashen-faced, we stood silently as a stern-looking major went in first, followed by the adjutant of the academy. "Jaswant, you take the lead and do the talking," whispered one of my petrified colleagues. We were marched in, with me in the lead. General Habibullah raised his eyes from whatever he was reading, looked each of us up and down, then asked the adjutant to read the charge sheet. That done, the general asked of no one, yet of all, "Do you have anything to say?" Almost reflexively, unrehearsed, I replied: "Nothing, Sir; we are guilty of the charges." He looked down. Was the general suppressing a smile? Like an illuminating ray, that hopeful thought flashed through my mind. "Unthinking fools, ruining your lives, and for what?" An ominous silence followed, lasting for what seemed like an eternity. A clock on the wall ticked the seconds by; they seemed as loud as rifle fire. Finally: "Go on, then, get out. I am letting you all join the parade. I don't know why I am doing this instead of . . ." He fell silent. Then, in much sterner tones: "As for you, Jaswant, I don't know what to do with you. Why did you lead them all into such damn foolishness, when it could have been a suicide mission? With what face will you go back if I throw you out? I should give you Field Punishment No. 1, and flog you with a horsewhip myself.[10] Now, go. And if you must do crazy things, then don't ask for volunteers to join you in that craziness. Go join the parade. Adjutant, take over." Were there whoops of relieved joy when we were all out of that office? No, rather a silent, reflective, united relief. An understanding general had given us another chance in life, and thus no whoops accompanied our sober farewell to the National Defence Academy.

The Academy and the World

The remaining two years of my training, this time specifically for the Army, I addressed in altogether a different manner. I came to some new agreements with myself—principally to demonstrate "excellence," not just meet whatever demands the system might make upon me. I was barely seventeen, still in the turbulent teens, but in some ways I was mature beyond my years. I was also continuously expanding my fields of inquiry now, into a wide spectrum of subjects, beyond the Army's duties and calls.

My riding skills became much more polished, decidedly more mature, but still reckless. I experienced many falls, and some injuries, too. I suffered two concussions, but the regiment medical officer of the academy, a straight-talking, no-nonsense, old-fashioned Army doctor with combat experience, pronounced me fit: "What is your skull made of, wood?" "No, Sir," I replied with cheeky flippancy, "it was made in Jasol." He had the grace and humor to laugh. His language was profane, but not his deeply human sensibilities. To every fresh crop of gentleman cadets—GCs, for that is what we were

---

10. In Field Punishment No. 1, the offender may be kept in irons; be attached to a fixed object by straps, irons, or ropes for a prescribed length of time (not more than two hours in one day, and for no more than three out of four consecutive days or for more than twenty-one days in all); or be forced to perform the equivalent of hard labor.

now termed, as against just "cadets" earlier—he was required to give instructions in personal hygiene, military style. His graphic instructions on the use of slit trench latrines invariably started with this advice: "GCs, first learn to align your shit holes with the slits"; or, "It is not an offense under the Army Act to ———, but if any of you bastards ever contracts a venereal infection, I will cut your ——— off." The language was graphic, but that made the message unforgettable.

I did take one rather bad and embarrassingly public fall. It happened during the preliminaries to a big polo match. I was scheduled to play, but first I was to take part in the preliminary events. One such demonstration required that I gallop fast in front of the spectator stand, stop my horse and quickly step off it, then turn with one foot still in the stirrup and fire my revolver at an imaginary enemy (two men from the cavalry) chasing hard to "capture" me. I had done all this on numerous earlier occasions with no trouble at all. As I had to play a polo match later that afternoon, I was wearing boots that were suitable for the game, but not at all suitable for trick riding. All went well through the firing of the shots, but as I swung to get back into the saddle, my foot slipped out of the stirrup. I fell hard, on the small of my back, which caused a whiplash effect. My head snapped back and hit the dry ground with so much force that I was knocked unconscious. I have no memory of how long I was out. When I came to, I saw a doctor peering at me with great concern. He had been in the spectator's gallery. "Well?" he said. "I am fine, Sir," I replied. "I will complete all the events." I could barely see the ball during the match. The next morning, the doctor spent a lot of time examining me. He concluded: "You are young now, but as the years advance, your back will give you trouble. Take my advice, remember: never agree to an operation." He was right; my back does trouble me now, irritatingly so at times, and against the advice of many doctors, I have never consented to an operation.

I was becoming increasingly aware of the much larger world outside my own. India was moving, but so were other countries. Tibet had been bleeding for some time. Pictures of all the military actions against Buddhist lamas had shocked India even earlier—in September–October 1951—but now sharp, questioning voices rose above the sycophantic drone of unthinking approval that the government in Delhi had become accustomed to. Suez 1956, Britain humbled, photographs of Soviet tanks in Budapest—it was all greatly troubling, even to this unlettered adolescent from the desert. But our government's reactions did not appear to be a shining example of the "moral force" of a "nonaligned" India. It seemed as if we were nonaligned about the aspirations of the freedom-loving. Why? I questioned some of the officers and professors in the academy. I could tell that they were troubled, too, but they pushed their disquiet aside, not wanting to have their certainties about Nehru questioned, let alone to permit a fragmentation of their comfort. Yet questioning voices were being raised and getting louder. I added mine to this simmering, amorphous disagreement, though I was still a GC and bound by the military code of "no politics." "No politics in uniform, yes, Sir, but that does not mean that I hold no political views," I had responded to my company commander. "Besides, what is happening in Ladakh, Sir?" I had also begun to write, in Hindi and in English, mostly for myself, on scraps and sheets of paper, without order or purpose. I found that I liked doing so simply for the sake of doing it, crafting words into coherent, readable thoughts, molding half-formed views into reasoned expositions. I knew that no one would publish the pubescent outpourings of an unknown youth. "Jaswant, a word of advice to you," my professor of English in the academy had said one day. I remember that we had no more than two or three classes in that subject each week. "You have a weakness in your expression but a strength, too. Remember that your ability to write, to express your views, to give voice to your beliefs, cannot be regulated. It is subject only to your own convictions. Even you will not be able to dictate to it if you lack conviction. But once you are convinced, your pen will flow with a life of its own. For even you will then be unable not to write."

On December 15, 1957, I was commissioned as an officer. I was a second lieutenant in the Indian Army. I had applied for the Central India Horse and was selected for it. Tradition required that I join the Poona Horse; my father and uncle had both done attachments with that regiment, and my cousin Hanut was now serving as an officer in it. But that was precisely why I would not opt for it. I had no desire to be a permanent understudy to Hanut, even though he was as close to me as a brother. What were my feelings about "passing out"? Relief at having done it, and a sense of quiet satisfaction; but again no whooping joy, no desire to toss my cap. I had become an under-officer in my final term, and I was among the top ten in the passing out order. So that, I thought to myself, was a bit of all right, was it not? At least for the time being. I already knew, had perhaps always known, that I was not going to be in the Army for good. At the time I was commissioned, I was still only nineteen years old. I did not inform my father that I had been commissioned until I got to Jodhpur. I would have been embarrassed if anyone from the family had attended my passing out parade. "Oh! Have you? Well, that's quite good," he responded. "I am joining the Central India Horse," I added. "CIH? Well, well; I knew them at one time as a great polo-playing regiment. I knew two of them rather well. There was Dalrymple—Hay . . . What was his first name now? A bold, dashing player; his handicap was as high as 9, I think, at one time.[11] And yes, Alexander, Jeff Alexander—he hit a very long ball, that Jeff. When do you have to report to the regiment?" And after a while, "Pity you are not going to the Poona Horse."

"Don't Forget Delhi"

I went to Jasol to meet my grandfather, Zorawar Singhji. The great stables in the House were now nearly empty—not entirely of animals, but certainly of spirit; even the few animals that remained appeared to have lost condition. Far fewer people lived in the House now, and with the bustle gone, a certain stillness had settled over it, a brooding silence whose hollows carried the echoes of time. I was immensely saddened by it all, and I went up to meet Grandfather with no joy in my heart. He was sitting almost slumped, in a patch of sun, in his fulgar.[12] His shaven head was covered not with his usual turban but with a skullcap of his own design, thinly padded and with ear flaps for protection against the cold. We talked of this and that, of the elections that had just concluded, of the changes that were taking place in Sindh. Then he asked: "When do you go to Delhi?" I replied that I would pass through it on my way to the regiment. After a bit, when I got up to leave, he said, "When you go to Delhi, let me know." And then I remembered—it all came back—and as I fumbled for a suitable response, he smiled wearily, adding, "You will go, that I know. I only hope it is not too late."

My joining leave was short, but to Khuri I had to go, and I was very glad that I did, for that world of my early years was still in place, still intact, with my grandfather, Mool Singhji, still very much his robust, hearty self, meeting change head-on, riding above it. But his spirit had wilted somewhat, and his magnificent frame, too, was not what it once was, not as upright as it had always been. He was sitting in a makeshift arbor spinning the mixed yarn of goat and camel hair that was so much a part of our leisure lives, of our daily occupations. Not one for sentimental

---

11. In polo, each player is assigned an individual handicap on the ascending basis of −2 to 0 and 1 to 10. This handicap reflects the player's ability and his value to the team—the higher the handicap, the better the player.

12. A fulgar is a dress consisting of a light wool layer sandwiched between two layers of cotton fabric. It is often worn to ward off the evening chill.

expression, he asked me to sit next to him, then said: "Come again soon; my body will not last much longer." He brushed aside my remonstrances, adding, "I know, you don't understand or accept it. But change is beating me now, moving faster than I can. You will see that, but mark my word, people will come to know of Khuri because of you."

I was to see them again, both of them, but each only once more.

When I saw my paternal grandfather in Jasol two years later, he complained of "feeling the cold much more these days," and also of too much coughing. "Yamraj is announcing his arrival with these signals.[13] That is why I tell these fools, 'Why do you want me to stop smoking my hookah? Why now? And how many years will that add to my life?'" After a pause he said, "Go and get me some grouse, and partridge, too; it has been a long time, and my teeth are aching for that taste." I brought him a full bag. He looked at it, looked up at me from where he was sitting, smiled his usual somewhat cynical smile, then said: "You will never change; you always do more than you should. I am old now, Jasu; who will eat all this grouse and partridge now? Look at the House!" But his cook was waiting and took them all. As I left, he added: "Don't forget Delhi." I did not see him again.

My maternal grandfather was already ill when I got to Khuri. His body had shrunk and he was unable to eat, but of course he would not go even to Jaisalmer for a doctor. "How many days are you here for?" he asked. "At least three or four," I responded. Instantly he said in relief, "Good. Now, Jasu, you organize this. My sons are all sentimental fools. Take a few men and camels, and collect enough firewood that my body will burn properly. There is not much time—the grim reaper is coming; I hear the sound of hooves." I had the needed firewood collected; it is always scarce in the sands. Satisfied, he saw it arrive in camel load after camel load, and he was able to bid me farewell with his mind at ease. About a month later, he too was gone. A great gateway of my life—of links, identity, and roots, of consciousness and connectivity—was now closed.

My nine years of commissioned service in the Army, from December 15, 1957, to November 22, 1966, has no place in this narrative. I joined during what I call the "golden age of cantonment soldiering" in India. We soldiered as we imagined that fabled cavalry must have done at one time; therefore, we too must follow suit: "Cavalry, Sir, is to lend color to battle, to add style to what is otherwise just an unseemly squabble." "Officers, Sir, are to lead men into battle, not to waste time on inspections and parades and all that." An officer at the Jhansi railway station, imitating

---

13. Yamraj is the Hindu god of death.

the legendary commander John Brabazon to the flustered and hapless sta-tionmaster, after being informed that the train to Delhi had gone: "Gone?" the officer asked in a gimlet-soaked drawl. "What do you mean, gone? Get another one this instant; get another train right now."

I realized soon enough that it was all empty posturing, this living as caricatures; that the Army had better awaken to reality. I sought a formal interview and asked permission to resign. I had barely two years of service. "Why?" a rather jovial, bon-vivantish colonel commandant asked. He was a great raconteur, and he truly couldn't grasp what I meant when I said: "To write, Sir. I need leisure to do so, and I am losing time." Astounded, he asked: "How old are you?" "Twenty-one, Sir." "Twenty-one! You are crazy! The maximum leisure is here in the Army, not outside. Look at me—I have all the time I want, so much that I don't know what to do with it." I did not succeed that time, but I was not deterred from my objective.

Reflexively, I volunteered for all the seemingly impossible missions, the many reconnaissances in the Himalayas that were then being ordered. I wanted to see, to experience, to feed my senses. This led to long spells in the mountains, glorious excursions, with the eternal silence of the mountains as my constant companion. "CHINESE FORCES CROSS INDIAN BORDER," screamed the newspaper headlines. Within twenty-four hours, if I remember correctly, "Throw Them Out, Says Nehru" followed. The year was 1962. The regiment, too, was ordered to the northeast. I was to lead the advance party. Nobody could tell me what I was supposed to do when we got there, or what our role, our task, was to be. My orders were simply to reach such and such a place with tanks at the earliest: opposite Dhubri, as I loaded the tanks on rafts, the Brahmaputra in spate was like a sea, the opposite bank of the river lost in the mists of distance. This was independent India's first mobilization.

The rest is history, for later reflection and comment: 1962 was trau-matic; it left an imprint so deep, we still have not shaken free of it. A short engagement with Pakistan in Kutch followed; the regiment then moved again, to Fazilka in Punjab. Then came 1965, and Pakistan launched Operation Gibraltar. The regiment was again in Punjab. That cease-fire established a pattern, but I had even more serious reservations about Tashkent.[14] "Can't anyone see?" I kept asking.

---

14. The 1965 armed conflict between India and Pakistan was formally brought to an end by the Tashkent Declaration, which was signed on January 10, 1966, at Tashkent, the capital of Uzbekistan, which was then part of the Soviet Union. Prime Minister Lal Bahadur Shastri of India and President Ayub Khan of Pakistan signed it on behalf of their respective countries in the presence of Premier Alexei Kosygin of the USSR, who mediated.

In 1966, I resigned. When asked to state my reasons, I responded clearly: "To get involved in politics." I had no pension; I did not want one, or any other "terminal benefits" from the Army. My service was the great benefit, and what the Army gave me, taught me, left with me, is my priceless pension.

With such an upbringing, such varied learning experiences, the enthusiasm of a naïve innocent, and with multiple chips of arrogance on my shoulders, I entered India's public life. I struggled for another fourteen years, again single-handedly, before I reached Delhi. I wrote in my diary then: "All of this, in retrospect, seems so inevitable, and now that I am finally here, so natural, it is as if this is where I have always been, where I must be. I felt so totally at ease then with myself and with my environs, too. This is where I belong; this is my métier; it is for this that I have struggling until now and preparing my entire life."

I was ready for the new challenges, this or any other. I was on the "dehlij," the doorstep of Grandfather Rawal Zorawar Singhji's "Dilli." It would take a great deal more effort on my part to reach Delhi.

2

Born of the Same Womb: Pakistan

The Birth of Pakistan

So many accounts now live on our bookshelves about the idea and birth of Pakistan: why and how it came about; the pain and agony that accompanied this new country's emergence from the body of the old. There really is no space left for more analysis. But this "Partition" has left a deep imprint on our sensibilities, on the memory templates of several generations—mine, too, even though Partition and Pakistan came about while I was still just a child. For all of us in the subcontinent, Partition was the defining event of the second half of the twentieth century. The name "Pakistan" hardly featured in our consciousness in Jasol or Khuri before it actually came into being. Culturally, linguistically, in social observances and adherence to customs, with respect to marriage and relationships, the districts of Thar and Nagar Parkar in Sindh were closer to us than, say, Ajmer, or even Jaipur to our east. Besides, we could not simply "unrelate" to the Muslims; they lived with us, and we with them. For so many centuries we had sat on one of the principal land invasion routes into India from the west. But perhaps for that reason, and perhaps also on account of our long history of testing one another, crossing swords, confronting each other robustly whenever challenged, we had now evolved the needed mutual accommodation. In our joys we were together, and in our sorrows, too.

We lived surrounded by the lawless Hurs of Sind; their religio-tribal chief, the Pir Saheb of Pagaro, had some years earlier raised a banner of revolt against the British, after which he sought shelter from those vengeful imperialists and found it in our midst. The Hurs raided and looted and sometimes abducted women, too, but never in our regions, and never, for that matter, around Jasol. One such bandit raid occurred after Pakistan had become a reality, and it was quite close to Khuri—too close, in any event, for my maternal grandfather's comfort. As he had always done, he immediately mounted a retaliatory "commando," to borrow an apt phrase from the Boer War. He reached deep into southern Sindh, which was by then a province of Pakistan, and tracked down the leader of the raiding party, who returned all the stolen goods, expressing regret for the action and blaming it on the impetuosity and ignorance of the "younger set." Grandfather camped there in the dunes for the night; his camels and his accompanying party had ridden a long way. In the dead of night, he was surrounded by a force representing the government of Pakistan. He was taken captive, for the first time in his life! The outrage we felt, even we children, was profound; blood rushed to our heads and darkened our vision. For years thereafter, we mounted retaliatory raids into Sindh, evading all law, whether Indian or Pakistani.

But as this news spread in the Thar and Nagar Parkar districts of Sindh—and such news tends to travel very fast indeed—a huge uproar arose. "You cannot hold Moolji of Khuri. It has never happened before." Relatives and other persons of prominence, now citizens of Pakistan, rushed to Karachi, to Lahore, to Rawalpindi. The mood in Sindh was clearly communicated. My grandfather was escorted back with due honor and protocol. I cite this only to emphasize that in large parts of undivided India, there was no desire to partition the country. We were content to remain where we were, not for the political convenience of some distant few who wanted to be "partitioned." That is perhaps why we could not understand this demand for Pakistan at first. And though most of us had relatives in Sindh, none migrated. "Communal riots"? There was no such obscenity in our region—not at all. "Why on earth do they want to give up India, which is so much larger, and opt for Pakistan—where opportunity will be a fraction of what they already have in India?" my grandfather in Jasol wondered repeatedly, in mounting exasperation. Until his dying day he sought an answer, but he never got one.

August 15, 1947, Early Morning, Mayo College, Ajmer

It was a rainy morning in Ajmer. Sporting turbans, we all assembled, fidgeting, in front of the main building of the school, near the flagpole. At the appointed hour, Principal MacCanlis lowered the Union Jack for the last time and raised the Indian Tricolor for the first time. Soon thereafter, MacCanlis left India. He was the first Englishman I had come in contact with. (As his name suggests, however, he was actually not English at all.) We then collectively shouted "Jai Hind!"—"Hail, India!" The ceremony over, we went skipping back to our respective houses, as the day had been declared a holiday.

"We are independent now," some said. "Of what?" I asked. "I have always been independent, whether in Jasol or in Khuri. We have never known servitude." I realized then that I had not even been fully aware of this entity called "British India," or of the fact that Ajmer, where we went to school, was "British India," but adjacent Jodhpur was not.

When I woke up the next morning, a couple of soldiers were standing guard inside the dormitory. "Who are they? Why are they here?" were the natural queries. Two of my dormitory mates were princelings (one was actually the heir apparent to a state in the eastern part of India), and soldiers from their respective state forces were now standing next to their beds. Others stood guard at the dormitory door. I finally got a reply to my persistent questions from our housemistress, a Mrs. Lall, who had a pet fox terrier, a mean little fellow who delighted in nipping at the calves of unwary boys. "Riots have broken out in the city," she said—"Hindu-Muslim riots." To my repeated queries, there was but one reply: "Because Pakistan has just been formed, and Muslims will have to go there now." I could not explain satisfactorily, then or even later, that where I came from, there had been no riots, no one had gone anywhere; and that the ills of one part of India were not necessarily the ills of all the other regions.

That morning, I witnessed my first "communal riot," a phrase routinely used thereafter as a convenient euphemism for a Hindu-Muslim fracas. Shouts suddenly went up in the House compound: "Smoke, smoke!" We rushed headlong, as only the young, uncaring, and unknowing do, toward the source of that smoke. Unable to see much, we then hurried en masse to the rooftop. From there we could finally see: just outside the barbed wire compound of the school stood a solitary, box-like, double-storied house, and smoke was pouring out of it. That scene has imprinted itself so indelibly on my mind that I can relive the experience as if it had happened only this morning. A crowd had surrounded the burning house, but from that distance I could not make out any details or establish any identities. Smoke continued to pour out of the house, and the crowd continued to shout, raining stones at that lifeless, inanimate thing, which, I imagined, was crying silently in helpless anguish. I, too, shouted, repeatedly: "Why doesn't someone help?" Finally came the reply, "Shut up, you fool! A Muslim lives there." "So what?" I protested. "You really are a fool." That afternoon, we heard that a large furniture store in Ajmer—the Empire Store, I think it was called—had also been set on fire and looted. "My grandfather would have whipped them," I said, but my remark was met with hoots of laughter, and a dismissive "You can go to Pakistan, too."

Inwardly I was growing bitter, and I began to lose conviction in my own beliefs. I was only nine years old, and I was in that ruthless, uncaring, concentration-camp-like establishment called a boys' boarding school and hostel. Vacations saved me, just in time.

This is what I felt on Independence Day in 1947, and in my mind, that is how Pakistan was born: out of the same womb from which India had reappeared, but as if it were missing some limbs. Two arms, perhaps? It certainly looked like that on the new maps in our geography class. Much, much later, I began to read everything I could get my hands on about this cataclysm, and to reflect deeply upon it. I think about it still and continue to search for answers; some I have found, but others remain beyond my reach even today. More than half a century after that great division, the trauma of Partition continues to haunt the subcontinent. It still deeply influences our minds, our thinking—the reactions of Hindus and Muslims alike. Did we not also seek freedom from fear of subjecthood in that August of 1947? Why, then, does fear continue to so afflict us all now that it has made us subjects again? So what if we are not subject to the British; we have instead become subject to mutual suspicion. Independent, sovereign Islamic states have now emerged, guiding their own destinies, masters of their own lands; so why does this torment and turbulence persist even now? What atavistic animosities inhabit our psyches? What, ultimately, is this "unfinished agenda of Independence"?

The Seed

In 1933, five years before I was born, Choudhary Rahmat Ali, an Indian (Punjabi) Muslim student at Cambridge who believed that a Muslim homeland should be established within India, coined the name Pakistan for the nation he envisioned. Supposedly an acronym formed from "Punjab," "Afghanistan" (including the North-West Frontier Province), "Kashmir," "Sind," and "Baluchistan," it literally meant "land of the pure." Initially the idea of a separate Muslim state drew little attention, but with time, and aided by continuing human folly, it began to gain acceptance. At the same time, however, there was a strongly voiced concern that if a Muslim state of "Pakistan" were to be created, it would be dominated by the Punjab. This apprehension never went away. When the question of separating Sindh from the former British province of Bombay Presidency came up, Ghulam Hussain Hidayatullah, speaking to the Sind Azad Conference in July 1934, said, "It would be a political blunder for Sindhi Muslims to form a group with Punjabi Muslims."

If it was only the provinces with a Muslim majority that were to come together to form Pakistan, then what about Muslims in the rest of India? For them, Rahmat Ali proposed that "half a dozen Muslim states" be established, and that they then be consolidated into a "Pakistan Commonwealth of Nations." This was an absurd suggestion. Organizations such as the Jamiat-ul-Ulema-i-Hind did not support the idea of even one Pakistan, let alone an indefinite number of them. Mohammed Ali Jinnah, the head of the Muslim League, was doubtless the tallest Muslim leader then, but even he did not command the support of all Muslims. Indeed, two religious leaders, Maulana Hussain Ahmed Madani and Maulana Hafiz-ur-Rahman of Delhi, were known to have berated him publicly "for having no beard, for not fasting during Ramzan [Ramadan] and for frequenting clubs and cinemas instead of saying his prayers."[1] Soon thereafter, Jinnah shed his Saville Row suits and began wearing a sherwani and a cap made of Karakul fur (a style that came to be known as a "Jinnah cap"). This form of dress became his public display of a "Muslim cultural identity." It was this same Jinnah who promoted the founding of a separate nation for Muslims. This was a rather expedient transformation, born of many factors and caused principally by his repeatedly feeling let down by the Congress. That sentiment of betrayal eventually became one of the most potent factors for the birth of Pakistan. The other, clearly, was the politics of the Congress Party and its several follies, some of which were unavoidable. Ironically, even while Rahmat Ali was articulating the sketchiest outline of Pakistan in 1933, Jinnah, in total sincerity, was advocating that "Hindus and Muslims were two arms of the Indian body."

The drift away from that position began in 1937, in the provincial elections of that year in the United Provinces (now Uttar Pradesh or UP, one of India's largest states). An agreement had been reached earlier whereby the Congress and the Muslim League would share office, and some elected representatives of the League would also hold ministerial berths in the provincial government. After the election results had been announced, however, Nehru went back on that agreement, asserting that the Congress had the required majority on its own. The League, its leadership, and Jinnah took this as a deliberate and planned betrayal. The divide of the 1930s widened further on the issue of joint or separate electorates, with the League favoring separate electorates for the Muslims and the Congress opposed. It was this divide that eventually manifested itself in the creation of the "political Hindu" and "political Muslim," who used their faith as an instrument

1. Ayesha Jalal, *Self and Sovereignty: Individual and Community in South Asian Islam since 1850* (London: Routledge, 2000), p. 441.

of political particularism, separating one human from another for political exploitation—far different in mentality and approach from the "religious Hindu" and the "religious Muslim," who lived simply by their faith.

Jinnah championed the Muslim League and the idea of Muslims as a different "nation," and was the founder of Pakistan. Yet despite all this, he was almost an agnostic, his bent of mind being purely political, and later in life bitterly cynical. He rejected religion-driven politics, as well as those who brought religion into politics. His opposition was not directed against either the Hindus or "Hinduism" as such; it was the approach and policies of the Congress that he opposed. He scoffed at its "holier-than-thou" and "more-patriotic-than-thou" attitude. Jinnah's faith in the ultimate national solution of the Hindu-Muslim question had been shaken in 1937–39, during the short period of Congress rule. Thereafter, he began propounding a thesis that India was not just a country but a continent inhabited by many separate "nations." Chief among these were Hindus and Muslims. Therefore, this "Muslim nation" in India had the right to a land of their own, not immediately as a separate, territorial "state," but certainly as a different, nonterritorial "nation." It was this theory that enabled Jinnah to transform what the Congress had termed "Muslim communalism" into what he himself liked to call "Muslim nationalism." It is here that the idea of communal autonomy was re-enunciated as the right of "national sovereignty." Astoundingly, the congressional leadership at the time went along with the proposition, contributing significantly to its many crippling consequences, both then and later.

The acceptance by the Congress of Hindus and Muslims as two separate nations was then superimposed on the earlier advocacy of separate electorates in the province of UP. Thereby was born an evil, entirely unwelcome, and unintended progeny: the "communalization" of India's political system. What had earlier been simply the identification of faith—be it Hindu or Muslim or whatever, as subscribed to and practiced by its adherents—became almost cemented into two "rival nationhoods" after the formal separation resulted in two electorates. What had been designative now became a separate identity, and the only reason for that separation was religion. This was a compound fracturing of Indian society, and once the segments of Indian society have begun to be separated electorally, they will continue to split, as cells do.

With a skill that few of his contemporaries could match, Jinnah elaborated his idea during an address to the Muslim League in March 1940:

> Our Hindu friends fail to understand the real nature of Islam and
> Hinduism. They are not religions, but in fact two distinct social
> orders, and it is only a dream that they can evolve a common
> nationality. Hindus and Muslims belong to two different religious
> philosophies, social customs, and literatures. They belong to two
> different civilizations . . . based mainly on conflicting ideas and
> conceptions. . . . Mussalmans are a nation according to any defini-
> tion of a nation, and they must have their homeland, their terri-
> tory and their state.

Though Jinnah remained willing to negotiate a settlement with the
Congress within the framework of a very loose federal scheme, even that
plan was finally abandoned. The dark shadows of deep-seated suspicions
and animosities had finally obscured all vision.

On August 11, 1947, after becoming the president of the Constituent
Assembly of Pakistan, the Quaid-i-Azam ("Great Leader"), as Jinnah is
commonly known, made an important speech, which is frequently
quoted now:

> A division had to take place. On both sides, in Hindustan and
> Pakistan, there are sections who may not agree . . . but in my
> judgment there was no other solution. . . . I am sure future history
> will record its verdict in favour. . . . Now what shall we do? . . . If
> we want to make this great State of Pakistan happy and prosper-
> ous, we should . . . work in cooperation, forgetting the past, bury-
> ing the hatchet . . . work together in a spirit that everyone . . . no
> matter to what community he belongs . . . no matter what is his
> colour, caste or creed, is first, second, and last a citizen of this State
> with equal rights, privileges and obligations.

Thus, "theocracy" would not be central to the birth of the new nation, and the
many non-Muslims still residing in the new state were all to be Pakistanis.

> If you change your past and work together in a spirit that every-
> one of you, no matter to what community he belongs, no matter
> what relations he had with you in the past . . . is first, second and
> last a citizen of this state with equal rights, privileges and obliga-
> tions, there will be no end to the progress you will make. I cannot
> emphasise it too much. We should begin to work in that spirit

and in course of time all these angularities of the majority and the minority, the Hindu community and the Muslim community . . . will vanish. . . . You are free; you are free to go to your temples, you are free to go to your mosques or to any other places of worship in this state of Pakistan. You may belong to any religion or caste or creed—that has nothing to do with the business of the state.

These were no doubt "noble sentiments," but alas, they had no effect. It was already too late. Even as Jinnah spoke, caravans of uprooted humanity were trudging hopelessly out of the new state of Pakistan, while others were pouring into it, coming to this new home, their own separate land. Many millions of haunting laments filled the air, both in India and in Pakistan. Individual pain gained a voice (which it still has today) in poetry and drama and songs and memoirs. This loss was not just individual, and it was not limited to Punjab and Bengal alone. Established geographical and economic entities, ancient cultural unities, having evolved over millennia into a distinct and unique oneness, had been fragmented. This historical synthesis of an ancient land, its people, its culture, and its civilization was deliberately broken into pieces.

The Radcliffe Mission

No one yet knew exactly how this ancient land now stood divided; it was not clear where the boundary would be delineated. By the summer of 1947, the British and the Congress and Muslim League leaders began serious discussions about the format and procedure for establishing a boundary commission. In effect two commissions were created, one for Bengal, the other for Punjab. Sir Cyril Radcliffe was the chairman of both. He was respected for his intellectual abilities, but he had never visited India, and he knew almost nothing about it. Paradoxically, this may actually have made him more acceptable, on the assumption that such ignorance aids impartiality. Each of these commissions was to have four judges, two selected by the Congress Party and two by the Muslim League. This format inevitably produced frequent deadlocks, leaving Radcliffe to make all of the most difficult decisions. His "judgments"—based on no knowledge, no experience, no understanding of the history, the geography, or the sociology of this ancient land—left consequences that still trouble the successor countries today.

Radcliffe did not arrive in India until July 8, learning only then that the boundary determination had to be completed before August 15.

Naturally he protested, warning that this restriction could "wreck the result." But other priorities prevailed; the establishment of an international boundary was the principal prerequisite for the transfer of power, and the dividing line had to be finalized before August 15, 1947, no matter what. This was Lord Mountbatten's diktat. Radcliffe's efforts were hampered by routine administrative deficiencies; he lacked even qualified advisors who could handle the complexities of boundary marking. His only help came from his private secretary, Christopher Beaumont, who was familiar only with the realities of British administration, which of course were not really germane to complex boundary delineations in a rather contentious India. This, and Radcliffe's natural predispositions, meant that it was primarily British interests that would end up being served. Besides, the unnaturally tight timetable rendered even the collection of needed information nearly impossible. In addition, Radcliffe found it difficult to acclimate to the monsoon-humid atmosphere in Delhi (which even "natives" find uncomfortable), and he suffered from dysentery for the entire length of his tenure there. There are no scientific studies that can inform us of the influence that such ailments have on political cartography.

In line with Mountbatten's, Nehru's, and Jinnah's collective requirement that his work be completed before August 15, Radcliffe submitted the Boundary Award on August 12 (four weeks for nation-making!). Mountbatten, as an afterthought, then asked Radcliffe to delay the award until after the 15th. Radcliffe, by now fatigued, feeling trapped, and wanting to escape from India, flatly refused. Nevertheless, Mountbatten chose not to release the award until August 16, at which time he discussed it formally with the Indian and Pakistani leaders, although he had shared it with Nehru informally earlier. It was only on August 17 that the award was finally published. When it finally trickled down to the districts and below, where it counted, is impossible to judge. But India had already been partitioned. Two days prior to the award, vast columns of displaced humanity were already on the move. This hasty "award" resulted in many indescribable crimes, causing incurable ills. To quote the poet Sardar Jafri, "Who is this cruel person who has with his burning pen 'Cut a deep line of innocent blood across the motherland's breast'?"[2]

---

2. From Ayesha Jalal's adaptation of Sardar Jafri's poem "Khoon ki Lakeer" ("The Line of Blood"). Poets and writers on both sides of the 1947 divide have captured the anguish of Partition. In "Khoon ki Lakeer," Sardar Jafri, one of India's leading leftist poets, rejected the newly demarcated boundary as an imperialist artifact. Jalal, *Self and Sovereignty*, p. 568.

I will share with you accounts of two out of the many thousands of incidents that occurred at the time of Partition. Both are based on official reports, checked and verified through subsequent investigations. The first is a shortened version of what happened to a caravan of some two thousand Sikhs who were attempting to migrate to India, based closely on *Divide and Quit* by Penderel Moon. The other, involving Muslims who were attempting to go to Pakistan, is from *Stern Reckoning,* a report compiled by G. D. Khosla.[3]

The Bhawalpur Massacre

A flare-up in the state of Bhawalpur, which had not yet acceded to Pakistan, made many of its residents uneasy, especially the Sikhs who lived there, who now sensed a serious threat to their lives and property. Believing that they needed to escape the situation, they made a decision to gather where they would have safety in numbers, then travel en masse to India. The state authorities in Bhawalpur rejected the use of the railway, because the routes, which ran to Hindumalkot by way of Rahim Yar Khan, were too exposed, they said, and thus too risky. They decided that it would be preferable for the caravan to travel through the desert to the state of Jaisalmer, accompanied by an escort party from the Bhawalpur State Forces.

Approximately two thousand Sikh men, women, and children set out for India on the afternoon of September 26. They were made to surrender their arms before leaving, which they did reluctantly, but they were assured by the Bhawalpur officer who was leading the escort party that they had no reason for concern.

After the column had stopped for the night, members of the escort party began taking the Sikhs' belongings. The Sikhs resisted, and in the altercation that followed, several of them were shot and killed, with many more injured. The commander of the escort party apologized for the actions of his men, characterizing it as a "misunderstanding," and promising that it would not happen again.

With some apprehension, the Sikhs resumed their journey in the morning. When they reached the desert and had nowhere to turn for protection, the commanding officer suddenly told them that they were going to be searched. Over their protests, they were relieved of all their possessions, on the pretense that Muslims were not being allowed to bring any possessions

---

3. Penderel Moon, *Divide and Quit* (1961), reprinted in David Page et al., *The Partition Omnibus* (New Delhi: Oxford University Press, 2002), pp. 127–41; G. D. Khosla, *Stern Reckoning: A Survey of the Events Leading Up to and Following the Partition of India* (1949), ibid., pp. 284–88.

into Pakistan, so the Sikhs should not be allowed to bring anything into India. Even their camels, horses, and donkeys were taken from them, leaving them no animals on which to ride across the desert.

On September 30, the caravan encamped for the night within two miles of the Jaisalmer border. The Sikhs expected to spend the night at that spot, then walk across the border the following morning and find safety in the nearby hamlet of Kishangarh. After midnight, however, the two Sikh leaders of the caravan, Bakhtawar Singh and Bhag Singh, were roused from their sleep and told that the column must move again immediately. They lodged a protest with the commanding officer, and in the commotion that followed, both men were bayoneted to death.

The remainder of the column quickly reassembled in the dark of night and moved out toward the border. They had not gone far, however, when they were ordered to halt by the escort party. Gunfire could be heard in the distance. The women and children were forcefully separated from the men—to protect them, they were told, "from the 'Hurs,'" a lawless tribe of Muslims who supposedly were the ones doing the shooting. In reality, however, the guns were being fired by a small number of the escort party who had gone on ahead and were now shooting into the air so as to make the Sikhs believe that they were in danger of being attacked.

After some of the younger women had been separated out and divided up among the members of the escort party to be sent back to the city of Rahim Yar Khan, the rest of the Sikhs—men, old women, and children—were told that they should quickly get across the border, before the Hurs arrived to attack them. The group made a desperate run for Kishangarh, but as they ran, the escort party opened fire. Only a few of the Sikhs reached Kishangarh, where they were able to get help. A group of armed men from that outpost were dispatched to bring back the wounded and those who had been left behind.

The Other Side: East Punjab and Delhi

Hindu and Sikh migrants from West Punjab recounted their own stories of unprecedented horror, such as had "not been heard of since Nadir Shah." Some of those accounts were undoubtedly exaggerated, but they played a huge role in stoking the desire for revenge and retaliation. With each new report in the newspaper, the flames of vengeance were fanned, "until the barriers of commonness, of a shared past, were torn apart, rendered inconsequential." Horror piled upon horror, and hatred fed more hatred. Revenge killings spread outward from Delhi and East Punjab into the rural areas. After two trains carrying Muslims were stopped near the railway station in Badli, the authorities found piles of burning bodies on both sides of the tracks. On September 4, workers on their way home from the Delhi Cloth Mills murdered a number of Muslims, for no reason whatsoever. Three days later, Muslim shops in Connaught Place in Delhi were looted and set on fire. The Army and the police were authorized to shoot on sight, if circumstances so warranted.

Muslims sought shelter in the growing number of refugee camps, forced to look to others for safety in their own home, as had Sikhs and Hindus in West Punjab. Torrential rains in late September added to their misery, as the Sutlej, Beas, and Ravi rivers overflowed. Two major tragedies occurred during this period. In the first, an eastbound train carrying Hindus and Sikhs from West Punjab was attacked at three different locations. When the train reached Amritsar and news of the attacks spread, the virulent outpouring of resentment overflowed the banks of restraint. On the evening of September 22, as a train carrying Muslim refugees attempted to cross Amritsar, a mob gathered and attacked. The consequent loss of Muslim life was terrible.

A few days later, there was a second attack, this time on a large contingent of some ten thousand Muslims who had entered Ferozepur District from the state of Kapurthala. They believed that they were traveling in safety because of a bribe that supposedly had been paid to arrange for a military escort, but as they crossed through the district, they were set upon by Sikhs who had recently arrived from West Punjab. A large number of girls were abducted, and between 500 and 1,000 of the Muslims were killed. Once the Army became aware of this column, the group was reorganized and given safe passage. Fortunately, about 200 of the Muslim girls who had been abducted were recovered and eventually reunited with their families.

The inclement weather, the unprecedented rainfall, and the lack of adequate food took their own toll on this contingent. Another 1,500 or so died from exposure and hunger. As a result of these flare-ups, almost the entire population of Muslims in East Punjab was evacuated to Pakistan. The misery and horror that occurred in West Punjab were repeated with equal ferocity in East Punjab. Now neither half of the Punjab had anyone of the other faith left on its soil.

Picking up the Pieces

In India and Pakistan, which were now independent countries, even the joy of being "free" had an undercurrent of gloom. It is impossible, even after the passage of more than half a century, to erase completely the scars of those deep wounds. Whatever was happening in the west, in the two Punjabs, was also being practiced, with added ferocity, in the east—in Bengal, in Calcutta, in Noakhali, in Bihar. Was this the pain that I had heard in my grandfather's voice even before it had occurred, when I was but a child? What price this great human folly, I continue to reflect, and what an enormous, incalculable loss this eventually became, for Hindus as well as for Muslims. It is a memory that cannot be erased, that will not simply sink into that "depthless pool" from which there is no return.

How did Pakistan fare? It has always been marked by high drama, by the dark and looming shadows of history, as well as myths, and thus by intense emotionalism and this sad absence of cold logic. Inevitably, since that time this "idea of Pakistan" has often been usurped, which is why Pakistan's "friends" have so often become its "masters," and which is also why the "state" of Pakistan remains fragile, so unsure, so tense. But there were other factors, too. Pakistan, founded on the notion of separateness, a nation distinctly apart from India, could do no more than to affirm an Islamic identity. It therefore adopted the identity of an "Islamic Republic." This seemingly logical evolution from "Muslims as a separate nation" to "Pakistan as an Islamic state" was not, as we shall see, as direct or as evolutionary an idea as it might at first appear. In reality, it has impeded Pakistan. From its roots as an Islamic state, Pakistan ultimately—perhaps inevitably—grew into a "jihadi state." No one foresaw this development—not India, not the West, and not even Pakistan.

Upon Independence, now freed of British rule, India had a continuing identity, a functioning administrative structure, and in that immense spread of land, sufficient mass and enough resilience and cushion to absorb repeated shocks, as it had done so often through history. Not so in Pakistan; the challenges it faced upon independence were formidable. After all, Pakistan had been more a "negotiating idea," a tactical ploy to achieve a greater political role, more say in the governance of India, and then a degree of autonomy within India. No one, including Jinnah, had ever defined Pakistan; the cry had always been only for Islam. That is why, when this dream finally became a reality, no one was prepared for it. There had been no prior assessment of potential problems or priorities, for not even Jinnah had known what shape Pakistan was going to take. Yet August 15 could not wait, and Jinnah dared not ask for a deferment.

"In just over two months," said a former Pakistani diplomat, "provinces had to be divided, civil and armed services bifurcated, and assets apportioned. This telescoped timetable created enormous problems for Pakistan, which, unlike India, had not inherited a capital, a government, or the financial resources to establish and equip its administrative, economic, and military institutions. The migration of millions of refugees imposed its own burdens on this fledgling state with an awesome burden of rehabilitation."[4] This would be one of the many challenges that Pakistan would face. For the fledging nation, a quick solution to these problems lay in a "confront India" approach; that was an obvious escape, but to where? And never for long. It is here, I believe with the benefit of hindsight, that India needed to give more; it needed to accept with greater generosity (of spirit, too) what had separated from its own body. It was a difficult call; the trauma of a searingly cruel partition had cauterized the sensibilities of an entire subcontinent. The manner of carving out the land, the shattering of the psyche of an entire generation (more than one, perhaps?), and the unprecedented uprooting of so many millions made accommodation nearly impossible. All true, and more: Pakistan was starting on its journey of nationhood neither with an abundance of options nor with the goodwill of an amicable settlement, a willing division of assets among disputant brothers. Great bitterness was added to what was already a very bitter partition. Under these circumstances, could India have been more understanding? That is now largely an academic query. But for Pakistan it was a major challenge just to stand on its own feet. It had practically no industry, and the market for its agricultural produce lay in India. Pakistan produced three-fourths of the world's jute, but all of the processing mills were now in India. The non-Muslim entrepreneurial class had moved away with its capital, uncertain of its future in the new state. The monetary assets apportioned to Pakistan were held by the Reserve Bank of India, and given the hostile environment, their transfer was not occurring smoothly.

Although the idea of Pakistan entailed a separate nation for Muslims, the movement for it actually left this struggling state with a number of identities. One was clearly Indian, in that the principal pillars of support for Pakistan were Indian and identified as such culturally, even though they were totally opposed to "Hindu India." This is a sensitive and difficult aspect of India-Pakistan relations overall, particularly the question of "national identity." What we routinely call India's "identity" axiomatically will continue to incorporate many aspects of what is today a "Pakistan identity," just as Pakistan will retain an "Indianness" in its identity. Pakistan both rejects and revels in its "Indianness." This is a facet of

---

4. See Husain Haqqani, *Pakistan: Between Mosque and Military* (Washington, D.C.: Carnegie Endowment for International Peace, 2005), p. 11.

Pakistan's continuing identity struggle that is largely overlooked; sadly, however, it cannot be rejected. How could the reality of one's geography be shed, sloughed off; how could a common historical past be totally pulled asunder? And yet, when citizens of Pakistan are reminded of this oneness, they understandably bristle and become instantly, angrily rejectionist. There are other ideas of Pakistan; some have worked and others not. Pakistan aspires to be "a modern extension of the Mughal dynasty," but such aspirations grossly misread both the present and the historical reality. The Mughals were able to rule a part of North India continuously only because they managed to establish a political coalition with the other dominant political force of that age—the Rajput kingdoms of Rajputana. The desire to be a legatee of British India in the tradition of the Raj became inverted, and Pakistan, unfortunately, is now much more a "rented state." Cultural links with Central Asia (which India has had for centuries) do not make Pakistan a boundary land between the "teeming masses of India and the vastness of Central Asia";[5] it cannot be that link with Central Asia because the geographical, historical, and cultural logic is entirely different. Pakistan's aspirations are much greater than the accompanying reality.

A "Nation" in Search of a State

There have been many attempts—and serious ones, too—to help Pakistan become a functioning state, but with no demonstrable success. Earlier it was essentially the "triad" of the Army, the bureaucracy, and feudal landowners that were central to the country. Now that reality is very different. Pakistan, always sensitive to the centrifugal energy of the "provinces," now finds that Islam in and of itself has not proven to be as effective a glue as was earlier assumed. Provincial identity, loyalty, and interests have always taken precedence, and that has not changed.

Jinnah's call to Muslims (primarily in northern India, Bengal, and Assam) was couched in Islamic terms, but though his words were unambiguously political, they often stoked nearly unquenchable fires of hate and roused atavistic furies. This, it is suggested, he did to keep his "Muslim constituency" together, but it unavoidably then led to the division of the two provinces that he most needed to keep intact—Punjab and Bengal. Without those two provinces as part of Pakistan, the country was bound to become what it eventually did—"moth-eaten." In consequence, it simply

---

5. Stephen Philip Cohen, *The Idea of Pakistan* (Washington, D.C.: Brookings Institution Press, 2004), p. 38.

could not have parity with India, an aspect that troubled Jinnah then and continues to gall even now.

The post-Partition experience has further cemented fears and prejudices about India, more so since the 1965 and 1971 wars. Pakistan has now become a fortress—what author Stephen Cohen has called "an armed redoubt guarded by the Pakistan army, safe from [a] predatory India."[6] Other factors also contributed to this siege mentality: Jinnah's early death, followed by the murder of Prime Minister Liaquat Ali Khan, rapidly caused a loss of authority in government, which in turn became impatient with democratic restraints. The other factor has been the politics of language. Which has priority: Islam or language? This became a deeply emotive issue, as it did in independent India, too. Above all, there was an added sense that India was "somewhat contemptuous of Pakistan's ability to survive." "Let us see for how long they last," Nehru remarked.[7] Since that time, it clearly is only hostility toward India that has kept Pakistan glued together.

Pakistan, like many Islamic populations, has found it difficult to establish or maintain a modern state. The sentiments involved are a complex mix. Muslims feel that the West is responsible, that it has robbed Muslims of dignity and honor, and that India is a party to this "conspiracy." Thus honor will be restored only in revenge, in violence. Overall, this is yet another shadow, suggesting that Pakistan is not yet complete, not really. What rankles in the depths of their psyche is the uneven migration of Muslims to Pakistan, the very large numbers who opted to stay behind in India. How, then, can Pakistan be complete? Are those Muslims not a part of the separate "nation" that was originally carved from India, Muslims being a nation apart? So why not another Muslim "nation" in India?

It has been a long and obstacle-ridden journey for Pakistan. Some of the dimensions that affect it today can be gauged by demographic and social indicators, which ordinarily do not attract as much attention as a nuclear program or terrorism. These indicators act concomitantly, according to Cohen: when such indicators are positive, so are the opportunities for significant progress, and when they are negative, Pakistan can go into a vicious downward spiral.[8] For example, the population of Pakistan is growing by 2.9 percent annually—the highest rate in the world—and is

---

6. Ibid., p. 81.

7. B. K. Nehru, *Nice Guys Finish Second* (New Delhi: Viking, 1997).

8. This and the following paragraphs rely on Cohen, *The Idea of Pakistan,* p. 80.

expected to reach 219 million by 2015. Admittedly, it is a population with a young profile, but the representatives of that profile will not find any opportunity for themselves within Pakistan. The resultant frustrations have a predictable enough content: they are fertile ground for political exploitation, already sown with seeds of hatred and anger. The magnitude of this problem has not been sufficiently appreciated. Assertions by some Islamists that this proves that Pakistan is a populous nation of "Islamic warriors," backed by an "Islamic bomb," are deeply troubling.

Pakistan was born of an artificially induced hostility toward India, a deliberate policy of separateness, supposedly on account of irreconcilable differences. This perpetual hostility has now become the "operational code of Pakistan's Establishment," to borrow again from Stephen Cohen. The central idea is that India is the chief threat to Pakistan, and therefore it must be checked in every possible way—militarily, strategically, and diplomatically, as well. Further, because Punjab is the "heart of Pakistan," it is preeminent with respect to preserving the national interests of Pakistan. As military alliances are a "strategic necessity," therefore "borrowed" power has a continuing purpose. The issue of Kashmir is helping to bleed India at a very low cost and with relatively low visibility, and therefore it must be endlessly pursued even if the Pakistani masses cease to think so, and even if the returns on this "investment" continue to diminish. Democracy may theoretically be desirable, but as the Pakistani people are "excitable" (according to President Zia-ul-Haq), the standards of education and public discourse have to be raised before the masses can be allowed to freely express their opinion. It is best to adopt "controlled democracy"; the Pakistani masses should be exposed only to "the correct history and . . . news." An excessive security consciousness has led to high militarization, and—again as if preordained—the prominence that Inter-Services Intelligence (ISI) has achieved as the guardian of national security and of the "ideological purity of Pakistan" adds to the military-security emphasis in the country.

The Bomb and Pakistani Identity

It was the late Zulfikar Ali Bhutto who made the decision to initiate Pakistan's nuclear weapons program. For him and his successors, it was an imperative in shaping Pakistan's self-image. Simultaneously, it rendered as "infinitely more complex an already complicated security situation in South Asia." Pakistan's nuclear program is entirely India-centric; it is always trying to match India, but at the same time to project an image of itself as possessing two great assets: Islam and technology, even if most of that technology has been either "stolen from a European nuclear facility or provided by China." But this nuclear program has already warped judgments about Pakistan's real strengths and weaknesses. Pakistan's bomb is in reality a "successful outcome of espionage and assistance from a friendly power." It is not, unfortunately, the product of a technologically advanced state, although for "deterrence and for war" that would clearly be a meaningless difference. In the context of Pakistan's deeper security, political, and social problems, however, the bomb has made it possible to perpetuate a delusion that Pakistan is a technologically advanced country; it is the "magic bullet which could resolve any problem."[9]

Cohen cites an officer of the Pakistan Army as the author of *The Quranic Concept of War:* "terror is not a means of imposing decisions on the enemy, it is the decision we wish to impose upon him," for it is terror that is sought to be imposed. That is also why a link between "terror and the Islamic conduct of war has found manifestation in the support extended to terrorism in Jammu and Kashmir." A strategy minus this "element of terror being imposed on the heart of enemy" will remain deficient. And this strategy, in its application, must go beyond "conventional wars," if necessary to nuclear war, and to making terror a necessary ingredient of it. Such expositions make chilling reading. It was with this Pakistan, this mindset, that I engaged in the period 1998–2004.

Strategic Depth to Strategic Dilemma

Of the several experiments in democratic governance that Pakistan has attempted to conduct, the last was stopped by the military again in 1999. Prime Minister Nawaz Sharif was relieved of all responsibilities by General Pervez Musharraf, whom Sharif himself had appointed to the top job in the Army. This resulted in some innovative developments, experiments of a sort to help formulate Pakistan's policy toward India, and all were initiated by Pakistan's new president. Another constant has emerged: employing terrorism as an instrument of state policy. It is perhaps no longer based on any explicit executive order from the president's office. But then whose will or order now determines policy about terrorism? Is Pakistan's ruling establishment not entirely in control? And if it is not, then the contagion of such troubling doubts will spread far and wide, causing even greater harm.

Right after 9/11 and the attack on the Twin Towers in New York, Pakistan, displaying adroit diplomatic nimble-footedness, reversed course,

---

9. These thoughts have been expressed by many, but most effectively by Stephen Cohen in *The Idea of Pakistan*. Quotations in this section from ibid., pp. 80, 118–19.

altering the very polarity of its policy. When that change was announced, a Pakistani diplomat exclaimed, "We are saved!" As a Western diplomat wryly observed, "How many times will Pakistan sell its soul? How many times *can* it do so?" Overnight, Pakistan—a known promoter of terrorism, the "crucible of terrorism," on the verge of further, more extreme classifications by a world shocked into awareness of this evil of "cross-border terrorism"—became a valuable ally for the West. This transformation has brought several problems and contradictions to the fore. Pakistan's present policy of ridding the country of terrorists must succeed; no other option exists, and failure in this endeavor will have unimaginably dire consequences. Yet even though the Taliban have been driven from Kabul, they are neither vanquished nor entirely out of Afghanistan. They continue to hold off the United States and NATO forces in eastern Afghanistan, and more damagingly are once again spreading their influence in the adjoining areas of Pakistan. An independent, self-confident Afghanistan is not a comforting thought to Pakistan, for such an Afghanistan will then be an assertive Afghanistan, which for Pakistan just cannot be. Yet, unless there is an efficient, effective, and self-reliant Afghanistan, capable of dealing on its own with any and all security challenges to the country, how can U.S. forces leave?

For Pakistan, this is an awkward reality. Entirely dependent on the United States throughout its rather checkered past, Pakistan is again a valued U.S. ally. This has been a great relief to Pakistanis; it has given them an economic transplant of healthier growth, a better financial situation, and a more reassuring balance of payments position. Though its economy cannot be described as booming, it at least is no longer sluggish. Tactically timing the handover of some of the terrorists most wanted by the United States, Pakistan simultaneously drip-feeds U.S. anxiety while also exacerbating it. The country has regained a greater sense of itself; it is more self-confident now, with an added sense of well-being because the peace process with India has progressed reassuringly. But many questions still hang in the air. They have not been answered principally because they have not even been addressed, and they are filled with a variety of ominous portents. What, therefore, does the future hold? The main pillars of today's Pakistan convey no assurance of permanence. Omnipresent or ubiquitous, Inter-Services Intelligence remains a troubling reality. Is it or is it not the guardian of the nation's ideological purity? Does Musharraf, as the head of the government and also the Army chief, retain both posts? Is the growing strength of the Islamic parties on the vulnerable periphery of Pakistan—the North-West

Frontier Province and Baluchistan—a reversible development? And most important, how durable is the mutual dependence of the United States on Pakistan for counterterrorism operations in Afghanistan, and Pakistan's assessment of the U.S. as its principal lifeline? Were any one of these pillars to give way, most unfortunate consequences could then follow, for both India and Pakistan. The region would spiral uncontrollably into a vortex of unforeseen and unpredictable complexity.

In recent years, most Western countries have based their foreign policies toward Pakistan on the fear of an "Islamic" threat. That has left them fixated on personalities: "So and so (whoever is in control at the time) is the best option. Support him or Pakistan will be thrown into turmoil, fundamentalists will take over the country and its nuclear weapons, and regional terrorism will escalate." Such apprehensions have led to continued support of the Pakistani military as the only institution able to contain that danger. Pakistan, sadly, has experienced more than its share of religious violence, both sectarian and jihadi; yet these law-and-order situations do not mean that the fate of the state is at stake. Those Islamic groups have never posed a political or military threat to the role of the sole center of power in Pakistan: the Army.

For Pakistan, there is an attendant need to create a pool of talent from within its society, to have a "power" outside the influence of the Army, which could then become a viable alternative. This is a dilemma for the Pakistan Army, for this creation of "human capital" would generate a middle class who would seek a much greater say in governance. For the Army this may be a "lose-lose" situation, but the path of development of Pakistan requires this "ultimate sacrifice" from an organization expected to make ultimate sacrifices in the protection of the country.

Pathos and Postscript

Altaf Hussain, poetically surnamed Hali, was born in 1837 in the northern Indian town of Panipat. Along with Shibli and Iqbal, Hali was be one of the great literary figures of modern Indian Islam. Iqbal's contribution to Pakistan is beyond controversy. Muhammad Shibli, called Numani, was a "genius of commanding importance." But among those who from the outset "worked amply for the new thrust to Islam, while giving to it a distinctive contribution from their own personalities, the most eminent is Hali. He was a prolific writer in prose and poetry, a great critic, a reformer, a preacher and a teacher." In his early days Hali moved to Delhi, where he got to know Sir Syed Ahmed. He "developed a close friendship with and a great admiration for that leader and afterwards wrote his biography. Sir Syed asked him to write a poem on the fallen condition of the Mussalmans. The result was Hali's epic *Mussadas* of 1879, *Madd-o-Jazr-i-Islam* (*The Flow and Ebb of Islam*). This was then printed and distributed in millions, and sung in assemblies, from pulpits, mosques and conferences."[10]

Sir Syed remarked, "It will be quite appropriate to say that this book starts a new era in our poetry. Many of its stanzas cannot be read without one's eyes getting wet with tears." The aim of Hali's *Mussadas* was to appeal to Indian Muslims to discard their ignorance, indolence, and selfishness and to forge ahead as a disciplined, industrious, and united nation. "No other modern Urdu book is so well-known. It is familiar to every educated Mohammedan in India, and many men of the previous generation knew it by heart. Its chief merit consisted in taking stock of the national virtues and vices; like a reformer, Hali put all the virtues in the past and all the vices in the present."[11]

Hali warned Muslims against Western democracy, pointing out that in the end it would make them strangers in their own land. And thus he bade farewell: "Farewell to thee, Oh evergreen garden of India. We foreigners have stayed long in the country as your guests."[12]

---

10. Syed Sharifuddin Pirzada, *Evolution of Pakistan* (New Delhi: Uppal, 1963), p. 59.

11. Ibid., pp. 60, 61, citing Ram Babu Saksena, *A History of Urdu Literature,* 2nd ed. (Allahabad: R. N. Lal, 1940), pp. 215–16; Khalid Bin Sayeed, *Pakistan: The Formative Phase* (Karachi: Pakistan Publishing House, 1960), p. 3.

12. I have relied greatly on Ayesha Jalal's interpretation and rendering of Hali here, and also on Pirzada, *Evolution of Pakistan.*

3

India:

The Journey from Nation to Statehood

Freedom at Myth-Night

Independence came to India in 1947, accompanied by joy and soaring expectations, but spiked, too, with several question marks. Several myths were adopted, some as protective mechanisms, others largely delusional: India's attainment of independence was acclaimed as a shining example of a nonviolent transfer of power, a great tribute both to the departing British for "transferring power" in such an orderly manner and to the people of India who had "won" their independence through nonviolent means. Some manner of self-adulation had to be there, understandably, but the persistence of such myths, which perpetuate invented beliefs as a part of the country's permanent portfolio of convictions, begins to color the national fabric in artificial hues. For 1947 was not by any account peaceful, and it did not usher in a "transfer," a handing over of "power." It was more a hasty abandonment of imperial authority by an utterly fatigued Britain, drained by the Second World War of both resources and the needed will to continue with the ever-increasing demands of ruling India. All of this is open to question now, as are assertions about a "peaceful, nonviolent revolution" and the thesis of independence gained only by "civil disobedience."

Besides, this "transfer of power" did not even occur in approximately 48 percent of India, home to almost two-fifths of the total population. These were the princely states, over which Great Britain had the right of paramountcy, with differing treaty obligations, but where it had no territory or power to transfer. All these things, of course, made it immeasurably more difficult for the British to remain in India. To question these or other aspects of India's freedom movement is not to engage in revisionist history; it is a matter of common sense asserting its right to interrogate delusional notions.

British governance in India had begun to wind down around the end of World War II, and an air of uncertainty had begun to prevail. The solid seat of the British Empire was finally shifting. Departure, change, "hurry, go quickly, leave before total chaos descends" had become the overriding sentiment. Britons in India were now filled with twin anxieties: a safe, orderly, and early exit, and making arrangements for themselves in an austere postwar Great Britain. In the last two to three years of British rule, the character of governance altered greatly as responsibilities were gradually relinquished. The will to achieve results was gone. Many factors had contributed to that—a mass freedom struggle was one of them, but it was not the only catalyst.

Between the political changes in Britain; the Atlee-Mountbatten combine in charge of the fate of so many millions in India; a vast erosion in Gandhi's own position and his authority to exert a meaningful influence over even his own Congress; an "interim government" in Delhi, first without the Muslim League, then with it, resulting in three rulers in Delhi—the British, the Hindu Congress, and the Muslim League—instead of the needed single authority; and then accelerated Partition, it was probably inevitable that violence followed. Undoubtedly it was an unintended consequence and not the result of any Machiavellian design, but it was unprecedented nevertheless. The strong anti-British sentiment that had simmered for decades rapidly transmuted and added to the existing bitterness between Hindus and Muslims—a fratricidal, hate-filled antagonism such as India had never seen before, not even in the mass killings of Nadir Shah or the great massacres of Mahmud Ghaznavi. The governor of undivided Punjab, Evan Jenkins, characterized the violence in his state as the "War of Succession."[1] That wise old man of Indian politics, the ancient druid C. Rajagopalachari, then told Mountbatten, "If you do not transfer power now, there may soon be no power left to transfer!" The violence in India during the final years of British rule was unprecedented; but so too was the vast displacement of humanity. Upon Partition, some 10 to 12 million people were forced to leave home and move elsewhere. The suffering that resulted is unimaginable today, and had never before been experienced in India. It was then that "peace" abandoned this land altogether; it has yet to return, to India, to Pakistan or to Bangladesh. The very tectonic plates of the identity of this ancient land had not merely shifted; they had been deliberately and knowingly splintered.

---

1. Paul R. Brass, "The Partition of India and Retributive Genocide in the Punjab, 1946–47: Means, Methods, and Purposes," *Journal of Genocide Research* 5, no. 1 (March 2003): 71–101; Jagat Mehta, "Two Cold Wars: The Crucial Hundred Days of 1947," *India International Centre Quarterly* (New Delhi) 23, no. 1 (Spring 1996): 3–24.

The sun finally set upon the mighty British Empire, with India gaining Independence on August 15, 1947. This momentous event also marked, in Andre Malroux's phrase, the end of 500 years of the "Age of Imperial Civilisation." Rajendra Prasad, later to become India's first president, said at the inaugural function in Delhi's Government House on August 15, "Let us gratefully acknowledge that while our achievement is in no small measure due to our own sufferings and sacrifices, it is also the result of world forces and events." What came into existence then were two countries: India and Pakistan, which in turn split yet again, resulting in the birth of the third, Bangladesh. One in 1947 became three by 1971.

One particular thought often interrupts our reflections on Partition. Why did no one—not Nehru, Patel, or Jinnah, or any other protagonist—ever assess the strategic costs of Partition, or its linkage with the global consequences of the Second World War?[2] At another level, why did the Congress leaders fail to anticipate Jinnah's rapidly declining health? There is a sense of regret-tinged irony here when we revisit the fateful coincidence of some of those epochal dates of early 1947. Truman proclaimed his doctrine on March 12, 1947, a year and a week after Churchill had announced the descent of the "Iron Curtain" on March 5, 1946; the Asian Relations Conference opened in Delhi on March 23, 1947, with Nehru eloquently advocating "Asian solidarity," "Third World unity," and the like. Ironically, however, this advocacy of unity was taking place after Mountbatten had already arrived, and after a "blueprint" for partitioning India had already been finalized. Divide India and announce Asian solidarity at the same time? The implications of a divided South Asia for "the strategic calculus of an emerging, imminent bipolar globe, did not feature in India's or Pakistan's calculations."[3] In that era of mushrooming bipolarity, almost blindly, both India and Pakistan got locked into much larger global conflicts; their bilateral relations also became intermeshed with superpower standoffs. And there they remained fixed, decade after decade. Was this necessary?

Who Are We? India, Bharat, Hindustan?

The new India was almost twenty years of age by the time I resigned my commission and plunged into public life. "Plunged" is the appropriate word, for in truth, I had no preparation other than years of solitary rumination. That was all I came equipped with. I had also, quixotically, chosen not

---

2. I owe this thought to Jagat Mehta.
3. Ibid.

to join a political party, remaining an "independent" for another decade or so. Of the questions that were surfacing post-Partition, one pertained to the manner in which the partitioning had been done. Whose choice was it to divide our land? Was it the consequence of some great referendum among all those who lived here? Far from the views of most of undivided India, the handful who "ruled" India at the time, and a few others from within, had sat down together, drawn lines on paper, and altered the lives of millions. This was not a settlement of family assets among disputing brothers; it was a willful rending of the very psyche of this land. And all in the name of faith? At least this is how a very large number felt then, those who lived far from Delhi, and held their own views, who definitely wanted the "white man" out of our land, but without causing India's physical or social frame to fracture.

It was only years later that I grasped the import of two rather unsettling details. First, the area that had become Pakistan was now cut off from its principal support base, the United Provinces. The Muslim League had received a great deal of support from the UP, but that support could not be transferred to Pakistan; it remained in India. Second, the provincial or Constituent Assembly elections of 1945–46 in the UP were being credited with having established this question of "popular support" for Partition, yet that "support" was from an electorate consisting of just 15 percent of only the UP's population, not all of India. This franchise was so tiny, so very restricted, that it could hardly be said to speak even for the UP. But neither the resulting decision to partition the country nor its consequences were restricted to the UP alone. All of India paid the price—or so it seemed at the time to a very large part of undivided India. Overnight, identities were altered; what had been one became the other. Along with uncertainty, uprooting, and death came great bewilderment. What were we now? Were we India, Bharat, or Hindustan?[4]

What I share now, therefore, are the thoughts of a child born less than ten years before 1947—but not in the British part of India—who grew into consciousness with Independence. While traveling, when I was asked where I was from, I had always responded simply "Jasol" or "Khuri." We proudly described Hindustan as "our land." We might also refer to it as our "mulk"—country, nation, home—but for us, at least, "our land" encompassed all those meanings. Bharat, too, often came up, but mostly

4. A thought process also outlined by Girilal Jain in his book *The Hindu Phenomenon* (New Delhi: UBS Publishers' Distributors, 1994).

in Sanskrit or in Hindi lessons, or in discourses by visiting holy men. The name India, however, was used (as well as I can remember) only in geography lessons to denote British territories, thus almost always as "British India." Upon Independence, however, India had "awakened," and when this was pronounced, there were many who questioned the preference. I began searching for the origins of this name, India. Where had it come from, and when was it first used? Did we give it to ourselves? Or was even our name someone else's creation? I still have no satisfactory answer. In any event, "Hind" was the name routinely used by the Arabs and others in the Middle Ages. Admittedly, the distance from "Hind" to "India" is a short one, easily the result of repeated mispronunciations. The names "Hind" and then "Hindu" were also given currency by early Portuguese and Dutch seafarers, and perhaps later by the British as well. Early travelers and geographers were the first to employ "Hindustan," a combination of "Hindu" with "stan" (or "sthan," a Sanskrit word for "place"), following the model of Afghanistan as the land of the Afghans, or Tajikistan and Uzbekistan as the lands of the Tajiks and Uzbeks.[5] "India," on the other hand, became a kind of double derivative: first from the Greeks, who referred to the river Sindhu as "Indus," and then later from the British, who, after they (as they modestly put it) "acquired the country," gave the name India its "official, formal recognition."[6]

Strange, I wondered then as I occasionally do even now, that my country, this ancient land, should be so casually named. And characteristically, no pre-European, "Indian" text or map using this name (India) exists. Why do I say "characteristically"? Because there was no tradition of mapmaking in the country, so there simply are no maps in existence that were based on India's geographical delineations. India was also not the name used by early pilgrims or travelers from China, such as Fa-Hian or Huen Tsang. They found local place names adequate for their purpose. To add to the confusion, the constitution adopted in 1950 completely omits the name Hindustan, which was much more commonly used internally (at least up to Partition) than the other two. In that venerable document the Constitution of India, we declared ourselves to be "India, that is, Bharat." Hindi is mentioned as the official language of the country, but not its etymological cousin, Hindustani. After Partition, a new salutation was adopted by the armed forces: "Jai Hind"—"Hail, Hind." But there was no constitutional

---

5. There is an entirely unintended irony here in the use of the name Pakistan. Despite the desire for separateness, the continuities of centuries are impossible to erase totally: the suffix "-stan" etymologically denotes attachment to India, not separation from it.

6. Attributed to a British East India Company official.

Hindustan, so what or whom were we soldiers hailing? And what was the origin of "Bharat"? Was it taken from those ancient Sanskritic invocations mandatorily used before all "yagna" ceremonies? Our Sanskrit teacher told us that it came from the classic line "Jambudveepe Bharat khande." Freely translated, this means "On the Island of Jambu (Jambudveepe) is the section of Bharat." There was also the other injunction: "This land inhabited by the descendants of Bharat, at the foot of the Himalayas, bound by the ocean, is 'Bharatvarsha.'" This was the name of the country, and so it had remained until the first Arab invasion in the seventh century AD, led by Muhammad Bin Qasim. It was the Arabs who first used the word "Hind." Scarcely any foreign invader or visitor ever used "Bharat." "Hind," later "Hindustan," was the name we used until the British officially announced that our country was "India." Then, of course, its official adoption was sanctified by the Constitution of Independent India.

This rather casual adoption, albeit over time, of "Hindi," "Hindustan," and various other derivatives of "Hind" led to the erroneous application of a rather simple, linear logic. It went something like this: If the country is Hindustan, as it indisputably is, and if it is inhabited by the Hindu, which is also correct, then the "religion" they practice must be Hinduism. It did not matter that this was an incorrect assumption, based on untenable logic, on account of a rather lazy adaptation of the name "Hindustan." The name of a country is never the basis for the name of the religion practiced by the majority of its inhabitants. By that same logic, now that the land is known as India, the name of its religion ought to be changed to "Induism." Furthermore, and perhaps most important, there is no "-ism" in Hinduism—it is a complicated system of beliefs and practices, not a singular doctrine or theory. This has been a most ironic and unfortunate oversimplification, perpetuated over time. An even greater irony is that even though the constitution dropped the name Hindustan, the official language is still called Hindi, and we continue to debate Hinduism, Hindutva, and Hindu nationalism! Misapplications notwithstanding, the names that are now current are India, Hindustan, and, less often, Bharat. Several consequences follow, the foremost of which—and one that continues to cause confusion—pertains to the civilizational core: What gives India its identity? Where does this core lie—in India, in Bharat, or in Hindustan? To avoid disputation, a compromise is often resorted to: "Whichever you prefer; they all mean the same thing." That is correct, and yet our search continues. Why is this clarity so important for India (or Bharat or Hindustan, whichever you prefer)? Why now, in these days of globalization and dissolving sovereignties? It is because the name you choose defines the civilizational construct of India; it identifies that core as the first building block of "nationhood." India is quintessentially a civilizational, imperishable, nonterritorial entity, obviously inclusive of its political dimensions, too. But if you empty this "nonterritorial nation" of its cultural distinctiveness or civilizational substance, what then is left of India, Bharat, or Hindustan?

There is another, related difficulty involved here: the word "Hindu" is not denominational. It was not so when it was initially adopted, and it is not so now. It was based entirely on geography, so it can scarcely serve as the basis for naming a faith of such unfathomable profundity. This is a sociopolitical observation, not at all ecclesiastical. And yet the word "Hindu" has today become the determinant of identity; it is the word that is now accepted by all, even by India. There is deep irony in accepting that all of this confusion is due to the lack of continuity in India's political thinking—principally because politics and political theory have always been subservient to philosophical and religious writings. Muslim invasions caused even further disintegration of this already enfeebled tradition. The assault continued with Macaulay's introduction of European political ideas and institutions in the nineteenth century, rendering classical "Hindu" thought even more peripheral. But the question remains: If not Hinduism, then what is the name of the religion that is practiced by 85 percent of the people of India? One of the most comprehensive yet concise explanations comes from A. C. Bouquet in *Chambers's Encyclopaedia:*

> Indian religion has always been hospitable, absorbent, and syncretistic. Hence within Hinduism as it exists there is an almost unbelievable tolerance of varieties of both belief and practice. Inside the social structure of Hinduism can be found philosophic mystics, who have no belief in a personal deity; pluralists, ranging from crude animists mainly interested in local godlings (such as the village-mother or the jungle spirit) to polytheists of the type familiar to students of Greek, Roman, and Egyptian antiquities; and, between these two extremes, fervent monotheists, who address their devotion to a single personal God, conceived in terms superficially akin to those used by many Christians.

"Hindu" and "Indian" share the same etymology. Thus both words are used to mean "the people of the whole continent," and in its primary meaning, the word "Hindu" denotes the same thing as "Indian." Historically, however, the word has come to embody much more than the "merely geographical notion" that it started out as:

> When the word "Hindu" is used, it evokes a cultural connotation. But a "religious" association to the word "Hindu" has been read into it quite recently in history. Now, therefore, most of us think that we are Hindus because we have a religion called Hinduism and that the word is comparable to "Christians" or "Muslims." In fact it had no such association for the Hindus in past. This crept in when the modern European Orientalists began to study the religion of India. They found that the Hindus had no other name for the whole complex of their religious beliefs and practices except the phrase "Sanatana Dharma"; they did not even have a word of their own for religion in the European sense; and so the Orientalists coined the word "Hinduism" to describe that complex of religion. Actually, we Hindus are not Hindus because we have a religion called or understood as Hinduism. On this analogy the Greek religion might be called Hellenism.[7]

Clearly, then, dharma and religion are not the same, and Hinduism is in reality a dharma, not a religion as that term is commonly understood. But what is dharma, then? Is it duty or social obligation, or is it yet another of the indefinably complex thoughts in which the philosophical concepts of India abound? Some have, in a loose, rather lax fashion, characterized it as the equivalent of "conduct." Hindu dharma gives absolute liberty in the world of thought; to quote Professor Sarvepalli Radhakrishnan, "it enjoins a strict code of practice. The theist and the atheist, the sceptic and the agnostic may all be Hindus if they accept the Hindu system of culture and life . . . what counts is conduct, not belief."[8]

I have spent a considerable time examining this only because I believe that it is central to our subsequent deliberations—for the words "communal," "secular," and "two nations" were the focus of Partition, were they not?

---

7. Nirad C. Chaudhuri, *The Continent of Circe* (Bombay: Jaico Publishing House, 1966), p. 29.
8. S. Radhakrishnan et al., *The Hindu View of Life: Upton Lectures Delivered at Manchester College, Oxford, 1926* (London: G. Allen & Unwin, 1927), pp. 28–29.

Two Nations: Communalism and Secularism

Two examples can be used to convey a better understanding of the political import, or more accurately the politicized use, of the words "communalism" and "secularism." Syed Ahmed Khan was the first Muslim of political prominence to project the idea of "two nations." He had earlier rejected the Congress as an option for Muslims. He also resented the uneven impact on Hindus and Muslims of the British economic and educational policies. Just before the formation of the Congress, Syed Ahmed Khan had asserted unequivocally that "Hindus and Muslims are words of religious significance; otherwise, the Hindus, Muslims, and Christians who live in this country constitute one nation." He did not believe that any religion, community, or group should be identified with a nation. And yet his call for Muslim nonparticipation in the early days of the Congress earned him the title of "separatist"! As scholar Ayesha Jalal notes, "this underscores the political nature of the distinction that was made between 'communalists' and 'non-communalist' postures in the retrospectively constructed nationalist pasts."[9]

Consider, too, the stance taken in the early 1900s by Abul Kalam Azad. At the time, he was unquestionably the most important Muslim "traditionalist" in the country. Yet according to Jalal, it is "Azad's somersaults on 'religion' and 'politics' that convey the paradoxes of 'communalism.'" In 1904, Azad described the Congress as a "Hindu" body. He was distressed that his coreligionists were not united, and were living "un-Islamic and irreligious lives without a leader." In the 1920s, he issued a fatwa stating that Muslims had an "Islamic obligation" to leave India. Such utterances have all been pushed conveniently aside, like so much else of pre-Independence history in India, and even more so in Pakistan. Politically "correct" alignments have been far more important in determining what is "nationalist" versus what is "communalist."

The contradictions continue. Maulana Mohammed Ali was an adopted ally of Gandhi in the 1920s against the abolition of the Khilafat (Caliphate) in Turkey. After Indian Muslim leaders drew up a plan for a separate electorate for their community and presented it to the Viceroy Lord Minto at Simla on October 1, 1906, Ali, from the Congress pedestal, termed the work of this deputation a "command performance." He also emphasized that separate electorates were "a consequence and not the cause of

---

9. Sugata Bose and Ayesha Jalal, eds., *Nationalism, Democracy and Development: State and Politics in India* (Oxford: Oxford University Press, 1997), pp. 5–6.

the separation between Muslims and Hindus." Yet few historians trace Mohammed Ali's "communal lineage" to this period. It was only after he differed with the Congress on the issue of the Nehru Report of 1928, which outlined a proposed new Dominion Constitution for India, that he conveniently showed his true "communal" colors to the Congress. The ulema, the most ardent believers in the one-nation theory, could not imagine an independent India without shari'a rule. This advocacy of Islamic law and "nonsecular" vision coexisted harmoniously with the Congress's oft-proclaimed "secular" program. "This clearly underscores the binary opposition between 'secular nationalism' and 'religious communalism.'"[10] The strangest marriage, of course, came when the Islamic cause for Pakistan was supported by Muslim communists and socialists! The deduction is obvious, and direct: even the statements of "communal patriots," if they were made from within the Congress fold, were regarded as "nationalist." But if they were made outside the Congress, they immediately became a "communal reaction." Anyone who articulated "politics of Muslim interests" was a rank "communalist" if he did not belong to the Congress, but otherwise was a great "nationalist."

Now try replacing the word "Muslim" with "Hindu." If a statement about Hindu interests is made from outside the Congress fold, then it represents "majority communalism," worthy of condemnation. Otherwise such conduct is clearly "nationalism" worth emulating!

Spirit of Nations

India, sadly, is a victim of the reactive consequences of the many traps of history. In 1947, when Pakistan was born in the name of Islam—indeed, *for* Islam—by deliberate design and through a free exercise of democratic choice, the Constituent Assembly of India rejected the notion of a "theocratic Hindu state." India is not, and cannot be, a theocratic state. The notion that the state of India has a faith called Hindu, which the state then espouses and practices—and that therefore this is the only faith, so that none other can exist—is the very antithesis of "sanatan," for sanatan means "for all"; it is the ultimate of inclusiveness. It is sanatan that subscribes to the noble concept of "sarvpanth sambhav."[11] Yet historical hangovers trap us here; reason is the only way out of this entombment. Reason is a fight against injustice and against blind prejudice, not against faith

---

10. Ibid., p. 9.
11. A Sanskrit phrase that roughly translates to "freedom of communal expression in the context of religion."

and belief and religious practice. There is another aspect: Can any state function without a deeply ingrained sense of the moral and the spiritual? Is it not worth our while to reflect on the possibility that Marxist thought expired within a single human lifetime partly because it had no answer to that great riddle "What is death?" and because it offered nothing to that deep spiritual yearning common to all of mankind?

The challenge in the context of India is somewhat different: "to achieve a secular state with a society whose primary motivation springs from the profound depths of faith,"[12] irrespective of the color of that faith. From the moment we wake up until the last thought we have before falling asleep, through the length and breadth of India, Pakistan, and Bangladesh (and so many other lands in the region), we are all governed and deeply motivated by faith, by an almost palpable consciousness of the creator, an innate spirituality that the late Acharya Narendra Dev, in an evocative phrase, once called "Bharatiya Dharma." He advised all those who sought it to look for it in the chaupals of the hundreds of thousands of villages that dot this vast and ancient land.[13]

Thus governance in India is presented with a continuing challenge: how to effectively address the needs of a "secular" state interposed between a faith-imbued society and a spiritual nation. For the real strength of India through the millennia—through war and pillage and occupation, through famine and suffering—has been the strength of this faith. Our citizens, inspired by deep and abiding faith, are the constituents of our society, and it is this society that constitutes the core of our nationhood. In between, we do have the political organism of the Indian state, now of one hue and then of another, but that alters neither the nature of our society, state, country, nor its special needs.

What does this amount to? Simply that in India, "secularism" is not and cannot be a separation of church and state. In sanatan thought (that is, in a "Hindu" India), there is no such thing as the kind of all-embracing, all-powerful "church" that is the basis of religious organization in Judaism. Christian nations struggled for centuries to free the state from the stranglehold of the clergy. Pakistan, in its search for Islamization, still declares that the state will be run only in accordance with the sacred law of the shari'a. It is not so in India, and cannot ever be, for we are not ruled by any clergy. Why would anyone want such an all-inclusive concept as

---

12. I am quoting Syed Shahabuddin here.

13. Acharya Narendra Dev was a nationalist and social reformer who was imprisoned several times during the freedom struggle. A renowned scholar and linguist, he believed deeply in the importance of India's cultural heritage. "Chaupal" means "village square."

Sanatana Dharma to be funneled into a narrow, ritualized Semitic mold? This great thought, "sanatan," does not discriminate; it is "sanatan" for all who are on our soil. Indeed, it is difficult to strictly apply the term "religion" outside Judaism, Christianity, and Islam. Religion, with its division between the believer and the nonbeliever, is essentially a Semitic enterprise. "Sanatan Dharmis," now commonly and universally referred to as Hindus, accept no such division, believing that every path leads to the "Ultimate Reality." There is no human aspiration, belief, or experience that lies outside the wide range of this thought called sanatan, and at the cost of being repetitious, even atheism, nonduality, and self-obliterating faith are acceptable.

No other faith has ever thrived in a country whose predominant religion is Judaism. India, on the other hand, has always been a welcoming host. The Zoroastrians came here after they were driven out of Iran by a rampant Islam. St. Thomas the Apostle established Christianity on the coast of Kerala, near Calicut, in AD 52, consecrating one of the earliest churches outside the Holy Land. Islam arrived with the invasions. All have remained—yet India cannot justifiably be characterized as a "confederation of religions." For one thing, accommodation is not incorporation. For another, Hindu thought, "sanatan," is unique. It gives India its all-inclusiveness, the great spread of its spirit: Hinduism is not, like the experiments of the Archbishop of Canterbury, "a multi-faith workshop." This is the core of "Hindu nationalism," not exclusion of any kind. That is the very nature of "Hindutva"— "Hindu-ness"—and thus it is vital that we not jib at the very thought of it. This "tatva"—this essence, this basic element or spirit of matter—is not denotative of any rigidly narrow, sectarian faith or thought. Except that arising from an unneeded politicization of this phrase "Hindutva," the term itself no longer remains innocent of biased politics. The word "Hindutva" is actually an extension of "Bharatava" rather than any flanking maneuver by this often derided "Hindu nationalism" as, for example, anti-Islam or anti-Christianity thought. But arguably this is not selling well now, irrespective of "Hindutva's" true meaning—or rather, notwithstanding that; through continuous political and other use, "Hindutva" has acquired a (totally undeserved) imagery of extremism. This is sad, and it is also the real issue. "Hindutva," in its essence, is so profoundly humanist that its reality will remain. It can never be altered, no matter what the prejudices, the propagated imagery, or the wrong practices. What, then, of a "composite culture"? The president of the United States is sworn into office by taking an oath with one hand on the Bible. No one in the U.S. or elsewhere has any difficulty with the idea of that symbolic act. In India, however, if an inaugural function were to be accompanied by the breaking of a coconut or the lighting of a lamp, it would be denounced as a "Hindu ritual." How absurd, and that too in India, where coconuts are ubiquitous? Should we break champagne bottles instead? The lighting of a lamp (*tamso ma Jyotir gamaya*—"from darkness lead us to light," goes the old mantra) is not an empty ritual. It is an act of ineffable beauty, especially as part of an inaugural ceremony; it is an integral part of our cultural inheritance, yet it is not the ritual of any one denomination alone. The only culture in India is Indian, Hindu, Bharatiya— by whichever name you choose to call it. But to separate, to discriminate, and at the same time to wish to integrate does great injustice to the essence of India. And essence has to be the tatva, that basic element or spirit of matter, not a mix, even if that tatva be of many integrates.

Nehru, an iconic proponent of the "composite culture," had many nagging questions at the back of his mind, several lurking reservations about the path on which he was launching India. He was in search of the "soul of India," yet he was handicapped in a variety of ways. As the late Girilal Jain put it,

> He did not know Sanskrit, or for that matter any Indian language well enough. He had no direct access to Indian tradition, no folklore lit Nehru's psyche, for Motilal Nehru had deliberately Westernised himself rearing Jawaharlal to fit that environ. Nehru himself was essentially not a deep thinker. To the extent he was interested in ideas, he was familiar only with ideas current in Britain in his impressionable years; Fabian socialism, for instance. . . . He approached India's past, historical as well as spiritual, through British scholars who inevitably saw India through their culturally coloured prisms.[14]

Nehru's intellectual background led him to take a synthetic view of Indian culture. This was largely inevitable in view of the Persianized cultural background of his own forebears and of his Kashmiri Pandit community. The idea of partitioning the country on the basis of faith provoked grave doubts in his mind, but by then it was too late for him to review and restate his basic position, even if he had been so inclined. Some of his later speeches deserve attention in this regard. We will refer only to one, his address to the convocation of the Aligarh Muslim University on January 24, 1948:

---

14. Jain, *The Hindu Phenomenon*, p. 91.

I am proud of India, not only because of her ancient, magnificent heritage, but also because of her remarkable capacity to add to it by keeping the doors and windows of her mind and spirit open to fresh and invigorating winds from distant lands. India's strength has been twofold: her own innate culture which flowered through the ages, and her capacity to draw from other sources and thus add to her own. She was far too strong to be submerged by outside streams, and she was too wise to isolate herself from them, and so there is a continuing synthesis in India's real history, and the many political changes which have taken place have had little effect on the growth of this variegated and yet essentially unified culture. I have said that I am proud of our inheritance and our ancestors who gave an intellectual and cultural pre-eminence to India. How do you feel about this past? Do you feel that you are also sharers in it and inheritors of it and, therefore, proud of something that belongs to you as much as to me? Or do you feel alien to it and pass it by without understanding it or feeling that strange thrill which comes from the realisation that we are the trustees and inheritors of this vast treasure? . . . You are Muslims and I am a Hindu. We may adhere to different religious faiths or even to none; but that does not take away from that cultural inheritance that is yours as well as mine.

The Integration of Indian States: Paramountcy; State Forces, Administrations

Newly independent India faced myriad problems, and the integration of the princely states with the Union of India ranked high on the list. The attendant difficulties were numerous. When Lord Mountbatten announced the Partition plan on June 3, 1947, with barely seventy-five days left for the grant of independence, he made only a passing reference to the princely states. There had been barely a mention of them in the Cabinet Mission Plan, too. This was not indicative of the importance of this issue.

For one thing, there was not sufficient recognition before Partition that failure to integrate the princely states with the Union of India could well Balkanize the country. There was also the vexed question of "paramountcy." Each of the princely states had a separate treaty arrangement with the British. All of those treaties recognized and accepted Britain as the paramount power. If Britain were to withdraw from or abrogate the treaties, what would happen to "paramountcy"? Was it "transferable"? To an independent India? And if paramountcy could not be transferred, then what would happen? The answer provided by constitutional experts was that paramountcy, being nontransferable, would then lapse, after which the princely states could conduct new negotiations about their future course with the two successor countries (India and Pakistan), or with neither of the successors, at least theoretically. It all sounds fairly straightforward. In reality, however, it was not so at all.

Recent accounts of Partition and of subsequent developments in independent India have not included a detailed examination of this first significant achievement, the integration of princely states. This is a sad omission. Historically, the principal common feature that distinguished the states from the provinces was that the states had not been annexed by the British. In their origin, the evolution and growth of the individual states represented different processes. The old, historically established states, such as those of Rajputana, had been in existence as historical, political, and social entities, with their own languages, traditions, and forms of dress and a distinctly separate administration, since well before the many waves of foreign invasions. The states with Muslim dynasties were founded by the nobles or the viceroys of the invading Muslim rulers. There were also states that had emerged in the period of decline of the Mughals and prior to the consolidation of the British. Then there were the newer states, which the British recognized. Only one state, Benares, had been set up and recognized since the assumption of the government of India by the Crown.

The problem was one of stupendous dimensions. First and foremost was the sheer scale of it. Including all the nonjurisdictional estates that abounded in Kathiawar and Central India, the princely states numbered around 600. And collectively they constituted a major slice of the pre-1947 Indian body politic—two-fifths of the area and one-third of the population of the erstwhile Indian Empire, excluding Burma. Moreover, many of them were of considerable size in their own right. "Jammu and Kashmir, with an area of 84,000 square miles, was bigger than France; Travancore, with a population in 1921 of over five million, had more inhabitants than Portugal or Austria; from the recesses of his Peshi Office, Nizam Osman Ali of Hyderabad presided over a kingdom whose income and expenditure, in 1947–48, rivalled Belgium's and exceeded that of twenty member states of the United Nations"![15]

---

15. Ian Copeland, "The Princes of India in the Endgame of Empire, 1917–1947," Cambridge Studies in Indian History and Society White Paper (1948), p. 8.

Because the decision to partition India was such a severe blow to the nation's historical, political, and geographical integrity, the unity of what was left of it afterward became vital, not just for the political strength, full economic development, and cultural expression of the Indian people, but also for facing the aftermath of the Partition. "India could live if its Muslim limbs in the northwest and northeast were amputated, but could it live without its heart?" asked Sardar Vallabhbhai Patel. The heart of India, the states, had to be preserved.

The Chamber of Princes, not a constitutional body but an organization established to consider issues pertaining to the collectivity of the princely states, was unable to decide on the question of joining the Constituent Assembly, which had been set up to draft a constitution for independent India. Nevertheless, the representatives from the states of Baroda, Cochin, Jaipur, Jodhpur, Bikaner, Patiala, and Rewa took their seats in the Constituent Assembly on April 28, 1947. By then, every state except Kashmir, Bhopal, and Travancore had sent its representative. Hyderabad had not yet acceded to the Dominion and had therefore not agreed to send anyone.

It was immensely saddening that, as a former ruler described it, "shepherds of their respective flocks, large and small, were all now behaving like lost sheep." The trapdoors of history yawned open, wide and cavernous. One by one, these ancient seats of power chose to fall into that dark cavern of oblivion. With patience, tact, firmness, and understanding, this amalgamation of the princely states was completed in an admirable manner. The statecraft of Sardar Vallabhbhai Patel and his leadership gave much to independent India.

Another task to be dealt with was integrating the State Forces into the Indian Army. This, too, was handled with ease and dispatch, and without any complications—an exception being Hyderabad, whose integration was accomplished through a police action, and thus is not relevant here. The Indian Army established a committee, and officers were deputed to visit the various states and offer to absorb their forces into the Army of the Union of India. Simultaneously, surplus and unabsorbable units were demobilized. That all this was achieved with fluency was largely due to the prevailing political atmosphere. The absorption of manpower provided no major hurdles; not only were there skilled and well-trained elements in the State Forces (in the larger ones, at least), but they came largely from the same rural backgrounds as did the basic stock of the Indian Army.

The question of the future of the State Forces gained primacy soon after the general pattern for integrating the states had been worked out. For those states that had transferred their full powers, authority, and jurisdiction to the government of India under their Instruments of Merger, incorporating the State Forces into the Indian Army was not a difficult problem. Immediate disbandment was ruled out. After the government of India had taken them over, they were allowed to remain in their original locations and on the same terms and conditions as had obtained until then. Arrangements were made thereafter for their gradual absorption into the Indian Army. Those not absorbed were granted generous "mustering-out" concessions.

Partitioning the Armed Forces

It could not have been a worse time to dismantle the British Indian Army, Navy, and Air Force. At Partition in 1947, the Indian armed forces, on return from assignments abroad during the Second World War, had been reduced to 400,000 personnel in less than two years. By August 15, the Indian and Pakistani governments were to control their own armed forces. The Partition Council announced the guidelines for the division of the forces, with only forty-five days to complete the task. This responsibility was entrusted to the Armed Forces Reconstitution Committee, chaired by Field Marshal Sir Claude Auchinleck, then the commander-in-chief in India, and included two future chiefs of the Indian Army—Field Marshal Kodandera Madappa Cariappa and General Kodandera Subayya Thimmayya. The actual process of splitting up the forces began only in the third week of July, when all departments of the Indian government had de facto been bifurcated under the two heads: India and Pakistan.

It had been agreed that the reconstitution of the armed forces would be carried out on the basis of territorial rather than communal considerations. Military personnel were given the choice of leaving the service altogether or volunteering for service in either of the successor countries. Equipment and movable stores were to be divided largely in proportion to the respective strengths of the armed forces, and the technical training establishments were to be allocated on the basis of geographical location. By August 15, 1947, they were to be reorganized into independent Indian and Pakistani armed forces. The army in India had been made up of British troops from Britain and the regular Indian Army, with an overall ratio of roughly 1:2. On August 7, 1947, British units started to leave India; the last one departed in February 1948.

Since 1748, when the 1st Madras Fusiliers were established by Stringer Lawrence, two centuries had gone by. That which had taken 200 years to put together was dismantled within twenty-one days. "The safety, honor, and welfare of your country comes first, always and every time."[16] Was that the case on August 14/15, 1947?

India between the Imperial Sunsets

For India, the period between the two sunsets—the end of the British Empire in 1947 and the end of the Soviet Empire in 1989–91—was a challenge, compressing in the span of four decades the experiences of almost an entire century. The end of the British Empire was preceded by the most categorical conclusion of any human conflict ever witnessed—the bombings of Hiroshima and Nagasaki. It marked the dawn of what I, in retrospect, regard as the short "Age of Human Unreason," to paraphrase Eric Hobsbawm; it spanned roughly 1945 to 1991. This was the era of nuclear competition: of developing doctrines that in all seriousness pronounced "mutually assured destruction." It was during this age that India entered upon its freedom, dewy-eyed, full of delusional innocence, and fired by impractical idealism. Mixed with a rather sentimental approach to statecraft—the slogan "Hindi-Chini bhai bhai" ("Indians and Chinese Are Brothers") being an example—was Gandhi's overpowering humanism; and yet it often was accompanied by an "incomprehensible and unreasoning obstinacy." For example, Gandhi, though not formally a member of the Congress Working Committee after the 1930s, continued to exercise enormous influence over it. This he chose to demonstrate through his rather "un-modern" methodology of indefinite fasts, days of silence, and even sulking withdrawals. On the other hand, elements within the Congress, including Nehru and Subhas Bose, who simply could not work together as both competed for the same space, were "modern, socialist and radically inclined." This Congress had many other elements—"radical thinkers, socialists, even conservatives."[17]

Yet this was not a particularly fertile bed in which to plant the tender sapling of democracy. Democracy was a very slow entrant into the conscience of India. In reality, there was not even inner-party democracy in the Congress. What it did have was, as Sunil Khilnani graphically puts it, a "formidable will to political power." But there was a price to be paid for that quest. As the fateful date of 1947 drew closer and the lure of office was within reach, with those luscious fruits of power hanging tan-

---

16. "The honor, welfare, and comfort of the men you command come next. Your own ease, comfort, and safety comes last, always and every time." Sir Philip Chetwode, from his speech at the inauguration of the Indian Military Academy at Dehradun, capital of the Indian state of Uttaranchal, on December 10, 1932.
17. Sunil Khilnani, *The Idea of India* (London: H. Hamilton, 1997), p. 27.

talizingly close, the fissures within surfaced. The Congress's "diversity of voices—Gandhian, socialist, conservative, capitalist, Hindu—meant that Congress, like so many other visionary nationalisms had no coherent programme of independent government. Obviously, democracy, its practices, its demands, obligations and restraints was hardly any priority; it stood 'in a lonely corner.'"[18]

There was also the question of the founding of the state of India. The British had introduced, for the first time ever in India's political consciousness, the concept of a viable working state. They had addressed it as conquerors, flexibly, and with a degree of pragmatism, as well as, if I might again quote Khilnani, a "relative unconcern with consequences." In independent India, with Indian leadership, the approach to the functioning of the state obviously had to be very different, but the Congress, which had inherited the instruments of "coercive power" from the British Raj, remained with that power, not any other. On the other hand, Indian society at that point was filled with aspirations; it was a society on the move, but for this our state was neither fully structured, nor inclined, nor therefore empowered. It was, as Khilnani observed, inevitable that the Indian state would emerge from the "deliberations of the Constituent Assembly as a parliamentary democracy based on universal suffrage, without religious affiliations and committed to social reforms." And that it did. Against this background, we have to admire the enormous craft that went into bringing together this state, the integration of the princely order and states into an egalitarian India, and simultaneously addressing the many questions that the British had left unattended, including the great challenges of the northeast, where Nagaland was the first to raise its voice.[19]

There was, and remains, another issue of fundamental importance: ignorance, or perhaps the more appropriate word is innocence, of the very concept of territorial integrity. Millennium after millennium, India has been a nation, but always a "nonterritorial nation." In all my study, I have yet to obtain even one accurate and geographically delineated territorial map

18. Ibid., p. 28.
19. Unlike the British provinces in India, the princely states were not directly under British control. They were sovereign entities whose rulers had entered into treaties with the British Crown. The Indian Independence Act of 1947 released these states from their obligation to the empire and freed them to join either India or Pakistan.

Under British rule, the territory that was home to the Naga tribes had been incorporated into Assam. After Independence, separatists concerned about preserving the tribes' ethnic identity demanded greater autonomy for their ancestral areas, as well as the right to self-governance. It took ten years and a series of violent clashes between Naga rebels and Indian security forces, but in 1957, the Indian government established a Naga administrative unit under Indian rule, and six years later, Nagaland was inaugurated as a self-governing state within India.

of India before the British entered the scene. This is an aspect we still pay little heed to. We assume, almost genetically, that this nationhood of India is immutable, unconquerable, transcending all else. We have this self-induced certitude: that this civilizational nation is not confined within any delineated territory or boundary. Sadly, in independent India this proved to be a critical shortcoming. It prevented the new rulers of free India from moving to define the territorial limits of the Union of India as their very first task. It is largely because of this great lacuna of statecraft, and of leadership, that almost six decades after Independence, India is the only country of its size in the world that does not have a defined, settled boundary. Many years later, in 2000, when I was seeking further details on the consequences of the Kargil conflict the year before, I was aghast to read in a border management report that the government had yet to conduct a census of India's island territories. Successive governments of India had actually ruled without knowing how many islands the Union of India possessed! And this was after the 1962, 1965, and 1971 border wars! This attitude explains why "disputes" over rights to territory remain unresolved in India to this day.

Security and Statecraft

It is one of those great paradoxes that from the moment of Independence, India became more prone to internal violence. The Partition riots were an inopportune statement, adding to a sense that there was no authority, no one in charge. Of course, this was a direct consequence of the lack of experience of India's new rulers, of a sense of statecraft combined with what I term a post-Gandhi ersatz pacifism. This was often an excessively flaunted attribute of the new order, projected loudly as a kind of certifying label of "loyalty" to the ideas of that great and mesmerizing leader. Yet the entire culture of security was thereby twisted out of shape. For one thing, India has always had an accommodative and forgiving "Hindu" milieu. It does sometimes descend into insensate violence, as is true of most societies, but only episodically. On this foundation, Jain, Buddhist, Vaishnav-Bhakti, and then Gandhi's nonviolence have successively been superimposed. The result has been a curious mixture of ideas and attitudes.

With unthinking allegiance to Gandhi, the concept of "state power" had become emasculated; its due and proper deployment in the interest of state and society, and at the correct time, had been relegated to a low priority. In consequence, independent India simply rejected the centrality of strategic culture as the first ingredient of vigorous and bold national security.

There was also no recognition of a sense of history, of recording, evaluating, and assessing it, then incorporating that into decision-making. This absence of a historical sense had a consequence: it, too, significantly impaired the development of strategic thought. Ancient Indian texts on every conceivable subject are filled with sex, art, dance, and drama, and most abundantly with philosophy. Yet there is none, other than the odd text by Kautilya, that has detailed the military science of India. There was another factor: of geography and a sense of territory. Indian nationhood was largely cultural and civilizational, and Indians did not fear the loss of it, for it was as unconquerable as the Indian spirit. Thus both were absent: a territorial consciousness, and a strategic sense about the protection of it.

It is a telling comment that independent India failed to build on a key resource that the ruling British had developed: a surplus of military power. It was this surplus that enabled the British to commit Indian troops to many assignments overseas—Afghanistan, Burma, the Gulf and the Trucial States, the two world wars—while simultaneously meeting internal obligations. But yes, about half of India, the princely states, was outside their area of direct responsibility for order. Since Independence, sadly, there have been several occasions that required the use of the Army within the boundaries of India (for example, Operation Blue Star at the holy shrine of the Sikhas in 1984; in the northeastern states of India; and in Jammu and Kashmir). This, too, is a comment, and a serious one. Employing the Army for such tasks or in support of civil authority has many consequences. It distracts the military from its primary role and seriously impairs its effectiveness. Its sense of prestige and of purpose also takes knocks, and it has suffered this consequence.

Such concerns perhaps seemed secondary when Nehru set out to achieve what he called "a just society through just means." There was, however, one great psychological interruption to this enterprise—the long skirmish with China in 1962 over unsettled territory. Nehru had continued to live in his rather unrealistic world, dreaming of "Asian solidarity," an "Asian civilization," even persuaded in his conviction that conflict between India and China was a "conceptual impossibility." Tragically, he adhered to this belief despite increasing evidence of China's true intentions and the glaring reality of an unsettled border. Even as evidence of Chinese intentions continued to mount, Nehru remained ambivalent. In the 1950s, therefore, when China invaded Tibet, Nehru did no more than to inform the Indian ambassador in Beijing, K. M. Panikkar, "I attach great importance to India and China being friends." I was in uniform in 1962, and I cannot sufficiently convey the sense of deep outrage and humiliation experienced by those of us who were serving at the time, whether or not we were in the northeast of India. It was totally incomprehensible as to what the prime minister really meant when, after the stunning fall of Sela and Bomdila to Chinese infiltration parties who had worked their way behind Indian lines, he announced over All India Radio: "My heart goes out to the people of Assam." Rude soldiery then voiced phrases that were, well, very rude. India witnessed a Nehru seized of pathetic fury, blustering to his Cabinet colleagues in impotent rage: "I would fight them with a stick!" Nehru's foreign policy was in tatters; "nonalignment" had died along with so many soldiers on the bleak heights of the Aksai Chin. It is also here that the foundation was laid for what we later accepted in Tashkent in 1966, and the signing of the Treaty of Peace and Friendship with the Soviet Union in 1971. In actuality, 1962 was the end of the dynamism of nonalignment.[20] It was too severe a blow; the Nehru premiership ended in 1964, and with his death, an era ended as well. From 1947 to 1964, it had been Nehru's time. He was dominant, not as an emperor or dictator, but as a searching, sensitive human, as full of the questioning uncertainties of life as was newly independent India. Nehru did not know all the answers; nor did he have the instincts of a decisive ruler. No one could help him, for he was already too distanced, too proud to ask. But he searched, with unvarying diligence, with transparent sincerity, with great patriotism, because he so very earnestly wanted to bequeath to this India all that he could.

Socialism Central

Nehru was not an economic intellectual, but he was governed by an intellect that had a sense of the ideas of his time. Principally, this was socialism, including state control and centralized planning. This is where Professor P. C. Mahalanobis entered the scene of India's macro-economic management. Very early, Mahalanobis had written to Nehru that the "heart of the problem is to make changes in all necessary directions at the same time, in a balanced way, so as to bring about structural transformation as quickly as possible." This became Nehru's guiding beacon. From the establishment of the Planning Commission until his death, this was the logic that persuaded him. Underlying it all was obviously a disputable proposition—the idea that "India's economy could be managed through human control," through policies and actions decided upon cen-

---

20. Y. D. Gundevia, *Outside the Archives* (Hyderabad: Sangam Books, 1984), p. 235.

trally, then handed down. Steps were taken to "acquire for the state near total control over all means of production." The Planning Commission was administratively a clever device. As a commission, it was not obligated to answer to the Parliament in the way that ministers and ministries did. Significant decision-making authority was built into its structure, but the chain of command went straight to the prime minister. In consequence, with the prime minister as chairman and a succession of distinguished economists who enjoyed Nehru's confidence as deputy chairmen, the Planning Commission became the nerve center of economic management, rather than the Ministry of Finance. Indian society came to believe in the Planning Commission and what it represented. Nehru's enthusiasm was infectious; he spoke eloquently of the "temples of the future," of the state sitting on the "commanding heights of economy." It was an evocative idea, and thus those "heights" were not contested by anybody, for the Planning Commission and the centralized economy had by then been drawn into the electoral rhetoric of the times. Like "nonalignment," "planned economy" became a shibboleth, to which successive generations of Indians, and of course successive governments in Delhi, were required to pay unquestioning homage. They still do.[21]

Reality was not as flattering. By the mid-1960s, the economy had begun to falter. India was already living beyond its means. Licenses and quotas, permits and exchange-control laws had converted even god-fearing housewives into currency and gold smugglers. The laws of the land persuaded the law-abiding to become lawless, if only by innocently tucking extra currency notes into the folds of their sarees. But things changed. Mrs. Gandhi's premiership lurched from one economic crisis to another. Lacking any kind of economic philosophy, she moved from one populist shortcut to the next. Almost all the subsequent problems of the Indian economy can be traced back to these first years of Nehru and Indira Gandhi. By now, planning had become the god that failed; the Planning Commission was now a kind of quango, a sinecure for the semiretired and the politically inconvenient. In the democratic sense, too, the social contract took on a totally different idiom. The citizen could no longer negotiate with political leaders; consequently, he skipped politicians and went directly to the state. The bureaucracy increasingly appropriated authority. By the time Indira Gandhi became prime minister in 1966, the consequences of the 1962 conflict with China and the 1965 conflict with Pakistan had left a deep mark on her psyche. For security, she reverted to

---

21. Khilnani, *The Idea of India,* pp. 88, 81.

"protectionist policy of the lowest kind." She also prepared the ground for what later came to be termed "the economic crisis of 1991."[22]

The Adventure of Democracy

In the meantime, how was democracy operating in independent India? "The great sway that the Congress had under the impulse of the freedom movement," indeed, the sheer veneration in which Nehru had continued to be held several years after Independence, had evaporated. Gandhi's nationalism had stood to disband the Congress Party upon Independence. "Its task is done. The next task is to move into villages and revitalize life there to build a new socio-economic structure from the bottom upwards."[23] But this did not happen, which prompted him to state after Independence, "Every Indian whether he owns up to it or not, has national aspirations but there are as many opinions as there are Indian Nationalists [about] the exact meaning of that aspiration."[24] After resounding victories in the first and second general elections of 1952 and 1957, the Congress began to lose its hold on the country. By the election of 1967, the Congress was swept out of office all the way from Amritsar to Calcutta, across the vast heartland of India. This was followed by the election of 1971, which was called in advance, in the process fracturing the system of simultaneous elections to Parliament and state assemblies. This has had serious long-term consequences for India. The great political landmarks of this phase of independent India's evolution into an integratedly functioning state are the adoption of the country's constitution; the first general elections; the Sino-Indian border standoff; the conflict of 1962; Nehru's death; succession struggles; 1965; Tashkent; the death of Lal Bahadur Shastri; the political ascendancy of Indira Gandhi; and the fourth general elections—1967—when the Congress was routed in North India. Fifteen years after the first elections in 1952, the Congress as a unifying all-India party was finished. Internal power struggles in the Congress post-Shastri, and the inherent contradictions in a party that had represented "all things to all men" but had now reached the boiling point, were actually the precursor to the ultimate fragmentation of Indian democracy into components representing religion, caste, region, and—only occasionally, and again accidentally—ideology. The Congress Party fragmented, but in the process it splintered the Indian polity, too.

---

22. Ibid., 90–91, 30.
23. Ignatius Jesudasan, *A Gandhian Theology of Liberation* (Ananda: Gujarat Sahitya Prakash, 1987).
24. Mahatma Gandhi, *Mahatma Gandhi and Leo Tolstoy Letters* (Long Beach, Calif.: Long Beach Publications, 1987).

With the prevailing populist mood, the economy was further paralyzed. Everything was being nationalized; the government even experimented with trading in wheat, but with disastrous results. Barriers were erected against foreign investment. A Voice of America radio station that had been proposed for Ceylon was termed an "outrageous encroachment." Severe restrictions were placed upon how much the industry could actually produce. Most unbelievable, penalties were imposed for those who exceeded their sanctioned production levels. Everything was licensed; everything required a permit. This equaled delay, plus patronage, hence corruption. Such was the Left intelligentsia's great contribution to India's economic development. Of course, I do not know whether Indira Gandhi ever recognized, as much as her Left supporters did, that she spoke a language that was solidly populist. Banks were nationalized, and the compensatory "privy purses" being paid to the former rulers of the princely states were withdrawn, against all solemn assurances and constitutional promises. It is ironic that the total saving in this process was less than rupees 4 crore per annum (less than $900,000 in today's U.S. dollars).

Indira Gandhi made many more socialist promises, extravagant and evocative, but only because they were "vague and could not be translated into action." Therefore, as an alternative she "organized loan melas, free distribution of milk, free sarees." Politicians of her party began to distribute both food and bank credit as "payment" for votes. In the process, she did gain electoral support, but she very rapidly then descended into authoritarian politics. This was the consequence of many factors, including the oil shocks of the 1970s. This economy spawned an illegitimate "black economy"; tax rates were raised, with the income and wealth tax combined increasing to 110 percent! Till then, India had managed to control inflation and also avoid high debt. But you could not continue to have populist announcements and yet none of these shortcomings. No new day dawned; electoral support began to evaporate. Inevitably, therefore, following an adverse court judgment in 1975, Indira Gandhi declared a state of emergency that gave her the power to rule by decree. The many consequences of this Emergency permanently destroyed the Congress and the administrative machinery of India. Indira Gandhi became a dictator: "she began to exude power, but power it was not"; it was but the empty notion of power. There were elections in 1967, 1971, 1977, and 1980, with the percentage of votes obtained by the Congress Party ranging from a high of 43.6 (1971) to a low of 34.5 (1977). But the door was closing very rapidly. "India had entered a phase of identity creation as the instrument of electoral success. This was a very dangerous development for it had come in the wake of authoritarianism." It is an old and accepted axiom that once you set your skis on the downhill slopes of such policies, you have to go faster and faster or you will perish. And even if you continue to go faster, you will still perish. During and after 1984–89, India endeavored to find an answer to that most difficult question in electoral democracy: how to effect a peaceful democratic succession. In 1989, Rajiv Gandhi lost his great majority in the House and saw his number of seats slump from 415 (out of 543) to just 197. The sole proprietary right of the Congress over India was finished.[25]

India at the Cusp

We ended our survey of the development of democracy in India in 1989, linking that date to the disintegration of the Soviet Union. If that is the determinant, then 1989 is equally appropriate because of, even if it is not exactly synchronous with, the fall of the Berlin Wall. But as Eric Hobsbawm once commented, "Exact dates are always matters of historical, didactic or journalistic expediency," and clearly 1989 could easily have been replaced by 1996 or 1998. Nikolai Kondratiev propounded the theory of long waves, which states briefly that periods are cyclical; a beginning (political-economic) always has an end at the trough of a "long wave." In like fashion, the wave of India's democratic evolution set in motion by the British in and around 1935—with evolutionary landmarks such as 1947 (Independence/Partition) and 1952 (the first general election)—had to end, to reach its apogee or trough, whichever can best explain that transition point. It is clear that 1989 was marked by two clearly visible events, both denoting a kind of finality—one internal to India and the other external. For the democratic evolution of India, 1989 marks the trough of the phase of single-party Congress domination. Internationally, that year marks the end of the Soviet Union. The world went into a global transformation: the relative equilibrium of two rival superpowers was no more. There was now only America, the hyperpower. A New World Reordering became the menu of the day.

Just then, characteristically, India became totally internalized, in a muddle as it tried to answer that most trying of questions: how to achieve an orderly, democratic succession. Between 1989 and 1998, India had four general elections and seven prime ministers (one of whom served twice).

---

25. A number of thoughts and ideas in this section have been more elegantly and eloquently voiced by Sunil Khilnani in *The Idea of India.* Quotes from ibid., p. 44.

New political forces emerged, competing to fill the space left by the Congress—which, lacking a central, unifying, inspiring idea, now represents no more than a family inheritance, sufficient only to keep the structure of the organization together, occasionally to be voted into office in some states, or in coalitions of convenience. Political parties born in the transformational trauma of the Emergency of 1975 have—since 1977, when it ended—been coming together, splitting and rejoining again, almost in a political replication of cell biology. Some have taken up the mantle as the voice of a specific state or region, combining the strength of newly emergent political classes in rural and urban society with invocatory localism. These forces and parties are now a coalitional constant in Delhi's governments, at least for the time being.

There is also the Bharatiya Janata Party (BJP), representing an alternative way of thinking, a self-confident nationalism with a pronounced emphasis on the civilizational and cultural identity of India as Hindu, and a meritocratic party structure and hierarchy. The BJP, which traces its roots back to the Janata Party—the combined non-Congress party of protest put together in 1977—and before that to the Jan Sangh (1950–77), has some members with connections to the Rashtriya Swayamsevak Sangh, too.[26] The BJP was formally launched in 1980, and now has an established electoral support base that varies, nationally, between 22 and 28 percent. After three successive parliamentary elections in 1996, 1998, and 1999, it formed the government at the center, but always in coalition. In the elections of 2004, it obtained 26 percent of the vote, won 138 seats in the Lok Sabha (Lower House)—seven less than the Congress—and demitted office after six years in government. To its political adversaries, the BJP is a "communal organization" and, variously, a "fascist body," "anti-minority," "Hindu extremist," "chauvinistically aggressive" in its approach to Pakistan, destroyer of India's secular tradition, etc. "Hindu nationalist party" is another phrase that is frequently used. Some of the supporters of the BJP, on the other hand—particularly while in government—regarded it as not sufficiently faithful to Hindu thought, not adequately committed to the core of Hindu interests, and too accommodating of Pakistan! The BJP's scorecard contains two major negatives. First, there was the dispute between Hindus and Muslims over the Ayodhya Ram temple, which was

---

26. The Rashtriya Swayamsevak Sangh came into existence in 1925. Described by *The Economist* as the largest noncommunist organization in the world, the RSS is organized hierarchically, with a single director at the top. Most of its work is done through its widespread network of branches, called "shakhas." Over the years, it gained prominence and political influence.

consequently vandalized, then forcibly destroyed by activists in December 1992. The government's failure to control this situation is accepted, and is greatly regretted. The other is the loss of state control in Gujarat in 2002, after a trainload of pilgrims returning from Ayodhya were trapped and the car they were riding in was set on fire in Godhra. Just under sixty men, women, and children died in that ghastly attack. This triggered rioting in Gujarat, killing 254 Hindus and 790 Muslims, according to figures that were provided by the government to Parliament in May 2005. These riots were a blot on Gujarat's face, and they sullied the BJP as well. Prior to this development, there had not been a single communal riot. The mishandling of events after Godhra gave substance to the worst imaginings about the BJP, as even those who remain sympathetic toward it were forced to observe. To the critics, these riots did more than sully the BJP's name; they "justified" the worst fears of the self-styled "secularists," and presented the worst possible face of what they called "Hindu nationalism." An impeccable record, of a riot-free India over six years, was compromised.

That, however, is getting ahead of the story. Diligently making its way up the electoral ladder, the BJP was in office in 1998, which is where we go next. I was deputy chairman of the Planning Commission at that point, though it was as minister of finance that I had earlier been slated to take over. In the short-lived BJP government of 1996, too, I had been the finance minister.

This has been a greatly condensed attempt at recounting independent India's democratic endeavors. A great many details have been omitted; that is inevitable. If I could be permitted an analogy here, today when I travel, I see much less than I saw earlier, for now I have to move with jet-propelled velocity; earlier it was one step at a time, with plenty of time to see, observe, learn, and understand. In the period that I am writing about, however, events, too, seemed to travel with terrifying velocity. Impossibilities became realities; the Soviet Empire, the greatest empire of the twentieth century, collapsed. And in a gesture of historical and poetic justice, this collapse was symbolized by the physical pulling down, by East Germans and East Berliners, of that great visual symbol of totalitarianism, the Berlin Wall.

It was the sunset of the Second Empire. It would change India's world forever, just as the imperial sunset of 1947 had done, or the collapse of the Ottoman Empire had following the First World War.

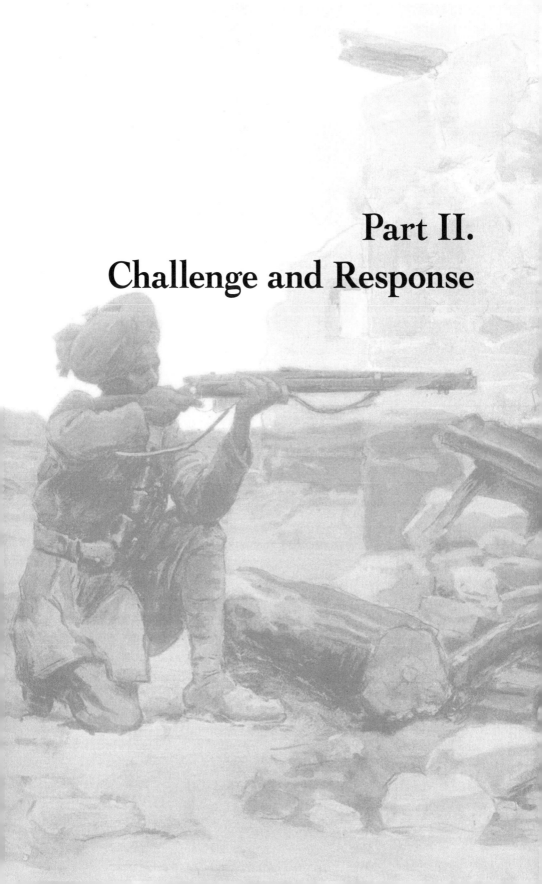

Part II.
Challenge and Response

4

Pokhran II:
The Implosion of Nuclear Apartheid

India Searches for Change

The decade 1989–98 was one of democratic transformation. The elections of 1989 had removed the Congress led by Rajiv Gandhi from office. A coalition of disparate parties led by V. P. Singh, a rebel congressman and former minister in Rajiv Gandhi's cabinet and his Janata Dal Party, was sworn in. Predictably, this government did not last long; major conceptual and structural faults in this untenable coalition led to its premature end. The Congress exploited the situation by propping up an unviable breakaway of this same Janata Dal. That cynical experiment, too, soon ended. The results of the election of 1991 were a shade more decisive, but sadly, Rajiv Gandhi was assassinated by a terrorist group while campaigning that year. The Congress gained seats and formed a rather tenuous government under the cautious and calculating P. V. Narasimha Rao. The BJP was the second-largest party, persuading a prominent international journal to remark perceptively: "the winner came in second." As per constitutional norms, five years later there was another election, after which the BJP was sworn into office, despite not having sufficient numbers to command a majority on its own.

I had been returned to Parliament in all these elections, and I was now the deputy leader of the party in the Lok Sabha. In 1996, the BJP's prime minister, Atal Bihari Vajpayee, invited me to take the finance portfolio. Yet again, other parties combined to oppose the BJP government, forcing it to resign. Two successive "United Front" governments—a collective of regional parties propped up by the Congress—followed, almost like seasonal change. In the election of 1998, the BJP emerged as the clear leader, though again not with an absolute majority. I was again to be sworn into office, but could not be immediately, because of a last-minute difficulty. This arose from a sudden objection that was raised by senior and responsible quarters about my inclusion in the ministerial ranks. When I was informed about it, I immediately stepped aside. I was sworn in as external affairs minister a few months later. This was the government, under the premiership of Vajpayee, that led the country until 2004, though in 1999 it was forced to face yet another election following a snap defeat, by just one vote, in Parliament. That led to a comment in the House: "Atalji, you may have lost the vote in the House, but you have won the heart of India!" This was prophetic. We were again returned to office, and I continued as minister for external affairs.

Regime Change in the Nuclear Orbit

The end of the Cold War transformed Europe but did little to ameliorate India's security concerns. The rise of China and continued strains with Pakistan made the early 1990s a greatly troubling period for India. At the global level, the nuclear weapons states showed no signs of moving decisively toward a world free of atomic danger. Instead, the Nuclear Non-Proliferation Treaty (NPT) was extended indefinitely and unconditionally in 1995, perpetuating the existence of nuclear weapons in the hands of five countries that were busily modernizing their nuclear arsenals. In 1996, after the favored five had conducted more than 2,000 tests, a Comprehensive Test Ban Treaty (CTBT) was opened for signature, following two and a half years of negotiations. This treaty, alas, was neither comprehensive nor related to disarmament. It did nothing more than ratify the nuclear status quo. India's choices had narrowed critically. It had to maintain its nuclear option, which had been developed and safeguarded over decades, by all eight prime ministers and eight successive governments of India between 1974 and 1996, and not eroded by self-imposed restraints. Such a loss would place the country at risk. Faced with a difficult decision, the government concluded that its lone touchstone would be national security. Not only were the nuclear tests that India conducted on May 11 and 13, 1998, inevitable, but they were a continuation of a policy from almost the earliest years of Independence. This policy was committed to a basic tenet: India's security in a world of nuclear proliferation lies either in total global disarmament or in exercising the principle of equal and legitimate security for all.

So why did we conduct tests? Nuclear technology had already transformed global security. Nuclear weapons, theorists reasoned, were not actually weapons of war but in effect were a military deterrent and a tool of possible diplomatic coercion. Thus India's nuclear policy was based on the logic that a world free of nuclear weapons would enhance not only our own security, but the security of all nations. In the absence of universal disarmament, India could scarcely accept a regime that arbitrarily divided nuclear haves from have-nots. With no international guarantees of security for India forthcoming, nuclear abstinence by us alone seemed increasingly worrisome. In 1968, India reaffirmed its commitment to disarmament but decided not to sign the NPT. In 1974, it conducted its first nuclear test—Pokhran I, as it has come to be called—but did not weaponize. Frankly, however, thirty years (1969 to 1999) of an often overtly moralistic but simultaneously ambiguous nuclear policy and self-restraint had paid no measurable dividends. The NPT had identified five "legitimate" nuclear weapons states: the United States, Britain, France, Russia, and China. If the possession of nuclear weapons by this so-called "Permanent Five" (P-5), had somehow enhanced the global architecture of security, then why and how would only India's bomb be dangerous? If the P-5 continued to employ nuclear weapons as an international currency of force and power, then why should India voluntarily devalue its own national security? If overt, unambiguous deterrence worked in the West, by what reasoning would it not work in India and our neighborhood?

Since Independence, India had consistently advocated global nuclear disarmament. Our country was the first to call for a ban on nuclear testing in 1954, for a nondiscriminatory treaty on nonproliferation in 1965, for a treaty on non-use of nuclear weapons in 1978, for a nuclear freeze in 1982, and for a phased program for the total elimination of nuclear weapons in 1988. Most of these initiatives were rejected by the nuclear weapons states. What emerged, in consequence, was a discriminatory and flawed nonproliferation regime that was detrimental to India's security. The imposition of an unconditional and indefinite extension of the NPT on the international community in 1995 was the watershed. India was left with no option but to go in for overt nuclear weaponization. The Sino-Pakistani nuclear weapons collaboration, in flagrant violation of the NPT, made it obvious that the NPT regime had collapsed in India's neighborhood. The situation only worsened as the decade wore on. In 1997, more evidence surfaced that nuclear technology was being shared between China and Pakistan, and that the United States was taking a relatively permissive stance on this issue. During a visit to Washington by Chinese president Jiang Zemin, the United States insisted on separate agreements with China regarding its provision of nuclear materials to Iran and to Pakistan. These the Chinese signed instead of professing their innocence. Both America's unease and

China's signature on this agreement attested to the threat posed to India by Chinese proliferation. Nevertheless, China continued to pass missile technology and components to Pakistan.

The end of the Cold War created the appearance of American unipolarity but also led to the rise of additional power centers. The fulcrum of the international balance of power moved gradually from Europe to Asia. But China's rise led to new security strains that were not addressed by the existing nonproliferation regime. The indefinite extension of the NPT in 1995, essentially a Cold War arms-control treaty with a hitherto fixed duration of twenty-five years, legitimized in perpetuity the existing nuclear arsenals, and in effect, thereby, an unequal nuclear regime. Even as the nations of the world acceded to the treaty, the five acknowledged nuclear weapons powers stood apart; and the three undeclared nuclear weapons states—India, Israel, and Pakistan—were unable to subscribe. Neither could the world succeed in halting the transfer of nuclear technology from declared nuclear weapons powers to their preferred clients. The NPT notwithstanding, nuclear proliferation continued in India's backyard. Since nuclear powers that assisted or condoned proliferation were not subject to any penalty, the entire nonproliferation regime became not just flawed but a sanctuary for proliferation! Nuclear technologies became at worst commodities of international commerce, and at best lubricants of diplomatic fidelity. Chinese and Pakistani proliferation was no secret, but neither was America's docile acquiescence. India, the only country in the world that was sandwiched between two nuclear weapons powers, faced a permanent legitimization of nuclear weapons by the haves, a global nuclear security paradigm from which it was excluded, trends toward disequilibrium in the Asian balance of power, and a neighborhood in which two nuclear weapons countries were acting in concert. Clearly, this was not an acceptable situation. India had to protect its destiny—and exercise its nuclear option.

Besides, the "ambiguous deterrence" that had been practiced by both India and Pakistan from 1989 to 1999 had run its course; it was now increasingly a potential source of danger in the context of the jihad that had been launched by external terrorists in Jammu and Kashmir, who, backed publicly by Pakistan, were capable of carrying out warlike interventions. It was also clear that, notwithstanding the loud cries of horror from the P-5 (in May 1990, the United States sent Deputy National Security Advisor Robert Gates to the region to defuse the so-called "crisis"), since May 1998 they had all been fully aware of the "ambiguous deterrence" or "recessed deterrence" (call it what you will) being practiced by India and Pakistan; the repeal by the U.S. Congress of the Pressler Amendment, which had barred aid to Pakistan unless the Pakistanis could prove that they did not possess a nuclear device; China's increased activity at its testing range at Lop Nur, where it had set off a Pakistani nuclear device; and Pakistan's own nuclear proliferation as part of the A. Q. Khan syndrome.[1] It is disingenuous for the P-5, and the United States in particular, to continue to assert that the A. Q. Khan Research Institutes and ISI in Pakistan were, and in the latter case are still, independent of the executive authority. This fiction may be a component of the United States' techniques for preserving its self-image, but it is morally indefensible because it is factually so incorrect.

The events of May 1998 resulted in transparency, openness, and the development of a publicly and mutually visible doctrine with supporting capabilities. This is precisely the "classical" nuclear deterrence that was practiced by the P-5 for more than forty years. India has, in addition, taken a conceptual leap by publicly limiting its intentions through the voluntary declaration of "no first use" and "non-use against non-nuclear states." This is far more than any of the P-5 have ever promised, either to their potential opponents, to friends, or to the global community.

One Morning in May

It was the morning of May 11, 1998. We waited expectantly, rather anxiously, on that fateful day in central Delhi, at the house and office of the Indian prime minister at 5 Racecourse Road. The underground test, slated for around 8:30 AM, had been postponed because the wind direction was not suitable—an important precaution, as approximately five kilometers east of the test site is an inhabited village. In the room, anxious minutes turned into hours; conversation faltered, for there is only so much empty talk one can engage in on such occasions. It was, after all, an event that would alter an existing order; it would confront us, we understood, with a phalanx of challenges the moment the formal announcement of it was made. What was scheduled for early morning had to be postponed several times, and for the same reason. By then, other worries and concerns had begun cropping up: about wandering cattle straying too close to the test

1. A country practicing "ambiguous deterrence" refuses to either confirm or deny that it possesses nuclear weapons. A country practicing "recessed deterrence" confirms that it has achieved nuclear capability but asserts that it does not plan to make offensive use of such weapons. Abdul Qadeer Khan is a German-educated metallurgist who was for many years the head of Pakistan's nuclear program. He is sometimes called "the father of the Pakistani bomb."

bore, too close to the "No Entry" sign. For the team at the test site—which included A. P. J. Abdul Kalam, then the head of the Defence Research and Development Organisation (DRDO), and today India's president—the possibility of death or injury to cattle was not acceptable. Ordinarily, those conducting tests of India's scientific and high-tech capability would not accord much importance to the safety of cattle, but this team of scientists did.

Of those present in the Prime Minister's Office that day, I was the only one totally familiar with Pokhran, its environs, and its testing range. The scientific team used the facility there on occasion, but Pokhran was not a part of their lives. For me it had a very different meaning. Pokhran is a historical township about 100 kilometers east of Jaisalmer. Although not part of the former Jaisalmer state, it was an important constituent of princely Jodhpur. Whenever I had traveled to Khuri from Jodhpur, it was via Pokhran. The train from Jodhpur used to terminate at Pokhran, and for the next hundred kilometers or so it was a track in the desert that led to Jaisalmer. Traveling a further fifty-odd kilometers, one would then reach Khuri. To the north of this track, now a road, lay vast, open spaces, largely uninhabited, pristine, and untouched for centuries. At one time there was an abundance of chinkara and black buck there, as well as grouse. It was also the home of the largest of our desert birds, the great Indian bustard, now so sadly depleted in number; and the migratory houbara bustard, which every winter hopped through the desert all the way from eastern Iraq, through Iran and Baluchistan, and into this part of Jaisalmer. In the 1970s, Pakistan, as part of its efforts to cultivate influential Arab sheikhs, had begun to organize falconry outings just across the border. Their main hunting ground lay on both sides of this "border." Pakistan police and customs agents, and the Pakistan Rangers, too, were free to ascribe as many attributes of inviolability as they wanted to these borders, which were actually nothing more than lines on paper. But for the hunted houbara or the swiftly swooping falcon, this human-defined border had no meaning whatsoever. Not infrequently, we would look after a lost falcon or two, which, unable to find a familiar wrist to return to, would instead seek shelter with us!

The Moment of Truth

We continued to wait. Then, as the shadows began to lengthen on that midsummer day, the "hotline" suddenly rang. Brajesh Mishra, the principal secretary to the prime minister, picked up the telephone receiver and listened without comment, the tension on his face visibly lessening as the conversation progressed. After quietly hanging up, he turned to the assembled ministers, in the midst of whom sat the prime minister, and announced: "The test has been successfully conducted." He looked at his watch and added, "At precisely 3:45 PM" Did we pop open champagne bottles, or cheer and rejoice? No, we did not. But I do remember walking up to the prime minister soon after Mishra had finished, shaking his hand, and saying simply, "Congratulations. You have acted with great courage, Atalji." L. K. Advani, rendered wordless by deeply felt emotions, shook the prime minister's hand silently. The draft of a statement that had been prepared earlier, in consultation with the scientists, had to be finalized. Brajesh Mishra and I worked together on it and produced what we thought the prime minister ought to share with the country—as indeed he did, and with the rest of the world as well.

On Monday, May 11, 1998—at 10:13:44.2 UCT ± 0.32 seconds; 6:13:44.2 AM EDT; 3:43:44.2 PM local time—as measured by international seismic monitors, India declared itself a nuclear-armed state. This de facto declaration was followed shortly thereafter by an official announcement. Prime Minister Vajpayee, at a press briefing, said, "I have an announcement to make: today at 3:45 PM, India conducted three underground nuclear tests in the Pokhran range. These were contained explosions like the experiment conducted in May 1974." He went on to say that the devices tested had been a thermonuclear device, a fission device, and a low-yield device, adding, "I warmly congratulate the scientists and engineers who have carried out these successful tests." In contrast to the 1974 explosion, no claims were made that these were "peaceful tests." Indeed, Principal Secretary Mishra told reporters, "These tests have established that India has a proven capability for a weaponized nuclear program." Just two days later, on May 13, two more nuclear devices were detonated simultaneously. Those explosions had to be simultaneous for convenience, for speed, and because the shafts in which the devices had been placed were only a short distance apart. If the tests had been conducted separately, the first detonation and its consequent shockwaves could well have damaged the second shaft, or even made its wall collapse. The entire test series was dubbed Operation Shakti 98, and the five individual tests were designated Shakti I through V. More recently it has become common to refer to the series as Pokhran II. ("Pokhran I" is used for the 1974 explosion.) After the explosions of May 13, Prime Minister Vajpayee announced a voluntary moratorium on further testing. He also declared India a "nuclear weapons state."

Health teams had made a preliminary inspection of ground zero soon after the detonations and, after conducting all necessary tests, had declared the area radiation-free. The instruments used during the experiments were collected for further study. Scientist Anil Kakodkar, now the chairman of India's Atomic Energy Commission (AEC) and secretary in the Department of Atomic Energy (DAE), called the explosions "successful tests of advanced and robust weapons designs. . . . Perfect." Several new weapons-related ideas and substances were tried out, most notably sub-kiloton devices. All the tests had been very carefully planned and conducted in close cooperation with the DRDO, thus involving the cumulative synergy of three of the great brain banks of India: the DAE, the Bhabha Atomic Research Centre (BARC), and the DRDO. At their suggestion, the prime minister was easily and quickly able to announce a moratorium on further testing: "With this series of tests, India has concluded what it set out to do."[2]

A press conference with the entire scientific and engineering leadership responsible for the tests was held three days after the second group of detonations. It was unprecedented in the amount of detail that was made public, which included information on yields and the general characteristics of the devices. The purpose was to demonstrate the scientific and technological competence behind the tests. In comparison, since the 1960s, the United States and the Soviet Union/Russia have kept the precise yields and purposes of a vast number of underground tests classified. Most of the information about the nature and intent of our tests was made available at this press conference itself. The briefing came primarily from two top scientists—A. P. J. Abdul Kalam and Rajagopala Chidambaram, then chairman of the AEC.

Sounds of Silence

Total secrecy had preceded the Pokhran tests. This was a source of considerable satisfaction to the scientific team, the Prime Minister's Office,

2. Technically, the seismic data reveal that the total magnitude of the first event was 5.4, one of the largest seismic events in the world in the twenty-four-hour period in which it occurred. The measured seismic center of the triple event was located at 27.0716° N latitude and 71.7612° E longitude, which placed it only 2.8 kilometers from the 1974 test site. The first three tests (Shakti I, II, and III) reported a combined yield of about 55 (or 58) kilotons (kt) and consisted of a two-stage thermonuclear weapon design (Shakti I) with a yield of 43 kt, ±3 kt (also stated to be 43–45 kt), a 12 kt test of a light compact weaponized tactical fission bomb, and a 0.2 kt tactical fission weapon. The three shafts were located about 1 kilometer apart and 3.5 kilometers from the control room. The second phase of two tests (Shakti IV and V) had yields of 0.5 and 0.3 kt, and were fired in shafts designated NT 1 and NT 2 (for Navtala, the area where they were dug). A third device and shaft (NT 3) was not fired, because the earlier five explosions were fully successful. The second group of tests were conducted to generate additional data for improved computer simulation of designs.

and the members of the Cabinet who had been given advance notice. However, our secrecy had some unexpected consequences. U.S. officials were greatly disturbed by the fact that the tests had been conducted at all, but they were even more riled by the realization that despite their intelligence agencies, their satellite surveillance, and an impressive array of technical gadgetry, they had failed to detect even an inkling of the detonations. Long after the tests had been completed, seismic monitors all over the world were still querulously refuting what was an irrefutable scientific fact. It had not been easy to maintain this secrecy. To conduct five nuclear tests in the course of just three days was asking for the near-impossible. To have done it in Pokhran, more than 1,000 kilometers away from major facilities of the DAE, and for a country so loquacious by nature not to have breathed a word about it—this was a situation that merited special mention. It had required the cooperation and assistance of so many—not just the scientific community, but all of the various military establishments en route, particularly in Jodhpur and, more significantly, the Range Organization in Pokhran. In retrospect, some of the precautions may evoke amusement, but they were serious business at the time. Each of the four principal scientists involved had to move on- and off-site frequently and for considerable lengths of time. They had to travel to and from the area repeatedly and under the cover of alternative identities. Having chosen to pass themselves off as members of the military, Kalam, Chidambaram, Kakodkar, and K. Santhanam donned Army uniforms and name badges, and ranks, if I recollect correctly, of a colonel and below.

In going over the entries in my diary from that period, I find that the first time Prime Minister Vajpayee spoke to me about wanting to "bite the bullet" and proceed with the test was in 1996. At the time we were part of a short-lived government in which he was the first BJP premier and I had been assigned responsibility for the Finance Ministry. He had taken me aside once and said that he really wished we had a little more time; all the "arrangements" had been made, but the previously enthusiastic scientific community had begun to balk at the idea when the possibility surfaced that our government could be voted out. There had been earlier attempts at testing back in the 1980s, when R. Venkataraman, later India's president, was defense minister in Indira Gandhi's government. Venkataraman shared with me that on two separate occasions, a date had been set, the preparations had been made, and the bore shaft had been dug, fully wired, and prepared. Indeed, he himself had once, out of curiosity, gone down a shaft. But Indira Gandhi then changed her mind and called the whole exercise off. In 1996, when P. V. Narasimha Rao demitted office as prime minister, he took aside his successor, Atal Bihari Vajpayee, and quietly said, "I could not do it, though I very much wanted to; so now it is up to you."

Sometime before Pokhran II, the prime minister telephoned me to ask where I was. I informed him that I was not very far away, but I was in a meeting. He suggested that I return via his house, because there was something that he wanted to discuss. If memory serves, he was still living at 7 Safdarjung Road in Delhi then, because the prime minister's residence on Racecourse Road was not yet ready for him to move into. Not one to be elaborately expansive, particularly in private conversations and when such explanation was not needed, he was cryptic: "It has been set for May 11 and 13, 1998." I knew instantly what he meant. Reading through my diary, I find that we then sat down at his dining table, and I took out a piece of paper on which I had listed some essential points that I thought the prime minister ought to consider. He might well have already decided on the issues I brought up, but he was courteous enough to sit through the briefing. Even then, we spoke of continuing to keep a very tight lid on information. This was of vital importance, for we knew how closely the world was watching what India, under its new prime minister and BJP-led coalition, was doing. To many, the BJP was an alien interloper, "extremist" by instinct, an unknown entity in the realm of governance and international affairs.

On March 28, 1998, the BJP-led coalition won a vote of confidence in the Lok Sabha, 275-260. The way was now clear. Within days, the prime minister met with Kalam and Chidambaram and sought their views on possible timing. Kalam informed the prime minister that everything was ready, and the prime minister in turn gave the go-ahead, assigning the task of coordinating the tests to Brajesh Mishra, his principal secretary. President K. R. Narayanan was scheduled to tour Latin America from April 26 to May 10. As the president was not part of the decision-making process, it would have been improper for him to be taken by surprise by such tests, particularly when he was traveling abroad. But advancing the test dates to before April 26 would not work for a compelling domestic reason: that was an auspicious period for weddings, which was likely to keep some of the principals away! Thus Kalam and Chidambaram told the prime minister that May 11 was the earliest practical date. As it happened, on April 6, Pakistan tested a new missile, the Ghauri, with a range of 1,500 kilometers (900 miles)—though it flew only 800 kilometers in the test—and a payload of 700 kilograms. The Pakistanis' missile pro-gram had been known since 1997, and on March 23 they had hinted that a test was imminent.

Unquiet Americans

When I reflect on those days, some fragments of memory cause both retrospective amusement and sadness. Not so much about the prejudices and preconceived notions about the BJP, but more about India—that the Western world viewed a land of such enormous ability and talent only in terms of a particular leadership, as if India were synonymous with individ-uals of one particular political ilk. It is a greatly mistaken notion that in the corridors of international diplomacy, the foreign ministries and diplo-mats who are assigned that responsibility are assiduous in the discharge of their duties, in the information and advice that they send back. That sadly is not so. On April 14 and 15, 1998, India had an important visitor from the United States, Secretary of Energy Bill Richardson. We knew that he was a close confidant of President Bill Clinton. A reception was hosted in his honor by Richard Frank Celeste, the U.S. ambassador to India, at Roosevelt House, his official residence in Delhi. My general reluctance to attend such functions and my utter disinclination for the empty routine of diplomatic inanities were well known. But this clearly was an excep-tion, so when Celeste suggested a meeting with Richardson before the reception, I agreed. A week earlier, prior to the energy secretary's arrival, Pakistan had conducted a test of its Ghauri missile.

It was known that Richardson was headed for Islamabad after Delhi, for in those days we still lived in the age of the "hyphenated relationship": "India-Pakistan." The Ghauri missile test came up during the conversa-tion, but I did not find it so irksome as to turn it into the principal issue, let alone to share with a guest any consequential concerns that India might have. After all, for decade after decade, the United States had consistently averted its eyes so as to avoid seeing such activities in Pakistan, and it was even then an ally of Pakistan; that was, and still is, the reality. However, it did come out at the meeting that a key reason for Richardson's visit was to ask our new government to initiate a strategic defense review, in the hope that if we intended to pursue nuclear tests or weaponization, we would not be able to do so until such a review had been concluded. I told him that India's overall security concerns would be central in any deci-sion that the government made. Perhaps because it was what they wanted to hear, or perhaps because President Clinton was planning a visit of his own, Richardson and his team took this to be an indication that any strategic review or related undertaking would *precede* the test. That may have been the essence of what Richardson shared with Sandy Berger and thus reported to President Clinton.

A few days later, Ambassador Celeste came to my house in Delhi. He was preparing to take a longish leave. We were discussing issues in a perambulatory sort of way when, somewhat tangentially, he expressed a thought, more in the air, implying that he wanted to go home assured that nothing "disagreeable" that might disturb his holidays was likely to happen. "I hope I am not going to be surprised," he said, because he wanted to "spend some quiet time" with his family. As the Ghauri had been tested in our neighborhood, I presumed that he was expressing concern about any possible step we might take in reaction to that launch. We had no intention whatsoever of engaging in any kind of "competitive testing of missiles"; besides, the BJP-led National Democratic Alliance had its own specific manifesto, which we were following, having announced it as our "program of governance."

By the time Celeste returned from the United States, Pokhran II was long over. Soon after his arrival, he sought to call on me, and naturally I readily agreed. An extremely genial and outgoing figure, the ambassador was totally at home with the kind of banter that is characteristic of the political community the world over. But on this occasion, he came in looking serious and rather reflective. I sat with him in my makeshift study. With great sincerity and concern, he voiced his thoughts in words that have stayed with me: "Jaswant, I have a young son; he is barely a year and a half. I do not want him to grow up in a world filled with such perils, such horrors." Silence followed. I did not know how to answer him. What he had expressed was my own concern, too, and I knew as surely as I know my own bones that the civilizational core of India shared such thoughts. India is not a warmongering country, but public duty will always take precedence. How was I to convey this message to Dick Celeste? What words could I use to tell him all this?

Because I could not find an immediate answer—or was it just that thoughts struggled with words to find suitable expression?—I excused myself and went inside the house. I shared my painful dilemma with my wife. After not more than a moment's thought, she came up with just the right response. With a woman's assured instinct, she gave me a small silver toy from Rajasthan, meant for infants and very young children. It was made of silver and had a built-in whistle that emitted a song-like sound.

It also had an attached cluster of tiny bells, like a bunch of grapes, which jingled merrily when shaken. "Give it to the ambassador," she said, "and ask him. Still better, ask him to give it to his wife to give to their son, with just a short message: 'If I give your son this gift, then how can you imagine that I have any intention of harming his future?'" Immediately I felt immensely relieved, and that is exactly what I did and said. Dick was also clearly moved. This was not part of his brief; he had expected a combative response from me, and may well have been carrying instructions to convey his government's views seriously, accompanied by an appropriate degree of grimness. But he knew me well enough by then to understand that there was no deceit in what I said, and that my gesture in giving him that gift for his son was as sincerely meant as was his concern.

I started by explaining all the measures that had to be taken to safeguard the secrecy of the tests. It is to the credit of Principal Secretary Brajesh Mishra that this had been achieved so irreproachably. That aspect of security was primarily his responsibility. But the search for information was real, it was relentless, it was very intrusive, and it had been going on for a long time. In 1995, for example, when I was in the Opposition and was the deputy leader of the BJP in the Lok Sabha, I was given a copy of a letter that had been sent that year to the U.S. In all these years, I did nothing with this letter. Our intent was to keep the proposed series of tests secret—and this we achieved.

The Day After

Immediately after May 11, 1998, world reactions exploded in our face. They were all, without exception, what I had expected them to be. What I had not accounted for was how much they would replay the global reactions to the "peaceful nuclear explosion" of 1974. If I repeat what my late friend the eminent scientist Raja Ramanna wrote about the reactions to Pokhran I almost a quarter of a century earlier in his autobiography *Years of Pilgrimage,* it would apply almost perfectly here as well: "embargos, sanctions." It appeared as if the P-5 and their followers "wanted to crush India for its temerity"![3] Approximately 120 countries raised some form of objection to the tests. Naturally, the language, the intensity, and the content varied. Of significance to India were the reactions of countries such as Canada, which had been one of our earliest suppliers of nuclear fuel and plants and was therefore justified in experiencing a sense of grievance. Then there was the Group of Eight (G-8), representing the collectivity

3. Raja Ramanna, *Years of Pilgrimage: An Autobiography* (New Delhi: Viking, 1991), pp. 92–93.

of the economic powers of the world. Their perception was of concern to India because it combined the economic and political viewpoints of the wealthy of the world. Japan was of particular concern to me personally, as the only country to have suffered the consequences of a nuclear strike. I understood the anger of the Japanese and have shared this viewpoint, in exactly these words, on several occasions with friends from Japan. Of great relevance to us was the reaction of the United States, which was at the forefront of world opinion in this condemnation of India. Then there were China, the United Kingdom, Germany, France, and Australia, as well as Russia, which was highly important to us as an ally of standing, and as one of our principal suppliers of nuclear fuel.

Eight years after the Pokhran tests, it is still interesting to reflect on the reactions they evoked from the international community. The Chinese government stated that it was "shocked" and "strongly condemn[ed]" the Indian nuclear tests and called for the international community to "adopt a unified stand and strongly demand that India immediately stop development of nuclear weapons." The French Ministry of Foreign Affairs said in an official statement: "France reiterates its commitment both to the cause of disarmament and non-proliferation and to the improvement of security and stability in south Asia. In this context, it expresses its concern and calls on all the region's states to show restraint." The G-8 statement said, "We condemn the nuclear tests which were carried out by India on May 11 and 13. Such action runs counter to the will expressed by 149 signatories to the CTBT to cease nuclear testing . . . [and] to efforts to strengthen the global non-proliferation regime and to steps to enhance regional and international peace and security. It has been met by immediate international concern and opposition. . . . We underline our full commitment to the Non-Proliferation Treaty and to the Comprehensive Test Ban Treaty as the cornerstones of the global non-proliferation regime and the essential foundations for the pursuit of nuclear disarmament." German chancellor Helmut Kohl noted, "This decision will make a contribution to increasing tensions in the region because it, too, is in a way a direct challenge to the neighbouring countries." Prime Minister Ryutaro Hashimoto of Japan called the nuclear tests "extremely regrettable," and announced that his country would cut off all aid, except humanitarian assistance, to India.

The case of Pakistan, of course, was different, because our relations with that country have always been on a different plane altogether. The undercurrent of hostility and tension between us has never really abated. Hence Pakistan's reactions to the tests were understandably harsher than those of other nations. Equally important are the developments that took place in that country immediately afterward. Prime Minister Nawaz Sharif began by addressing his people: "I wish to assure the nation that Pakistan has the capability to respond to any threat to its security. . . . We will take all necessary measures to safeguard our security, sovereignty, territorial integrity, and national interests." Foreign Minister Gohar Ayub Khan said, "Indian actions, which pose an immediate and grave threat to Pakistan's security, will not go unanswered." He told the press that Pakistan had "a superior technology than India's in both missile and nuclear fields." Pakistan's Defense Committee termed India's three nuclear tests of May 11 "reckless and highly provocative." In Islamabad, Foreign Ministry spokesman Nadeem Kiyani said that Pakistan condemned India's two nuclear tests on May 13, adding, "We are looking into the situation." A. Q. Khan, the father of Pakistan's nuclear research program, said he only needed orders from the government to carry out a nuclear explosion, which he could do within ten days. "It is a political decision," he said. "Now it all depends on the government." Benazir Bhutto, the former prime minister who in 1998 was the Opposition leader, said, "India has now gone ahead conducting three nuclear tests and I expect Pakistan to follow the suit." Lieutenant General (Retd.) Hamid Gul urged the government to devise an "equally matching and powerful response" to the Indian nuclear tests.

On May 13, returning from a trip to Central Asia, Nawaz Sharif met for several hours with senior military officials and members of his government to discuss India's actions, which appeared to have taken Pakistan's security establishment by surprise. "We didn't have any advance information on these explosions," admitted a member of Sharif's cabinet. Another cabinet member said, "Not surprisingly, many ministers thought it was the ideal moment for Pakistan to test its nuclear device." The Pakistan Army informed Sharif that it would be ready "within a week" to conduct an "underground nuclear test on twenty-four hours' notice." But officials familiar with the deliberations spoke of a division within the cabinet over an appropriate Pakistani response. According to an aide, the prime minister appeared to favor "a balanced and moderate response" and ordered a report on the cost the country would have to bear if a Pakistani nuclear test resulted in international sanctions. The same day, President Clinton telephoned the Pakistani prime minister and urged him "not to respond to an irresponsible act in kind." By the week's end, however, American spy satellites, at last fully alert, had detected an influx of equipment at a previously prepared test site in the Chagai Hills in the desert of southwestern

Baluchistan Province, barely fifty kilometers from the border with Iran. The Central Intelligence Agency, having learned from earlier lapses, now began predicting that a "test could occur as early as Sunday, May 17." That weekend, Nawaz Sharif consulted various parties and factions, and remained under enormous pressure to test. Meanwhile, public reaction continued to favor an immediate response. Benazir Bhutto advocated not only that Pakistan immediately carry out a nuclear test, but also that India "be disarmed by a preemptive attack"!

Meanwhile, the United States was working on putting together an incentive package to persuade Pakistan not to test. The offer included repeal of the Pressler Amendment, which had cut off military aid to the country, as well as the delivery of $600 million worth of F-16 fighter-bombers that Pakistan had ordered and paid for but not yet received. Discussions also began on how much aid to offer Pakistan over and above these concessions. In the case of a test, it was clear that a nearly total embargo would automatically be imposed, as had happened with India, but it was also obvious that the much smaller Pakistani economy could hardly afford such a penalty. The tension was ratcheted up on Saturday, May 16, by Gohar Ayub Khan when he told reporters that a nuclear test by Pakistan was "just a matter of timing and the government of Pakistan will choose as to when to conduct [it]. A nuclear test by Pakistan is certain." He repeated those remarks the next day, telling the Associated Press that Pakistan had decided to go ahead with the testing of a nuclear device: "It's a matter of when, not if, Pakistan will test. The decision has already been taken." The frenzy reached a peak on Sunday, May 24, when the nuclear device was believed to have been put in place for a test. There was even a brief flurry of excitement caused by a false alarm that day, when Helmut Kohl said that he had "reliable information" that Pakistan had already detonated a bomb—a report that was quickly denied. But by the beginning of the following week, Pakistan appeared to have backed off from any immediate decision to test, and was content to bargain instead, to see how much aid it could extract from the United States.

On May 25, it was reported by the Associated Press and Reuters that American intelligence officials had said that Pakistani preparations had accelerated in recent days at a site called Ras Koh in the Chagai Hills. Tunnels were being dug, and explosives-monitoring equipment was being set up. "At this point, they could conduct a nuclear test at any time," one U.S. official was quoted as saying. At the same time, it had become increasingly likely that any American aid package would fall short of

Pakistan's demands. The major inducements suggested at this point—delivery of twenty-eight F-16s and the rescheduling of loans—were not tempting. Pakistan seemed to be after explicit U.S. security guarantees, which were unlikely to materialize. Late on May 27, the U.S. administration reported that Pakistan had been observed pouring cement into a test shaft in the Chagai Hills. This indicated that nuclear devices were being sealed in, the final and necessary step before an actual test. Officials then predicted that tests could take place within hours. Many last-minute efforts were made, including by Deputy Secretary of State Strobe Talbott, who said, "India is isolating itself and should be allowed to stew in juices of its own making." But these were to no avail. On May 28 at 15:00 UCT, Nawaz Sharif announced that Pakistan had detonated five nuclear devices. Seismic readings indicate a detonation time of 10:16:17.6 UCT (±0.31 sec). The Pakistan prime minister then telephoned President Clinton and "apologized" for the tests in a rather unbecoming conversation between two heads of government. There was one more rather bizarre scare raised by Pakistan. Satish Chandra, India's high commissioner in Islamabad, was called at midnight on May 27–28 by the Pakistan Foreign Office. He faced this charge: "India was going to attack Kahuta and other targets in Pakistan in a midnight/dawn aerial raid, in collusion with Israel; also that aircraft had already been placed on 'runway readiness' for being launched."[4] It was so tragically comic, so pathetically untrue.

Meanwhile, reaction to India's tests was solidifying. President Clinton said, "They clearly create a dangerous new instability in their region. And, as a result, in accordance with United States law, I have decided to impose economic sanctions against India." (See Appendix 1.)

The Russian Foreign Ministry said that it viewed the Indian nuclear tests "with alarm and concern," adding, "As a close friend of India, this action has caused us to feel great regret." It assessed the tests as "contradicting the efforts of the international community to strengthen the nuclear non-proliferation regime on the global and regional level." The statement called on India to reverse its nuclear policy and adhere to the NPT and the CTBT.

Taking up the Gauntlet

This frenzy of critical rhetoric against India had descended to rather unfortunate levels when I was deputed by Prime Minister Vajpayee to head a delegation to the United Nations. It was not yet a month since the tests, and I was to attend both the regular session of the General Assembly and a

---

4. Press release, Ministry of External Affairs, May 28, 1998.

special session on narcotics. Secretary of State Madeleine Albright greeted me with a cutting remark upon my arrival in New York. Inevitably, I was asked to respond. *The Times of India* of June 11, 1998, reported on the exchange:

> Jaswant Singh has criticised US Secretary of State Madeleine Albright's comment that India and Pakistan should "climb out of the hole they have dug themselves into," after their nuclear tests. "I must point out that civilisationally, we in India do not dig holes to bury ourselves in, no, not even metaphorically speaking. Therefore, this observation exemplifies yet another fundamental lack of comprehension about the Indian stand and about addressing Indian sensitivities," he said when asked to comment on Albright's remark during a news conference at the UN headquarters." By then, a "war of words" had broken out between the United States and India. Distinguished members of the State Department had already opened proceedings. Strobe Talbott, for example, had said that the sanctions were "not designed to punish or isolate the two countries, but to send a message to them and any other country thinking of going nuclear that there are heavy economic costs in such a decision."

It was under these conditions and with a large package of responsibilities that I headed for the United Nations in June 1998. I was carrying with me India's message for the world.

5

Pokhran Looks East

ASEAN Drama

In July 1998, I headed for Manila to attend a meeting of the Association of Southeast Asian Nations (ASEAN). The chairmanship of the body turned over annually, and that year it was the Philippines' turn. I knew that for me personally, as indeed for all the ASEAN nations, the principal issue at that year's meeting was Pokhran II; those tests loomed above all other items on the agenda. In one capacity or another, the participating countries had all opposed the tests, whether on account of a principled opposition to nuclear tests as such or because they were pushed by the United States. They would all be there, to singly and collectively convey their disappointment, disapproval, or condemnation. Almost invariably Gandhi would be invoked, how "the land of Gandhi has abandoned his path of peace and nonviolence." I found this wearisome, because in every way it was so utterly irrelevant. The "legacy of Gandhi" was not connected in any way to the current situation, and there was no justification for citing it as the basis for admonitory criticisms of India. However, I did share their concern about the indiscriminate spread of weapons of mass destruction; that subject I would certainly address. I considered it India's obligation, its duty, to respond to the just and valid anxieties of the international community. But as for those who themselves had either violated the provisions of relevant international treaties or contributed to such violations, and who in any event had not fulfilled their own commitment to adhere to the duties and obligations of the Nuclear Non-Proliferation Treaty—their admonitions I was certainly not going to accept. After all, we were not in violation of any international treaty, nor of any obligations or commitments. Not being a signatory to either the NPT or the CTBT, India had not gone back on any commitments whatsoever. The policy and program that India adhered to was as open and transparent as is customary. It had to account for that program to Parliament, and confidentiality on national security issues was obviously not subject to any regime of prior international approvals. This was as much the right of India as of any other country.

I had been assigned responsibility for managing the country's international relations and engaging with the principal global players at a time when India was both the object and the subject of a major assault ("the Charge of the Invective Brigade," I had once called it privately). The catalyst for this "charge" was, of course, the nuclear tests of 1998; they had opened a Pandora's box. This box, which had been closed for decades, contained a whole set of questions that had long confronted India, but that India, in typical fashion, had shut away, hoping that they would simply vanish. They did not. Instead they had lain dormant, their complexities inhibiting us. That was now no longer an option.

Running into the Great Wall

On May 12, China's reaction to our three nuclear tests of the previous day was relatively muted. Foreign Ministry spokesman Zhu Bangzao expressed the government's "grave concern about India conducting nuclear tests," which "runs against international trends and is detrimental to the peace and stability of the South Asian region." After we conducted two more tests on May 13, the Chinese government expressed shock and condemnation, calling on the international community to unite in demanding an immediate halt to our development of nuclear weapons. Why had the tone changed? Was it a response to the repeat tests? China rapidly upgraded its reaction phraseology from "seriously concerned" to describing as "strongly condemnable" India's "outrageous contempt" for the world community. Although we had prepared for the certainty that the United States would hit back, and hard, we had not factored in the possibility that a confidential correspondence between two heads of governments would also be employed as a "weapon of offense." Yet that is precisely what happened. A letter from Prime Minister Vajpayee to President Clinton, sharing thoughts on the 1998 tests and India's assessment of its strategic neighborhood, was deliberately leaked to the press:

Dear Mr. President,

You would already be aware of the underground nuclear tests carried out in India. In this letter, I would like to explain the rationale for the tests.

I have been deeply concerned at the deteriorating security environment, specially the nuclear environment, faced by India for some years past. We have an overt nuclear weapon state on our borders, a state which committed armed aggression against India in 1962. Although our relations with that country have improved in the last decade or so, an atmosphere of distrust persists mainly due to the unresolved border problem. To add to the distrust that country has materially helped another neighbour of ours to become a covert nuclear weapons state. At the hands of this bitter neighbour we have suffered three aggressions in the last 50 years. And for the last ten years we have been the victim of unremitting terrorism and militancy sponsored by it in several parts of our country, specially Punjab and Jammu & Kashmir. Fortunately, the faith of the people in our democratic system as also their patriotism has enabled India to counter the activities of the terrorists and militants, aided and abetted from abroad.

The series of tests are limited in number and pose no danger to any country which has no inimical intentions towards India. We value our friendship and cooperation with your country and you personally. We hope that you will show understanding of our concern for India's security.

I assure you that India will continue to work with your country in a multilateral or bilateral framework to promote the cause of nuclear disarmament. Our commitment to participate in non-discriminatory and verifiable global disarmament measures is amply demonstrated by our adherence to the two conventions on Biological and Chemical Weapons. In particular we are ready to participate in the negotiations to be held in Geneva in the Conference on Disarmament for the conclusion of a Fissile Material Cut-off Treaty.

I enclose for your information the text of the press statement issued after the nuclear tests were carried out today. I close with the expression of my highest consideration for your country and yourself.

Yours sincerely,
A. B. VAJPAYEE

The leak was clearly intended to embarrass India, a retaliatory strike for our tests' having embarrassed the United States.

The scheme succeeded. I was more taken aback by the method employed than by any consequence of this low blow. The Chinese, inevitably, employed the leaked letter as an additional irritant in our bilateral relations. There was also the question of what role the People's Liberation Army (PLA) would play in determining China's reactions. This has seldom been fully examined or commented upon. The PLA's role in the post–Pokhran II phase was very important but seldom visible or explicit. As a consequence, I had to deal with a joint announced position, but seldom with sufficient knowledge of the internal inputs that had gone into a structuring of that position. This was a consequence of inadequate intelligence about China, its government, its decision-making. In comparison, India was a book that lay open for the entire world to read, if it felt so inclined.

The dates for the ASEAN Regional Forum meeting were not of my choosing, having been determined well in advance. India could have been, indeed was invited to be one of the founding members of ASEAN in 1967, but for reasons that have remained rather obscure to me, we declined to join at that time. By 1998, however, after some lobbying, India was finally a member. Because participants had to be at the level of foreign minister or the equivalent, I was obliged to attend, even though I had only just returned from the United States. I knew that the central challenge would be to face the collective barrage of critical references to India's nuclear tests; that was inevitable. It was also clear that the United States would lead the charge, as it would enjoy the support of a substantial number of nations at this gathering. China, although somewhat aloof from the rest, would be among the critics, wanting to know where things stood. Then there would be Japan, in a category by itself. To my amusement, I found that the team of Ministry of External Affairs (MEA) officers who had accompanied me were far more occupied with preparing and rehearsing the skit that each country had to present at the end of the conference. I did not really object to such prioritization, because I much preferred collecting my own thoughts instead of going over lengthy briefing notes of variable content, questionable language, and repetitive bureaucratic syntax. Thus they were left busy rehearsing, and I with my thoughts.

How do nations relate to one another? This question remains in my mind, unanswered, unresolved. I have always endeavored to discern patterns in the great sweeps of history, but as yet fruitlessly. My search continues. Is there some underlying pattern to history's seemingly arbitrary oscillations, or is it all random? Is it no more than a chance encounter of events and forces in a particular geographical location, in a particular context, at a particular time? Does human will ever, even marginally, shape history, or is the reverse true, with events, autonomous by nature, always molding human destiny? I ask this because the responsibility that I carried needed a philosophy, a policy, and an instrument. It was difficult for me to alter the mindset of the officers of the ministry. Their views understandably reflected the residue of years of official caution, the distillate of institutional experience, and hence "steer a safe course" timidity. This, too, was inevitable. Decades of management of foreign policy had left us, particularly the ministries of Defence and External Affairs, with many scars, a host of problems, and several shelf-loads of prejudices. The British-imparted civil service tradition of reasoned independent thought had been so diluted by then that to elicit views, whether dissenting or not, required repeated persuasion. Too many political changes internally, born of political uncertainty and India's continuing search for democratic transition, had bred into the Indian Administrative Service and the Foreign Service a deep suspicion of the entire political leadership: their vagaries, their short "shelf life," and their pronounced provincialism.[1] The system was simply not working at its best; the needed fuel of inspired thought and leadership was just not there.

With these thoughts, I flew into Manila in that final week of July 1998. My diary notes for July 24 record:

> A tropical seaside; Manila, humid, hot, an entirely Asian city; a vast sprawl . . . with a certain insouciant abandon and vitality. There is a near total absence of "natural order," for nature itself is so fecund and abundant that it overgrows any imposed boundary. Naturally thereafter, the people, too, are exuberant, unrestrained and excitable—also compulsively unresponsive to voluntary order, just as much as we are: as in India so here in the Philippines, too.
>
> At the airport, an airport workers' strike was busy immobilizing movement instead of facilitating it; their aggrieved "sit-in" (again *à la* India), most uncomfortable in this humid heat under banners that proclaimed "workers' rights" and their "demands" and so on, all totally unconvincing. In Delhi, on the afternoon of my departure had also been in progress a strike—of all things, of some "medical workers"!
>
> The road from the airport to the hotel was clogged with traffic, jerking forward in fits and starts, accompanied by a ceaseless honking of horns and ragged youth, entrepreneurially selling wares to this trapped and congealed mass. The cultural symbol of the

---

1. Shri T. C. Raghavan, who worked with me in the Ministry of External Affairs and is presently the deputy high commissioner in our high commission in Islamabad, Pakistan, commented after reading this chapter of my manuscript that the paragraph regarding the "mindset" of MEA officers merited revision. He said, "At one level this is, of course, entirely true. At another, it obscures a more fundamental factor. All Foreign Service officers are essentially conservative. This often is 'timidity' but equally often is born of the regimen of the doctrine of 'estoppel.' In brief, precedents in domestic policy can be over-ridden, not in foreign affairs. It is possible for the Ministry of Finance to say 'not to be quoted as a precedent.' A Foreign Office cannot do so."

Philippines is the "Jeepanni"—a modified jeep, as public transport—festooned with a bewildering variety of garlands and exag-
geratedly colored (also colorful) announcements.

In the foyer of the hotel, the owner, the reception staff, garlands
of marigold, some fragrant Champa.[2] The room, just that little
bit chipped, slightly untended, comfortingly inefficient. Latticed
windows to keep the sun out—and there beyond the window lay
the South China Sea, hazy and dull in the torpor of this midday
heat.

Center Counter Game

In the end, my meetings with all the principal interlocutors could well
have resembled a Center Counter Game.[3] The first was Evegenii Primakov,
then the foreign minister of Russia. (I was to meet him on several other
occasions later, in all his changing roles and incarnations.) He was an old
India hand with long roots in the KGB, in which capacity he had often
visited India, where he had a wide range of contacts. He had spent long
periods of time—wisely, I think—enjoying the salubrious beaches of
Goa. Beneath his gruff exterior and his "Soviet granite" appearance, there
dwelled a very sharp mind and a deep understanding of global currents.
Many years in this field had left him with few illusions. His *basso profundo*
must have been among the deepest of all such voices, even in Russia, a
country that excels in this attribute. He was often provocatively direct,
and when necessary, he could be rude, too. In an encounter with a colleague of mine who was on a visit to Moscow, Primakov had impatiently
and directly demanded: "You must sign the CTBT."

"How can we?" my colleague had remonstrated.

"How? How . . . how—how, you ask? I will show you how." Primakov
had then leaned across to pull the pen out of my bewildered colleague's
pocket, uncapped it, and, making signing motions, said forcefully: "This
is how you sign, like this—do you see? Like this! Now do you know how
to sign?"

In our bilateral meeting, though, he was politeness itself, for he is an
innately courteous man, and I reckon he had knowledge by then that he
was being considered for promotion to the premiership of Russia. He did
go through the routine of post-Pokhran protestations, to which I had
become fairly acclimatized. At one point, however, impatience pushed

2. A flowering tree of the magnolia family, *Michelia doltsopa*.
3. "Center Counter Game" is the name of an opening move in chess.

aside his reserve. We were discussing the geopolitical structure of South Asia and India's contentious neighborhood when suddenly, in the context of a particular country, he interjected, "What is this? What is this preoccupation with such midgets?" And more followed, until he concluded: "It is as if we in Russia were to always worry about . . ." Hunting for a suitable example, he paused, and then it came like a cannonball: ". . . to worry about Latvia!" I liked him, rough ways and all, and I knew that I could do business with him. But it was with his successor, Igor Ivanov, that I was to interact in the years that followed.

The opening dinner of the ASEAN Regional Forum is usually an informal affair designed to settle unresolved points of the agenda or other such routine trivia. In Manila, it took on a rather different hue. The team of officers who had accompanied me were markedly worried. For one, I was new to the ministry. They themselves were not permitted in the conference hall, and they were not at all confident about what I would do, say, or not do when I was under "attack"—for an "attack" they apprehended was coming. No such anxiety assailed me. I held then, as I always did later, that India had no obligation to "explain" anything, and certainly not in response to a demand. But I did consistently hold, and advocate, that it was our obligation to come forward, to in fact volunteer to meet the valid concerns of any member of the international community in this regard. I would not, however, acquiesce to peremptory demands made upon India, as if with a gun to my temple. As it transpired, the occasion ended up being a little bit of everything: a touch of theater, some low farce, and some collective protest, too, followed by private disclaimers. But mostly it was a repetition of positions that had already been enunciated. We sat around a large round table. There was no head of the table, yet there was an attempt to create that kind of an atmosphere. It was important that there be an air of high seriousness, as if a grand ecclesiastical council were in session to inquisitorially examine the questionable behavior of an aberrant lay member. Thus, after all the "ayatollahs of nonproliferation" were fully seized of the heretical conduct of one, a pronouncement would be made, ex cathedra, by the high priestess. Sadly, perhaps inevitably, an Oriental casualness crept in, absorbing Occidental intent. As the evening progressed, the attendees began to address themselves to issues of real import: bilateral matters that needed airing outside the confines of a formal conference; travel schedules; and, most important, making plans to play golf during the days that stretched ahead.

Manila has an air of languid sensuality, a casualness bordering on indifference to most issues that otherwise trouble the rest of the world. And yet this attitude contains a degree of fragility, too, and a volatility of spirit. All of this, in combination with some municipal untidiness and the mix of races, lends the city and its environs an exceptional charm. I came to the conclusion that it was entirely a fortuitous circumstance that the first "collective inquisition" of India was being carried out in this rather laidback coastal town: the sea, the sky, the air, and the comely beauty of the Filipino women smoothed many of the sharp edges of tension, well before I even had to do anything. In the plenary session, therefore, there was not much the participants could forcefully articulate that had not been said earlier. For me, the gathering and the occasion provided yet another invaluable opportunity to put across India's view clearly (I think) and with conviction. After all, in the "nonproliferationist" lobby, almost all had feet of clay. In one fashion or another, they had all violated their respective obligations to the NPT. India had not violated any treaty. This knowledge was a source of immense strength to me. Here, for the first time, I observed the great and powerful hegemony of the United States in action. A hint, a mere suggestion, and some of the participating members would rise, almost like automatons, competing to obey. That is why Madeleine Albright could sing so unblushingly, so coquettishly, that she "enjoyed hegemony"! This she did with abandon in a joint skit with Primakov: America and Russia performing *West Side Story*—or, well, a certain special version of it.

Important bilaterals had preceded these concluding amusements. The one with the United States was a rushed affair in a corner of the main conference hall itself. I had first met Madeleine Albright in the early 1980s, when, as a much younger MP, I had been invited to participate in a global program for young leaders at Georgetown University in Washington, D.C. Albright was one of our professors. Subsequently we continued to meet at the program reunions. But in Manila, our paths truly crossed. We had already exchanged moderate invectives, via the press, in New York. Clearly Manila was no occasion for pleasantries. She opened the proceedings with a charge that, if true, would have been searing: "You have betrayed us, Jaswant. You gave us false assurances." I would ordinarily treat such an accusation as an egregious slur, but this one was lodged more to provoke, to wound through exaggeration. It was a retaliatory blow for the injury apparently caused to her pride by the secrecy of the tests. Instead of anger, therefore, her farfetched opening gambit actually caused me to smile. Thus I was also able to easily rebut what she said: "No, Madeleine, far from it.

Your agencies betrayed you. India, and I, will never knowingly go back on what we commit ourselves to doing. And I just cannot betray my given word. That is a statement of fact, nothing else." Thereupon she said something slightly arch about my dialogue with Strobe Talbott, leaving me with the impression that she was not entirely at ease with the fact that my dialogue was with her deputy secretary, not her, that we had somehow invaded her territory. But that had been her president's decision, not mine.

My bilateral with Australia was somewhat pugnacious. Foreign Minister Alexander Downer and I later grew to be good friends, and I became a great admirer of Australia—of its wide, never-ending spaces, of its people, and of its superb wine—but the contentiousness in that discussion was not agreeable for either of us. Don Mackinnon of New Zealand was more moderate and modulated his protest with restraint, a style that now characterizes his role as secretary general of the Commonwealth. Lloyd Axworthy of Canada had a firm, principled stand, a national commitment. He stood by it loyally; Canada remained unswayed till the last.

The immediate circumstance of the meeting with my Chinese counterpart in Manila in July 1998 was, of course, Pokhran II. There was a much larger dimension, however. This meeting had great significance for me; it had a singularity that only India-China relations can have. My instincts told me that the situation held something in reserve, as a potential for India-China relations, that was markedly different from what New Delhi had assessed. Headquarters are almost always far more cautious and pessimistic than field formations. In the Sino-Indian context, many inhibitions crippled our decision-making, primarily the psychological effects of the defeat of 1962. Fear of another failure generated extremes: either extreme caution or a kind of exhibitionist foolhardiness. The climate of political decisiveness and of clarity of military purpose or objectives had long been obscured by a veil of indecision. This had inevitably resulted in a rather adversarial attitude. In consequence, our decision-making suffered, becoming confused or irresponsibly disjointed and jerky. As I went in to meet my counterpart, Tang Jiaxuan, the salient features of the environment surrounding Sino-Indian relations already existed. I was seeking more than just a resolution to the post–Pokhran II impasse; my quest was markedly different. I was in search of the deeper meaning of good relations between our two nations, and that quest includes so many more ingredients—geography and history and inherited biases, separate civilizational norms, and above all how to resolve an encounter of philosophical disagreements. Thus I had many contradictions to disentangle, and there was much that had come with us as part of our respective legacies. When the two of us met, we did not have a clean slate on which to write.

My China Syndrome

The baggage of Nehruvian legacies was primary, but there were assets, too—some individual and others self-acquired, whether on account of my different circumstances or because of what I had had to do in life, learning the hard way one step at a time. That is perhaps why I had a clearer grasp of what we were engaged in. I did not feel at all psychologically defeated, not by any memories of 1962. I searched for that one opening "code" that would enable me to disentangle the many complexities of the past, to go directly to the human in this great civilization, our eastern neighbor. Thus my central task lay in addressing the challenge of bringing together two estranged countries, two peoples that had been converted from "bhai-bhai" (brothers) into adversaries because of inept handling of the diplomatic and military challenge of those early years. Every problem—military, dip-lomatic, or domestic—has a core, a heart, which if addressed effectively helps in resolution. Where, then, did the "center of gravity" of India-China relations lie in 1998? Was it in the disputed interpretation of a faulty imperial legacy, an unsettled border? Or was it in competition over other issues, rival aspirations in a military or nuclear standoff where two giant nations aggressively grate against one another? What was it that was to be resolved? If it was purely 1962 or the unsettled border that needed settling, then was the focus on that entirely a "technical" matter, simply a cartographical issue? If not—if there was a larger question of primacy in the region—then did China want to keep the pot of the border problem constantly boiling? What, then, was the hierarchical priority of respective national interests? But more than that, what was the core? Was it land, or boundary, or national prestige, or all of these? As we went headlong down this path of contention to confrontation, were we always in command of the situation? Or did the situation so propel us onward, faster and ever faster, that no one in India even knew where we were headed? What about China? Was it clearer in its purpose? My instincts were telling me that the answer lay in these seemingly innocuous queries.

In both diplomatic and military terms, what 1962 exemplified to me, and not just in retrospect, was ill-thought-out, ill-prepared ad-hocism. I had not only lived at the ground level of the consequences of the mili-tary policy in 1962, but since then I had delved extensively into a study of the issue. I have still not been able to determine what the focal point of the government's policy was at the time, both military and diplomatic. Oddly enough, it was Stalin who once said something to the effect that it is the choice of establishing the focal point (military or diplomatic) that determines nine-tenths of the fate of a (policy) campaign. We had no clarity about that "focal point." There was also a near-total absence of understanding of the local correlation of forces, and here I do not mean simply the ratio of troops deployed; rather, it was the focal point of emphasis that was absent. The Chinese, on the other hand, are "scientists of equilibrium, artists of relativity," clearly grasping that as the balance of power between nations is constantly shifting, as circumstances change, so too must attitudes. This cannot be neglected, even for a moment, because the cost of neglect could be as high as the loss of independence. Besides, national survival ought never to be dependent on the assistance of another. A country must immediately address danger, real or potential, to prevent an adversary from amassing overwhelming strength. That would be tantamount to a rank failure of leadership.[4]

Even a cursory examination of any theory of congruent interests would lead us to a clearer understanding of the foundations of good relations. As neighboring countries, though history is not very encouraging on this score, can India and China break their historical pattern and live in peace and harmony? Or will they follow the example of great civilizations such as Greece and Rome, or Greece and Persia? Having settled borders between two countries is obviously of crucial importance. That is undoubtedly an essential requirement for good relations between neighbors, as central to nations as it is to farmers with adjacent fields: good fences do indeed make good neighbors. Another important factor involves respective value systems, social norms, civilizational and cultural equations, similarities of language: all these help greatly. India and China must try and fit these criteria. Do they? It is a historically established fact that when the state of China is stable, it is a practitioner of power. It expands by extending the spread of its power. This Chinese state has never demonstrated any romantic humanitarianism; it has never confusedly used that notion as an instrument of state policy, as, for example, Nehru did in his early dealings with China. I considered myself extremely fortunate that I was now granted an opportunity to address some of these great issues confronting India. After all, diplomacy is mostly about improving relations between countries, obviously without compromising national interests. Thus it is important

---

4. These thoughts are much more eminently and elegantly expressed by Henry Kissinger in *Years of Upheaval.*

to acknowledge that this "congruence of interests" is not possessed of any attribute of permanence; it is a transient in time. When such moments of congruence occur, they present only fleeting moments of opportunity. The trick is to catch the great opportunity that a fleeting moment provides, and then mold it to national advantage. That is where the central challenge lies: in judging the moment, then seizing it. Thereafter, the scope for diplomatic creativity expands enormously. The greater the complexity of the challenge, the greater is the scope for creativity. Yes, even in the dull old world of diplomacy.

In governance, in order to meet any form of challenge, decisions will always have to be made, and always in a relative void of information. Information is never complete, never timely, never focused, and never entirely relevant, because no brief, however well prepared, will ever be adequate; no theory, however astute, will or can provide the needed insight, certainly not for long; and theory by itself is never sufficient to enable one to absorb information and then convert it into a series of effective actions. Most theories require "full information," but that raw material is simply never available; believe me when I say that it is the scarcest commodity in governance. Let us acknowledge that governments usually act on hunches, not on facts; and let us also acknowledge that most information sheets are actually only part fact—the rest is guesswork. Decisions have to be made on this basis, whereas the ex post facto magnifying glass will always be ruthless in its judgment. After all, history has all the information that it needs, as well as all the time in which to judge. Thus, after a decision has been made, it is extremely difficult to prove convincingly that it was the vital decision at the time, that it was absolutely unavoidable, that it was the step that needed to be taken so as to preempt many larger national wrongs later. Should this consideration of "who might or will say what" be allowed to hinder decision-making, then a government, any government, will remain crippled by indecision.

The Middle Game

Preoccupied with such thoughts, I went to meet the distinguished foreign minister of the People's Republic of China. I had not known him well earlier, but there was something about Tang Jiaxuan that I instinctively knew I could work with. He had long years of field experience working in the realm of international affairs, especially in Japan. He had risen up the ladder in the Foreign Office in Beijing. He appeared to be a very able, astute, and diligent representative, well informed about India, and somebody I could reach. It was not a very large room in which we met, but I suppose it was the only one available at the time in the hotel. A long, rectangular table, laden with flowers, made the space feel even more crowded. In the corridor leading to the room was a great crush of the press—Indian, Filipino, international, and some from China, too. In keeping with Chinese custom, Tang Jiaxuan invited me to speak first. In response, I repeated what I was by then rather used to saying. After I had said what I had to, and some routine words of welcome and the usual pleasantries, Tang Jiaxuan launched into a direct attack, and with vigor. Table-thumping and finger-pointing accompanied his brief; I learned later that this was standard Chinese procedure for expressing major disagreement. My own assessment, not fully shared by official wisdom, was that it was not so much the tests per se that troubled them—it was the larger context in which the tests had taken place, exacerbated by some rather inadvertent and not wholly needed Indian comments. What had wounded China's self-esteem and resulted in embarrassment for India was, of course, the unwarranted leak to the press of what Prime Minister Vajpayee had written to President Clinton after Pokhran II. That troubled China greatly.

China's—and therefore Tang Jiaxuan's—emphasis was on delegitimizing this linkage with the tests, for that clearly had several rather embarrassing ramifications for Beijing. Thus Tang Jiaxuan consistently attempted to set his country's protest in a much wider international context. China had deliberately and persistently steered clear of placing India's tests within narrow bilateral confines and a country-specific context, because of which they could now hardly accept a further dilution of their protest by a second linkage: the unresolved border dispute. It was China's aim all along, and has remained so, to come across as a responsible member of the international community, not as some kind of "threatening neighbor" to India. Projecting itself as a "responsible member" was now vital for both China's self-image and the global role it aspired to. The current imbroglio for peace and stability had placed China squarely within the limited confines of South Asia, which it did not relish. But for this, too, it had an inverted caveat: that this was entirely the result of inherent and rather incurable Indian "irresponsibility." Repeated pronouncements of this kind suggested that such behavior on India's part could overflow and become a global danger. For China, this would be a beneficial arrangement. If the allegation stuck, the Chinese would be on the other side of the divide. In any event, they were already one of the P-5, among the "legitimates." As on earlier such occasions, Tang Jiaxuan suggested that such tests by India were part of the country's aspirations to be the "hegemon" of South Asia. This not so subtle trap was not something that I was going to fall into. That would diminish India and make Pokhran II totally country-specific; for China, this was an uncharacteristically direct fly to cast, and a bold fly at that.

There came a moment during the meeting, after all the finger-pointing and table-thumping, when my Chinese counterpart suggested that as India "had tied the knot, it had better untie it also"—because we had created the problem, we had better find the exit route. I liked this statement; this one sentence of simple directness conveyed what many sentences of complex diplomatic jargon could never get across with such direct clarity. In a rather subtle and allusive way, characteristic of the Chinese civilization, Tang Jiaxuan was perhaps sending a message. In essence, he was saying: "The door is not tightly closed. You closed it first by what you did; now take that first step which will open it." Had I waited for a detailed analysis from the Ministry of External Affairs of what the comment meant and what my response ought to be, it might well have taken many weeks and produced several possible responses. An opportunity, a possibility, had unexpectedly opened up: our neighbor was making an offer. There was another aspect, however, that did not strike me immediately; it came to me somewhat later. In the new priorities that the People's Republic of China had now adopted, any continuing confrontation with India was out. The new priority was to put the past behind us. As a corollary, therefore, Pokhran II would also be accepted as an overt transformation of what China had always considered India to be: "a silent nuclear power."

My sense of the offer urged me to seize the moment. This I did by responding positively, for I had truly not been alarmed by all the table-thumping and finger-pointing. I offered to my very able Chinese counterpart and interlocutory: "Yes, that door needs to be opened, but where I come from in India, which country you know so well, in the vernacular they would say that you need two hands to untie a knot. It is very difficult to do so single-handedly. You give your hand, I will give mine. And together, with two hands, we will untie that knot." Soon thereafter, our bilateral meeting was over. I sensed immediately that the post–Pokhran II ice between India and China had begun to melt. Even though it may not have been immediately discernible, the thaw was under way.

I do wish to add how much I enjoyed and benefited from my interactions with this wise and astute Chinese foreign minister in subsequent meetings. Later he also took to complimenting me in a rather fulsome manner, which in the unfeeling world of diplomacy is both uncharacteristic and unusual. But whenever he expressed something complimentary about my rather "military style," I could never decide whether he was being approving or gently saying something else! We were to meet again, Tang Jiaxuan and I, in 1999 when I went to Beijing, in July 2000 when he visited India, in the General Assembly meetings at the United Nations in 2001, and when I inaugurated the Delhi–Shanghai flight on March 29, 2002. By then we had become friends. I value this association. In July 2002, when I moved to the North Block, I remember his telephone call, during which he spoke warmly of what we had achieved together.[5] I know that I could have done a great deal more with him for India-China relations. For this reason alone, even now I sometimes wish that I could have added some years to this bilateral relationship.

---

5. The Central Secretariat houses the various ministries of the government of India and consists of two wings separated by a wide road that links Rashtrapati Bhawan, the residence of the president of India, and India Gate, a memorial devoted to the Indian soldiers who made the supreme sacrifice in the two world wars. These two wings are called the North Block (which houses the Finance Ministry and Home Ministry) and the South Block (which houses the Prime Minister's Office and the ministries of External Affairs and Defence).

6

The Asian Two: India and China

Destiny's Perennial Twins

In the awesome oscillations of history's clock, the pendulum swings once more toward these two Asian neighbors, India and China. The world watches riveted, fascinated by the epic dimensions of the endeavors of two ancient civilizations, two great races almost synchronously addressing the many challenges of today, even as they emerge from the disorder of historical legacies. Their problems are similar—poverty, want, disparity—yet their methods to correct these wrongs are different.

Whereas India pursues democratic gradualism, China has taken recourse to what Roderick MacFarquhar and others have called "market Leninism." These two ancient nations have always been neighbors, yet their social and political intercourse has never been consistent. It has gone through several phases, mostly benign. Historically, the Chinese have been self-confident about having devised an ideal polity and society. Except for the journeys of the Buddhist monks and the extraordinary voyage of the eunuch Zheng He in the early sixteenth century, China has remained internally focused. Both India and China then inclined toward a kind of self-righteous insularity; now, of course, they both thirst for full knowledge of the wider world. Equally, they seek global recognition, considering it a rightful due, denied to them by the historical unfairness of an order dominated by the West.

For its part, India is a "nonterritorial cultural nation"; it has always been so. In that sense, it can never be "conquered"—not ever. But it has often been invaded, and parts of it have been occupied on occasion—though always only in part, never as a whole. India also, exceptionally, has never needed and seldom had a functional "state"—a "state of India"—governing all of its territory. The British Indian state was the first, but even it did not govern the whole of India. So often through history, for many centuries, India has gone along without a unitary state. That is again an exceptional attribute, because the roots of India draw their sustenance directly from the nutrition provided by Indian society. China, on the other hand, vitally needs a strong central state, all-powerful and all-controlling. This is absolutely essential; otherwise the Chinese nation will fragment. This tendency has been demonstrated time and again. It is this fundamental difference that gives the two countries their characteristic distinctiveness. It is this difference that sets China and India apart.

With a total combined population of almost 2.4 billion, China and India are home to more than a quarter of all the humans on Earth (6.5 billion). This is a humbling thought, and an onerous responsibility. The causes and consequences of our border dispute in 1962 have colored relations between the two nations, almost indelibly. Regrettably, this episode almost defines the relationship, and certainly influences it deeply.

India's path into the future is fairly discernible, but not so China's. India will continue down this relatively disorderly path of participatory democracy: raucous, contention-prone, often exasperatingly slow, and somewhat tardy when compared to the tight hand of totalitarian governance. India will always be a vivid kaleidoscope, inhabiting many centuries simultaneously, at first accommodating, then absorbing its several contradictions. The People's Republic of China, on the other hand, has obliterated most of its distinctive individualism. Will the creativity of the Chinese cause it to surface again? In time, yes. For the present, however, the Chinese state reigns supreme; in India, the individual can (and often does) command the state. But "money," cynically, is indifferent to such philosophical or ideological esotericism. Money needs to multiply, and to do so constantly. Otherwise it will diminish or escape to where it can grow rapidly. Money as that essential lubricant of "growth and development" will go only where it can move easily and in large volumes—ever-increasingly at that, multiplying compulsively.

Look Back in No Anger

Through the centuries, China and India have never confronted one another in anger, and certainly not in prolonged conflict. So what happened in 1962? And *why* did it happen? That question is always dominant, compelling us to reexamine the assumptions about 1962 that have become fixed verities. Soon after the civil war and the revolution of 1949, China's emphasis remained focused on consolidating internally, quelling pockets of disturbance, settling the peripheries while shelving complex border issues for later—as, for instance, with the Soviet Union or India. But wherever it was vital for national security, China acted unilaterally, without any regard for legality and irrespective of consequences. The most notable examples of this approach were clearly Tibet and the road across the Aksai Chin.[1] There were exceptions to this general assessment, of course—for instance, the issue of Taiwan.

By 1998, however, following India's tests of May 11 and 13, those early attitudes about the border had mellowed. White papers published by the Chinese government in 1998 and 2000 confirm this assessment. A half-century had gone by, and China had already largely taken India's nuclear posture into account in its security assessments. In any event, I had held to the view for some time that the peaceful nuclear explosion of 1974 had sent a message abroad, and those who had read the message had already incorporated India into the category of "nuclear-weapons-capable countries." Besides, after 1962, the chances of another such Sino-Indian military encounter were almost negligible. Were it ever to recur, China had assessed that its conventional force superiority would be adequate, and that its capability in nuclear weaponry and delivery systems was markedly ahead of India's. Leo Rose, the doyen of South Asian commentators, astutely wrote that China regarded India as "a 'quiet' nuclear power."[2] Thus Beijing was not particularly disturbed by the tests of 1998, preferring instead to feign a degree of studied indifference toward Pokhran II—portraying it as a development of not much consequence for a "far superior" China—and yet articulating protests, especially after Prime Minister Vajpayee's letter to President Clinton was leaked to the press.

Our bilateral relationship with China is endowed with considerable emotion for me personally, because my understanding of its background was colored by my experiences as a soldier in India's northeast in 1962. What I sought was much more than an answer to the problems of the here and now. I wanted a deeper understanding of the historical and civilizational impulses of the People's Republic, the political dynamics of that country, the personalities who decided policies there. All this I sought to grasp. I knew that without such an understanding, I conceivably could not—nor could anyone—move toward the goal of stable relations. In the

---

1. Aksai Chin is the site of one of the two main border disputes between India and China, the other being Arunachal Pradesh. Aksai Chin (which literally means "desert of white stones"), also called the Soda Plain, is a vast desert of salt and is almost uninhabited. One of the proximate causes of the Sino-Indian War of 1962 was India's discovery of a road that had been built through the region by China to connect Tibet and Xinjiang. Aksai Chin is currently under the occupation of the People's Republic of China. India asserts that the area is a part of the Ladakh District of the state of Jammu and Kashmir.
2. Leo Rose, "India and China: Forging a New Relationship in the Subcontinent," in Shalendra Sharma, ed., *Asia Pacific in the New Millennium: Geopolitics, Security, and Foreign Policy* (Berkeley, Calif.: Institute of East Asian Studies, University of California, 2000).

intervening years, since resigning my commission in the Army and stepping into political activism, I had read a great deal, trying to gain a sense
of the history of the interrelationship between these two Asian giants.

Why, for example, had history conferred upon the southeast of Asia that
age-old designation of Indochina? Why is it "*Indo*china," not some other
name? There is obviously a great imprint of Indian culture in the region;
its influence is all-pervading, clearly and unmistakably present, not just in
the great Hindu monuments and architecture that dot those ancient lands,
but in their customs, their manners, even their observances, all the way
down to Indonesia (Indian—Asia?) and the idyllic island of Bali (which
now, sadly, has experienced a series of terrorist bombings). And it was
not just Buddhist thought that had traveled or influenced Boro-Badur,
the incomparable temples of Angkor-Vat, or the customs and observances
in that land of the Kamboj (now Cambodia); these are all so evocatively
Hindu. And where, I often wondered, is Champa, that ancient outpost of
Hindu civilization? I searched long and hard for that line, which is not
physical or geographical so much as a line of cultural separation. Is it discernible? Is there a dividing line at some spot where the Indian imprint
clearly fades and the mark of the great Chinese civilization begins to assert
itself? Although I have no historical or any other basis for thinking so, my
own observance suggests that the line that divides India's cultural imprint
from China's may run through the Plain of Jars in Laos.[3] I say "may" only
because at this point, who could penetrate the dense obscurity of the past
and find out for certain? Perhaps it is the lost ancient kingdom of Champa
in central Vietnam through which the divide runs.

There has been, to my mind, a kind of cyclical movement in the relationship between India and China. Even a cursory reading of history reveals that
there have been discernible contacts between these two great civilizations
since the advent of Buddhist thought. No account exists of maritime trade
or contact between these two Asian giants. Travel between them as neighbors was overland, the route mostly across Ladakh, or later through Tibet.
Faith in Buddha, his thoughts, teachings, and place of birth, was the great
draw for early pilgrims from China. Buddhist monks from India traveled
far and wide, including to China, to spread the message of that great faith.

I first went to China in the early 1980s. I went on my own, not in any
official capacity, before it became fashionable to go there, and before China

---

3. The Plain of Jars is located in the highlands of northern Laos. Its name comes from the hundreds of huge
stone jars that are mysteriously strewn across it. The jars, some of which weigh several tons, date back at least
1,000 years, but historians have not been able to explain how they got there or what they were used for.

exploded with such prodigious economic growth. I went on a journey of discovery, and found so much. But that visit only whetted my appetite for more. Encounters between India and China, even when only civilizational or cultural, have consistently involved two competing philosophies. That philosophical contradiction turns into contention only when one country fails to consider its relations with the other in that light. When I came to the Ministry of External Affairs, it was not with any fixed notions about China, and this was despite 1962. The ministry itself had both an institutional fixity of views and a continuing difficulty with the "Nehruvian legacies." I was searching for a distillate of that experience much more than reams of analysis.

Take, for example, Henry Kissinger's insightful observation when he described the Chinese leadership during Mao's regime as a truly remarkable group of people: despite having no hope of victory, they valiantly undertook the Long March; they confronted Japan when attacked; they endured a civil war; and then, in 1949, in the most improbable of circumstances, against every possible adverse factor, they achieved their revolution and drove out the Kuomintang. The more deeply I studied this history, the more I was struck by the ironies of India's multiple contradictions. On March 23, 1947, the Asian Relations Conference was inaugurated in Delhi under the auspices of the Indian Council of World Affairs.[4] By that third week of March, however, Mountbatten had already arrived in India, and a plan for Partition, with Nehru's knowledge, was on the anvil. Nevertheless, India took on a kind of leadership role for Asia, at a time when there was not yet a People's Republic of China. This had several consequences, the logic of which became clear with time. The most unfortunate of these, perhaps entirely unintended on Nehru's part, was the presumption that India had a responsibility to encourage China, promoting and projecting it as a great "new" nation. This presumption was demonstrated at the Asian-African Conference in Bandung in 1955; it was unnecessary and counterproductive. For one, China resented the patronizing attitude that Nehru seemed to project. For another, India's stature was dented, not enhanced, by even an impression of such an attitude.

In the intervening years, from 1949 to 1955, several events occurred that, in truth, anticipated the shape that this bilateral relationship was to take.

---

4. The Asian Relations Conference was attended by delegations from twenty-eight countries, including some of the Asian republics of what was then the Soviet Union. Observers came from the United Nations, the Arab League, and institutes of international relations in Australia, Great Britain, the U.S., and the USSR. The conference helped strengthen the solidarity of Asian nations, but when Independence came on August 15, 1947, urgent internal problems, such as ending communal clashes and resettling refugees, pushed everything else into the background.

At the time, we were not really seeing the hard-headed pragmatism of Mao Zedong, Marshal Chen Yi, or Premier Chou Enlai. We approached our immediate post-Independence years fired by idealistic zeal. Sharply distinct from this and standing clearly apart was China's no-nonsense realistic approach. When viewed against the People's Republic's total preoccupation with settled boundaries, India's relative indifference to borders is in itself a lesson in statecraft. Increasingly, China began to distance itself, impatient with the woolliness of India's policy approaches. Of course, it never avoided engaging with India, because it had grasped early on how India could develop. The landmarks were, I believe, the annexation of Tibet (1950), the Dalai Lama's seeking shelter in India (1959), and our adoption of Panchsheel, a formalized code of conduct between our two countries that entailed five principles: (1) respect for each other's territorial integrity, (2) mutual nonaggression, (3) agreement not to interfere in each other's affairs, (4) equality and mutual benefit, and (5) peaceful coexistence.

At about this same time, in the mid-1950s, China began to distance itself from its other great neighbor, the Soviet Union, just as India, guided by other global considerations, was seeking a closer relationship with the Soviets. This jangled Chinese sensitivities. Perhaps it appeared to be a page out of their own book: containing a possible adversary through the leverage of converting that adversary's own neighbors into hostiles. From this, in a fashion, was born China's cultivation of Pakistan, a countermove on Asia's strategic chessboard. At another level, we somehow failed to understand the essential nature of the revolutionary regime, or its many personalities. Following the border skirmishes that began in the late 1950s, it became increasingly difficult to study China. Sino-Indian relations underwent a great freeze; China became even more of a closed society to us. India remained what it has always been—an open society, as open to study and scrutiny as to spying. It is also possible that we did not fully grasp the subtlety of expression of the Chinese civilization. It is not as if India suffers from the coarseness of the Occidentals, but our neighbor is given much more to elliptical, subtle, rather indirect and allusive statements than to brazenly direct pronouncements in the manner of Western foreign offices. Our experience and learning was of the West; our current problem was with the East. China experienced its own agonies in the 1960s and 1970s, which I would think affected the course of its India policy, as much as if not more than our own internal political confusions or failures affected our China policy. China's India policy may have been a victim and part of Mao's inner-party struggle against his enemies. A great deal of this came out in wall posters and in the Red Guard attacks on Foreign Minister Chen Yi during the Cultural Revolution. Unfortunately, no Indian scholar has really put all this material together and drawn lessons for us, even though we are the party directly concerned.

There were then the great fixities, the great rigidities of the "legacy of 1962," over and above the legacy of Nehruvian thought. I was to meet Tang Jiaxuan, my Chinese counterpart, with both of these legacies, which were very much a part of the mindset of the Ministry of External Affairs. I did not share this legacy, at least not entirely, and though I had come from the military, memories of 1962 did not weigh upon me. They rankled, but they did not cripple my thinking. What load, then, did I carry? What psychological burden from 1962 was on my shoulders? I found that my anger had dissipated with time. That grievance was no longer there, certainly not against the People's Republic. It was a feeling of betrayal that I was experiencing, that we had been let down by our own kind, by our system. Therefore, what little bile I did possess I sought to save for "Delhi," with none directed at Beijing.

Moving Forward by Rearview

In the Sino-Indian context, the shadow of 1962 still hung over Pokhran II. That fateful year was in itself a kind of climacteric for the inept handling of the unsettled border between India and China. We had asserted the McMahon Line as the border, and also accepted the principle on the basis of which the Line was drawn on maps, so it only made sense to conduct a physical survey and delineation on the ground. India had recently gone through Partition. We had already experienced a boundary dispute with Pakistan. Thus there is no convincing explanation for our neglect of this duty on the Chinese front. And if there was ambiguity about the McMahon Line, then why escalate contention to the point of a military conflict? The border war of 1962 is partly attributable to the phases that the India-China relationship has gone through. India's "Age of Innocence" was the first, lasting roughly from the 1947 Asian Relations Conference and India's Independence that year, and the Chinese Revolution in 1949, until the startlingly "immediate action" initiated by the revolutionary government to move into Tibet in 1950. This was the first signal, but we did not properly read it, for it contained much embarrassment for Nehru. Whereas the government of the People's Republic of China was less than two years old, it was already demonstrating the clarity of purpose of a pragmatic regime of long experience, with defined goals, clear objectives, and a sense of national direction. We in India were moving differently. Of course, this PRC government had the power of the communist movement of those times, and also the unstinted support of the Soviet Union, at least to start with. Nevertheless, some of China's early decisions are still noteworthy.

India, too, faced formidable challenges in 1947. The handling of some of them added lasting value to the Union of India, particularly the integration of the princely states. However, there were areas where idealism often obscured purpose. I do not intend to be distracted here by the mistakes of Partition itself, or of Jammu and Kashmir, but it is clear that establishing defined international borders—for a country that had just gained independence and had not inherited settled boundaries—was a task to which insufficient attention was paid. We were preoccupied with imagery, and with how we were viewed by the rest of the world. In contrast, China withdrew into itself, sought no international recognition, and never stopped working toward the establishment of fixed boundaries. Regrettably, Nehru's high international flights did not leave behind the secure landing fields of established borders. China consolidated its borders; we talked about doing so—in fact, we talked about it nonstop. China took what it needed of India's territory, particularly in the Aksai Chin, because it considered the area to be of vital national importance. Across that plateau lay the access to a strategic area, the Central Asian province of Xinjiang (Sinkiang). India, for its part, remained ignorant; we did not even learn about this incursion until several years later, because we were patrolling the area only periodically. China moved into Tibet, which it regarded as its rightful due, then claimed it unhesitatingly. It refused to be sidetracked by any consideration other than national interest. For China, that was the highest morality. While Nehru looked on almost as a bystander, he advised the Indian ambassador in Beijing, K. M. Panikkar, that "India valued greatly relations with the People's Republic." Of course we did, but how did that spirit serve our national purpose? It is that which persuaded Deputy Prime Minister Sardar Vallabhbhai Patel to write to Nehru in protest on November 7, 1950. His letter read in part:

My dear Jawaharlal,

Ever since my return from Ahmedabad and after the cabinet meeting the same day, which I had to attend at practically 15 minutes' notice and for which I regret I was not able to read all the papers, I have been anxiously thinking over the problem of Tibet and I thought I should share with you what is passing through my mind. I have carefully gone through the correspondence between the External Affairs Ministry and our ambassador in Peking and through him the Chinese government. I have tried to peruse this correspondence as favourably to our ambassador and the Chinese government as possible, but I regret to say that neither of them comes out well as a result of this study. The Chinese government has tried to delude us by professions of peaceful intention.

Our ambassador has been at great pains to find an explanation or justification for Chinese policy and actions. As the External Affairs Ministry remarked in one of their telegrams, there was a lack of firmness and unnecessary apology in one or two representations that he made to the Chinese government on our behalf. It is impossible to imagine any sensible person believing in the so-called threat to China from Anglo-American machinations in Tibet. Therefore, if the Chinese put faith in this, they must have distrusted us so completely as to have taken us as tools or stooges of Anglo-American diplomacy or strategy. This feeling, if genuinely entertained by the Chinese in spite of your direct approaches to them, indicates that even though we regard ourselves as the friends of China, the Chinese do not regard us as their friends. With the Communist mentality of "Whoever is not with them being against them," this is a significant pointer, of which we have to take due note. During the last several months, outside the Russian camp, we have practically been alone in championing the cause of Chinese entry into UN and in securing from the Americans assurances on the question of Formosa. We have done everything we could to assuage Chinese feelings, to allay its apprehensions and to defend its legitimate claims in our discussions and correspondence with America and Britain and in the UN. In spite of this, China is not convinced about our disinterestedness; it continues to regard us with suspicion and the whole psychology is one, at least outwardly, of skepticism, perhaps mixed with a little hostility. I doubt if we can go any further than we have done already to convince China of our good intentions, friendliness and goodwill. In Peking we have an Ambassador who is eminently suitable for putting across the friendly point of view. Even he seems to have failed to convert the Chinese. Their last telegram to us is an act of gross discourtesy not only in the summary way it disposes of our protest against the entry of Chinese forces into Tibet but also in the wild insinuation that our attitude is determined by foreign influences. It looks as though it is not a friend speaking in that language but a potential enemy.

In the background of this, we have to consider what new situation now faces us as a result of the disappearance of Tibet as we knew it and the expansion of China almost up to our gates. Throughout history we have seldom been worried about our north-east frontier.

Thus, for the first time, after centuries, India's defence has to concentrate itself on two fronts simultaneously. Our defence measures have so far been based on the calculations of superiority over Pakistan. In our calculations we shall now have to reckon with communist China in the north and in the north-east, a communist China which has definite ambitions and aims and which does not, in any way, seem friendly disposed towards us.

It is also clear that the action will have to be fairly comprehensive, involving not only our defence strategy and state of preparations but also problem of internal security to deal with, which we have not a moment to lose.[5]

Such caution was timely and relevant, but that phase has passed. It cannot be ignored that a real struggle on China policy took place within the Ministry of External Affairs in the late 1940s and early 1950s, until the victory of what is now regarded as the "Nehru line" in the late 1950s. There was actually considerable argument on China policy, and Sardar Patel's letter was not the last word on the subject. Unfortunately, the political leaders at that time did not take kindly to well-argued and cogent reasoning that differed from their own policy preferences. One by one, all those who had direct experience in dealing with the Chinese after the 1940s, in China or in Tibet, were removed from the division of the Joint Secretary East in the MEA; the North East Frontier Agency (NEFA) section was actually closed down, and the post of undersecretary was abolished.

The "Age of Innocence" was over. It was followed by the period of "Hindi-Chini bhai bhai," Bandung, the Non-Aligned Movement (NAM), and Panchsheel. The theory of unintended consequences began to operate at Bandung itself, at the Asian-African Conference of 1955, where the first seeds of NAM were sown. Instead of marking a great new beginning for Sino-Indian relations, however, those proved to be the seeds of significant change. This judgment, though born of the harsh scrutiny of hindsight, is inescapable. Chou Enlai was increasingly coming across as an astute and affable practitioner of statecraft. Although he never showed it, it became clear that he greatly resented the implied patronage that Nehru exhibited

---

5. The full text of this letter is reproduced in Appendix 2.

at Bandung in wanting to introduce the Chinese premier and the People's Republic to the rest of the international community. This caused unstated outrage. I often reflect that had Chou Enlai at the height of Hindi-Chini bhai bhai said to Nehru, "I notice that our maps and yours both claim Aksai Chin. As you know, there is virtually nobody living there, but it is strategically important for us because we can build a road to Tibet across it. Would you consider conceding that piece of land to us, in exchange for our agreeing to the McMahon Line and other border delineations as you would prefer?" I think Nehru might well have agreed. Instead, the Chinese did it behind his back. When India discovered what had happened, Nehru was embarrassed and humiliated, and thereafter, of course, an angry Indian public would not let him compromise, even though he clearly wanted to.[6] Some correctives from Nehru did follow, but the damage had already been done. Thereafter, the relationship between India and China went rapidly downhill. Tragically, this decline took on a life and a momentum of its own.

1962

The Sino-Indian border conflict of October 1962 was the result of many factors, a culmination of several accumulated errors, some inherited and others added on. Principally, there was continuing ambiguity about where the McMahon Line actually ran, as well as whether it had indeed ever been formally accepted by all, for this fact itself was disputed by China. Worse, independent India did not even move into the territory that it had announced as its own, relying instead on established imperial practice and assumed "good intentions" on the part of a "bhai-bhai" neighbor. Soon enough, criminally faulty intelligence and timid military and Foreign Service advice—or worse, an absence of it altogether; or worse still, criminal cowardice and sycophancy—replaced dispassionate and objective considerations. On such suspect foundations was established the edifice of a "forward policy." Nobody stopped at the time to ask "forward" of what, or indeed, "forward" to where? All those records, unless they were deliberately purloined or spirited away, now gather dust among the archival material of the Ministry of External Affairs, or in the dim, unlit corners and crevices of history. There were two principally disputed areas—Aksai Chin and the NEFA. I find it tragic and also symptomatic that whereas military appraisals of the developments and events that led to 1962 do

---

6. Y. D. Gundevia recounts in *Outside the Archives* that Lord Mountbatten exerted pressure on Nehru to resolve the issues with both Pakistan and China.

exist, no corresponding official study focused on the diplomatic or the political is yet available. This is a great lacuna, born possibly of built-in hesitation and embarrassment about not opening too many closed doors in our diplomatic history. Truth breaks many idols and shatters many myths. It will here, too.

Some dates and events do stand out, however. In September 1961, there was a major appraisal by the Intelligence Bureau (IB), which formally advised the government that if military posts were established in a "forward position," India would not meet with any challenge from the People's Liberation Army after those posts had actually been set up. On November 2, Nehru, along with his defense minister, V. K. Krishna Menon, and the Army hierarchy, took this as a formal policy decision. This was an unforgivable lapse on the part of the IB, a grievous wrong by Nehru's government. Up to that point there had been a prohibition on any operations by security forces or the military within three kilometers of what India treated as its "frontier." This restriction was now lifted. A local commander was ordered to "fill the gaps" with a "systematic advance" toward India's own interpretation of the McMahon Line. I found it instructive to examine the Chinese government's approach in this regard.

> Chief-of-Staff Luo Ruiqing relayed the Chairman's eight-character comment on the situation: *wuzhuang gongchu, quanya jiaocu* (armed coexistence, jigsaw pattern); presumably Mao was contemplating the long-term persistence of the situation that had begun to develop already, whereby Indian and Chinese posts were on the "wrong" side of each other. Chinese accounts stress that because of the diplomatic implications of a border clash, all decisions were taken at the highest level: No matter to do with border defence to be considered as small; every matter must be checked with Beijing. . . .
>
> Sometime earlier, Mao had complained that the Indians had been pressing the Chinese along the border for three years, 1959–61; if they tried it a fourth year then China would strike back. The Dhola clash apparently decided the Chinese leaders that a military engagement was [now] inevitable. On 6 October, the order was sent to the border forces: "If the Indian army attacks, hit back ruthlessly. . . . If they attack, don't just repulse them, hit back ruthlessly so that it hurts." During fateful discussions held by the Chinese leadership in October, Mao and Zhou were

in charge, but Liu Shaoqi and Deng Xiaoping also participated, along with Marshals Liu Bocheng, He Long, and Xu Xiangqian, and General Luo Ruiqing as chief-of-staff. In the light of subsequent events Marshal Liu's recommendations were clearly taken very seriously. He rejected the idea of simply dealing with border troops by removing them, forcing them back, breaking up their attack, and surrounding them. Rather, he advocated taking on India's best troops and swiftly beating them. Only that could be called a decisive victory.[7]

Before that, however, the Chinese were clear in their directives to their forces:

> The Chinese rules of engagement, which began to be laid down by the Military Affairs Commission on February 1, 1961, were quite strict. Within the band of territory thirty kilometers inside their line of control, Chinese units were not permitted to fire weapons, patrol, go hunting, or even put down rebellious Tibetans; within the thirty kilometers band inside their line of control, there were additional restrictions: no target shooting, manoeuvres, or demolition. If Indian troops penetrated its lines, a Chinese unit had first to issue a warning and try to push them into retreating; if this did not work, it had then to confiscate their weapons according to international custom, and after an explanation, return their weapons and allow them to leave. "All easier said than done," was probably the comment of the average PLA platoon commander.[8]

There were clearly other reasons for exercising caution. China was dealing with a variety of concerns, all at the same time. There was, for instance, the real threat of an invasion from Taiwan. A significant underlying fear concerned deteriorating relations with the Soviet Union. Whether there was any examination of this important aspect in India is still not clear from available records. But from a very early stage, China had determined

---

7. Roderick MacFarquhar, *The Origins of the Cultural Revolution* (New York: Columbia University Press), 3 vols., vol. 3, p. 307. "The Dhola clash" refers to a conflict that occurred after the Indian Army established a forward outpost at Dhola, on the Chinese side of the McMahon Line. In response, Chinese forces entrenched themselves atop the adjacent Thagla Ridge, then dispatched 800 soldiers to surround the post. Neither side opened fire for twelve days. When the Indian troops were ordered to retake the ridge, a firefight broke out on September 20, with casualties incurred by both sides.

8. Ibid., p. 300.

that India might have the support of both the United States and the Soviet Union. That is another reason why China was apprehensive about a two-front war: the possibility of having to face Taiwan and at the same time confront India on the Himalayan border. The great droughts and indescribable ravages of the preceding years were not just incidental; these two internal developments had significantly affected China's moral reserve. Yet nowhere do I find sufficient proof that there were any in-depth analyses of such factors by India, as its own assessment of the situation.

Over and above all these, there was the crisis in the Caribbean. The world's attention was focused on the confrontation between U.S. president John F. Kennedy and Soviet premier Nikita Khrushchev over the movement of Soviet nuclear missiles into Cuba. The resulting standoff led the Soviet Union to quickly change course with regard to India. Shortly after the Chinese attack began on October 20, 1962,

> Nehru received a letter from Khrushchev in which the Soviet leader [alluding] to earlier reports of India's intention to initiate hostilities, urged him [instead] to agree to Zhou's offer of talks. Soviet officials followed through on Khrushchev's undertaking to Liu Xiao on the Mig-21s, telling the Indian embassy in Moscow that the Soviet commitment to sell these to New Delhi would not be fulfilled. The closest that Khrushchev came to a public commitment to the Chinese was a *Pravda* editorial on 25 October, which said only that the McMahon Line had been imposed on both Indians and Chinese, that the Chinese had never recognised it, and that Beijing's statement of the previous day constituted a satisfactory basis for opening negotiations.[9]

The Cuban missile crisis clearly restrained the Sino-Soviet dispute, or at least the timing of it. Just as China did not want a two-front war, neither did Khrushchev want to have to confront both America and China in the autumn of 1962. When facing Kennedy, he vitally needed total communist unity. The accompanying comparative chart of the chronology of events of this period (Table 1) illustrates the overlapping developments in the Caribbean and on the Himalayas.

To identify the principal military events that sparked this conflict is not entirely relevant here. It is educative, however, to underscore some of the conclusions of the military, its assessment of the conflict, and its outcome.

9. Ibid., p. 314.

TABLE 1

TIMELINE FOR THE HIMALAYAS AND CARIBBEAN CRISES, 1962		
	HIMALAYAS	CARIBBEAN
October 14	Khrushchev pledges support for China	US discovers missile silos on Cuba
October 20	First Chinese attack, Khrushchev letter to Nehru	
October 22		Kennedy reveals Soviet missiles, demands removal, imposes naval quarantine
October 24	China proposes talks	Soviet ships halt en route to Cuba
October 25	*Pravda* editorial tilts to China	
October 26		First ship stopped by US Navy
October 27	First Chinese offensive ends	
October 28		Khrushchev agrees to remove missiles
Early November	Moscow resumes neutrality	
November 5–14	Chinese criticized at Bulgarian Party Congress	
November 14	Indian reaction; Soviet ambassador conveys good wishes to Nehru (Before 21st: MiG-21 sales confirmed)	
November 16	Second Chinese attack	
November 21	Chinese ceasefire	
December 1	Chinese withdrawal commences	

Source: Jaswant Singh, *Defending India* (Houndmills: Macmillan, 1999), with credit to Roderick MacFarquhar, "War in the Himalayas, Crisis in the Caribbean," in MacFarquhar, *The Origins of the Cultural Revolution,* vol. 3: *The Coming of the Cataclysm, 1961–1966* (New York: Columbia University Press, 1999).

I am struck by the cautionary analysis of a retired Army chief who told the Indian government in January 1961, "Should the nature of the war go beyond that of a limited war . . . and develop into a full-scale conflagration amounting to an invasion of our territory, then it would be beyond the capacity of our forces to prosecute war . . . beyond a short period." In July 1962, a respected former Army chief, General K. S. Thimmayya, under whom the above appraisal had been drafted, wrote: "I cannot, even as a soldier, envisage India taking on China in an open conflict on its own. China's present strength in manpower, equipment and aircraft exceeds our resources with the full support of the USSR. It must be left to the politicians and diplomats to ensure our security." It is ironic that the director of military operations at Army Headquarters, Brigadier D. K. Palit, also concluded that the government's proposals for countermeasures against the Chinese threat were "perfunctory" to the point of being simplistic: "It seemed incredible that so grave a matter could have been despatched so heedlessly." This was in 1962. In similar terms, the military's conclusion was that the implementation of the forward policy was faulty. "That is why it is so vital," the assessment stated, "that a political direction must always be explicit on the available military means should a situation be created in which these two are necessarily interdependent or correlated."[10]

Most strangely, for all the meetings and the decisions that were made in connection with the operations of 1962, no minutes were kept and none issued. It is telling, as well as symptomatic of the moral erosion that had set in by then, that the defense minister had actually instructed that official records of his meetings were not to be maintained. Obviously this resulted in unrelieved confusion and conflicting interpretations of instructions given. Records were seldom available of what decisions had actually been made, what was said by whom, or even what the instruction was. In all this, the Ministry of External Affairs played hardly any role. This is extremely disquieting, as it comes on top of the knowledge that the military had not played its role properly. Even the routine elements of staff work and the most basic coordination with Army Headquarters at each formation level, in an otherwise highly professional army, were criminally abandoned; it is incomprehensible how the very veins and arteries of military functioning were so casually severed. Even in 1962, to those of us in the lower echelons of the Army, the whole enterprise smacked of whimsical and criminal negligence; but there is little point in revisiting those painful years in detail. All those errors took an onerous toll; the price that India paid was heavy. And it is a price that is still being paid even now, decade after decade, so many generations later.

There was one other great failure in the moral realm. Leaders at the very top—military, diplomatic, and political—failed India, in a criminal

---

10. Chandra B. Khanduri, *Thimayya: An Amazing Life* (New Delhi: Knowledge World, 2006), p. 318.

and unforgivable way. They besmirched the country's honor, yet had no remorse for what they had done. This was the first real test of independent India. Those who did not measure up had to accept responsibility. Not a single one volunteered to do so; and an indulgent nation simply looked the other way, largely in embarrassment, as we do when we come face to face with an ugly deformity. No one wanted to cause more hurt to Nehru. We are still paying for that act of national generosity. No political, diplomatic, or military commander—other than one or two who resisted by not acting speedily enough, but not any more forcefully—ever took that final and irrevocable step of protest, of stating views that, if not found acceptable, would have led to his stepping down. Nor did anyone voluntarily accept any responsibility. The Communist Party, particularly the CPM—the Communist Party (Marxist)—demonstrated and recorded its allegiance to the People's Republic of China. But it did not stand up and say so in India, the land of its birth; it did so in the land of its mentors.

For India, the result of all this could not have been otherwise. The humiliation of it, the moral rot that set in, still rankles.

> There [would] admittedly [be] cases where a senior commander [a leader] cannot reconcile with his responsibility to carry out an order that has been given. Then like Seydlitz at the Battle of Zorndorf, he has to say "After the battle the King may dispose of my head as he will, but during the battle he will kindly allow me to make use of it." No political leader, diplomatic head or general can vindicate such humiliation by "claiming that he was compelled against better judgment to execute an order that led to defeat."[11]

Just as no political leader, not even a prime minister, can transfer responsibility for national loss and humiliation, no general can shift the blame for the loss of a major encounter.

The Himalayas and the Superpowers

There are two additional aspects of this epochal conflict of 1962 that I wish to highlight: the roles of the United States and the Soviet Union. These have continuing relevance, though major transformations have obviously taken place since 1962 in the respective attitudes of the U.S. and Russia. We need to assess the small part played by Pakistan, too. It is

---

11. Erich von Manstein, *Lost Victories* (London: Methuen, 1958), p. 361.

fascinating to study the changing footwork of these countries, their shift-ing positions, as the situation (whether developing or deteriorating) evolved. India and China; China and the Soviet Union; the giants, the Soviet Union and the United States; China and Pakistan (as a price of Partition?); the United States and Pakistan; then add India to this duo. It is instructive to reflect on how much greater flexibility and dexterity all these countries demonstrated in the face of situations that were undergo-ing rapid transformation—all, that is, but India. I cannot help but com-ment that this demonstrates, above all, a marked contrast between the pragmatic imperatives of national need and interest in a given situation, versus rigid, fixed policy positions, or unconvincing and false idealism—refusing to accept dualism as the reality of most international situations, both then and now. I recognize that this could create a conflict between foreign and domestic policy in India, rendering the former a subservient player. Tragically, 1962 was an example of this; it became the ultimate Nehruvian legacy. There was another great difficulty that democracies such as the U.S. and India faced: how to manage international relations, to negotiate and implement foreign policy in the public eye, under constant media scrutiny, in contrast to those countries where policy is conceived and implemented in seclusion, originating from single-point sources. India was in error on another account: the tendency to always reduce for-eign policy to a single formula. In international relations, alas, there is no such thing as a straight line.

In the Sino-Soviet context, it is noteworthy that Beijing did not have the support from Moscow that New Delhi assumed it did. This is rele-vant because unless there is a clear understanding of the interplay of vari-ous forces in this region in 1962, it will be difficult to understand today's dynamics. On October 2, 1962, Khrushchev gave his views on the Sino-Indian border issue:

> I have to admit I wasn't at all enthusiastic about flying to Peking when hostilities broke out between China and India in 1959. I knew my official welcome would be laid on according to form, but I didn't expect to be greeted with the same fraternal goodwill I'd encountered in 1954, on my first trip to Peking.

The Indians maintained that the frontier was defined by the McMahon Line which they had inherited from the British. According to Peking, the McMahon Line was an imperialist hangover which had never been accepted by any central Chinese government, but Chou Enlai indicated that China was prepared to acknowledge reality and accept the status quo. Implicit in his position was the assumption that the precise boundary line would have to be negotiated and formalised in a treaty, but he did not spell this out. For his part, Nehru appears to have preferred to let sleeping frontiers lie, on the assumption that if Chou did not press the matter, it could legitimately be concluded that the Chinese accepted the Indian demarcation. . . .

The McMahon Line section of the frontier would probably have been easily settled, but Chou may have anticipated difficulties in the western sector where the maps of the two countries indicated disagreement over the ownership of a large segment of territory. At this time, the Chinese were about halfway through building a road from Sinkiang into western Tibet, and over 100 miles of it lay across the Indian-claimed Aksai Chin. This road was of critical importance to the Chinese for communications with Tibet, partly because the route from Szechwan across the mountains into eastern Tibet was a difficult one anyway, more importantly because the first rumblings of the Khampa revolt carried the threat that the latter route would be cut.[12]

America on the Himalayas

The response of the United States was equally complex, of course, reflecting its own very distinct agenda. The superpowers of those years, the USSR as much as the U.S., were attempting to set up the "chess pieces" of the region in a way that would be as favorable to their own national interests as possible. The United States was not a bystander in the conflict of 1962; it was very much a player, a very interesting and a very interested player. On November 3, 1962, in a memorandum to President Kennedy, Deputy Special Assistant for National Security Affairs Carl Kaysen rendered this assessment:

> The rapid Chinese advances in both NEFA and Ladakh have had a profound effect on Indian political thinking. The Indian leaders are being forced to re-examine some of the basic assumptions which have been central to Indian political life and attitudes. The great exponent of peaceful coexistence has been attacked by a nation which ostentatiously shared this attitude. The effectiveness of nonalignment as a policy has been clearly brought into

---

12. MacFarquhar, *The Origins of the Cultural Revolution,* vol. 2, p. 256.

question. The Soviet Union's action in supporting an unaccept-able Chinese Communist offer to negotiate the conflict has led the Indians to rethink their thesis that they could count on the Soviet Union to restrain the Chinese Communists and to provide India with substantial quantities of military equipment.

And in a telegram to the State Department dated November 17, 1962, John Kenneth Galbraith, the ambassador to India during the Kennedy administration, laid out the situation thus:

3) Even if the Chinese have no forward ambitions and even though they negotiate a settlement, no Indian Government can soon assume their peaceful intentions. Public opinion has now taken hold on this issue with the greatest firmness. Any Indian Government must be prepared for the contingency, of a long-continuing forward Chinese military policy in NEFA, the border countries, UP, Kashmir and it must assume that this will be com-bined with flexible claims as to what is Chinese territory.

4) In light of our past lecturing on the aggressive designs of the ChiComs, we cannot now reverse the field and tell them to confine their preparations as we will confine our help in accordance with the assumption that the Chinese are basically lambs.

5) It follows that beyond the equipment for five divisions for the next few months the Indians must have a policy of procur-ing weapons for regaining ground or holding open terrain, basic transport including transport aircraft, plant for arms manufacture, raw materials for the foregoing, and air power.

6) We must have a policy on assisting this for they are already asking us for help. There are many reasons for taking a deliberate view of this assistance. But we cannot decline it on the grounds that we do not believe the Chinese are a serious threat to India.

7) The issue is an urgent one for the Indians are now coming for-ward with requests of very large magnitude. Some of these I have persuaded them to withhold on the legitimate ground that they are not well considered and that first things be put first and the first thing is ready infantry equipment. But this is not substitute for a policy.

I turn now to recommendations.

1) The Indians must clearly realize, as they are only now dimly realizing, that our decision to help them beyond the ready combat requirements of the next few months involves political and financial issues of the highest order. This help in the magnitude contemplated will not be easy for us to provide.

2) This means that very senior Indian Minister should go to Washington (and London) to negotiate the arrangements including political understandings.

3) Our help must be related to a sense-making defense plan which reflects the realities of the military situation, does not commit the Indians to impossible tasks (e.g. the recovery of all the Aksai Chin), involves a realistic view of the weaponry and is related to actual as distinct from our imagined capacity to assist.

4) There must be a clear understanding that India (not the US) will take up the Pakistan problem. Pakistan in the past has been regarded as an American problem. Now it is serious Indian business. Our ability to help India is circumscribed while tension continues. India has an exposed flank and is handicapped in helping herself. We can help by restraining the Pak appetite but leadership in the task of making the subcontinent secure and unified belongs to India.

5) Given the foregoing, we should, I believe, help the Indians on a very substantial scale to organize their continuing defenses and build the supporting industry so far as this is clearly within their capacity. We shall, as the London decisions make clear, have to work with them patiently and with understanding. The major responsibility must remain in their hands. But we shall have to be severe on all wasteful nonsense.

6) We should be as tolerant as our own political climate allows to obeisances to nonalignment. These will probably disappear in the next few weeks or months. The Indians now want, in fact, an intimate and confidential relationship with the United States. Sophisticated concern is already turning to whether we will insist on nonalignment.

7) We stand on the edge of great opportunity here—reconciliation between India and Pakistan, security for the whole subcontinent, a decisive reverse for communism in its area of its greatest opportunity. We could lose the chance by not helping the Indians defend themselves according to their view of the Chinese danger. We could lose it by rushing in indiscriminately either with help or with unreal conditions. But given patient work and some luck with the Pakistanis and firm bargaining on essentials we can bring it off.

In light of foregoing considerations, which we know to be much in the mind of the British High Commission New Delhi, we strongly urge that London decisions, especially those in Annex A, be not communicated now to the Indian or Pakistan Governments and we have in mind visit of Duncan Sandys. Instead we urge prompt consideration which obviously must be at highest levels reflecting the foregoing considerations and resulting guidance.

Strictly FYI except for reference to Sandys, foregoing conveyed very informally to British Deputy HICOM.

Galbraith[13]

Extremely tragic—and I do mean tragic—were two letters that Prime Minister Nehru sent to Kennedy on November 19, while the United States and its president were still deeply immersed in the Cuban missile crisis. The first was conveyed in a telegram from Galbraith to the State Department. Captioned "Eyes Only President, Secretary and SecDef. Verbatim Text," it began: "Following is text of message dated today from Prime Minister to President, to be delivered by B.K. Nehru. Copy handed me this evening by M.J. Desai." The second was also delivered to the White House by B. K. Nehru, who was the Indian ambassador to Washington and a nephew of the prime minister.[14] The text of this letter was transmitted that same day to the embassy in New Delhi. These letters have not been declassified, either by the U.S. administration or by the Indian government. In his biography of Jawaharlal Nehru, S. Gopal provides the following summary:

13. Both the memorandum and Galbraith's telegram are available online at http://www.state.gov/r/pa/ho/frus/kennedyjf/46454.htm, Documents 190 and 199.
14. The telegram conveyed to Kennedy by Galbraith is commonly known as telegram 1891. The telegram delivered by B. K. Nehru was numbered 2167.

Nehru, apparently without consulting any of his cabinet colleagues or officials, apart from the foreign secretary, M.J. Desai, wrote two letters to Kennedy describing the situation as "really desperate" and requesting the immediate despatch of a minimum of 12 squadrons of supersonic all-weather fighters and the setting up of radar communications. American personnel would have to man these fighters and installations and protect Indian cities from air attacks by the Chinese till India personnel had been trained. If possible, the United States should also send planes flown by American personnel to assist the Indian Air Force in any battles with the Chinese in Indian air space; but aerial action by Indians elsewhere would be the responsibility of the Indian Air Force. Nehru also asked for two B-47 bomber squadrons to enable India to strike at Chinese bases and air fields, but to learn to fly these planes Indian pilots and technicians would be sent immediately for training in the United States. All such assistance and equipment would be utilised solely against the Chinese.[15]

The American response came promptly, but in two installments. The first, sent by Secretary of State Dean Rusk, was received later that very evening. The relevant paragraphs read as follows:

> 4)   We are prepared to dispatch twelve or more C-130's at once to assist in any necessary movement of forces and equipment to Assam area or to Ladakh. This would be US operation with planes, crews support. Request your urgent advice whether Indians prepared to use this transport immediately. Also earliest estimates men and tonnage involved. Special airlift team being dispatched at once. This provides another opportunity for you to remind Indians about importance of moving troops from Pakistan border. Urgency of situation underlines anomaly of Indian reluctance in this respect.
>
> 5)   For continuing build-up Indian airlift capacity we also prepared urgently airlift at least critically needed spare parts C-119's. Best procedure appears send maintenance team already named at once to assess need and determine effective measures.

---

15. Sarvepalli Gopal, *Jawaharlal Nehru: A Biography* (Cambridge, Mass.: Harvard University Press, 1976–1984), 3 vols., vol. 3: *1956–1964*, pp. 228–29.

6) This as far as we can see to go on basis of facts now available here. However, supply actions urgently needed and assessed as valid need not be delayed despite lack of clear picture Indian capabilities. View possibility India now ready use tactical air, one airlift requirement may be bombs request of UK. London should raise this and ascertain availability and British air shipment capabilities.

Rusk[16]

Rusk summarized the U.S. response to these letters from Prime Minister Nehru in an assessment sent to Galbraith on the same day, November 19, 1962:

It is not our purpose now to rehash the past but to look at present situation in its fullest reality. The essential question is whether Peiping is now engaged in an all-out assault on India or is pushing its territorial claims up to the extreme limits of Chinese pretentions. Nehru's latest message indicates his assessment that the Chinese are determined to push far beyond disputed areas and that this is in fact a genuine attack on India.

If this is so then it is apparent that India is faced with the necessity of mobilizing every possible resource in its support and that every other question must be subordinated to its own defense and national existence. It seems that, therefore, PriMin must now consider maximum diplomatic, political and military effort to encompass the following:

1) The enlistment of full Pakistani cooperation at whatever cost in terms of lesser question between the two countries including Kashmir. The United States cannot give maximum military support to India while most of India's forces are engaged against Pakistan over an issue where American interest in self-determination of the peoples directly concerned has caused us since 1954 to be sympathetic to Pakistan's claims. To put it in most brutal terms, India may now face a choice between Pakistani assistance in the defense of India and some kind of satisfaction of Pakistan's interest in the Kashmir question.

16. Available online at http://www.state.gov/r/pa/ho/frus/kennedyjf/46456.htm, Document 2170. Paragraphs 1 through 3 are not relevant and so are not included here.

2) We have seen little evidence thus far of India's attempt to mobilize the traditional commitments of the British Commonwealth. We believe the defense of India is in the first instance a Commonwealth problem though there are no formal treaty commitments within that structure. If India considers that it is faced with a war against China, it would be very difficult for the United States to give maximum assistance without the fullest participation of at least the old Commonwealth and without the elimination of such anomalies as normal Commonwealth relations with Peiping and the shipment of large supplies of foodstuffs from Canada and Australia to Red China. India must, we think, insist upon maximum Commonwealth support in its struggle against China. Specifically, any requests for assistance made of us should also be addressed to the British.

3) A third factor is the United Nations. We can understand that Nehru might have been reluctant to raise question of Chinese aggression in United Nations so long as he had any hope that Russia would not be forced to support Peiping. On the other hand, the full mobilization of world opinion against Red China could bring to bear political, economic and psychological pressures on Peiping which would add strength to the relative ineffectiveness thus far of Indian arms. In any event, full United States support for India would be much easier and more palatable to the American people if there were near unanimity in the United Nations that this was an aggression rejected by the entire world community, and on which India had the widest possible international support.

4) Further, we have seen little evidence that India has attempted to mobilize the political and practical support of other nations in southern and Southeast Asia also bordering on or near Red China and interested in resistance to Red Chinese expansion. India's heretofore cavalier attitude toward communist penetration Southeast Asia is obviously an obstacle to Asian solidarity in this situation, but a maximum diplomatic effort to trade support for support with these countries is clearly called for.

5) Latest message from PriMin in effect proposes not only a military alliance between India and the United States but complete commitment by us to a fighting war. We recognized this might be

immediate reaction of a Government in a desperate position but it is a proposal which cannot be reconciled with any further pretense of non-alignment. If this is what Nehru has in mind, he should be entirely clear about it before we even consider our own decision.

There are strong reasons why the United States should not appear to be the point of the spear in assisting India in this situation. The most impelling of these is that our role might force Moscow to support Peiping. We shall be considering here whether there is anything we can constructively say to Moscow about China's reckless and provocative action because there is some reason to believe that Moscow is also very much worried about the dangerous possibility. I would emphasize, however, India must mobilize its own diplomatic and political resources, seek the broadest base of support throughout the world and, more particularly, enlist the active interest and participation of the Commonwealth.

Please let us have your comments on the above urgently before we reply to the PriMin's latest letter to the President.

Rusk[17]

The United States Embassy in New Delhi confirmed the need for the C-130s on November 20, and the State Department responded the same day that the Department of Defense was dispatching twelve C-130 aircraft to India.

The American position was further elaborated in a telegram of November 20:

Eyes Only for Ambassador from Secretary. We have just forwarded to you second letter from Nehru today anticipated in your 1889. As we read this message it amounts to a request for an active and practically speaking unlimited military partnership between the United States and India to take on Chinese invasion India. This involves for us the most far-reaching political and strategic issues and we are not at all convinced that Indians are prepared to face the situation in the same terms. I recall that more than once in past two years I have expressed to various Indian representatives my concern that their policy would lead to a situation where they would call upon us for

17. Ibid., Document 206.

assistance when it is too late rather than give their and free world policy any opportunity for preventive effectiveness.[18]

It is tragic that the great champion of nonalignment had to experience such a denouement—not just to see the demise of nonalignment on those bleak plateaus of the high Aksai Chin, but to actually be a participant in bringing it about. This was in 1962. Also tragic is that the trauma of the event took Nehru's life, too. By 1964, he was gone.

Freeze and Thaw

After 1962, events between India and China fell into a familiar and predictable cycle. A small freeze set in, which lasted about fourteen years. After the peaceful nuclear explosion of 1974, Indira Gandhi felt sufficiently confident domestically to make another attempt to create at least an opening with China, and in 1976 the two countries exchanged ambassadors again. It was three years thereafter that Atal Bihari Vajpayee, the minister of external affairs in the Janata government, paid the first official visit to China in almost a quarter of a century—since Jawaharlal Nehru's visit in 1954. The last high-level visitor to India from China had been Chou Enlai in 1960. Unfortunately, the Vajpayee visit clashed with a Sino-Vietnam conflict. He therefore cut short his trip and returned to India. Yet another freeze occurred, not to be broken until a decade later, when Prime Minister Rajiv Gandhi paid a highly significant visit in 1988. That trip opened many new doors. Slowly normality began to return to Sino-Indian relations, until the interruption of May 1998. Two months later, I sat down with Tang Jiaxuan in Manila.

Manila was only the first of many meetings with the Chinese foreign minister. In June 1999, I visited Beijing on an invitation of some months' standing. Quite without my intending it to be read in that fashion, my trip coincided with the Kargil conflict. Not for that reason, but owing to a real movement of intentions in both countries, this visit brought about several transformations. I believe that a new chapter in Sino-Indian relations was thereby commenced. Thereafter our two countries conducted a regular exchange of visits. I visited China again in March 2002, and Tang Jiaxuan came to India in July of that year. K. R. Narayanan, India's ambassador to China in 1976, traveled back to that country in 2000, this time as president. The defense ministers exchanged visits. Of great significance were visits by the two prime ministers: Zhu Rongji in January 2002 and

---

18. Ibid.

Atal Bihari Vajpayee in June 2003. Most recently, Wen Jiabao came to India as the new Chinese premier. It is as if, the gates of necessity having finally opened, no opportunity ought now to be lost. We have come a long way from the days when China regarded India as an "imperialist dog." The intervening years have brought an India-China security dialogue, China's recognition of the Himalayan state of Sikkim as belonging to India, and now the announcement that India and China have a "strategic and cooperative partnership for peace and prosperity."

In the Fast Lane

Today, the People's Republic is desirous of transforming our relationship but continues to be somewhat perplexed by the concerns it harbors about the evolving relationship between India and the United States.

As for India, we need to shed any defensiveness or timidity in our approach to such evolving relationships, both with China and with the United States. Persuaded by the promise inherent in my initial meetings with Tang Jiaxuan, I reflected often on how to promote a conceptual evolution of Indo-China relations. I am not convinced that the relationship should continue to follow the path of "incremental gradualism." It has been my consistent view that these visits ought to be considered not as individual events separated in time, but as a consolidated whole, as indicators of a direction. We should vigorously pursue this consolidated synergy of visits and inherent intent on a path of ever-improving bilateral relations. Of course, this has to be done in accordance with national goals; that is a given. Yet a more highly activist approach is needed. For that reason, I wrote to Foreign Minister Tang Jiaxuan proposing greater and more deliberate movement on the Line of Actual Control (LOAC), and also offering a time frame. Subsequent developments carried a reassurance about these fundamentals. It did take time for Tang Jiaxuan to react, but when that reaction came, it was positive, it was purposeful, and even though there was slippage on the time frame—after all, as Mao had said, "I can wait a hundred years for Taiwan!"—a mechanism did finally evolve. That mechanism, with refinements, is now the methodology being followed.

During my second visit to China, in 2002, we progressed much further on the Sikkim issue than ever before. I brought up the subject tentatively, near the end of my talk with Tang Jiaxuan, as the meeting was coming to a close. Yet again this was contrary to the official advice of caution: one step at a time, or perhaps half a linguistic pirouette. Such an approach I treated as anathema, all these wearisomely petty maneuvers. Tang Jiaxuan's instant reaction was, if I recall correctly, in English and direct: "I am an expert on Sikkim. Should I give my views?" This eventually resulted in the assurance that during the next visit to India by the Chinese premier, such an announcement would be made. Sikkim has now finally been accepted by China as a state of the Union of India. Tang's assurance has been fulfilled. The two countries have also made significant progress on the mechanism devised for the Line of Actual Control. I have consistently held that neither the border nor the LOAC ought to hold this relationship back; it also should not be the only key that can open the relationship. It is unwise to treat this issue as a pacesetter for the entire gamut of bilateral relations. There is need for both China and India to recognize that the LOAC clarification is only a subset of a much larger framework. Necessary technical clarification of the Line is important, of course, both for mutual confidence-building and for a final boundary resolution. But it cannot, and should not, be the principal engine in this process of developing bilateral relations. There is a message inherent in the primacy accorded to the LOAC clarification: that the two Asian giants still bear the burden of the past, and are therefore adversarial, dispute-led, and hence routinely contentious. This is not correct; that approach needs to be abandoned as so much excess baggage.

We should expect the emerging Indo-American relationship to be a matter of concern to the Chinese. India certainly ought not to react defensively by explaining it to China. This is an inevitable process, an evolution of international relations, as the India-China equation now is. There is no reason why India should jump on the bandwagon with the sharp critics of U.S. policies. Soapbox diplomacy is neither India's idiom nor its style. In truth, it is what Jiang Zemin advocated that we should do: "scale the heights and look far." Besides, the Indo-U.S. relationship is not and should not be seen as an attempt to "isolate" China. We are not prepared to be a party to "encircling" China so as to serve any possible interest that the United States or anyone else might have in attempting such an enterprise. China is our neighbor and will remain so.

An Exorcist for 1962

A single chapter does not offer sufficient space for analyzing the complexity of the India-China relationship. In the preceding pages we have traveled from 1947 to the end of the Cold War and the turn of the millennium, roughly from when barriers went up to when they were pulled down.

Bilateral relations have fluctuated in this period (1947–2005) between conflict, accommodation, and contest. A self-sustaining balance has not yet been achieved. This absence has its roots in many factors, some permanent, others transient. We have dealt here primarily with the "reactives": issues, events, and occurrences that led to a chain of action and reaction. This cycle now overlays the nonvariables, rendering an already challenging geopolitical situation infuriatingly more complex. How do we impart a confidence that will generate a built-in balance? At the heart of it all is a grinding of the tectonic plates of overlapping interests, of spheres of influence, of an intersection of the regions of cultural spread, of security zones and their primacy in national interests; a policy or approach of strategic encirclement; the reality of economic muscle as the principal coefficient of national capability and power. As long as our two countries fail to consider this reality, we will fail to give the relationship equilibrium. Only such an objective and noncompetitive examination can lend the strength of a stable acceptance of mutuality.

Is this desirable? Clearly so. Is it attainable? If so, how? China and India both need concord and cooperation, not contention and conflict. The footprints of two cultures do overlap in Southeast Asia, but there is no clash of national interests in that area. It is equally undeniable that because Tibet and Taiwan are aspects of China's identity and part of its security considerations, there ought to be due recognition of such by India. The reverse, however, does not obtain. India is not the "hegemon" of South Asia, but it *does* have undeniable security interests. China needs to fully accept this fact. The nuclear issue was only one of India's concerns. There are others, including Myanmar, Gwadar, and, most significantly, China's quasi-alliance with Pakistan in the military and nuclear realm. Undoubtedly, there has been a reexamination of this quasi-alliance since the 1990s, but it has generated the theory of a "strategic encirclement of India." India has accommodated this reality; now it is necessary for China to also appreciate India's view. There is a geopolitical angle to South Asia, which China accepts at times—as it did, for example, toward the end of the 1980s. At other times, however, it moves away.

From its side, India has to purposefully readdress itself to relations with its immediate neighborhood. It is this area that has seen perhaps the greatest lack of conceptual clarity on our part. India has not inherited the mantle of the imperial British. Our neighboring countries are proud sovereigns seeking their own space in today's world. India, as much as China, has to accept that the essence of power is to know the limits of power. India needs also, finally, to cross the psychological barriers of 1962. India need not react to every Chinese move, whether in South Asia, bilaterally in its relations with Pakistan, or globally, as if each and every Chinese initiative is born of some latent hostility. As China now endeavors to "stand high and look far," so too must India. Such mutual accommodation, paradoxically enough, is thwarted by China's enhanced national power, by the fact that in terms of economic growth it is now well ahead of India. India set out on this path in the 1990s, but China had a significant head start. During a visit to Beijing in October 1994, as part of the delegation accompanying Vice President K. R. Narayanan, I asked President Jiang Zemin what, in his view, were the principal challenges faced by the state of the People's Republic of China. Instantly he responded: "Displacement, disparity, and the state enterprises." Not only have these issues not been healed, they are now running sores. Remove the factor of "displacement," and India faces almost exactly the same challenges.

Since the end of the Cold War and the great meltdown, China's principal concerns have focused around its relations with the United States, Japan, and Taiwan; where after managing North Korea, the equation with Russia, South and Southeast Asia are its concerns. What is shared with India is the potentially problematic demand for energy, to fuel national and individual growth. It is necessary for India and China to work jointly in this regard so as to optimize existing energy sources and to develop new, innovative ones, to the greater benefit of both. The Indian Ocean presents a concern, but not in any hierarchy of priorities. To meet the conflicting needs of managing such a portfolio of priorities, every now and then a triangular equation is proposed consisting of Russia, China, and India. This initiative has significance and potential, but it has a long way to travel yet.

In our age, issues of international concern are being redefined; national sovereignties and boundaries are being downgraded; human rights, the environment, and globalization are gaining primacy. We have to recognize this new agenda and work together to meet the challenge. India, its concerns, and its international standing are relevant in meeting these challenges. China must accept this aspect of India's status, both within the United Nations and in the context of the much larger international community.

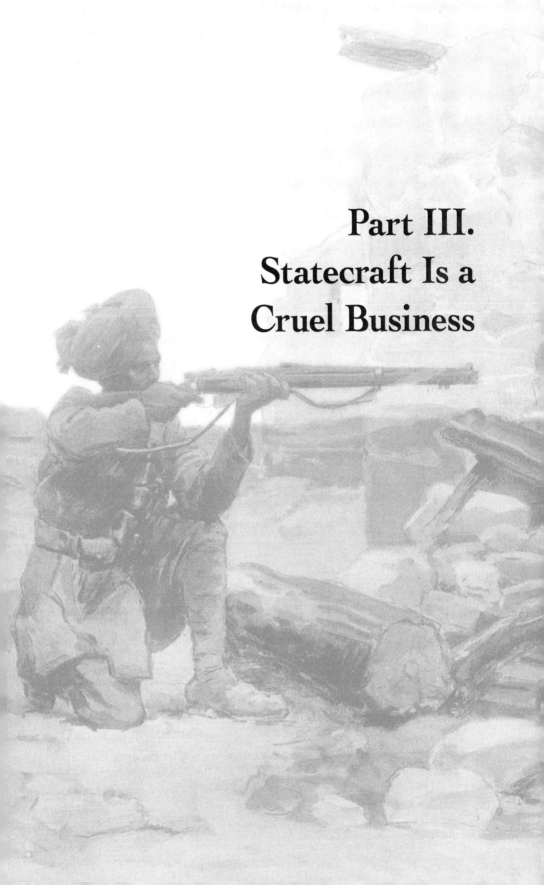

Part III.
Statecraft Is a
Cruel Business

7

Troubled Neighbor, Turbulent Times: 1999

Page from the Book of Aftermaths

For the entire period I was in government, 1998–2004, doubts about the relationship between India and Pakistan continued to assail me, as we oscillated from one dramatic event to another. The more we sought peace and resolution, the more that peace eluded us. Guided as if by some unknown, invisible hand, the final script was always far removed from the much-desired accord. The destinies of the two nations are intertwined and yet perversely divergent. At the time that (avoidable?) Partition was sought in 1947, neither could have reckoned that "perpetual hostility and occasional conflict" would end up as the policy baggage that both would have to carry. That a deliberately induced hostility would be adopted as a policy posture for maintaining this "separateness of identity" was clear enough, but surely not stretched to such limits as to suicidally obliterate that identity itself!

The Overture

It was against the backdrop of the nuclear tests of May 1998 that the two prime ministers, Atal Bihari Vajpayee of India and Nawaz Sharif of Pakistan, met in New York. Such meetings ordinarily take place on the sidelines of the United Nations General Assembly, which meets between September and December every year. This is a great annual jamboree, at which presidents and prime ministers, heads of governments and foreign ministers congregate. It offers a convenient occasion to fulfill the obligations of pending meetings. So it was at the 53rd session of the General Assembly, which commenced on September 15, 1998. I well remember that luncheon meeting between the two prime ministers. Both had agreed to meet in a relaxed atmosphere, preferably over a meal. Their respective schedules permitted no other option than lunch on September 23. It was not a small gathering. Among others, the foreign minister of Pakistan was there, along with the two foreign secretaries and the Indian prime minister's principal secretary.

The lunch was marked by an atmosphere bordering on bonhomie, which in fact is characteristic of almost all Indo-Pakistan meetings held outside the bondage of officialdom. Travel between the two countries was being talked about when Nawaz Sharif recalled that he had gone to India in 1982 to witness the Asian Games, driving in his own car to Delhi and thereafter even on to Agra. At the time, he reminisced, he was a minister in the Punjab government. One of my officers—Vivek Katju, if I am not wrong—murmured that bus service could be initiated between Lahore and Delhi. "Those were the days," Nawaz Sharif reminisced somewhat sentimentally to Prime Minister Vajpayee. "We can rediscover those days," I then interjected, and followed up with an impromptu suggestion: "Why don't you start a daily bus service at least between Delhi and Lahore?" Nawaz Sharif immediately fancied the idea, and greatly. He is, after all, from West Punjab, and it is difficult to find a people more parochial in this entire subcontinent than the Punjabi. (Some will assert that the Bengalis beat all others at this attribute, always and every time. The Punjabi do sometimes get beaten out by the Bengalis, but not by anyone else.) I must confess that I put in a word about my parochial concerns, too, something I had been doing on every such occasion, decade after decade. For example, I suggested that Nawaz Sharif reopen the road and rail link between Munabao (on the Indian side) and Khokhrapar (on the Pakistan side), which had been severed in 1965. My plea was met with a kind of polite and somewhat tolerant assent, neither serious nor particularly enthusiastic. My suggestion about the bus to Lahore seemed to have caught on, however, and soon enough the conversation returned to that theme. Prime Minister Vajpayee welcomed the idea, not with Punjabi-style acclaim but with a more reasoned assent: "How should we go about it?" he asked. I responded that upon our return to our respective capitals, the two foreign ministries could pick up the baton. Thus was born the Lahore bus project.

There was a brief Pakistani press statement following the meeting. It described the conversation as "very friendly and cordial." Immediately afterward, Nawaz Sharif went to the UN General Assembly to meet Secretary-General Kofi Annan and urged him to take "appropriate initiatives" to implement the Security Council resolutions on Kashmir. This disconnect is almost an established procedure for Pakistani interventions at the United Nations, a pattern of behavior that India, too, has followed over the years, though less often now.

I knew Nawaz Sharif from before. Curiously, the first time I met him was at a conference in Washington on September 24, 1997. I was in the

Opposition then, and so was Nawaz Sharif; Benazir Bhutto was the prime minister of Pakistan at the time. We were sitting on adjacent chairs and were both to speak on "the merits of democracy and freedom" or some such uplifting theme; we were being hosted by the National Endowment for Democracy, in honor of the fiftieth anniversary of freedom and democracy in India. We chatted amicably enough in the post-lunch session as the meeting droned on and on—not the most invigorating setting for mental activity, whether one is in Washington, New Delhi, or Islamabad. It was then Nawaz Sharif's turn to intervene. He went up to the podium, pulled out a prepared text, and, as they say colloquially, "let India and Jaswant have it." I was more amused than either alarmed or astonished, but I was, I must admit, at least a bit of all three. Upon returning to his chair, Nawaz Sharif, transformed into politeness itself, said, "Sorry, Jaswantji, I had to say all those things. You know I have to send a message back home." I responded, "Do not give it another thought, Nawaz Sharif, sahib. These are the merits and perils of democracy, but you need not worry, because the theme on which I speak will not even use small arms fire against Pakistan." I don't think he caught on to my use of this somewhat military metaphor. But much later—in different circumstances and when both of us were in positions of some responsibility in government—I was struck again by how he demonstrated the very same tendency: peace and accord and goodwill during meetings; invective and abuse, even conflict and war, afterward. That year in Washington, when I first met him, I did not know how we would meet again. Thus I was astonished when we did, and in such very different circumstances. Who could have foretold at the time that so many events were to follow—events of such great significance to both our countries, and certainly for the personal and political fortunes of Miyan Nawaz Sharif.

The 11 O'clock Bus to Lahore

It did take some months, as it always does in arranging high-profile diplomatic visits, to get the Lahore bus scheme fully on the road—initially because of the bureaucratic systems that the British had left us, and thereafter because of our genius for complicating even the most elementary business. During Foreign Secretary Krishnan Raghunath's visit to Islamabad in October 1998, Nawaz Sharif inquired about the progress of the project in the presence of Foreign Minister Sartaj Aziz and Foreign Secretary Shamshad Ahmed. Raghunath demurred, because in the follow-up, it had been the Pakistan officials who were not kindly disposed toward the idea. Sartaj Aziz mentioned that the matter was being looked into. Nawaz Sharif then expressed regret that decisions between two prime ministers were not being acted upon. Thereafter there was willingness all around. What could have been a simple executive decision followed by an order instead became a complicated, multi-ministry job.

Finally, in February 1999, the bus to Lahore was ready to leave. Prime Minister Vajpayee was to inaugurate the first run. He was advised, for reasons of distance and time, to fly to Amritsar and take the bus to Wagah from there, and that is what we did on February 20, 1999. The departure from Delhi was not without its share of drama, as dramatic as the arrival in Lahore subsequently became. In Delhi, everything had been done, all the formalities were over, we were all aboard, and the special aircraft flying the prime minister and his party to Lahore was already revving its engines, when suddenly they stopped, and silence descended. I saw the exit door of the aircraft being reopened. I was sitting in the cabin with the prime minister and could not make out why, so I asked the Air Force crew. They mumbled something that irritated me because of its lack of clarity. I then asked the prime minister's personal staff: "Have you left something behind?" The prime minister's faithful attendant, who had been with him for many years, replied sheepishly in Hindi: "Yes, I left his hearing aid behind!" There we stood, having ceremonially departed, already boarded and in runway readiness, but unable to leave until that vital piece of equipment arrived. The car that was carrying it was already speeding out of the prime minister's residence on Racecourse Road, all traffic in its way cleared by Delhi's harassed traffic policemen!

At Amritsar, the reception line was long, full of smiles and enthusiasm and back-slapping Punjabi informality. We went through the characteristic bhangra troupes one after another, and women dancers performed the gidda.[1] Prime Minister Vajpayee then boarded the bus. The mood was truly, irrepressibly infectious; the party accompanying the prime minister on the bus represented India in all its vivid richness and its geographical diversity, its beauty and its brains. With us, for instance, were Dev Anand, a veteran actor who had left West Punjab when he was barely at the doorstep of youth, and a greatly talented danseuse, Mallika Sarabhai. As the bus moved on, the mood continued to pick up. On both sides of

---

1. The bhangra is a lively folk dance that originated in Punjab. Originally performed at harvest festival celebrations, it has now become part of such diverse occasions as weddings and New Year celebrations. Women perform a different but no less exuberant dance called the gidda.

the road, all the way from Amritsar to the village of Attari, there was an almost unbroken chain of men and women, boys and girls, waving spontaneously and cheering at the tops of their voices. The bus and its symbolism had caught the imagination of the land. The journey to Wagah was scheduled to last forty minutes; it felt like just a fraction of that. At 4:10 PM Pakistan time, Prime Minister Vajpayee, accompanied by twenty-two representative Indian citizens, arrived at the border checkpost. As the gates were thrown open at Wagah, reporters gave their pens full rein: "Prime Ministers Atal Bihari Vajpayee and Nawaz Sharif created history today by opening the gates of friendship at the Wagah border and demolishing the walls of hatred that have symbolized India-Pakistan relations for the last 51 years." On the Pakistan side at the border crossing stood Nawaz Sharif and his brother Shahbaz, then chief minister of the Pakistani state of Punjab, Foreign Secretary Shamshad Ahmed, and others. Typical of a ceremonial arrival, there were gun salutes, a guard of honor presented arms, and national anthems were played. It all seemed so familiar, all so similar and yet so separate: these gates dividing Attari from Wagah appeared so unnecessary, at least to my eyes.

"This is a defining moment in South Asian history, and we will be able to rise to the challenge," the Indian prime minister said. "It is with a sense of elation that I find myself on Pakistani soil after a gap of twenty-one years." He paused, adding with some feeling, "I bring the good wishes and hopes of my fellow Indians who seek abiding peace and harmony with Pakistan. I am looking forward to a substantive program and talks with Prime Minister Sharif." In a statement later, Prime Minister Vajpayee said that India welcomed "sustained discussions on all outstanding issues, including on Jammu and Kashmir. . . . the solution of complex, outstanding issues can only be sought in an atmosphere free from prejudice and by adopting the path of balance, moderation and realism. . . . I am convinced there is nothing in our bilateral relations that can ever be resolved through violence." My diary entry of the day records:

> An Army helicopter—of the Special Forces no doubt, for the Colonel who flew us wore the red beret of the paratroopers—lifted us easily and transported us fluently to Lahore—setting us down directly upon the lawns of the Punjab Governor's House.
>
> Flying in from Wagah I looked down below at the fertile land, the clay pits and brick quarries, the buffalo ponds which even from that height looked (and felt) squelchily the same. What was different?

Out in the sky were kites—of myriad colors and various sizes.[2] At first I had thought they were birds, but I looked again, for they were not flitting past, instead they floated kind of lazily across our flight path. And expertly our pilot weaved us through them, with insouciance almost, for as we were coming in to land he asked his Havildar assistant over the intercom to open the door, lean out of the helicopter and check if there was enough clearance against the trees that bordered the lawns. And the Havildar did so.[3] I was sitting next to the door rather enjoying the sure touch of the Pilot when the governor of Punjab, sitting next to me in the helicopter, enquired if I was "a good flier." And when I had, somewhat non-committally shrugged my shoulders in response, he had added: "Well, I am philosophical; I leave everything in God's hands." "So we were doing, were we not?" I had responded inwardly.

From the Governor's House I came to shower and to change. I was not satisfied with the manner in which negotiations had been handled by the advance party. I wanted to sit and discuss with them. Our high commissioner then spoke of possible law and order problems, and though he was simply doing his duty I treated the caution almost as an irritant, wrongly though. Punctually at the appointed time, I was back at the Governor's House.

But here there was a delay, the High Commissioner had been correct after all, but nobody could or perhaps would explain why. And thus we waited and waited and still waited, until the PM sent for me in his suite. There had been some street demonstrations against our visit by the Jamaat-e-Islami.[4] Tension had also deliberately been built up by the Jamaat.

When finally we left, order on the streets had been restored but up to a point only, for shops remained forced shut by the Jamaat. Though it was already close to 9 PM and dark—knots of people kept standing and looking curiously as they would in any of the cities in South Asia. In the Fort, the arrangements unfortunately went completely awry, not because there was not adequate arrangement, there was an abundance of that and of military efficiency but there was simultaneously an abundance of guests and

---

2. The prime minister's visit coincided with the festival of Basant, which is still celebrated with great enthusiasm in Lahore and the surrounding areas. Kite-flying is a part of Basant in India as much as in Pakistan.

3. A Havildar is a noncommissioned officer, equivalent to the rank of sergeant.

4. The Jamaat-e-Islami ("Society of Islam") is a fundamentalist Pakistani political party.

visitors, too.[5] The system was straining as it tends to do in all of South Asia. The setting though, was incomparable; the idea of having dinner there, with ancient musicians playing some rather tearful tunes of old Hindi (circa 1950s or '60s) film songs was a bit kitsch but it was sheer, unrestrained Punjabi enthusiasm. Besides, far too many guests had been invited, or had just arrived, for there they were all spread out on the lawns of the Shalimar Gardens where Shah Jahan had lived in the early seventeenth century.[6] The food was Punjabi, the service ditto enthusiastic. But the setting and the mood (despite the short, put-up riot, or perhaps because of it), was bursting with enthusiasm. There could not have been any different beginning, or a better start. It was long after 1:45 AM that finally I caught sleep.

The next morning—February 21, 1999—things fell into place as they generally do. I was formally briefed by the officers about what I knew would happen, but only at the very last moment. The last of the bilateral agreements had been finalized. We concluded three documents: the Lahore Declaration, a joint statement of the two prime ministers, and a memorandum of understanding between the two foreign secretaries. The mood had by then become almost euphoric. In the afternoon, at the garden party-cum-public meeting, Prime Minister Vajpayee spoke without notes and with great feeling; his unmatched eloquence then flowed. He talked of peace and amity and accord. "We will not let war happen. We must not spill blood again," at which he was cheered wildly and repeatedly, and with great acclaim, for all present there truly shared a hope that we could finally put an end to all this continuing madness, and especially to induced hostility. It was a very good feeling, and I felt it personally, too, of having contributed something, hopefully something lasting, to the India-Pakistan relationship. The press conference thereafter was expectedly overcrowded— overflowing would be more appropriate: "I have never seen such a press conference in Pakistan," was Nawaz Sharif's simple observation. Our convoy of cars moved out of the Governor's House, a long, meandering snake on the road to the airport. The security was excessive, and all military. As we neared the airport, the cavalcade slowed, and suddenly there were loud reports. With me in the car was Sartaj Aziz, the foreign minister of Pakistan. Immediately, he tensed in reaction. The security escort, too, sat up; the air

5. The banquet was held in the Diwan-e-khas of the Lahore Fort.
6. The Shalimar Gardens, containing three terraces and hundreds of fountains, were built by the Mughal emperor Shah Jahan, who also built the Taj Mahal.

inside the car thickened with anxiety. "Koi nahi sahib, woh to gun salute hai"—"It was nothing, Sahib; that was a gun salute," someone said. The tension deflated, like air suddenly let out of a balloon.

There are a few things that I must add to my admittedly sketchy account of that momentous visit to Lahore, all taken directly from my diary notes of that period. Lahore and Amritsar are two cities that have a particularly poignant attitude toward Partition. They are separated at their outskirts by only some twenty kilometers, which is why people reminisce about the "old days" when they could and often would often travel between the two cities in a horse-drawn tonga. It is for this reason that Prime Minister Vajpayee's journey caught the imagination of so many, and so vividly. Since Jawaharlal Nehru's visit in 1960 to sign the Indus Waters Treaty, no other Indian prime minister had been to Lahore.[7] Rajiv Gandhi went to Pakistan in 1989, but that was to Islamabad. To Prime Minister Vajpayee's everlasting credit, he used great imagination in throwing open the gates at Attari and Wagah, even if the action was more symbolic than permanent. It was a rather more substantial gesture than merely lighting candles of nostalgia at Wagah. He conveyed a much more potent message of peace than any that had previously been attempted. At the banquet hosted at the Governor's House, Prime Minister Vajpayee said, "As we approach a new millennium, the future beckons us. It calls upon us, indeed demands of us, to think of the welfare of our children and their children and the many generations that are yet to come." It was this thought that lay at the root of his endeavors.

We knew that there was dissent against this move in Pakistan, as was also the case in India. We also had to take in our stride the obstacles and problems that we knew we would encounter on this adventurous journey of peace. Prime Minister Vajpayee demonstrated foresight and vision whenever he spoke of this journey. Prime Minister Nawaz Sharif displayed courage by agreeing to travel down this road. That is why such uproarious scenes of enthusiasm greeted Vajpayee in Lahore when, on the splendid lawns of the Punjab Governor's House, he said in Hindustani that the bus on which he had just journeyed was "not a bus made merely of steel and iron, it is a bus of sentiments and of emotions." That truly is the kernel of the India-Pakistan relationship; all aspects of it are loaded with sen-

---

7. At the time of Partition in August 1947, the boundary line was drawn across the Indus Basin. Two major irrigation headworks that fed the irrigation canals in Pakistan Punjab were then in Indian territory, which gave rise to a dispute over water rights. Under the terms of the Indus Waters Treaty, the Sutlej, Beas, and Ravi rivers were allocated to India, and the Indus, Jhelum, and Chenab rivers were largely allocated to Pakistan.

timent, because of which there can be both so much animosity and also so much fraternity, both great hope and sinking despair. As expressed so beautifully by the Punjabi poet Bulle Shah, "Our tears we shed together as we share laughter too."

On February 20, even as we were proceeding to Lahore, news reached us that terrorists had killed seven members of a wedding party in the village of Bajrala in the Rajouri district of Jammu and Kashmir. In another incident, four had been killed in the village of Khudbani, under the Kalakot police station of the same district. There was yet a third incident, in which nine people were killed at the village of Badiani in Udhampur district. The All-Party Hurriyat Conference, pursuing an incomprehensible path, had announced a demonstration against Prime Minister Vajpayee's visit to Lahore. The Jamaat-e-Islami had caused disturbances in Lahore and delayed the official banquet. While the intention was to defeat the purpose of the visit, it did not have that effect. The two prime ministers did sign the Lahore Declaration, the essence of which permitted the two countries to intensify their efforts to resolve all pending issues, including that of Jammu and Kashmir. The visit was greatly acclaimed, in India and elsewhere in the world.

Shortly afterward, in the final days of February 1999, Parliament convened for the Budget Session. In one of those totally inexplicable quirks of fate, in April the Vajpayee government was defeated in the Lok Sabha by a single vote. I felt particularly aggrieved, as the decisive vote had been cast by a member from the state of Jammu and Kashmir itself, who ought ordinarily to have been delighted at the initiative taken by Prime Minister Vajpayee, and also because his own party, the National Conference, was with the government. The other vote I felt disturbed about was perhaps technically correct but morally entirely wrong. It was cast by a member of the Congress Party from Orissa. He had been sworn in as chief minister of that state, but by law he was allowed to retain his seat in the Parliament for an additional six months. Thus technically he could still vote, but there was something morally reprehensible about the situation. And it was those two votes that cost us the motion. A well-liked senior MP had then remarked: "Atalji, you may have lost in Parliament by one vote, but you have won in India by many, because you have won the hearts of India: they are yours."

India now awaited mid-term elections, scheduled for the late summer of 1999. It is then that Kargil intervened.

Challenged in Kargil

The route from Srinagar to Ladakh winds along the foot of the Shankaracharya Hill, then skirts the northeastern bank of the Dal Lake, turning east into the Sindh Valley. It then travels on the left bank of the Sindh River toward Sonamarg ("meadow of gold"), from which some great walking trails radiate out to the surrounding ranges. From October to March, the area is a delight for those inclined to fish for trout or to hunt sloth bear or other game. From Sonamarg the road climbs steeply, upward to the Zojila Pass. I had crossed the Zojila Pass into Ladakh for the first time in 1959, in an Army 15 CWT light truck, as part of a small convoy that I was leading, crawling up on the steep incline. The road was not blacktopped then, being little more than a track that permitted only one-way traffic. I cannot remember what month of the year it was, but it had begun to get dark, and the light was fast fading. There was a sudden rumble on the hillside, and soon boulders came rolling down. One fell through the tarpaulin cover of the truck; it landed on the thigh of one of the junior commissioned officers accompanying me and smashed his thigh bone. I could do no more than administer first aid, after which our only option was to keep inching forward on the wet track, in the gathering dark with rain falling continuously; we could hardly have reversed all the way back to Sonamarg. By the time we reached Dras, it was pitch dark, and the rain had turned into sleet. The military authorities had a Vehicle Recovery Post there, and they were able to give the injured man some more rudimentary medical assistance, after which he was taken to a shelter in preparation for being evacuated after daylight. Even in the dark, as I headed for Kargil, I could see the towering peaks on my left, with the track snaking its way through. I had no idea then that this region would one day become a battleground that would test me in an altogether different fashion.

Years passed, and I resigned my commission. By March 1999, Pokhran, Washington, Manila, and Lahore were already behind me. Very soon after my return from Lahore, shelling and infiltration across the Line of Control (LOC) had started; the usual and "normal" had recommenced. The firing of shells across the LOC from Pakistan-occupied Kashmir was a routine activity. That year, the shelling began earlier and in a more aggressive manner. I was struck by this, but not so markedly as to ask the Defence Ministry about it. As the weeks went by, the intensity of the shelling continued to increase. Finally, I was troubled enough to ask the vice-chief of the Army staff, "What on earth is happening?" I did get an answer, but it did not satisfy me; the reasoning was too standard, too neat: "This shelling is the usual cover for pushing in infiltrators, Sir." I was not at ease with that reply, but I let the matter drop. After all, he was the professional, and he was on his ground. In May, the snows began to melt. Spring came early, knocking on the doors of the beautiful valley of Kashmir. Terrorist activity had begun again, since infiltration from across the LOC would now be easier.

The Early Doubts

In the beginning of May, in what is known loosely as the "Siachen sector"—where the highest Indian post, and probably the highest in the world, is at 22,000 feet—a shepherd brought news of some movement of unidentified people in the area of Batalik, a tiny village on the LOC. A patrol sent out on May 4 could not reach the suspect area because of heavy snow. Another patrol was sent a day later. The men were walking into a trap; the adversary already knew that they had been spotted. Inevitably, this patrol was ambushed, resulting in four fatal and five nonfatal casualties. The first shots in the Fifth Battle of Ladakh, for the Kargil sector, had been fired.[8]

On May 7, 1999, the Infantry Brigade Group with responsibility for this sector communicated relevant information to HQ. On May 8, the Pakistan Army chief, Pervez Musharraf (who incidentally is still Army chief today), made an unannounced visit to his forward areas opposite Kargil. A day later, an ammunition dump was blown up in Kargil by enemy artillery shelling, destroying about 5,000 metric tons of ammunition. Though I had no formal intimation of any serious situation developing, I had become concerned and made individual inquiries. I recommended that we discuss the situation in this sector in the Cabinet Committee on Security. Two days later, the 70th Infantry Brigade of the Indian Army launched Operation Vijay in the Batalik sector.

I have given some detail of these first few days so as to briefly recount and then attempt to recapture the atmosphere of those opening dates. It was not anxiety that I was feeling so much as uncertainty and an exasperating absence of clarity, which I often expressed by asking, "What on earth is happening?" What was Pakistan attempting to do by focusing such aggression in the Kargil sector, particularly so soon after the Lahore bus journey? I could not fathom why the hopes that had been generated by Lahore now had to be abandoned. Why should the promise of peace be choked so soon?

---

8. India has had to battle thrice with Pakistan in this region (1948, 1965, and 1971), and once with China (1962).

The next few days saw some rather premature and localized actions by commanders in the area. It was clear, however, that something unusual was afoot. But the assessment remained focused on infiltration, and that continued to be the judgment of the military until about the middle of May. I assumed that some action would be directed against our lines of communications in the region, calculating that such aggressive measures would raise the morale of the infiltrators, and they did appear to be unusually better trained this time. Some early intercepts then began to indicate the involvement of the Pakistan Army. It was on May 18 that the prime minister was formally briefed by the director general of military operations (DGMO) about the situation in Kargil.[9]

I did then inquire about the nature of this intrusion, in response to which I was informed by the vice-chief that the action was being carried out by irregulars and terrorists. To my further query as to how long it would take to clear the area, I was given an assessment of "about two to three weeks or so." There was, however, a clear contradiction between the assertions of "early intercepts" involving the Pakistan Army and then simultaneously "irregulars and terrorists"; all this I just could not reconcile. During this period, I was scheduled to make a number of visits, their dates having been decided earlier. These were to take me to Uzbekistan, Turkmenistan, Russia, and thereafter to France. There was some discussion as to whether I should be undertaking such travels, considering that Kargil was so obviously troubled. It was decided that to cancel these visits would send an altogether unintended message, one of anxiety, and therefore I must continue with the schedule.

Up until this stage, there had been no political assent to the use of the Air Force. It was my view that involving the Air Force at this point was not good policy. My reservations were born of two or three principal considerations. Should the adversary be determined to escalate the conflict, as all his early actions demonstrated, then we ought to be prepared for air casualties. The difficulty with air casualties, as against casualties on land, is principally one of imagery. The sheer optical value of the Air Force is significantly greater, particularly in a limited and contained conflict. That is why the loss of a single aircraft catches the public eye so much more quickly than the loss of even a full platoon of infantry. There was another

---

9. At the meeting of the South Asian Association for Regional Cooperation (SAARC) Ministerial Council held on March 18–19 in Sri Lanka, I met with my Pakistani counterpart, Sartaj Aziz, to issue a Joint Statement. To my knowledge, it is the only document that sets forth an agreed interpretation of an Indo-Pak declaration. Many officers who were involved in the process were asking the same question at the time: "What is Pakistan up to?"

aspect that concerned me greatly: undertaking these air missions within the narrow, tight confines of the LOC would amount to sending the Air Force on a virtual suicide mission. And there was no way that the political leadership would permit cross-LOC operations. Thus there were but two routes of operation for the Air Force, and both were extremely narrow funnels. Our air missions could fly in this narrow air corridor, either east to west or the reverse. The fact that the LOC was not a visibly marked line on the ground further compounded difficulties. Pilots in high-speed aircraft, even at low altitude, or even in helicopters chugging along peaks, would have difficulty determining exactly where the LOC was. A minuscule mistake of a few seconds could convert into several nautical miles of flying. Some years later, it was precisely such a mistake that cost the Indian Air Force one of its most promising officers.[10]

The Heat Is On

By now it was becoming increasingly clear, day by day, what the intentions of the infiltrating troops were. I shared my own assessment with my colleagues in the Cabinet Committee on Security, the defense minister, and the Army chief. The strength, the equipment, and the nature of the operations made it obvious that this was not a ramshackle gang of infiltrators being pushed across the LOC. These were regular troops of the Pakistan Army. Clearly the intention behind all this was to choke the lines of communication that linked Srinagar, Dras, and Kargil with the Siachen sector.

It was patent that any force that commanded the heights of Kargil would have total observational control of all activity over the highway that provided for the essential needs of Indian troops in virtually the entirety of Ladakh. This route carried nearly 70 percent of the needed supplies during the locked-in winter months, too. Supplies are normally stocked here before the arrival of autumn, and in any case well before the snows choke traffic. Thereafter, until the route reopens the following spring, it becomes extremely difficult to travel or to bring anything in by road. Air transport is then the only alternative.

It was in this frame of mind that I left on my diplomatic missions to Central Asia, Russia, and France. By May 23 I was in Paris. On that day George Fernandes, India's defense minister at the time, called me from

---

10. Air Marshal V. K. (Jimmy) Bhatia, the former commander-in-chief of the Western Air Command of the Indian Air Force, was moved to Air Headquarters as inspector general for flight safety after an incident involving an unintended violation of air space in February 2002. While flying an AN-32 transport aircraft, he inadvertently strayed across the Line of Control in the Kargil region of Jammu and Kashmir and was fired upon by the Pakistanis. Air Marshal Bhatia was known to be among the best in the force.

Delhi to inform me that the Kargil intrusion was continuing to escalate. Further, on account of the Army's repeated demands, the Air Force was finally being given the go-ahead to carry out air missions. Those commenced a day later. It was considerate of my colleague to still consult me. With all these developments, I thought I must return home immediately. By then we were already into the third week of May; the skirmishes were intensifying, and it was also clear that even as the Lahore Declaration was being executed between prime ministers Vajpayee and Nawaz Sharif, preparations for the intrusions by Pakistani troops into Kargil must already have been in full swing. Prime Minister Vajpayee spoke to Nawaz Sharif at this juncture and informed him clearly that India was aware that the intrusion into Kargil involved the use of regular troops from the Pakistan Army, that this was totally unacceptable, and that he would compel India to take all necessary steps.

By now, international concern was beginning to mount, including on the part of the secretary-general of the United Nations. The United States, too, had begun to issue statements about the situation. In view of some rather erroneous and mistaken announcements, whether to the press or elsewhere, the Ministry of External Affairs released a detailed statement on the situation. The ministry also conducted its first press briefing on Kargil. Just prior to some informal deliberations by the Security Council, India's permanent representative to the UN conducted several briefings. Our embassies were also engaged, particularly in Washington, and our ambassador there undertook extensive briefings on Capitol Hill and to the media.

On May 27, the first of the aerial losses took place; a MiG-27 on a routine mission developed engine trouble in the Kargil sector and crashed. The accompanying MiG-21 was then shot down by a ground-to-air missile fired from across the LOC by Pakistani troops. To prevent the situation from getting out of hand, Pakistan began to call for a "meaningful international engagement." The pilot of the MiG-21 that had crashed, Squadron Leader Ajay Ahuja, was taken prisoner. It was only much later that I came to learn that he was tortured and put to death while still in captivity. I was back in India on May 27. The very next day, a Mi-17 helicopter came under missile fire in another sector, and was downed. The visual impact of the air casualties now took over, and both national and international concerns grew. Prime Minister Nawaz Sharif called Prime Minister Vajpayee again, repeating what he had said earlier, and suggesting that he send Foreign Minister Sartaj Aziz to Delhi for talks "to defuse the current situation and to pave

the way for a peaceful settlement of the J&K issue." This was a disingenuous formulation, and to me personally it was a matter of some considerable
resentment. The patronizing attitude of the message, its very language,
the offer to discuss "peaceful settlement" even while fully involved in an
armed violation of the LOC—this was extraordinary. Nevertheless, Sharif
repeated his readiness—or perhaps anxiety?—to send his foreign minister
the next day, denying that the Pakistan Army was involved in "any fashion." Prime Minister Vajpayee counseled his Pakistani counterpart "not to
abandon facts altogether." It was with some disquiet and disappointment
that he informed Sharif that the body of a Pakistani soldier had been recovered with Army documentation and identity papers on him.

Madeleine Albright then called me on May 30 to express her "regret"
about developments in Kargil and to indicate that she had spoken to
Nawaz Sharif. She told me that the United States knew "full well" how
the chain of events had started. She did hint at the possibility of a ceasefire, following which a withdrawal of troops would be possible. India had
gone down that road several times earlier and had learned that a ceasefire
under such conditions was always converted into a ploy for remaining in
occupation of the land being encroached upon, leading to endless, fruit-
less, and largely purposeless dialogue. I offered to Albright that were the
Pakistan government to restore the *status quo ante,* then we certainly would
examine the feasibility of a ceasefire. She expressed some apprehension that
"things could get out of control." It was important, she said, to initiate a
dialogue. In response, I said that we were never averse to a dialogue, and
never would be in future, either, but we found it difficult to agree to such
a step so long as an aggression was still being committed against India and
the aggressor was still on Indian land.

Recognizing the importance of the media—which were by now almost
a player in the contest—and how important it was for India to get its
viewpoint across to the country and to the international community in an
effective, timely, and correct manner, I decided that all subsequent briefings to the press would be conducted jointly by the ministries of Defence
and External Affairs. This was India's first "media war." It was essential
that even as the conflict continued, we gained proficiency in the use of this
additional tool, employing it for national purpose. For the entire duration
thereafter of this conflict, whenever I was in Delhi, the briefing team from
those two ministries, Defence and External Affairs, would invariably come
to me first, and we would then decide what was to be projected and how,
and also the phraseology to be used.

By then, employment of the Air Force had stabilized. The Indian Air Force had acquired the needed additional ability to operate under such tight and difficult conditions. To have to fly at high speed in an extremely narrow air corridor, in which the enemy knew our aircraft would be operating and therefore could very easily determine its own retaliatory tactics—these were true suicide missions, and the Indian Air Force continued to conduct them with great determination and a remarkably innovative spirit. I do not believe that any other air force in the world had ever operated under such conditions.

The position of the United States was to clarify with time, its opinion firming up by the beginning of June. Yet it was a matter of considerable concern to me that there was as yet no distinction being made publicly between the historically inherited issue of Jammu and Kashmir, and this blatant armed aggression in the Kargil sector. Until the beginning of June, we heard expressions of concern from the United States, but no categorical and unambiguous acceptance, in private or in public, about who the aggressor was, what they saw as the status of the LOC, and what, therefore, were the essential obligations of the international community regarding the aggressor. It was only then that Assistant Secretary of State Karl F. "Rick" Inderfurth articulated clearly and categorically "that the Line of Control has to be respected, [and] the intruders will have to first leave what they have occupied."[11] This was perhaps the first ever articulation by the U.S. of an unambiguous position in regard to the LOC. Some years later, I came to learn that when the then Pakistani ambassador to Washington, Riaz Khokhar, had visited Inderfurth and suggested that the LOC itself was unclear, Inderfurth's first response was apparently to "pick-up the mosaics of the LOC, duly signed by Lt Gen Abdul Hamid Khan and by Lt Gen P.S. Bhagat, VC, respectively on Pakistan and India's part, on December 11, 1972, at Suchetgarh and thereafter to ask Khokar to point out the precise portion of the LOC where Pakistan felt it was not sufficiently clear."[12] Pakistan's strategy was clearly beginning to backfire. So too were the rather simplistic suggestions—in other circumstances, they might even have caused amusement—by Foreign Minister Sartaj Aziz to the effect that the infiltrators might be "fighters" from Afghanistan who had "crossed the LOC in support of the local mujahideen forces"!

---

11. From a classified diary maintained by the Ministry of External Affairs, entry on the Kargil conflict, dated June 2, 1999. Apparently, Riaz Khokhar, Pakistan's ambassador to the United States, had gone to see Inderfurth, and had told him that the LOC was unclear. Inderfurth's response was to pick up the full forty-three-page LOC agreement and offer it to Khokhar, asking exactly which part of it Khokhar felt was unclear. It was obvious that the stratagem of questioning the LOC was backfiring badly on Pakistan.

12. From a confidential U.S. report.

With such statements as the backdrop, plus Sartaj Aziz's iteration of what Khokar had said in Washington—that the LOC was "vague or unde-fined in some manner"—it became abundantly clear to me why Pakistan was repeatedly seeking a ceasefire, followed by talks to clarify that very LOC which they had violated! Until that was done, the Pakistani intruders would remain where they were, continuing to dominate, by observation and with intermittent fire, India's strategic lifeline into the interior of Ladakh. This is not a retrospective judgment. This is actually what I had assessed their aim to be within days of Pakistan's misadventure, and I had hence structured the responses of the Ministry of External Affairs accordingly.

When I was informed by the ministry that the Pakistan high commis-sioner in Delhi was proposing that his foreign minister visit Delhi on June 7, I found the date unfeasible, and offered that we would come up with an alternative. I have gone to considerable length in describing even minor incidents in the early stages of this untidy effort by Pakistan, which wanted to gain through subterfuge and deceit what it was impossible to do by other means, for it is necessary that there be clarity about the aggressor's intent. Pakistani suggestions to start talking were now always accompanied by another forced opening of their hand. Sartaj Aziz's arrival plans had to be postponed for one more reason: Prime Minister Vajpayee was to address the nation, and I had a visit scheduled to China. This visit had nothing to do with our knowledge that General Musharraf had left for a visit to China in the final week of May 1999. My own visit was a pure Sino-Indian initia-tive. It had long since been scheduled, it was to take place from June 14 to 16, and I could see no reason why I should put it off. The choice for me was clear: Aziz and I could meet either before I left for Beijing or after. To have postponed his visit to the middle of June would have been inadvisable, and that is why, and how, the date was fixed for June 12.

Heroism on the Heights

Events now began gathering pace. The planned redeployment of the Indian Army in the Kargil sector had been completed. All earlier and temporary tactical setbacks of the kind that are unavoidable in the early stages of any conflict were long over. I was, by then, very clear in my mind that it was only a matter of time before all Pakistani forces were either choked into submission because of an absence of water and supplies, or compelled to withdraw, driven off one peak after another in a process of slow and painful attrition. The first option was very clear and would require the Indian Army, along with the Air Force, to mount special efforts to seal off the supply routes to the Pakistani troops who already occupied some heights. The second was for the Indian Army to fight what, in retrospect, I consider to be the most outstanding demonstration of infantry assaults in mountain warfare anywhere, by any army, at any time. Merely to reach such heights—most of which were above 5,000 meters (17,500 feet), and where some of the cliff faces were nearly vertical—required not only determination and courage but also great mountaineering skill. To perform such unbelievable feats of climbing in battle conditions, against armed fire, while carrying full equipment plus weapons; and then to fight an entrenched enemy, sometimes hand to hand, and finally evict him from one height after another—all this our valiant infantry did, day after day, absorbing casualties, hanging on to gains, not yielding an inch, with no surprise, no benefit of force ratios—winning back one peak after another, with no other preponderant asset than sheer grit.

Long after this conflict was over, when students of military science from other countries visited the Kargil sector, they found it impossible to believe that our simple, unassuming Indian soldiers, not always equipped with the most advanced of personal weapons, had scaled these heights, mostly in the dark—so as to avoid direct, aimed fire—and had fought battle after battle, winning each of them and gaining back each of those heights. (By God! It makes me very proud to be of this fraternity.) There were many among the doubters. Henry Kissinger, for example, who had stopped in India on his way to China, just to call on me and perceptively inquire, "Will you be able to evict them from those heights?" I did not know how to answer. Had I affirmed my faith in the Indian soldier, my worldly wise and experienced visitor might well have scoffed at me inwardly. And I could not and would not say that our soldiers would fail, because I carried an internal conviction about them, an abiding faith; my instincts assured me that they would not fail—not fail me, not fail us, not fail India.

When, on June 13, the 2nd Battalion of the Rajputana Rifles regiment attacked and captured Tololing, I knew that it signaled the beginning of the end of the Pakistani intrusion, and that the tide had begun to turn. I estimated that it would take us no more than three weeks or so to clear out the Pakistani invasion. It was with this conviction that I prepared to leave for Beijing. I had no intention whatsoever of even raising the question of Kargil when I met my counterpart, Tang Jiaxuan. But before I went, I did have a formal visit from Foreign Minister Sartaj Aziz to take care of.

I had gone to the Delhi airport to receive him, not because protocol so demanded but out of courtesy, which in both of our lands is not dictated by the antiseptic methodologies of the Western world. But I carried within me very deep disappointments as I reached Palam Airport. I had little anger—no, I would not be totally honest if I said "I had little anger," for I had very deep anger. It was born principally of the violation of trust that this attack on Kargil represented—and before the ink on the Lahore Declaration had even dried! I did not know how to shrug off this sense of having been betrayed. "It is not just the Line of Control that has been violated, it is the territory of trust that has been transgressed," I said at the time. Additionally, on the eve of Aziz's visit, the Ministry of Defence informed me that as our troops moved forward, they were recovering more and more evidence of the involvement of Pakistan's regular troops, more and more equipment belonging to the Pakistan Army. But most disturbingly, Pakistan had handed over the bodies of six of our soldiers taken prisoner earlier and killed in captivity, in violation of all conventions and norms of civilized conduct. The bodies had been mutilated and disfigured, an outrage that I could scarcely countenance. It was extremely difficult for me to contain my emotions; I was appalled by the mutilation of my soldiers.

At a press conference on June 11, on the eve of Aziz's visit, I shared with the press the position of the government of India. The full text is reproduced below. In response to a reporter's question about the treatment meted out to Indian soldiers, I was unable to restrain myself: "I feel personally violated, as if my own body or a body of a near and dear relative of mine had been so desecrated. Anger is not my total reaction." Later, very much later, Prime Minister Vajpayee gently corrected me, simply by inquiring, "You lost your temper, did you?" I knew immediately that it was not a question that he was asking; he was nudging me, reprimanding a colleague in his own fashion.

STATEMENT AT PRESS BRIEFING IN DELHI, JUNE 11, 1999

Foreign Minister Sartaj Aziz will be visiting Delhi tomorrow. His visit is taking place in the context of Pakistan's armed intrusion and aggression in the Kargil sector of Ladakh, in Jammu and Kashmir.

I wish to share with you, Ladies and Gentlemen of the media, and through you, with all the citizens of our country, as also the international community, some, and I repeat that this is only some, of the incontrovertible evidence that we have obtained about many aspects of this armed intrusion and aggression in the Kargil sector. This establishes beyond any doubt the involvement and complicity of the Pakistani establishment in this misadventure. It raises serious doubts about the professed aim of "defusing tension" as averred by Foreign Minister Sartaj Aziz. The evidence will also establish that the management of this enterprise is in the hands of those who put it in place in the first instance. It raises doubts about the brief that Minister Aziz carries and at whose dictates he is actually working.

The making public of this evidence at this juncture, is to expose the Pakistani game plan to the entire world; to pre-empt any designs that Pakistan may be nurturing about obscuring the central issue of their involvement, complicity and continued support to an armed intrusion and aggression in which Pakistani regular troops are participating; to defeat in advance the Pakistani aim of dangerously attempting to reopen the sensitive and settled issue of the Line of Control; and above all, to re-emphasise and reassert the Indian position. There is only one aspect of this Pakistani misadventure that can be discussed: earliest restoration of the *status quo ante* and reaffirmation of the inviolability of the Line of Control. This is the very minimum imperative for the maintenance of peace and security in the region.

Ladies and Gentlemen, I will now ask that two recorded conversations between the Chief of Army Staff of the Pakistani Army and his Chief of the General Staff be played. The first conversation took place on 26 May, the second on 29 May. The transcripts of these conversations will be distributed simultaneously.

Transcripts of conversations between Lt. Gen. Mohammad Aziz, Chief of General Staff and Gen. Pervez Musharraf, Chief of Army Staff, Pakistan.

Aziz spoke from Pakistan to Musharraf, who was on a visit to China.
Pakistan: Lt. Gen. Mohd Aziz, Chief of General Staff
China: Gen. Pervez Musharraf, Chief of Army Staff
First recording—26 May

AZIZ: How is the visit going?
MUSHARRAF: Yes, very well, okay. And what else is the news on that side?

AZIZ: Ham-dul-ullah. There is no change on the ground situation. They have started rocketing and strafing. That has been upgraded a little. It has happened yesterday also and today. Today high altitude bombing has been done.

MUSHARRAF: On their side, in those positions?

AZIZ: In those positions, but in today's bombing about three bombs landed on our side of the Line of Control. No damage, Sir.

MUSHARRAF: Is it quite a lot?

AZIZ: Sir, about 12–13 bombs were dropped, from which three fell on our side, which does not appear to be a result of inaccuracy. In my interpretation, it is a sort of giving of a message that if need be, we can do it on the other side as well. It is quite [a] distance apart. Where the bombs have been dropped, they have tried to drop from a good position where they are in difficulty, from behind the LOC but they have fallen on our side of the LOC. So I have spoken to the foreign secretary and I have told him that he should make the appropriate noises about this in the press.

MUSHARRAF: They [Indians] should also be told.

AZIZ: That we have told, foreign secretary will also say and Rashid will also say. He will not, generally speaking, make any such mistake about those other bombs falling on the other side, our stand should be that all these bombs are falling on our side. We will not come into that situation. The guideline that they have given, we have stressed that we should say that this build-up and employment of air strike, which has been done under the garb of [. . .] us (?), actually they are targeting our position on the LOC and our logistic build-up, these possibly they are taking under the garb having intention for operation the craft (?) Line of Control, and this need to be taken note of and we would retaliate in kind [. . .] is what happened. So, the entire build-up we want to give this colour.[13]

MUSHARRAF: Absolutely okay. Yes, this is better. After that, has there been any talk with them? Any meetings, etc?

AZIZ: Yesterday, again, in the evening.

MUSHARRAF: Who all were there?

AZIZ: Actually, we insisted that a meeting should be held, because otherwise that friend of ours, the incumbent of my old chair, we

13. The use of [. . .] denotes garbled speech.

thought lest he give some interpretation of his own, we should do something ourselves by going there.

MUSHARRAF: Was he [a] little disturbed? I heard that there was some trouble in Sialkot.

AZIZ: Yes, there was one in Daska. On this issue there was trouble. Yes, he was [a] little disturbed about that but I told him that such small things keep happening and we can reply to such things in a better way.

MUSHARRAF: Absolutely.

AZIZ: There is no such thing to worry.

MUSHARRAF: So that briefing to Mian Saheb [Nawaz Sharif] that we did, was the forum the same as where we had done previously? There, at Jamshed's place?

AZIZ: No. In Mian Saheb's office.

MUSHARRAF: Oh I see. There. What was he saying?

AZIZ: From here we had gone—Choudhary Zafar Saheb, Mehmood, myself and Tauqir. Because before going, Tauqir had spoken with his counterpart. We carried that tape with us.

MUSHARRAF: So, what was he [Indian counterpart] saying?

AZIZ: That is very interesting. When you come, I will play it for you. Its focus was that these infiltrators, who are sitting here, they have your help and artillery support, without which they could not have come to J&K. This is not a very friendly act and it is against the spirit of the Lahore Declaration. Then Tauqir told him that if your boys tried to physically attack the Line of Control and go beyond it [. . .] and that the bombs were planted on the Turtok bridge and the dead body received in the process was returned with military honours and I said, I thought that there was good enough indication you would not enter into this type of misadventure, and all this build-up that you are doing—one or more brigade strength and 50–60 aircraft are being collected. These are excuses for undertaking some operations against the various spaces, so I had put him on the defensive. Then he said the same old story. He would put three points again and again that they [militants] should not be supported, and without your support they could not be there, they have sophisticated weapons and we will flush them out, we will not let them stay there. But this is not a friendly act.

MUSHARRAF: So, did they talk of coming out and meeting somewhere?

AZIZ: No, no, they did not.

MUSHARRAF: Was there some other talk of putting pressure on us?

AZIZ: No. He only said that they [militants] will be given suitable reception. This term he used. He said they will be flushed out, and every time Tauqir said that please tell us some detail, detail about how many have gone into your area, what is happening there. Then I will ask the concerned people and then we will get back to you. So whenever he asked these details, he would say, we will talk about this when we meet, then I will give details. This means, they are possibly looking forward to the next round of talks, in which the two sides could meet. This could be the next round of talks between the two PMs which they are expecting it [. . .]

MUSHARRAF: So, many times we had discussed, taken your [PM's?] blessings, and yesterday also I told him that the door of discussion, dialogue must be kept open and the rest, no change in ground situation.

AZIZ: So no one was in a particularly disturbed frame of mind.

MUSHARRAF: Even your seat man?

AZIZ: Yes, he was disturbed. Also, Malik Saheb was disturbed, as they had been even earlier. Those two's views were that the *status quo* and the present position of Gen Hassan, no change should be recommended in that. But he was also saying that any escalation after that should be regulated as there may be the danger of war. On this logic, we gave the suggestion that there was no such fear as the scruff [*tooti*] of their [militants'] neck is in our hands, whenever you want, we could regulate it. Ch. Zafar Saheb coped very well. He gave a very good presentation of our viewpoint. He said we had briefed the PM earlier and given an assessment. After this, we played the tape of Tauqir. Then he said that what we are seeing, that was our assessment, and those very stages of the military situation were being seen, which it would not be a problem for us to handle. Rest, it was for your guidance how to deal with the political and diplomatic aspects. We told him there is no reason of alarm and panic. Then he said that when I came to know seven days back, when corps commanders were told. The entire reason of the success of this operation was this total secrecy. Our experience was that our earlier efforts failed because of lack of secrecy. So the top priority is to accord confidentiality, to ensure our success. We should respect this and the advantage we have from this would give us a handle.

MUSHARRAF: Rest (*baki*), is Mian Saheb okay?

AZIZ: Okay. He was confident just like that, but for the other two. Shamshad as usual was supporting. Today, for the last two hours the BBC has been continuously reporting on the air strikes by India. Keep using this—let them keep dropping bombs. As far as internationalisation is concerned, this is the fastest this has happened. You may have seen in the press about UN Secretary General Kofi Annan's appeal that both countries should sit and talk.

Second recording—29 May

AZIZ: This is Pakistan. Give me room number 83315. Hello.

MUSHARRAF: Hello Aziz.

AZIZ: The situation on ground is okay, no change. This area but it is not brought down by attack. One of their Mi-17 arms was brought down. Further the position is, we had approached to our position, it was brought down. Rest is okay. Nothing else except, there is a development. Have you listened to yesterday's news regarding Mian Saheb speaking to his counterpart. He told him that the spirit of [the] Lahore Declaration and escalation has been done by your people. Specially wanted to speak to me thereafter. He told Indian PM that they should have waited instead of upping the ante by using Air Force and all other means. He [Nawaz Sharif] told him [Indian PM] that he suggested Sartaj Aziz could go to New Delhi to explore the possibility of defusing the tension.

MUSHARRAF: Okay.

AZIZ: Which is likely to take place, most probably tomorrow.

MUSHARRAF: Okay.

AZIZ: Our other friend [Lt. Gen. Ziauddin, DG ISI, or it could be the United States] might have also put pressure on. For that, today they will have a discussion at Foreign Office about 9.30

and Zafar Saheb [Lt. Gen. Saeeduz Zaman Zafar, GOC 11 Corps and acting Army chief] is supposed to attend.

MUSHARRAF: Okay.

AZIZ: Aziz Saheb [Sartaj Aziz] has discussed with me and my recommendation is that dialogue option is always open. But in their first meeting, they must give no understanding or no commitment on ground situation.

MUSHARRAF: Very correct. You or Mehmood [GOC X Corps, Rawalpindi] must have to go with Zafar. Because, they don't know about the ground situation.

AZIZ: This week, we are getting together at 8 o'clock because meeting will be at 9.30, so Zafar Saheb will deliberate it. We want to suggest to Zafar that they have to maintain that they will not be talking about [the] ground situation. All that you say, so far as the ground situation is concerned: subsequently, DGMOs can discuss with each other and work out the modus operandi.

MUSHARRAF: Idea on LOC.

AZIZ: Yes. Hint is that, given that the LOC has many areas where the interpretation of either side is not what the other side believes. So, comprehensive deliberation is required. So, that can be worked out by DGMOs.

MUSHARRAF: If they are assured that we are here from a long period. We have been sitting here for long. Like in the beginning, the matter is the same—no post was attacked and no post was captured. The situation is that we are along our defensive Line of Control. If it is not in his [Sartaj Aziz's] knowledge, then discuss it altogether. Emphasise that for years, we are here only.

MUSHARRAF: Yes, this point should be raised. We are sitting on the same LOC since a long period.

AZIZ: This is their weakness. They are not agreed on the demarcation under UN's verification, whereas we are agreed. We want to exploit it.

MUSHARRAF: This is in Simla Agreement that we cannot go for UN intervention.

AZIZ: Our neighbour does not accept their presence or United Military Observers Group in India and Pakistan UNMOGIP arrangement for survey for the area. So, we can start from the top, from 9842 [NJ 9842]. On this line, we can give them logic but in short, the recommendation for Sartaj Aziz Saheb is that he should make no commitment in the first meeting on [the] military situation. And he should not even accept cease-fire, because if there is ceasefire, then vehicles will be moving [on the Dras-Kargil highway]. In this regard, they have to use their own argument that whatever is interfering with you. That we don't know but there is no justification about tension on LOC. No justification. We want to give them this type of brief so that he does not get into any specifics.

MUSHARRAF: Alright.

AZIZ: In this connection, we want your approval. And what is your programme?

MUSHARRAF: I will come tomorrow. We are just leaving within an hour. We are going to Shenzhen. From there, by evening, we will be in Hong Kong. There will be a flight tomorrow from Hong Kong. So, we will be there at Lahore in the evening, via [a] Bangkok flight.

AZIZ: Sunday evening, you will be at Lahore. We will also indicate that, if there is more critical situation, then it [Sartaj Aziz's visit] should be deferred for another day or two. We can discuss on Monday and then do.

MUSHARRAF: Has this Mi-17 not fallen in our area?

AZIZ: No, Sir. This has fallen in their area. We have not claimed it. We have got it claimed through the mujahideen.

MUSHARRAF: Well done.

AZIZ: But top-wise side, crashing straight before our eyes.

MUSHARRAF: Very good. Now are they facing any greater difficulty in flying them? Are they scared or not? This also you should note. Are they coming any less nearer?

AZIZ: Yes. There is a lot of pressure on them. They were talking about greater air defence than they had anticipated. They can't afford to lose any more aircraft. There has been less intensity of air flying after that.

MUSHARRAF: Very good, first class. Is there any build up on the ground?

AZIZ: Just like that but the movement is pretty sluggish and slow. One or two are coming near no. 6. Till now only one call sign in which one has not reached the valley so far. Now the air people and the ground people will stay back and then the situation will be okay.

MUSHARRAF: See you in the evening.

Treatment of Lt {Saurabh} Kalia and Five Soldiers

The entire nation has been outraged by the savage treatment of our soldiers who were taken in custody, by Pakistan, in the ongoing action in the Kargil sector. The government shares the outrage of the nation totally. A post mortem was conducted on the six bodies which were handed over by Pakistan three days ago. The post mortem confirms that the soldiers were tortured and then shot at close quarters. We will demand of Pakistan that the perpetrators of this heinous crime be identified, caught and brought to justice. We had made the same demand in the case of Sqn Ldr [Ajay] Ahuja. Such conduct is not simply a breach of established norms or a violation of international agreements, it is a civilisational crime against all humanity; it is a reversion to barbaric medievalism.

Meeting Sartaj Aziz

Sartaj Aziz was flying in a small aircraft that did not have the standard Pakistan Air Force markings. I had reached the airport in advance; the high commissioner of Pakistan to India, Ashraf Jehangir Qazi, was also there. He got up to greet me cordially, but upon seeing my demeanor, he perhaps desisted. I felt bad that I did not have my feelings under control. Ashraf Qazi is an officer of distinction, ability, and learning and has served his country with great dedication. A very great pity, for I would have liked to know him better. Soon after Sartaj Aziz landed, the usual formalities and greetings followed. I informed him that we would meet very shortly at Hyderabad House, where he would have an opportunity to say whatever he wished to; thereafter a small lunch that I had organized would take place, and then, if he so wanted, either a joint press conference there or an opportunity for him to hold one in his own time and wherever he chose. He informed me that he would be returning the same day and concurred with the broad program that I proposed.

A day earlier, on June 11, I had released the text of the taped conversation between General Musharraf and General Aziz, his chief of general staff. The visiting foreign minister knew well enough the contents of the tapes; his assumed mien of unconcern seemed to me somewhat casual and uncaring. The situation was serious, and that is the only way it could be, and had to be, addressed. He had obviously not been in the know about what was happening, but that was his own or his government's responsibility. When we sat down before going in to lunch, I suggested that the visiting dignitary say what he had to. My phraseology then was also not what it should have been: "Yes, what do you have to say, then?" This was abrupt, and not warranted, but I really did not know how else to start. For him to respond by proposing that we have a ceasefire, that we reopen the whole question of the LOC, then decide upon a time frame, and so on and so forth, struck me as so totally irrelevant that I could scarcely hide my impatience. The talks were soon over, and we adjourned for lunch, after which the visiting foreign minister left for his high commission. He was scheduled to depart later that evening. I met the press and shared what had happened:

> Today I met H.E. the Foreign Minister of Pakistan, Janab Sartaj Aziz Saheb. Essentially I made only two points. Firstly, vacation of aggression in Kargil and secondly inhuman treatment of Indian soldiers in Pakistani custody. I emphasised that armed intrusion, amounting to deliberate aggression that has been committed by Pakistan, is not acceptable. Indeed their spokesman admitted that the Pakistani Army has crossed the LOC and is occupying positions on the Indian side. This point was not denied by Foreign Minister Sartaj Aziz. I also told him that tension has been created because of violation of the *status quo*. De-escalation requires the restoration of *status quo ante*. Line of Control which is intrinsic with Simla Agreement and which is clearly delineated has not been questioned for twenty-seven years. Questioning it now is a disingenuous attempt to find *ex-post-facto* justification for aggressive action. This is unacceptable. Sanctity of the LOC must be restored and respected. I also specifically demanded that those responsible for perpetrating barbaric action of torture and of killing of Indian soldiers when in captivity must be brought to justice. Being the initiator, India is committed to the process of dialogue. The purpose of the dialogue is vacation of aggression. We do not have the luxury to engage in talks about talks.

I left for Beijing at midnight on June 13. My diary records:

June 15: Diaoyutai State Guest House, Beijing

Delhi was hot when I left on the near midnight of June 13, and across the Bay of Bengal monsoon turbulence made the flight uncomfortable. I slept hardly a wink. Singapore was wet and much cooler where we changed flights. On 14th at about 1515 local time, I landed at Beijing. This ancient capital was surrounded in a strange midsummer mist. So many years back I had come here as a young MP. I did not then know, nor imagine that I would ever return as foreign minister of my country, someday.

Between Paris and here all my time, and energies, and thought has gone into combating the Pakistani aggression in Kargil. They have betrayed my trust; they have violated my soldiers . . . !

Therefore, when Sartaj, their foreign minister, sought a meeting and came to Delhi on June 12, it was not an opportunity to settle anything, it was an occasion really to let him know the depths of my feelings.

It is in that background that I came here yesterday.

By God's grace my talks yesterday with my hosts have been fruitful. Sino-Indian relations are back on the rails of normalcy.

I have a full day today. It is morning. Tomorrow I fly back to Delhi.

In Beijing, I had a four-hour-long session with Foreign Minister Tang Jiaxuan. When, however, the Chinese foreign minister brought up the question of Kargil, on his own, and said that the situation was part of the overall question of Jammu and Kashmir, adding that he had told Sartaj Aziz—who had made a rushed, unscheduled visit just a day prior to mine—that "Pakistan must resolve the problem through peaceful means and dialogue," I gently informed my distinguished counterpart that the present situation in Kargil was not related to the overall question of Jammu and Kashmir!

The Tide Turns

The military situation in Kargil began to deteriorate rapidly for Pakistan. One height fell after another; it was as if the entire invading force had been seized by the psychology of defeat and withdrawal. I was following this conflict on more than just a daily basis; by then I was engaged with it much more intimately. I knew that Pakistan simply did not have the needed resources of time, commitment, and overall balance of local and international forces favorable to it. Therefore, if it did not withdraw at the right time, its forces would suffer major losses. Just share with me for a moment what I wrote in my diary on June 20:

> 1 NAGA captures Pyramid and Thumbs-up while Pt. 5140 finally falls to 13 JAK RIF after a hand-to-hand combat.[14] The defeat of Pakistan's intruding forces is now inevitable. By now the United States has also taken a very fair stand, as it has never earlier done.

The Pakistani misadventure was doomed. Pakistani troops would have to withdraw, in consequence of an "agreed step back." If that was not done, they would still have to withdraw, but in that case in near-total disorder. The choice was entirely with the intruder. In any event, the conflict was now more than a month old; the Pakistani troops had been deployed on these heights without any turnover or relief for at least two months, if their logistical chain was any indication. For those two months they had gone without rest and were living in conditions of scarcity, with low rations, a limited supply of water, and prolonged exposure to high altitude, even if it was summer. The accumulated diplomatic pressure was also beginning to take its toll, particularly as a consequence of my visits to China and the United States. Brajesh Mishra, principal secretary to the prime minister, had also gone to Geneva to meet his American counterpart, Sandy Berger. The United States had certain worries about India crossing the LOC. For instance, Mishra had called Berger's attention to the point that a stage had come in Pakistan's continued misemployment of its relationship with the United States where the U.S. now had to temper it by sending a clear message to Pakistan: to publicly urge it to withdraw. Berger's reaction was cautious. He felt that for the sake of de-escalating the situation, as well as for restoring the spirit of the Lahore Declaration, Pakistan needed an exit clause. There was a need, too, he felt, to give Pakistan a chance to save face, so that it could withdraw its forces with some degree of credibility. For the present, clearly, the United States continued to want Nawaz Sharif's face to be saved somehow. But this tender consideration of a Pakistani invasion could go on forever and ever. Besides, as Inderfurth had rightly pointed out, there was but a fine line between giving voice publicly to disapproval and deliberately internationalizing the situation.

---

14. "1 Naga" is shorthand for 1st Battalion of the Naga Regiment. "Pyramid" and "Thumbs-up" are operational code names used to designate geographical features. "Pt. 5140" is shorthand for the height in meters as denoted on a topographical map. "JAK RIF" is short for 13th Battalion of the Jammu and Kashmir Rifles Regiment.

For once, America earnestly wanted to avoid this, and so, of course, did India. There was another angle: the United States did not wish to publicly embarrass Sharif, because the latter insisted that he had a "personal relationship with President Clinton," and therefore the Americans did not want him to feel "abandoned." The United States was also of the view that under the circumstances, Sharif remained the best option for it, as well as for Pakistan. Still?

Meanwhile, Ambassador Celeste came to meet me in the third week of June. He shared his perception of what the United States wanted: in substance, he said that an early resolution was vital, and that the sanctity of the LOC, as expressed by India, ought to be fully accepted. Celeste also informed me that the United States was working on a time frame for withdrawal, which would actually be a matter of "days, not weeks." From Washington, we got news that the State Department would be sending Deputy Assistant Secretary of State Gibson Lanpher and General Anthony Zinni. Zinni knew General Musharraf, and his military Area of Responsibility at the time was the U.S. Central Command, which included Pakistan. India was part of the U.S. Pacific Command, and thus was outside Zinni's jurisdiction. The ambassador wanted to know whether India would be ready to receive General Zinni if he flew in from Pakistan specifically to brief us. I advised against this. But I did agree that Lanpher could come to Delhi to apprise us of discussions in Islamabad. By then, the Americans had already assessed that India was militarily well placed. India had (tactically) achieved very rapid ground deployment and advance, and thus the "balance of power" was very much in our favor. The international community, too, by and large, saw no merit in Pakistan's continued intransigence. The International Monetary Fund route had also been activated. To India's request that the IMF send out a "strong message," Michael Camdessus, then the Fund's managing director, let it be known that "the signal had already gone out": "the IMF will look with a cold and searching eye on the fulfillment of the IMF conditionalities and full adherence to the integrity of the members, which is an integral part of the IMF arrangement."

By the end of June, the situation for Pakistan was desperate. General Zinni had by then left Islamabad, and Lanpher, who had come to brief Indian officials, said that on June 19, Nawaz Sharif had already sent a letter to Clinton about "meeting with the conditions that India had laid down." I assessed that the realization had finally begun to dawn in Pakistan that General Zinni could not go back to Washington with "no" as a response.

The beginning of July saw Indian advances very close, in some cases up to the LOC. Yet some pockets of Pakistani elements remained, and thus the State Department volunteered to share with us the information that it was now time to "ratchet up the pressure." Not only was the Indian Army rapidly regaining those heights of Kargil, but the pressure on Nawaz Sharif from the United States was also beginning to take its toll. He sought to visit Washington. It is not as if President Clinton had invited or advised him to do so; in fact, he had cautioned the prime minister of Pakistan to undertake such a visit only if he recognized "what great mistakes Pakistan had made and moved in for an immediate rectification."[15] Besides, Clinton was absolutely clear that there was simply no way that at the end of this uninvited visit to Washington—and on July 4, at that—the total output could be just "routine fudge."

On the battlefields of Kargil, in the meantime, continued action by Indian troops was beginning to achieve even more. The gallant action by the 18th Battalion of the Grenadiers Regiment in capturing Tiger Hill Top just prior to Nawaz Sharif's flight to Washington had already concluded in victory. The names of those peaks spoke for themselves, and of the valor of Indian troops. Spare but a few minutes to savor some of those successful recaptures: on June 20, Thumbs-up was captured; that perhaps was a signal for a rapid advance, because many such heights continued to fall. The hills known as Lone Hill and Saddle and Point 4700, Jubar, fell by July 4. The 18 Grenadiers had by then captured Tiger Hill, a location the media had made a totem of, as it were, in a gallant action led by Lt. Colonel Ramakrishnan Vishwanathan, who paid with his life. Symbolically, this was the final defeat for Pakistan. Thereafter, victories began to come to the Indian Army even more rapidly. On July 9, the DGMO of the Pakistan Army called his Indian counterpart on the hotline to inform him that Pakistan wanted to begin withdrawing. He therefore sought a meeting on July 11. Appropriately enough, Prime Minister Vajpayee addressed India's senior generals a day later, after which a meeting of the two DGMOs took place, as agreed upon, at the Attari post, on the Indian side of the international border. General N. C. Vij, the Indian DGMO, outlined to his counterpart the procedure that was expected of Pakistan. The withdrawal was expected to be completed in less than a week.

---

15. Strobe Talbott, *Engaging India: Diplomacy, Democracy and the Bomb* (Washington, D.C.: Brookings Institution Press, 2004), p. 160; Bruce Riedel, "American Diplomacy and the 1999 Kargil Summit at Blair House" (Policy Paper Series, Center for the Advanced Study of India, University of Pennsylvania, 2002), p. 7.

A week earlier, a joint statement had been issued by President Clinton and Prime Minister Nawaz Sharif. President Clinton had continuously kept Prime Minister Vajpayee briefed, at one stage even inviting him to join the other two in Washington. That invitation was naturally declined. For Pakistan, even the end game was at an end; the aggression was being vacated. What I had spelled out to Foreign Minister Sartaj Aziz when he came to Delhi in June 1999 was categorical:

1. Immediate vacation of the aggression
2. Reaffirmation of the validity of the Line of Control
3. Abandoning cross-border terrorism
4. Dismantling the infrastructure of terrorism in Pakistan-occupied Kashmir
5. Reaffirmation of the Shimla Agreement and the Lahore Declaration

India had achieved the substance of all that it had sought, both militarily and diplomatically. Not one inch of Indian territory was "negotiated away"—such a contrast to all previous engagements: 1948, 1962, 1965, and 1971. What irked, as bothersome continuities, were cross-border terrorism and the supporting infrastructure for it inside Pakistan. India's fight against this menace continues.

Diplomacy's War Dividend

It was not our intention to humiliate Pakistan in any way. It had, ill-advisedly, undertaken this extremely rash, "throw of a dice" adventure. Unfortunately for the Pakistanis, the dice did not roll at all well. Initially, Pakistan did achieve tactical surprise, but that too was the case for only a limited period. Indian intelligence had been unable to pick up any signals, and Pakistan had maintained appropriate secrecy. It had calculated the tactical advantages but, characteristically enough, had failed to take into account the larger, strategic aspects. Clearly, what it wanted was to sit on the heights of Kargil; to somehow hustle India into a ceasefire, which implicitly would be an acceptance of the intrusion; and to thereafter negotiate the LOC all over again. "What a boost that would be to the terrorists," Pakistan must have thought. In our assessment, never at any stage was there a question of a full-scale war. This even though we had information regarding some deflective activity in the Tilla ranges near Jhelum, indicating that Pakistan might be operationalizing its nuclear missiles. We treated this move as merely a desperate gambit. A nuclear angle to this conflict simply did not exist. This aspect, though, subsequently featured in the Clinton-Sharif meeting in Washington. It was denied by Pakistan, then authoritatively confirmed by the United States; Bruce Riedel of the National Security Council shared with the international community that Pakistan had indeed resorted to nuclear blackmail.[16]

The greatest challenge to Prime Minister Vajpayee during this nearly sixty-day trial was surely his continued conviction not to expand the field of combat beyond the LOC, whatever the provocation. This obviously cost India dearly; many gallant officers and soldiers had to lay down their lives because of this enormous restraint that India had placed upon itself. It cost us time, too. Perhaps this was also part of Pakistan's miscalculation that we would once again be hustled into expanding the scope of the conflict. Such an escalation, while tactically advantageous, would have been a strategic error of incalculable dimensions, principally because of the nuclear status of both India and Pakistan, which for the world was the foremost worry. We had assessed this carefully and were clear that there was to be no internationalizing of the issue; we wanted no repeats of Tashkent. We therefore resorted to diplomatic maneuvers to ensure that the matter did not even go before the Security Council. For the first time, a subcontinental conflict elicited from the United States a clear pronouncement of Pakistani wrongdoing. This had not been seen in 1948, in 1965, or in 1971. This step, along with recognition by the United States and other nations of the menace of cross-border terrorism, was another significant strategic gain.

It is not part of my preoccupations to dwell on whether Nawaz Sharif knew of this misadventure. To those of us who accompanied Prime Minister Vajpayee to Lahore, this was a great betrayal. Pakistan could—in its reckoning, I suppose with some justification—seek to explain all this away as revenge for 1971, or for Siachen, or for any Indian action earlier, say in the Neelam Valley, but this kind of discussion could go on forever if pursued in terms of retaliation and revenge for every real or perceived wrong. What then remains in the category of "Lessons of Kargil," as distinct from the "Memories of Kargil," is that Pakistan needs to recognize that continued conflict, confrontation, and bloodshed will not gain it any lasting advantage. There is also no future in promoting the Frankenstein of "state-sponsored terrorism," then exporting it across the border or the LOC. Jammu and Kashmir is inhabited by human beings. That is the most important fact, yet it is often overlooked. Today, after the earthquake of 2005, they assert themselves and demand that in the face of this great tragedy inflicted

---

16. Riedel, "American Diplomacy and the 1999 Kargil Summit," pp. 3–4.

on Pakistan-occupied Kashmir, the LOC be made nonexistent. I found it humbling that what has been prevented by human obduracy was on the verge of being achieved by the hand of God and human suffering. There are several important lessons here, provided that we are able to grasp their essence.

I have engaged often enough in this macabre casualty count of the Kargil misadventure. The most telling casualty, though, was, yet again, truth in public life and the practice of democracy in Pakistan. A hapless Nawaz Sharif was summarily removed and now spends his days in exile, in bitter loneliness, in Saudi Arabia and the UK. The brief shelf life of power has once again been clearly demonstrated. The greatest irony was that General Musharraf ended up gaining the most from the massive misadventure of Kargil. India fought this aggression under a democratic government; in purely parliamentary terms, it was simply a caretaker government during that entire period of conflict, awaiting an election that had been called. We in government were so tightly confined by the code of conduct that had been into operation since the elections were announced that even necessary and appropriate broadcasts about the successes of our troops had to be tempered by that overriding code. Prime Minister Vajpayee was not fighting what the British call a "khaki election"—one that is overshadowed by wartime sentiment. The election that year was as vivid and varied as Indian elections always are. On October 13, 1999, in the forecourt of Rashtrapati Bhawan, Vajpayee was sworn in as prime minister of India for the third time.[17] I have a photograph recording that moment.

I also have a photograph dated October 12, 1999. It shows soldiers of the Pakistan Army clambering over the iron gates of the residence of the prime minister in Islamabad. A military coup had taken place there, and Nawaz Sharif was to be arrested and put in jail by the very soldiers whose allegiance he had earlier claimed.

An Afterword as the Reverse of a Foreword

On January 4, 2000, Strobe Talbott wrote me, saying, "During Kargil, India held fast to the moral high ground throughout the crisis, in the face of enormous provocation, and resisted the temptation to take retaliatory steps which would at best have cost India its unprecedented international support." That was not all. During the Asian Regional Forum meeting in

---

17. Rashtrapati Bhawan is the official residence of the president of India, located in New Delhi. Until 1950 it was known as "Viceroy's House" and served as the residence of the governor-general of India. "Rashtrapati" is Hindi for "president."

Bangkok on July 27, 2000, I met Madeleine Albright again. In contrast to 1998, she greeted me with great warmth, and I got the appropriate hug and kiss on my cheeks. She was graceful and complimentary: "Jaswant, it was a masterly handling of the Kargil crisis. You did not put a foot wrong." But Kargil was followed by Kandahar.

Flight 814 to Kandahar

On December 24, 1999, an Indian Airlines airbus was hijacked by terrorists in Indian airspace and eventually was diverted to Kandahar, Afghanistan. Before writing about this event, I reflected long and hard on how best to do it. How could I convey the enormity of the challenge that we faced at the time, as a nation and not simply as a government? Wounded as perhaps never before, I went through a searing experience. But how did my countrymen and -women confront this challenge? As a great tragedy, or was the overriding reaction in the political community one of *schadenfreude*? I still do not have the answer. How could I share this experience clinically, dispassionately, perhaps even unfeelingly, and without permitting any subjective clutter? I went back to my diary notes of the period. One of them, dated December 31, 1999, I jotted down during a flight to Kandahar. I have not corrected the syntax, the mistakes, errors, grammar, punctuation, anything. I have left out, I believe, a prayer or an invocation, but that, being private, is of no relevance to others. This is perhaps the best I can do, for the account has at least the vividness of the immediate, which in recollection is impossible to recapture. It sums up quite aptly the substance of the challenge that was thrown up to all of us. How did we measure up? We need to ask that question of ourselves, both individually and collectively.

December 31, 1999: On board a special flight to Kandahar

It is simply impossible to not jot down impressions on board this special flight. I do not really know what to term my mission— a rescue mission; an appeasement exercise; a flight to compromise or a flight to the future?

I do not know if this coincidence of it being the last day of Dec of 1999, indeed of this century, and, as has become a cliché phrase, of the 2nd millennium adds irony to my journey or rings down the curtain on this evil in our lives, ushering in a new, more benign and beautiful beginning starting from tomorrow, the first of January 2000?

But such is my prayer and my hope, too. As for this journey itself more as we proceed but it certainly could not be any more dramatic and momentous; indeed unique as this is.

On board with me are three TADA detenues, along, of course, with other staff—engineering, security, aircraft maintenance for that hijacked airplane, plus spare crew, doctors for emergency and so on.[18]

And by all that hangs this tale.

That day—Christmas Eve—the 24th of Dec, at around 5:20 PM I was informed that an IA flight had been hijacked. There have been hijacks earlier but this instantly had entirely a different "feel," even the announcement of it sounded more sinister. It somehow, at least to me, felt graver, of much deeper import.

How, therefore, the plane traveled the Indian skies and how Lahore denied permission the first time, the landing at Amritsar, the sudden take off after about three-quarters of an hour, the CCS [Cabinet Committee on Security] meeting called urgently, denial of permission—Lahore, a second time, a forced landing by the pilot on a darkened runway; my urgent calls to [Pakistani foreign minister Abdul] Sattar, the rushed take off from Lahore; the tension of landing permission being denied at Dubai, finally granted—the landing—parleys, some 27 or 29 women and children finally offloaded, the plane leaves again and Kandahar is the destination. By then it had become Saturday 25th, Christmas day and on this Christmas day at around 9:30 AM, Afghanistan time, this airplane designated officially as IC-814, finally landed and parked, with 5 hijackers and a passenger manifest (including crew) of around 161 on board. [This count, it later transpired, was wrong.]

Then started a most demanding and emotionally a most draining period of my life.

On the 24th itself was born a daughter to Manvendra and Chitra. She was born around 3:18 PM, the hijack occurred just about an hour or so later.

---

18. TDA is short for the Terrorist and Disruptive Activities (Prevention) Act. The three détenues were Maulana Masood Azhar, a religious evangelist of the Deobandi school who received training in Afghanistan before arriving in India in 1994 and is currently said to be operating from Muzaffarabad, Pakistan; Mushtaq Ahmed Zargar, a Kashmiri and Indian national responsible for more than forty murders who headed the Al-Umar Mujahideen and was a key figure in the terrorist ascendancy in downtown Srinagar; and Ahmed Umar alias Syed Sheikh, a British national who organized the kidnapping of four foreign tourists from a hotel in Paharganj to secure the release of Masood Azhar and later shot a UP police inspector in Saharanpur during a commando operation to free the hostages.

Also, in this very period, my poor dear mother, not well in any case, became even more poorly and had to receive yet another transfusion of blood, alone—for I could not leave Delhi.

Starting on the night of this Friday 24th I went through torment. What is the right answer, where does it lie, how to reach it?

That is how these three terrorists became passengers on this airplane—Because all else is already so widely and extensively reported it scarcely merits reiteration. Besides being filled with utter revulsion at the prospect of reliving (in writing about) those minutes, hours, days, I am also bone weary now.

For 3 terrorists, 161 men, women and children. Is it right? Wrong? A compromise? What?

Between two moral rights: saving the lives of the innocents; and a fight against terrorism falls this hollow, unfilled space of the undetermined.

At first I stood against any compromise, then, slowly, as the days passed I began to change.

Thus this flight. I go to "conclude," rather to have the hijacking terminated and take back the passengers safely.

And so to Kandahar.

Also tomorrow to 1 January, 2000/ 1.1.2000.

For the hostages, their families and many others a joyous beginning, at least I hope and pray.

For me, 1999 will end on this note of humble and deep questioning.

The next entry in my diary reads as follows:

January 11, 2000: Aboard BA flight Delhi-London

Excessive fog has delayed all flights for the last so many days. In consequence this flight too, which ordinarily should have left for London early in the morning at 0030 hrs, took off, finally, almost 14 hours later—at 1400. I am actually transiting through London—for it is Rome to where I am headed, on a "bilateral" to Italy.

The last entry, in the last notebook, was also aboard an aircraft—that which was taking me to Kandahar on a rescue mission. And that was 31st Dec '99.

Kandahar and the hijacked aircraft—that bleak, abandoned sort of runway, the skeletons and that litter of derelict planes, Taliban

ruffians lounging in a variety of poses on an assortment of vehicles. I am received by and then drive with Muttavakil, their "foreign minister," and another somebody of enormous girth who, he
announces, is the minister of civil aviation. And there was a third
in that new Toyota from the seats of which not even the plastic
covers had been removed; he was a rather effeminate Afghan, shy
of manner, who, he said, "interpreted." We drove along the runway and through the airport building—more Taliban of various
sizes, all lounging, all festooned with all kind of weaponry. And
soon the airport complex roads gave way to a dirt track. That FM,
Muttavakil, made some remark about discomfort, and I gave "my
rural origins" reply, and thus to a concrete building of the standard South Asian CPWD [Central Public Works Department]
ugliness, where on a table were spread out canned juices and some
variety of cola; so unutterably sad, out of place biscuits and such
other depressing condiments.

Some desultory talk, stilted, rehearsed and insincere. I mouthed
appreciation and some (sincere) gratitude for what they had done
(well, they had actually goaded the negotiations on the hijackers, at
least up to a point). We agreed to meet the press jointly. It was getting dark. I was beginning to be nervously impatient. The whole
system here at Kandahar is chaotic, on top of which the hijacked
plane, the hostages, the relief aircraft and now the one on which I
was—I wanted the hostages to leave. And I wanted to meet all of
them again—after they had boarded the relief crafts. So we ended
this absurd ritual, I forced a termination of it. Then back to
the tarmac, where hilariously (under these circumstances, too),
the "civil aviation minister" informed me that he drives slowly,
mindful of my "comfort." I urge him to shed his inhibitions!
First, to the Boeing. Patent relief amongst the hostages, gratitude, profuse expression of it. Then the Airbus. Similar scenes.
Then back to the building. A scramble by the assembled press—
largely Pakistani, some foreign. I make a brief statement; announce
"no questions." Back to the Airbus. In the meantime, even as I am
with the press, and the dark is deepening, night descending, with
a roar the Boeing, with all lights blazing, takes off for India—on
a runway with no lights. On the Airbus, farewells by Muttavakil
and the "civil aviation minister." A "corps commander"(!) also
makes a brief farewell appearance.

Clapping inside the aircraft as we take off. Trauma appearing during flight, some come and cry, some berate me—abuse me, some in profound gratitude.

Loud clapping and "Jai Jai kars" [victorious shouts of joy] as we land at Palam. It was just after 9:30 PM on 31 Dec '99.

I have jotted all this down, not having had a chance to do so any earlier, for I do not want to lose the memory of this most trying and searing of experiences—the first, and I pray my last, encounter with a hijack. My memory is still fresh—11 days after—for those impressions have been etched, as with acid, on my consciousness. It was a most troubled period this Christmas '99 to 31 Dec '99. By the time I reached home it was well past 10:30 PM I had asked the MEA team to come home and share a glass of Champagne. They left, we sat down to eat. Just then the telephone rang again. Now what? I thought. It was Vivek [Katju]: "Sir, the hijacked aircraft cannot leave Kandahar, not yet, what should I do?" Where was any option? "Don't let them take off—not before a full check," I urged. I sat down. The telephone rang again—exasperated I said: "Yes, what is it?" "Jaswant, this is Strobe. I want you to know how glad Brooke and I are. You did the right thing—there was no other way. Congratulations. And a happy new year." It was midnight. AD 2000 had arrived. Thus, through trauma to resolution and tranquility and hope—I hope.

On 4 Jan I went to Jodhpur. Mother has been really poorly, bed ridden all the time, hardly eating, groaning with pain. I was guilt ridden, then also impatient with her, for she craved attention—understandably, but I lacked that. . . . Bitter with myself and ridden with guilt.

Back to Delhi on Fri, 7 Jan 2000. Political opponents baying for my blood; "national prestige," "security," "Compromise with terrorism," "why to Kandahar," etc., etc.

Striking, in contrast, the congratulatory messages and telegrams and sentiments from the world.

And thus even as the century ended and the millennium turned and AD 2000 arrived, starkly got posed ancient conundrums—old dilemmas, all over again, in the backdrop of Kandahar:

How, in governance, do you choose between two equally valid, and relevant "moral rights"? Here as posed, between this "right" act of saving 166 lives, or standing up against terrorism and letting them all "go," for all to die—will that be another "right" act? By choosing that which is otherwise extinguished for always— Life; for, in any event this fight against terrorism will continue, from one challenge to another.

And the other—

Between public and private duty: here the calls of office or attending to sick and lonely mother, which does one choose?

This, in comparison, is easy.

And thus with all these thoughts crowding my consciousness and in this backdrop I wing my way to Rome, London, Tel-Aviv, Jerusalem, Oman, Dubai, all during this visit, then I have a round of talks with Strobe (18/19) all the time in London, too. And yet the scars of that hijack travel with me.

London

It is quite possibly amongst the longest stays at one place ever since I became minister. But I arranged it thus. Kandahar had taken a great deal out of me—and thus after the bilaterals and work I attempted a short, week-end holiday. Fri 14 Jan to Mon 16 Jan—AM In any event Rome, that great and eternal city had passed in a whirl of irritable and dazed fatigue. A great crime to treat Rome thus.

London, cold, cloudy—also some patches of brilliant, crystal-line sunshine. And those parks and galleries and brooding intro-spection, this search for anonymity.

In my search, my many searches—the spirit, the mind, the quest—the goal—and the time for it. Reading the *TLS* of 7th Jan, I stumble upon some quotes from St. Augustine:

"What, then, is time? I know well enough what it is, provided that nobody asks me; but if I am asked what it is . . . I am baffled. . . . 'Time?'—'Can only be coming from the future, passing through the present, and going into the past. In other words it is coming out of what does not yet exist, passing through what has no dura-tion, and moving into what no longer exists' . . . and then the great lament: 'O! Lord I do not even know what I do not know.'"

That great vedantic—St. Augustine.

The Final Week of 1999

My diary notes miss out on some landmarks that I feel are necessary to recount. The first, of course, is the great torment I went through. On the afternoon of December 24, the first girl child in the family was born, to Chitra and Manvendra, my daughter-in-law and son. We have a custom (largely in Rajasthan) whereby the mother and father choose someone to give the newborn baby a drop of consecrated water from the Ganga, with possibly a small portion of honey and jaggery. Harshini, who had not yet been given that name and who is now a bouncingly beauteous creature who stuns all into submission through sheer charm, was but a weakly, rather mutedly mewing baby. She could not be fed, even by her mother, until she had been given that ritual "first drop," and they had decided that I should be the one to do it. The belief is that whoever dispenses that first drop will transfer his or her attributes (or misattributes) to the newborn. I don't know why it was felt that I should do it. But that was the position. This was conveyed to me, by telephone, around 4 PM, when I was at work in the Ministry of External Affairs. Filled with joy, I promised that I would soon be at the hospital.

Fate had decided otherwise. Very soon thereafter, news came of the hijack. As my diary records, even then I felt a strange disquiet. It did not sound, if I can use such a phrase, like a "normal hijack." I was planning to leave, because handling the hijack was not directly the charge of the Ministry of External Affairs. I wanted to go home, wash up quickly, dash to the hospital, and then go to the prime minister's residence. Telephones had by then begun to ring with increasing frequency and decreasing patience. Some of the calls came from family members, whose obvious joy at the baby's arrival was marred, in their minds and hearts, by my insensitivity in keeping her waiting and wailing. Said one: "You truly have no heart. I don't believe a word of what you or the doctors might say in this regard; in the left of your chest cavity there is no heart—it is either stone or just emptiness. You just do not have those feelings. If you can torture a newborn baby with hunger, what else will you not do?" she justly remonstrated. I could not share with her, or anyone else at that moment, that a hijack had taken place. And so it went tortuously on. By the time I was finally able to visit the hospital, it was between 7:30 and 7:45 PM. Little Harshini had paid a price for this hijack, too, and so undeservedly.

But before that, just after I arrived home from the ministry, information reached me that the hijacked IC-814 had landed at Amritsar. I almost yelled into the telephone, forgetting all diplomatic decorum, my Army days resurfacing, and in a language that brooked no misunderstanding: "Get your bloody fingers out now! For heaven's sake, do whatever it takes, but don't let the f——g aircraft leave Amritsar!"

But it did leave Amritsar. From there it was flown to Lahore, and then on to Dubai. There the hijackers permitted twenty-eight passengers—primarily women and children—to disembark. The plane was then flown to Kandahar.

Some accounts have already been written of the terrible agony of those who were kept confined in that aircraft from December 24 until almost 9:30 PM on December 31—eight days and seven nights. It is impossible to share that agony, even to fully grasp the horror, the torture, and the sheer dehumanizing impact of 166 human beings confined in that narrow, tubular, suffocating space, sharing a single toilet that was already overflowing, with the doors shut, no air conditioning at times, bitterly cold temperatures at night, and frequent malfunctions of the aircraft's auxiliary power. If there is such a thing as a hell on earth, that certainly was it. I shared almost every moment of it with the passengers, but only by proxy. Now that the aircraft was in Kandahar, it had become the responsibility of the Ministry of External Affairs, which was responsible for working for the passengers' release. How did we do it? We had no diplomatic representation in Taliban-held Afghanistan; obviously, therefore, we had no representative in Kandahar, either. This ancient and historical city had been conquered by armies from India, including that of Maharajah Jaswant Singh I of Jodhpur, and later, in the nineteenth century, by Maharajah Ranjit Singh of Punjab.[19] This city is more than 200 kilometers from Quetta, connected now by an all-weather highway. It was clear to us from the beginning that the aircraft had been deliberately maneuvered to land at Kandahar, so that the situation could thereafter be managed by forces inimical to India, specifically the ISI. That became obvious and visible as events began to further unfold.

Deliberations on options were agonizing, prolonged, and extremely testing. The pulls and counterpulls of the options weighed on us. The threat was real; it could not be brushed off: What if the airplane were to be blown up? There was no way that I could accept the responsibility of letting 156 innocent men and women and one child, some of whom were not even Indian, be blown apart at midnight on December 31 as the millennium changed, for such was the information that had firmly and convincingly

19. When I returned to Jodhpur after the hijack to visit my mother, there were a few mocking references in the local papers: "Jaswant Singh I won Kandahar—what has this Jaswant Singh done?"

come our way in an intelligence briefing—that if there was no resolution, the hijackers would do just that, "preferably in a suicide mission, with the aircraft in the air." That was to be their welcome to AD 2000. That this was a kind of forerunner of 9/11, using civilian aircraft with passengers as weapons of terrorist action, no one then saw, or even guessed. I certainly did not; I had concluded that this was not a simple hijack, but I had no idea that it was a rehearsal of sorts for what was to follow in New York.

To start with, I had no telephone contacts in Kandahar, no officers there, no other way of knowing authoritatively what was happening. Our earliest contacts were with the Air Traffic Control (ATC) in Kandahar. The ATC and the airfield, ironically enough, had been built by the United States in the 1960s, prior to the Soviet occupation; but so, for that matter, had the Taliban been midwifed by the United States. But what use was it to go back to that past? What confronted us was the now, though the shadows of "then" do continue to torment now and again. The ATC either did not or deliberately would not speak in English, preferring to use the local Darri language or Persian. We had language resources at the ministry, but they were not adequate, and conversations between Delhi and Kandahar via the ATC were conducted exclusively in those two languages. I got nothing accomplished in those first two days. On December 27, however, I was finally able to get an officer to Kandahar from our mission in Islamabad, on a special UN flight. I had spent the whole of Christmas and Boxing Day making urgent phone calls all over the world to my Western counterparts, some of whom did not even know about the hijacking yet, because it was the Christmas holiday season. There was another coincidence, and a rather insidious one at that: this was also the month of Ramadan. When I inquired why such evil was occurring at such a holy time, those who were knowledgeable scoffed at my ignorance, and responded that in Islam, the period of Ramadan fasting is the true period of struggle and sacrifice.

It is a different story altogether how I was able to finally reach some intrepid and able officers from the ministry who could guide me from Kandahar, inform me about the condition of the passengers, conduct basic negotiations with the hijackers, and advise on the status of the hijack. Up to that point I had been blind and deaf, dependent on factors that were totally beyond my control, attempting to "negotiate" the release and rescue of the hijacked humans and craft from the worst possible location on earth—at least for us from India. I am immensely saddened when I think back on that time: Was I strengthened by the demonstrated resoluteness of my countrymen and -women? I am ashamed even now, as I recollect how—initially perhaps spontaneously, but thereafter as part of some sponsored embarrassment to the government—gangs of political activists were persuaded to block roads, interrupt press briefings, and, to my mind and memory, roll around on the roads as if in a kind of collective hysteria. I still don't know what they were demonstrating with this undignified and demeaning behavior. But it certainly did succeed in shaming India in the eyes of the international community. We were making a spectacle of ourselves, and in this hour of such trial.

The day the demands of the hijackers came to me—$200 million as ransom money, the release of some thirty-six proven terrorists, and the interred bones of at least one terrorist—I shared them with the Cabinet and sought advice: What should I do? The Cabinet spoke with one voice: "Reject the demands. Go and tell the press in appropriate words." It was a tense day. The press was waiting outside, and I had to brief them, so on completion of the Cabinet meeting, I repeated the demands and simply added, "I now urge all in my country and abroad to reflect on these demands." There really was nothing more to say.

That Journey into a Dark Night

It was not an easy decision to go to Kandahar, but somebody had to do it. Vivek Katju, Ajit Duval, and C. D. Sahay were not unanimous in saying, "Sir, please depute somebody to come to Kandahar, for even though we have agreed to release three when thirty-six had been wanted, there is no knowing what obstacles and problems may arise at the last minute. We want somebody to be able to make decisions on the spot. There will not be time to keep referring matters to Delhi." Naturally I was inclined to go, as it was the MEA's responsibility. My younger son in Jaisalmer, whom I called just before leaving for Kandahar, immediately volunteered, as he had done earlier during those trying, uncertain blind days and nights of the hijack, and in all sincerity said, "Let me come with you." Earlier he had, again totally sincerely, said, "Offer me as the hostage, your son for all those innocents." Of course I could not do that, although not because I would not. I had tried to during the telephone call. I asked Vivek Katju (we had by then established a satellite phone facility) to talk to Muttavakil and inquire whether I could personally meet Mullah Omar. Within minutes, Muttavakil's reaction came: "Yes, why not? I will make contact." And soon enough his response came: "Sorry, you can't; don't fly to Kandahar." Muttavakil's minders in the ISI must have upbraided him for even this little relenting.

There were some ironies still to come.[20] I had earlier decided to send a back-up aircraft, but it developed a technical problem soon after take-off and had to return. This was also the day that I had offered to share my views on the episode with some of the press. What else could I do but laugh bitterly as the relief aircraft returned to Palam?

The airport at Kandahar was rudimentary and littered with the debris of war, exactly as in my diary notes. Four aircraft were about the most it could handle. Our plane was asked to go to one end of the airport and stay there. The agreement with the Taliban authorities about the sequence of events was that first the détenues were to be "identified." Then the passengers would be deplaned, and only then would the détenues be handed over to the hijackers. This agreement was violated. At the very last minute, the contract was stood on its head. I waited and waited and waited in the aircraft, but there was no communication either from elements of the Taliban or, what was more worrisome, from officers, until finally the walkie-talkie crackled and a worried-sounding Vivek Katju said, "Sir, we have to decide what to do. Do we let go of the prisoners first?" What do you do under such circumstances? The knife was not just at my throat; it was now, yet again, at the throats of the 156 passengers and crew who remained on IC-814. By then they had heard, some had even seen, that their relief aircraft had arrived, and that it was now only a matter of minutes until they would be released. So I agreed, with hardly any time for reflection or debate—and in any event, with whom was I to discuss it? As soon as the three men went down the steps, they were warmly embraced, and there were shouts of joy. I don't have to explain who greeted them. Meanwhile, this issue of "identification" of released TADA détenues was another giveaway of the ISI hand. The friends and relatives of the détenues to be exchanged were brought to Kandahar by ISI from Pakistan, and they confirmed the "correctness" of each released person. Only then were the hijackers assured that the TADA détenues were genuine and that a "trick" was not being played on them by the wily Indians. I continued to wait, for the stepladder that had been used to deplane the three prisoners had instantly been whisked away—and as I was later to learn, there were only one or two of them at Kandahar. And so there I stood in the open doorway of the aircraft even as the evening dark began to gather, gloom deepened, and the cold began to close in. Finally, Muttavakil arrived. The rest is as my diary records.

---

20. A commando raid was one of the options that had been considered. The problem was that over-flight permission would require a passenger list manifest, which over Pakistan would have been a giveaway. Going over Iran and then over a Taliban Afghanistan into Kandahar presented a similar range of problems.

Of the return flight, what memories do I carry? There was relief, because so much accumulated pain and agony had burst open, like a long-throbbing carbuncle. My officers and I had a place in the first row, but I didn't even want to sit. Many of the released passengers were visibly traumatized; there was no way I could do anything other than meet each of them, individually, to welcome them and do the best that I could to absorb their pain and try in some small way to assuage it. There was, as I recall, a young Frenchman who could not stop crying. I knew, of course, what the cause of his breakdown was, but why was he the only one? His girlfriend, who was also French and had been sitting next to him, said: "This became his state in the aircraft itself after the fourth day of captivity." I also recall a Swiss man, a gentleman of dignity and reserve. I knew that he worked in international finance. He would be returning safely to his country along with his girlfriend. It is he who subsequently said that he "marveled at the stoic reserve and courage of the Indians; had it been a plane full of Italians, what chaos there would have been! I have learned a great deal from the Indians." There was a young lady from Nepal who was traveling with a companion from Germany, who had kept up the spirits of the other passengers. She came up to me and said with great feeling: "Thank you. Now I will be able to find out where my children are. On the 24th they were traveling from Dehradun by train to Delhi, and I by air from Kathmandu to Delhi. I was supposed to meet them at the railway station. Does anyone know where they are now and what might have happened to them?" Of course I did not. There was also a rather overwrought young mother, still trembling with anger and suppressed fear. She came up to me in the aircraft, and with her tiny hands, grimy from her eight days of confinement, she clutched at my throat and yelled as loudly as she could: "Why have you come so late? Where were you all this time? You have betrayed all of us! Where are my children? Where is my family?" She angrily banged her head against my chest and finally broke down, crying bitterly. I stood there in the aisle and just held her; Vivek Katju stood next to me, and we watched. What else could we do? Today a pair of night binoculars sits on one of my shelves, a grim reminder of that night.[21]

---

21. Ajit Duval describes the binocular episode: "Around 5 PM, before the released prisoners were handed over to the hijackers, I wanted to make sure that the hijackers who were still in the aircraft were not up to some larger mischief. The three prisoners having arrived from Delhi had seriously limited our tactical options. I met the hijackers in the aircraft, where they confirmed the understanding. I also addressed the passengers and tried to boost their morale. When I was returning, Berger and Sandy, two of the hijackers, came to me and handed over a small binocular, by which, they said, they were monitoring developments outside. As the proof of vacating the hijack, they presented the binocular to me as a souvenir. Later, when we were on our way back from Kandahar I showed the binocular to the then EAM. He felt it would remind us of our bitter Kandahar experience and kept them as a souvenir."

The Final Puzzle

The hijacked aircraft could not be taken out of Kandahar that same evening. I had received an alarm that something was planted on it that would blow up at midnight. I could not risk the lives of the relief pilots and crew. Besides, it had to be given a technical inspection before it could take off. The aircraft had been kept confined for eight days. There was also the mystery of the "red bag." What was this "red bag"? Who owned it? Why did the hijackers return for it? The mystery was cleared up after Muttavakil's arrest by the United States following the defeat of the Taliban in 2001. The "red bag" belonged to one of the hijackers; it contained explosives, and possibly the terrorists' real passports, as well. In their hurry, they had forgotten it in the hold. By the time they came back to retrieve it, the hostages had been released. Yet Muttavakil himself acted illegally; he betrayed our trust by having the hold forcibly opened and all the red bags taken out until the one they were looking for had been found. It is all there in the report of A. R. Ghanshyam, the diplomat sent to Kandahar from Islamabad. I share an extract:

Winding up of the visit to Kandahar

> I stayed back at Kandahar to arrange the refueling and return flight of the hijacked aircraft IC-814. A crew of 14 members, including one flight engineer and two pilots—Capt. Rao, deputy managing director of Indian Airlines, and Capt. Suri of Indian Airlines also remained in Kandahar. While the hand baggage of the passengers on board IC-814 were taken by the passengers to the new aircraft, the baggage in the hold was retained. . . . I went on board the aircraft at 1900 hrs. The interior had an unbearable stink. The cockpit panel had left over chicken bones, peeled skins of fruits and other dirt. The toilets were choked and were absolutely unusable.
>
> I returned to the lounge and sat down for a while when I had occasion to meet Rehmatullah Hashmi. We sat down for a cup of tea in a corner of the lounge. At this time I asked what the Taliban wanted to actually do with the prisoners and the hijackers. He said that all of them would be put in a vehicle and that vehicle would be escorted by two armed vehicles—one in the front and one in the back—till the Pakistan border. He also said that they would not be

using the normal border passage but instead use one of those Pak-Afghan secret routes which the mujahideen used during the Russian occupation, where there would be no border formalities like immigration and customs. When I asked him whether at any time, the Taliban authorities were distressed enough to consider storming the plane, he said that while the inevitability of such a course of action was discussed in the beginning it was shelved once I arrived on the scene and it became known that India was sending its negotiating team. He offered to host me if I visited Quetta while he is there.

At around 2100 hours Capt. Suri came to the lounge and conveyed to me that the Taliban were not prepared to let IC-814 fly and they were delaying the refueling and were also keen to take out one bag that belonged to the hijackers. Mr. Muttawakil was still in the airport and I rushed to him with Capt. Suri and apprised him of the problem and requested him to advise the authorities to assist us in facilitating an early departure of the aircraft. At that time, I also came to know that one of the hijackers had mentioned that they had left a "millennium present for the government of India on board the aircraft." I then advised Capt. Suri that we better vacate the plane and get back to the lounge. But the Taliban authorities were still trying to see the hold and look for a red suitcase of the hijackers. I brought this to the notice of Foreign Secretary (FS) and Joint Secretary (JS) Iran, Pakistan, Afghanistan (IPA) who advised that I should ensure that all the crew and the two captains are not found anywhere near the aircraft and that I should also ensure that everybody stayed in one place and slept over in the lounge along with the other diplomats and the UN staff till the next morning.

Around 2300 hrs, I found that Capt. Rao had still not returned. When I looked around for Capt. Suri and asked him where Capt. Rao was, he told me that he was still there in the aircraft and was refusing to come back. I rushed with Capt. Suri to the aircraft. It was at that time that I found the red Pajero (which was used by Muttawakil all through my stay in Kandahar) parked right in front of the hold with its head lights on. It could not be confirmed as to who was in the aircraft as it had tinted glasses. Capt. Rao had started the engine with a jet starter and the APU was still running. Some workers were still working in the hold. Capt. Rao told me at that time that he had seen people taking every red bag from the hold and showing it to the car and then taking it back to the hold. Two and two put together, we both felt that perhaps either one of more or the hijackers or someone close to them who could identify the famous red suitcase were comfortably parked in that car and were trying out every red bag to identify the real bag and take it out. Capt. Suri found out from a local worker that they had found one bag and there were five grenades in it. The Control tower also told the captain that the minister for civil aviation had cleared the aircraft about 15 minutes before midnight and had said that they could leave if they wanted. At any rate, the requisite fuel was still not on board. The aircraft had 14 tonnes of fuel and needed another 16 to 18 tonnes of fuel before it could safely take off. Finally, I was able to bring back Capt. Rao and we all stayed in the lounge for the night. The next morning fuel was supplied to the plane, the engine was checked and it took off at 0943 hrs, Afghan time. The departure of the flight was conveyed to FS at the same time.

January 1, 2000

The entire officialdom of Taliban never came back to the airport on the New Year's Day. I sent a message through the airport manager that I wished to see anyone from among the minister for civil aviation or the minister for foreign affairs to thank them and also to take over the hijacker's bag. The airport manager consulted his seniors and came back to tell me that no one could be contacted. Then I insisted that if they were not likely to come to the airport, I could go and see them in the city which was about an hour from the airport. I did not receive a satisfactory answer even for this request. Around 1000 hrs, I was told that CCK and Hashmi would come to see me off and I could meet them at that time. I waited for them and even missed the first UN flight to Islamabad which took off at 1030 hrs. I was practically alone in the place with most of the diplomats and UN staff taking the first flight. Around 1100 hrs, while I was still waiting for CCK and Hashmi, one of the young officials of the Control tower who spoke English, came and whispered in my ear that nobody was likely to come to see me and no one knew what had happened to the famous bag after it was unloaded and taken to the city. He also handed over a packet containing some almonds and raisins, a pocket comb, a nail cutter, a handkerchief and a pair of nylon socks saying that the minister for civil Aviation had sent [these] for me as a gift because he knew that I never had time to go to the city throughout my stay at the airport in Kandahar.

I boarded the second UN plane at 1200 hrs and returned to Islamabad at around 1500 hrs.

Repeatedly India has asked the United States, now the virtual ruler of Afghanistan, to hand over Muttavakil for prosecution. The United States has provideed limited access but no more. That is the extent of its cooperation with India so far in this "joint fight against terrorism."

8

Troubled Neighbor, Turbulent Times: 2001

The Agra Initiative

The India-Pakistan meeting in Agra between July 14 and 16, 2001, was yet another opportunity created on the initiative of Prime Minister Vajpayee and his government. This was despite setbacks such as Kargil, Kandahar, and the many other incidents of terrorism in between, almost all of which originated from Pakistan, where there was now a proliferation of terror seminaries, sponsored, trained, and financed by Pakistanis. The products of these schools were then infiltrated into India, either across the LOC or in one of the myriad other ways in which, almost effortlessly, an ever-open India's security could be breached. For example, in the case of the hijack to Kandahar, one of the hijackers had arrived in India after obtaining a visa in Portugal! Still, efforts for peace had to continue, for there is no alternative to peace.

Between Lahore 1999 and Agra 2001, the political scene within Pakistan had changed beyond recognition. Included in the long list of Kargil casualties, sadly, was the permanent orphan of Pakistan, a fledgling democracy. It was now General Musharraf with whom we dealt, the man who had been the chief of Pakistan's army during Kargil. On May 23, Prime Minister Vajpayee, Deputy Prime Minister L. K. Advani, and I had lunched together. During this luncheon meeting, a number of issues were discussed, but we focused principally on Jammu and Kashmir, on Pakistan, and on what should be done. A slew of collective decisions were then made, one of which was to extend an invitation to General Musharraf to visit India for talks. The six-month phase announced earlier by Prime Minister Vajpayee, in November 2000 on the eve of Ramadan, about not initiating combat operations against terrorists in Jammu and Kashmir, had come to an end; the response to it from terrorist organizations had been disappointing.[1] These set in motion a whole chain of events, culminating

---

1. "Non-initiation" meant that the counterinsurgency forces would not initiate any hostile action against the militants; but obviously they would react to provocations.

in a visit by General Musharraf, who until then had styled himself as the chief executive officer of Pakistan. Before he arrived in Agra, however, he declared himself the president, demonstrating admirable adaptability. An appropriate press statement by the MEA was accordingly issued.

As a follow-up, a meeting of the Cabinet Committee on Security was held that same evening, and the proposal to invite Musharraf was formally approved. A letter of invitation followed the next day. I was required to brief the press about all this; the quest upon which India was yet again embarking was communicated in three brief paragraphs:

> India's commitment to peace, dialogue and cooperative co-exis-tence with Pakistan remains unaltered. Prime Minister Vajpayee had set in motion a peace process by his historic and path-break-ing visit to Lahore in early 1999.
>
> In pursuance of [the] Lahore Declaration and the Shimla Agreement, Prime Minister Vajpayee has decided to invite General Pervez Musharraf, the Chief Executive of Pakistan [as he still was at that point], to visit India at his early convenience. A formal invitation will be delivered shortly.
>
> India is yet again offering the hand of friendship, reconcilia-tion, cooperation and peace to Pakistan, in the expectation that this opportunity shall be positively and purposefully utilised by them.

I was due to leave for an official visit to Moscow soon thereafter. On June 2 I woke up, as usual very early, but that morning I was imagin-ing that I heard a telephone ringing somewhere—or was it really ring-ing? Instead, was I dreaming? Then yet again, just before 7 AM, another call came. An unprecedented, horrific tragedy had been visited upon Nepal: the heir to the throne, Prince Dipendra, had shot to death King Birendra, Queen Aiswarya, and several other members of the royal family, after which he had turned the gun on himself. Shortly thereafter, Prime Minister Vajpayee called from Manali, where he had gone for his usual summer break of about a week. Nepal had been thrown into a deep crisis. I was then holding two charges, as both minister of external affairs and minister of defense, and it is in that second capacity that I was undertak-ing the visit to Russia—but only after doing what I could in terms of tak-ing immediate steps to be by the side of Nepal in those hours of national trauma. On return from Russia in mid-June, I visited Mumbai to brief the prime minister, who was in the hospital for his second knee operation. It was a monsoon-drenched Mumbai I arrived in, wet and huddled, so different from the oppressive, pre-monsoon mugginess of Delhi.

We had set in motion very thorough preparations for Agra. On June 19, we released a formal press statement on General Musharraf's visit to India. It was brief and to the point, yet it contained all that needed to be said at the time, outlining the welcome planned in Delhi, the retreat in Agra, and a visit to the Dargah Sharif, the shrine of Khwaja Moinuddin Chishti at Ajmer Sharif.[2] Until then, Delhi had not been on the itinerary. We had proposed to the prime minister that it would be far preferable to have this "retreat" in Goa, which in July, although it was often subject to heavy monsoon rains, would be a far more suitable venue, offering greater privacy than the demanding environs of a capital city such as Delhi. This issue of possible venues became a bit of a football. As it always happens, a number of alternatives were discussed. I did not wish to push Rajasthan too much, having already had President Clinton go there in 2000. Although it was eminently suitable, I could be accused of parochialism for making such a suggestion. Our discussions were cut short quite soon, because we received a message from Islamabad that General Musharraf would himself prefer to arrive in Delhi and make that his first stop. After that, there was not much of an option; a guest's wishes must always prevail.

In a discussion with Prime Minister Vajpayee, I suggested that even before General Musharraf arrived, we should take some initiatives as overtures for the Pakistan president's visit. The PM assented, and a series of decisions were announced. Pakistani poets, academics, writers, and artists would be invited, individually or in groups, for a month-long visit as guests of the government of India. Groups of Pakistani students (school to university, boys and girls) would be invited by the government to visit and tour Indian academic establishments. Technical education was not overlooked; twenty scholarships were announced for Pakistani students attending Indian technical institutions. Concessions were announced for Pakistani fishermen, who from time to time were taken into custody because they had strayed into Indian territorial waters. In future they would be turned back after due warning. The prime minister also instructed the Ministry of Home Affairs to take expeditious action for the release of all Pakistani civilian prisoners currently in India, after due process of law. To enhance trade and encourage

---

2. Ajmer is venerated as a holy place by both Hindus and Muslims. The Dargah Sharif is the mausoleum of the Sufi saint Khwaja Moinuddin Chishti, who died in AD 1235. His blessings are eagerly sought by pilgrims who visit the shrine. Legend has it that the Mughal emperor Akbar went there in the sixteenth century, in quest of an heir, and was granted a boon.

Pakistani imports into India, the Ministry of Commerce was instructed to reduce or eliminate tariffs on fifty tariff lines. These announcements covered the entire range of interpersonal contacts between the two countries; they made travel easier. Certain decisions relating to the LOC and what was termed the AGPL (Actual Ground Position Line) in Jammu and Kashmir were also announced. (All these were declared, unilaterally, to be India's initiatives. It is ironic that so many of them remain unimplemented.)

Musharraf and the Media Circus

It was difficult to tell whether it was premeditated, or accidental, or perhaps a forerunner of things to come. Hours before Musharraf was to reach Delhi, after a gap of almost a year, Indian troops exchanged fire with their Pakistani counterparts across the LOC. Those with astrological inclinations did not find the incident propitious; I treated it as merely a reversion to routine, an old habit. Media interest in the event, which had been slowly building up from the speculative, now became highly excitable. Not only was there a real danger that the event would be hijacked by the media, but there was a serious apprehension in my mind that the agenda of the meeting—and therefore the outcome of it—could well be both decided and then dictated by the media. This I had first experienced during the Kargil conflict, and thereafter again on several other occasions; whether it was the Kandahar hijack or President Clinton's visit or terrorist attacks, twenty-four-hour coverage pushed the television channels into actually "demanding" news, at least every hour, always something new and different, and always an "exclusive." And when, as so often happens, there was nothing newsworthy to share, fiction often replaced facts.

There was nothing much, certainly nothing concrete by way of news, to report on that first day, the day Musharraf arrived in Delhi, for there was little else other than ceremonials. Thus a great deal of television time and newspaper column space was devoted to interpreting "body language," the perceived "warmth" or absence thereof, speculation about what was to be discussed and what would not even be touched upon. All the media time went into the symbolism of what was happening; there was, after all, nothing of substance till then. I find it interesting, as I go over my notes and diary entries for that period, to reread what the newspapers wrote at the time. It is all still very educative. One venerable newspaper, for example, decided knowledgeably that the first day's consultations had "helped to clear the air." Another informed us that the prospects for a productive summit "appeared to have improved." Yet another daily, supposedly more observant and acute of vision than others, commented that the two heads of government were "visibly tense at the first meeting, shaking hands without looking into each other's eyes." But, it reassured its readers, "over lunch, the atmosphere lightened." "This," it then forecast, "is the spirit that will now guide the summit." What else should I quote? How many more such examples? Yet another prominent daily, in a comment somewhat removed from what the others said, reflected that General Musharraf "appeared to be in an unfamiliar territory. He hardly smiled," and "his handshake appeared to lack warmth"! Without batting an eye, as they say, this same newspaper then added: "He projected the image of a leader on a charm offensive." Remarkable; but then they had already decided that the general had "taken centre stage instead of standing in the wings," that he was a "determined general, a confident CEO, an image conscious politician . . . who knows how to soft sell his hard talk!"

The venue in Agra had presented some security problems, along with all the attendant administrative minutiae. The host country on such occasions is always a harassed lot. An India-Pakistan meeting of this nature takes on a uniquely South Asian flavor: large, unrestrained, loud, and much like an upcoming *baraat* (wedding party), with all kinds of arrangements to be taken care of. Indeed, requirements must always be anticipated rather than met after being asked for! The first day, July 14, was spent almost entirely on the obligatory ceremonials: arrival rituals, a brief introductory meeting, and a visit to Rajghat, the Gandhi Memorial. There was also a trip down nostalgia lane, down Naherwali Galli, the area in Delhi's Old City where General Musharraf's family had lived until 1947, a reception at the Pakistan High Commission, photo opportunities, and so on, but nothing of substance. I decided, therefore, to advise Prime Minister Vajpayee that instead of flying early on the morning on July 15, the day for which the meeting had originally been scheduled, we should go on July 14. I take shelter behind my diary notes of that date:

July 15: Agra

It was late last night that I reached here with Atalji, in his special flight, from Delhi. We left directly from Rashtrapati Bhawan for the airfield, after the presidential banquet for the distinguished visitor, General Pervez Musharraf, had concluded.

This visit is in itself a consequence of the May 23 invitation. In between, of course, a great many weeks have gone by, also a great many things have happened. For one, an avalanche of statements by General Musharraf has been descending upon us all after that invitation and his acceptance of it.

I have kept deliberately quiet, have given just one press conference, if I recollect right, on June 14, and, thereafter, it was only the official spokesman who, under my supervision, handled it all. The second and final pre-visit, pre-summit conference I then held on July 11, 2001. We did, however, engage in what the Pak commentators, quite needlessly, began to term as "deflective diplomacy," by unilaterally announcing a number of steps successively on July 4, 6, and 9. Though there was nothing at all that was "deflective" in what was announced, it was focused, relevant, and a correct initiative. Yet, this troubled our prospective guests greatly, who in retaliation played the "Hurriyat" hand, which actually troubled the media much more than it did us.

Late on the 14th afternoon a storm had gathered in the skies; dark, low clouds, heavy with rain, rumbled overhead. Thunder, lightning, and gusts of wind lashed the environs, making me wonder if we would be able to fly in such conditions. The day's program had been entirely routine, though the media, visual and print, were totally unrestrained in their state of an induced hysteria of expectations. Predictably so, I suppose, being an India-Pak event.

Slept late in consequence of reaching Agra so late, only by about 1 AM.

The whole day has gone by as most initial days of India-Pakistan talks do. (I am after all a veteran now, and I can tell.) It is now evening. Only now have we got down to serious talk, discussing and sparring through an exchange of the "first draft" of what could be an agreed text. It is, I am afraid, a non-starter. So, as always this volleyball of drafts and counter-drafts will go on until late. I do not suppose I will be called in to judge until tomorrow morning, besides I so lack sleep by now that I would scarcely be able to "judge" anything, also shortly there is a banquet by the governor of Uttar Pradesh (Vishnu Kant Shastri)—with Rajnath Singhji as chief minister. Best, therefore, to leave this until tomorrow.

The whole of July 16, we kept working on how to reach a decision. Sadly, a display of grandstanding by the visiting dignitary had thrown a major wrench into the works. Every India-Pakistan event draws a disproportionate amount of interest. Perhaps inevitably, though mostly without foundation, every media channel works from a basket of stock phrases: "breakthrough"; "brotherhood"; "India (or Pakistan, depending on which country's media you work for) standing firm"; "India and/or Pakistan obstinate against establishing peace." We met early in the morning of the 16th to try and work out an agreed text, which with refinement could then become the document released at Agra, as a successor to Lahore.

Musharraf's interaction with the editors that morning was recorded on videotape by the visitors and was thereafter telecast by an Indian channel. When the visitors were informed that this violated unwritten codes, they intimated that the channel was at fault. This was a pathetically feeble attempt to deflect responsibility. Once telecast, it aroused great indignation throughout the country, because Musharraf came across as overly belligerent. It was this that made negotiations over the draft so much more difficult. This grandstanding fever had induced General Musharraf into a great deal of unrestrained comment in front of a select gathering of editors. Perhaps he had been mesmerized by the media. To be the recipient of such rapt attention is always an exceedingly heady wine. It bypasses the gullet and goes directly to the head, causing instant befuddlement. Thus, when the assembly began to applaud the visiting general, and all in anticipation, he rejected the presence of terrorism as an issue; continued to emphasize only the centrality of Jammu and Kashmir; was almost dismissive of Lahore; refused to accept the reality of what Kargil was, or what he had done; and seemed almost to dismiss the Shimla Agreement, too.

This was getting to be too heavy a load for any conference to carry. General Musharraf seemed not to understand the debilitating impact that Kargil had had on the atmosphere, and he appeared not to grasp the essence of what Prime Minister Vajpayee had offered—a new beginning. Instead, Musharraf began playing to the stands. He wanted to go home with a victory, to be able to say: "We straightforward, direct-dealing military men achieve results; we do not beat around the bush." There was a degree of rhetorical overstatement in all this, which in small doses is not too difficult to overlook. But if engaged in while on an important bilateral visit, it can cause deep embarrassment to the host and place a strain on negotiations. The critical point in Agra came at this breakfast meeting between the visiting general and the Indian editors. I had knowledge that such an engagement had been organized. Musharraf and his entire party had been lodged in a newly built hotel, the luxurious Amarvilas, with every room overlooking the Taj Mahal. That did not seem to have mellowed the military enthusiasm of the visiting president. That aside, our guest had persistently refused to decide upon the agenda for the Agra meeting, the importance of which had repeatedly been emphasized to the Pakistan High Commission in Delhi, and also by our high commissioner in Islamabad to the Pakistan Foreign Office. As everything had become so totally centralized in the hands of Musharraf, nobody was free to make decisions and share them with us. The proposal(s) by India for an agenda had thus continued to languish: "There is no decision yet from the president." In consequence, we had congregated in Agra without any agreed schedule on which to work.

Prime Minister Vajpayee had asked all his senior Cabinet colleagues to accompany him. Deputy Prime Minister Advani was there, as were the finance and commerce ministers and, because of the large media attendance and global interest, the minister for information and broadcasting. The press contingent from Pakistan was packed and demanding, and wanting very much to transmit a success story back to their readers and viewers. That, I rather suspect, had been suggested by the establishment around Musharraf. Diligence about such reporting would then be treated as some kind of an index of loyalty to Pakistan. In fact, at his news conference once he was finally back home, Musharraf complimented the Pakistani press for "patriotism in reportage." Naturally, therefore, they all clamored for news. And the clamor was not structured around any particular development; it was constant. Here I made an error: I remained conservative in my approach, not taking into consideration the high demand for "something," anything, that could be projected by these twenty-four-hour news channels—any trivia, even the menu or the style of the furniture. Instead of taking note of this insistent demand, I worked on the basis that when I had something to say, I would ask the minister for information and broadcasting to share it with the press. No such consideration restrained the general's entourage. They made frequent visits to the Press Assembly Hall in order to say something or other, whether it was fact, fiction, hearsay, or just rumor. None of them was sitting in on the meetings; impressions and surmises were all they had to share.

Dodged by the Draft

At the meeting itself, Prime Minister Vajpayee was accompanied by his deputy, L. K. Advani, and as his minister for external affairs, I was there, along with the principal secretary and officers from the MEA. Perhaps inevitably, there was a similar military-heavy contingent from Pakistan. I found it somewhat reminiscently amusing when the president of Pakistan, in the style of the military and its minor staff duties, expounded on his various theses about how the intractable problem of Jammu and Kashmir could easily be solved; and of course, he asserted, there was "no terrorism from Pakistan." As it happens, such diplomatic meetings do not easily lend themselves to the style and fashion of military maneuvers. It was therefore left to the two foreign ministers to sit down afterward and attempt to come up with a draft. That is where this whole theory of a "draft that had been agreed upon" surfaced. Musharraf was keen that some agreement be reached anyhow, that very afternoon. He wanted to leave, either that evening or early the following morning, for Pakistan via Ajmer, after a visit to the Dargah Sharif. However, neither he nor his team had fully assessed the consequences in the Indian public's mind of the rather free-ranging breakfast meeting he had already had with the Indian media. Neither was he able to grasp why others were hesitant about his various theses. This was a perfectly understandable military tendency, but it was workable only in a purely military environment.

Let me cut the agony short. Abdul Sattar was far more experienced in terms of length of service in the Pakistan Foreign Office than I was as a minister in the Ministry of External Affairs. Together we tried our hand at writing something on a piece of paper. When Sattar showed it to me, I mentioned somewhat jocularly that it would be best if we wrote it in English, not "Punjabi English." Being from Punjab, he took that with his characteristic Punjabi sense of good humor, and said, "Most definitely." I attempted something in pencil on a piece of paper; he corrected and amended it; I did likewise; and so we went back and forth like that for quite some time. Finally, he said that he would have to consult his president before he could assent or disagree. The two heads of government had by then retired to their hotel rooms. Abdul Sattar went to General Musharraf's room, and when he returned, he said that a few changes had been made on the paper: "Now do we agree?" I responded. I, too, would have to obtain the clearance of my Cabinet colleagues and the prime minister. He then added what I thought was a remark of characteristic wisdom, born no doubt of experience. I was touched by it, for the mood was neither relaxed nor mellow; the inherent tension of India-Pakistan talks had begun to manifest itself. With the wisdom of the East and his years in the Pakistan Foreign Office, Sattar said, "Jaswantji, I must share something with you. You have many years of service to your country behind you and many ahead, which you will perform with great distinction. But the task on which you and I are now set as 'negotiators of an agreement,' also 'messengers of that agreement,' is a perilous task. In such tasks, believe me, quite often it is the messenger who gets shot." And he laughed. I remembered those words later, when the story as it was reported in the Pakistani media was subsequently picked up in India, and inevitably was presented as an example of "tardiness" on the part of the Ministry of External Affairs.

This piece of "paper" has been variously cited as evidence of discord within the National Democratic Alliance government, of my own personal "soft approach" in comparison with some others, and a variety of other speculative flights of fancy, all so entirely unnecessary. This diplomatic negotiation was no different from any other. Those very preliminary notes would have been refined, shaped, expanded, or explained, and would then perhaps have led to some forward movement. This was an exercise aimed at finding a starting point; it was not an agreed document. Besides, a draft is no more than a "draft," so what is all the controversy about?

I went and showed this paper to the prime minister, who then called his Cabinet colleagues to his suite. The collective view expressed there was that without an adequate and sufficiently clear emphasis on terrorism, and a categorical acceptance that it must cease, how could there be any significant movement on issues that are of concern or are a priority only to Pakistan? And none that are in the hierarchy of priorities for India? How can we abandon Shimla or Lahore? Or forget the reality of Kargil? I went back to Sattar and reported our failure. He took it understandingly, as if he had known in advance that this was a long shot. He said words to the effect of "I am sorry this has happened. I really wish, Jaswantji, that we had been able to do something, but then this has been the fate of India-Pakistan negotiations—many hopes have been belied in this fashion." I went back, and a short while later the high commissioner of Pakistan, Ashraf Jehangir Qazi, came to talk to me. He was direct: "Is there any chance of salvaging a statement?" Yet again, I rely only on memory of this conversation with Qazi. I could not share anything with him other than facts, and so I told him, "I am sorry; I do not see much possibility on this basis." He persisted, asking just once more, "Why, Mr. Minister? Why not?" I replied, "I cannot because my Cabinet colleagues present here in Agra, who actually make up the Cabinet Committee on Security, cannot get themselves to assent." To that the high commissioner agreed immediately; he knew how effectively the Cabinet system worked in the Vajpayee government.

Some last-minute efforts were made. General Musharraf's departure was postponed, and he sought a special meeting with Prime Minister Vajpayee.

I thought that was an error on his part, but at that point he did not yet know Atal Bihari Vajpayee very well. The meeting took place at the hotel where the prime minister was staying. After all, he had recently had surgery on his knee. It was still very painful for him to walk; to be able to hold meetings and attend them with such regularity was in itself an act of great courage. I knew that a mistake was being made by our guest, for when I later asked Prime Minister Vajpayee what had happened, he said quietly, "Nothing." He said it in Hindi, in effect to mean, "The visiting general sahib kept talking and I kept listening." This is an art in which Atal Bihari Vajpayee specializes, and it is often disconcerting to the unfamiliar.

Later that morning, I was asked to meet the press.[3] Of all the questions that were put to me, two remain etched in my memory, along with an issue that troubled me. Through no fault of either Sushma Swaraj, the able minister for information and broadcasting, or Nirupama Rao, then the spokesperson for the Ministry of External Affairs the first woman to hold the job both were criticized for what had been my lapse in not informing them in time of events as they were unfolding. I had to stand up and protect them. I was informed just before the press conference that Nirupama Rao had been "pushed around" by the visiting media. This was extremely objectionable. I said all this in response to various questions. One question that has stayed in memory was whether our efforts at peace with Pakistan would continue. Without a moment's hesitation, I said, "Yes, of course, they will." The other was a query from someone who wanted to know why we had prevented Musharraf from going on a pilgrimage to the dargah of the revered "Garib Nawaz."[4] I responded by saying that it was well known that you could reach that dargah only if the great Garib Nawaz summoned you, and perhaps that "summons" had not yet been issued for the general! This answer was received with such totally unexpected applause by the entire assembly composed equally of Pakistani and Indian media that I was taken aback. I had not said anything clever, only that which I believed. I later wondered whether this one question and its reply had not encapsulated an essential and continuing aspect of the India-Pakistan relationship.

The media war continued for several weeks, the general holding forth in his domain, and I in the humble media briefing room of Shastri Bhawan, the office of the Indian Ministry of Information and Broadcasting. A controversy then arose about the text of what had been "agreed upon," again needlessly and fruitlessly. A curious thesis was thereafter put across, that

3. See Appendix 3.
4. Khwaja Moinuddin Chishti was also popularly known as Khwaja Garib Nawaz.

if another meeting were now to be held between India and Pakistan, the starting point would have to be the "piece of paper" that Abdul Sattar and I had worked on together. This was truly curious. How could that paper validate what had been done in Agra if it had not actually been done? There were, however, some things, albeit unstated, that both India and Pakistan post-Agra did agree upon. The principal one was that grandstanding was not the best way to inaugurate an India-Pakistan summit.

Democracy under Direct Attack

There are certain dates that I have never forgotten. Less than five weeks after Agra, a great tragedy occurred, a kind of forewarning, as if all that had already happened were not alarming enough. A stalwart fighter for freedom, a valiant soldier of Islam and of Afghanistan who had resolutely stood up against the invading Soviet troops and later the depredations of the Taliban, was assassinated at Khoja Baha-ud-din, Afghanistan, just outside and to the north of the Panjsheer Valley. Ahmad Shah Massood had agreed to be interviewed by two journalists, unaware that they were assassins in disguise. This was on September 9, 2001. In August, Massood had visited India as my guest, and had stayed with us for several days. I had spent a very useful two hours or so in conversation with him one morning, discussing the prevailing situation in Afghanistan in some detail. I was shocked and greatly saddened at this loss. Just two days later, on September 11, I was working in the Ministry of External Affairs when T. C. A. Raghavan, who was helping me with my work in those days, rushed in and informed me that a terrible event had just occurred in New York. He conveyed the essence of what the two aircraft had done to the Twin Towers, and told me about the other incidents at the Pentagon and the flight that apparently had been headed for the White House but had been forced to crash into a rural field in Somerset County, Pennsylvania. I was instinctively horrified. This was an attack by terrorists on what had hitherto been viewed as an impregnable fortress, the United States. Those great symbols of America New York, the World Trade Center, economy and commerce; the Pentagon, military power; the White House, the seat of authority—had all been simultaneously attacked or threatened. Instantly I telephoned the U.S. ambassador, Robert Blackwill, and conveyed my own sympathy and that of the government and people of India. I also said that India was ready to help, in whatever manner we could.

Some months later, I traveled to the United States on official business, carrying with me, as a gesture, jars containing water from each of the major rivers of India and soil from each of our states. In New York I presented these to Mayor Rudolph W. Giuliani, as symbols of India's commitment to this fight against terrorism and our solidarity with all the victims of this great menace. My request was that these jars be buried in the foundation of whatever would eventually be built in place of the Twin Towers. I was in Washington when, on October 1, 2001, early in the morning at about 7:30, I got a call from Delhi telling me that the prime minister wanted to speak to me right away. When a prime minister calls and wishes to speak, it is obviously an urgent matter. I asked the operator in Delhi what had happened. He very briefly informed me of developments in Jammu and Kashmir, upon which, instead of immediately returning the prime minister's call, I asked the operator to first connect me to the PM's principal secretary, Brajesh Mishra. He came on the line and succinctly informed me that the Legislative Assembly of Jammu and Kashmir had been attacked that morning in Srinagar, and that the chief minister, Farooq Abdullah, and his colleagues had escaped only because they had left the building moments earlier. The prime minister was very upset by this and wanted to express his sense of outrage to the American president. I told Mishra that it would be best if the prime minister did not speak to me. He would no doubt be extremely upset, and knowing that I was in Washington, he would ask me to prepare the ground for this task; but I must caution against it, for in any event, I was due to meet Secretary of State Colin Powell and National Security Advisor Condoleezza Rice later. Brajesh Mishra then said that he had already spoken to Condoleezza Rice. "What does the prime minister wish to do?" I asked. He wanted to speak to President George W. Bush, to tell him "how aggrieved we are," that "our patience is now running out." I advised against all this, suggesting that I would do all that needed to be done, and that it would be preferable to do it this way than to have the prime minister speak to the president.

Even the sketchiest possible outline of what happened in Srinagar that day made for horrifying reading. A car bomb was detonated just outside the Jammu and Kashmir State Assembly, killing at least twenty-seven people. It was a dastardly attack on a democratic institution. A terrorist organization, Jaish-e-Mohammad, had claimed responsibility. It named as one of the terrorists Wajahat Hussain from Peshawar, Pakistan. This claim was made from Pakistan within minutes of the attack. The Jaish-e-Mohammad had been created mainly from the cadre of the Harkat-ul-Mujahideen by its former ideologue, Masood Azhar. It was well known that Masood Azhar was the general secretary of Harkat-ul-Ansar later renamed Harkat-ul-Mujahideen which, with Osama bin Laden, was a co-signatory to the notorious call for a Holy War against all Americans, Christians, and Jews. India was also listed as an enemy. I pointed out the enormity of the attack to both Colin Powell and Condoleezza Rice. President Bush dropped in during my meeting with Rice. After this visit, the second time that I had met the president and his team since his swearing-in, I returned to Delhi on October 2, 2001, greatly satisfied. There was already a much greater recognition of the demon of terrorism, which India had been facing and cautioning against for so many years now. A month or so later, Parliament was due to meet.

Parliament in Peril

It did so about the third week of November. My office in Parliament was then in room 27. The entrances to Parliament are identified by their gate numbers, and my office was the closest room to gate number 12. On December 13, 2001, I was working at my desk, Parliament having just adjourned for the day; it was approaching noon. Suddenly I heard the unmistakable sound of rapid fire from an automatic weapon. I was not disturbed, thinking rather cynically that perhaps some sentry on duty, sitting on a stool, had dozed off in the soothing warmth of a balmy sun, and had inadvertently pulled the trigger. This was followed almost immediately by what clearly was the sound of a grenade burst. "Aha!" I thought to myself. "So it's finally happening." This truly was my first reaction. Raghavan rushed in. "What is it, Sir?" he asked with some anxiety. I said with concern now, not any flippancy, "Raghavan, I am afraid that what I have long feared has finally happened. This is surely a terrorist attack." The Parliament of India, the seat of my country's democracy, was indeed under attack. The first gate to be targeted was number 12, barely twenty feet from my office. A valiant member of the Watch and Ward Staff, stationed just outside the gate, was killed; the other, acting with some presence of mind, instantly bolted the gate. (Members of the Parliamentary Watch and Ward Staff have never carried arms within the precincts of India's national legislature. They will not do so in the future, either. This is an essential aspect of parliamentary propriety.) My diary notes record for that day:

> And thus, unusually, I record briefly: 13 Dec. Around 11.40 or so, the House had got adjourned over some stupidity about a C&AG Report. I was in room 27, doing something routine, when there was a rattle of fire. So it has at last happened. Booms of grenade bursts followed, more automatic fire, Parliament doors shut, etc.

Later I had walked out—saw the bodies, met the NSG commandant, Hoshiar Singh, and his officers. The rest is history. But the
aftermath of it is the current challenge. The crisis with Pakistan is
deepening. Calling back the high commissioner from Islamabad
is only the first step. From here where?

Saw the sun go down on 2001. Diplomatically the screw tight-
ened on Pakistan—more action has been taken by the US—the
public mood remains very angry and itches for action. But is that
to drive policy? Is the street to determine policy? And what is the
right thing for me to do in these testing times?

The rest of what happened has been recounted many times. As reported
officially to the Parliament by Home Minister L. K. Advani:

> [This] terrorist assault on the very bastion of our democracy was
> clearly aimed at wiping out the country's top political leadership.
> It is a tribute to our security personnel that they rose to the occa-
> sion and succeeded in averting what could have been a national
> catastrophe. In so doing they made the supreme sacrifice for which
> the country would always remain indebted to them.
>
> It is now evident that the terrorist assault on the Parliament
> House was executed jointly by Pak-based and supported terrorist
> outfits, namely, Lashkar-e-Taiba and Jaish-e-Mohammad. These
> two organisations are known to derive their support and patron-
> age from Pak ISI. The investigation so far carried out by the police
> shows that all the five terrorists who formed the suicide squad
> were Pakistani nationals. All of them were killed on the spot and
> their Indian associates have since been arrested.
>
> The investigation at this stage indicates that the five Pakistani
> terrorists entered the Parliament House complex at about 11:40 AM
> in an Ambassador car bearing registration number DL-3CJ 1527
> and moved towards building gate number 12 when it encountered
> the car-cade of the vice-president of India which was parked at
> gate number 11. One of the members of the Parliament House
> Watch and Ward Staff, Shri Jagdish Prasad Yadav, became suspi-
> cious about the identity of the car and immediately ran after it. The
> car was forced to turn and in the process it hit the vice-president's
> car. When challenged by the security personnel present on the spot
> all the five terrorists jumped out of the car and started firing indis-

criminately. The Delhi Police personnel attached with the vice-president's security as also the personnel of CRPF and ITBP on duty immediately returned the fire. . . . An alarm was raised. . . . The terrorists ran towards gate number 12 and then to gate number 1 of the Parliament House Building. One terrorist was shot dead by the security forces at gate number 1 and in the process the explosives wrapped around his body exploded. The remaining four terrorists turned back and reached gate number 9 of the building. Three of them were gunned down there. The fifth terrorist ran towards gate number 5 where he also was gunned down.

Interrogation of the accused persons has revealed that Afzal was the main coordinator who was assigned this task by a Pakistani national, Gazi Baba of Jaish-e-Mohammad. Afzal had earlier been trained in a camp run by Pak ISI at Muzaffarabad in Pak-occupied Kashmir.

The incident once again establishes that terrorism in India is the handiwork of Pakistan-based terrorist outfits known to derive their support and sustenance from Pak ISI. The hijacking of IC-814 flight to Kandahar, the terrorist intrusion into the Red Fort and attack on Jammu and Kashmir Legislative Assembly complex at Srinagar on October 1 this year were masterminded and executed by militant outfits at the behest of the ISI. Lashkar-e-Taiba and Jaish-e-Mohammad in particular have been in the forefront in organising terrorist violence in our country. The Pakistan high commissioner in India was summoned to the Ministry of External Affairs and issued a verbal demarche demanding that Islamabad take action against the two terrorist outfits involved in the attack on the Parliament House.

Last week's attack on Parliament is undoubtedly the most audacious, and also the most alarming act of terrorism in the nearly two-decade-long history of Pakistan-sponsored terrorism in India. This time the terrorists and their mentors across the border had the temerity to try to wipe out the entire political leadership of India, as represented in our multi-party Parliament. Naturally, it is time for all of us in this august House, and all of us in the country, to ponder why the terrorists and their backers tried to raise the stakes so high, particularly at a time when Pakistan is claiming to be a part of the international coalition against terrorism.

The events of December 13, 2001, outraged India. The nation clamored for immediate retaliatory action. I was not sure if that was what our response ought to be, but I was in the minority; and I did not continue to constantly repeat myself. Of course, statements of outrage came from all quarters of the world, from all political parties. President Musharraf, too, condemned the attack. As for the terrorists, all five of them had been killed, and all five had come from Pakistan. Indeed, one of them had carried a cell phone of Karachi origin, and had used it to call a number in that city only minutes before invading Parliament. It was this outrage that finally resulted in the standoff of 2002, which in turn caused anxiety in some international quarters, and generated fears of a nuclear war—fears that were totally unfounded, as subsequent events demonstrated. What we did adopt was coercive diplomacy, a combination of diplomatic and military pressure. Despite Pakistan's strenuous efforts, the most representative election was then conducted in the state of Jammu and Kashmir in the months of September and October 2002. The long standoff, with full troop mobilization between India and Pakistan, was thereafter called off by Prime Minister Vajpayee, who affirmed that "we achieved the aim that we set out to achieve."

Afghanistan, Two Decembers Removed

But this is getting ahead of the story. As a consequence of 9/11, Pakistan was presented with a charter of very stark choices, black or white options: either stand up unequivocally against terrorism and be counted, or face the international consequences. It stood up to be counted, and in a matter of months the Taliban regime in Afghanistan had been removed. President Hamid Karzai was to be sworn in on December 22, 2001, and I was to represent India. I would not have missed this event for anything, and so I flew to Bagram on the afternoon of December 22, jotting in my diary:

> Similar to other important happenings this year, 22 Dec. shall also feature prominently—for on this day the Northern Alliance government was sworn in; and it is to attend that ceremony that I flew into Kabul early this morning, and after it now fly homewards.
>
> A slight haze, cool but comfortable, a 0700 hrs takeoff. The sun rose behind us and by the time the first of the rays touched the treeless mountains (after Kohat, in Pakistan) of Afghanistan only an hour had elapsed. A dusting of snow all around the higher slopes. Landed at Bagram a shattered, war-torn land, cratered, carcasses of MiGs strewn all over: So this is that Bagram, it is across

this field that desultory artillery duels had taken place and which had become the photo opportunity area after Oct. 7, and on the western hills of which the B-52s had pounded so much arsenal.

Propelled into Kabul airfield, heart in mouth in a helicopter, which, I was told, "was late Ahmed Shah's own." I was not reassured by that piece of intelligence; my flying companions smoked with joyous insouciance next to the auxiliary fuel tank!

Kabul: Was asked, "Excellency, have you been to Afghanistan earlier?" "Almost to the day, two years back," I had responded looking directly at the questioner. Light dawned upon him—suddenly—then. "Ah," he said. "Kandahar—hijack—1999." I had only smiled but also reflected inwardly on the inscrutable ways of the workings of fate. From Kandahar to Kabul, in two years, this has been both a personal odyssey and the fruition of a policy, possible only by immense Grace.

And thus Kabul, though brief and hurried and limited, gave me a feel of itself. A curious mixture of west Rajputana and Russian heaviness, and an attempt to lay avenues and create boulevards in French style and fashion. You can transfer the design of a road or a building, but can you of a people? Their history and culture and their entire inheritance? Or their ethos?

The ceremony was worth all this trouble. It was alive, it was authentic, colorful as only this part of the world can be, dramatic and emotional, full of enthusiasm and disorder and confusion and camaraderie. It ran only about 90 minutes late, which considering everything (and not at all patronizingly) was a remarkable achievement.

And thus from Bagram, with the comforting order of the IAF, back to India.

Early during Operation Parakram the name given to the mobilization of Indian troops following the attack on Parliament on December 13, 2001 Raghavan had asked me about our own aims. I remember the question, coming as it did just after the crisis, because I had had to postpone a rather leisurely tour of Kenya, Tanzania, and Mauritius, with some game parks thrown in! But back to the aims. These I had written on a scrap of paper: "to defeat cross-border infiltration/terrorism without conflict; to contain the national mood of 'teach Pak a lesson'; and in the event of war, to destroy and degrade Pakistan's war fighting capabilities." In this I faced two, really three, challenges. The internal was the most taxing, for it involved carrying conviction with colleagues. This sapped my internal resolve and resources. An adjunct of this was to carry the three service chiefs with me, also convincingly, and to get them to recognize "restraint" (in that context) as a strategic asset, for avoiding conflict. Again, this was not easy. The chiefs so wanted a chance, "to have a crack" at it, as the military would put it—I not only had to persuade them, but also to convince them otherwise.

There was then the external challenge. I had to carry conviction with and thus carry the opinion of the international community. At the same time, India had to contain Pakistan diplomatically and yet continue to defeat terrorism on the ground. The third challenge was to convey the country's mood, to contain its belligerence, its desire for revenge and retaliation, but to give it a sense of achievement, of having diplomatically defeated the enemy.

Looking back, there were discernible, recognizable gains on all these fronts. These aims were, if not fully, at least substantially achieved. To some degree, success was a function of India's ability to work with the United States. That signals, inevitably, a new chapter, although even a brief look back informs us encouragingly of what was done.

The process that Prime Minister Vajpayee started with the Lahore bus journey of 1999 continued to move forward, to gather pace, and to be gradually accepted by all. To "peace," however you spell that word, there is no alternative, and this was slowly becoming accepted in Pakistan, too. Clearly there were setbacks, but each setback became the springboard for a renewed and more zealous effort. Agra 2001 resulted in SAARC Islamabad of 2004. What was earlier treated as "deflective diplomacy" by Pakistan became milestones in improving relations between Pakistan and India. Some infiltration continues, and terrorists still cross the borders, but the guns on the LOC have finally fallen silent, after years of booming constantly. Pakistan is now endeavoring valiantly to adopt a new role, a new mantle, a development that I watch expectantly; it is now, once again, a committed ally of the United States. Is this truly the dawn of a new day?

9

Engaging the Natural Ally

Uncle Sam's Cavil

That the nuclear tests of May 11 and 13, 1998, would cause a storm of protests was patent. We also had a fair assessment of the possible reactions of various countries and regional groupings; some certainly would be more like a formal re-registering of concerns than any forceful assertion of a new principle. A large segment of the international community had already accepted India as a de facto nuclear-weapons-capable country. Most felt that because India was by nature a status quo-ist country, explosives testing and (implicitly) weaponization did not constitute the announcement of a newfound aggressive design. There were several countries that congratulated us—although not publicly—expressing sentiments such as "Only India could have done it"; "You have broken a monopoly"; and "This is a great relief to us." Reactions of the P-5, notwithstanding their communiqué, were also varied. Some were strident, at times almost intemperate; others were somewhat modulated.

The American reaction included several elements. The principal objection arose from what Washington saw as a challenge to the nonproliferation regime that the United States and other nuclear weapons states had established, primarily to preserve their own monopoly. India had not heeded the "No Entry" sign they had posted. Meetings of the P-5 and the G-8 that followed the tests saw orchestrated condemnation under American initiative; though some of the P-5—Russia and France, for instance—were not fully in agreement with the imposition of punitive measures. While in Birmingham, England, attending the G-8 summit of industrialized nations, in a joint BBC television interview with Prime Minister Tony Blair, President Clinton painted a nightmare scenario of escalating conflict in South Asia. "It is a nutty way to go," he said. "It is not the way to chart the future."

That the United States should react as if piqued did not take me by total surprise; it perhaps found its inability to detect the tests in advance more troubling than the tests themselves. National Security Advisor Sandy Berger and State

Department spokesman James Rubin alleged, totally without foundation, that New Delhi had "deliberately misled" the United States in "twenty or more meetings," by giving "assurances" and "guarantees" that it would "never" exercise its nuclear option. These accusations were so wrong that Shri S. Mukherjee of the Ministry of External Affairs immediately and sharply refuted them:

> We have noted statements of senior US Administration officials that they have been "seriously misled" by Indian interlocutors. We completely disagree with this characterization of the discussions between the two countries. India has refrained from commenting so far, keeping in mind the confidentiality of diplomatic exchanges. It has, however, now become necessary to refute this allegation. We have welcomed the broader interaction with the US over the last several months. During these discussions we have conveyed our readiness to work with the US government to deepen and broaden our mutually beneficial relations. . . . In the twenty or more meetings referred to by US Spokesman, India never gave any assurances or guarantees. On the contrary, it was clearly pointed out that no assurances can be given.

India took particular exception to a remark that Rubin made about Home Minister L. K. Advani in response to a reporter's question at a U.S. Department of State daily press briefing on May 19:

> Let me say that yesterday's remarks by Home Minister Advani, like India's recent nuclear test—these are remarks about urging Pakistan to back off on Kashmir, which I thought you were going to ask me about—seems to indicate that India is foolishly and dangerously increasing tensions with its neighbors and is indifferent to world opinion. We call upon India to exercise great caution in its statements and actions at this particularly sensitive time, with emotions running high.

The official ministry spokesman responded sharply once again:

> We have taken note of the remarks made by James R Rubin, spokesman of the State Department of the United States, regarding a senior cabinet minister of the government of India. We had earlier drawn attention to intemperate outbursts by the State Department spokesman. Such language is not used in allusion to senior political leaders

of any country, even those with whom there may be disagreements. We would expect that courtesy, which is standard practice in responsible diplomatic communication, would be extended to India.

Notwithstanding such remarks, there were several senior American dignitaries and members of the U.S. media who did not view this development as a disaster. Notable were the reported remarks by Energy Secretary Bill Richardson, who had just been to Delhi: "Nuclear tests by India were accelerated to a certain extent by Pakistan's launching of its Ghauri missile." Former president Jimmy Carter offered a similar response: "Washington had no moral right to criticize India when it had 8,000 odd nuclear warheads."

In an address to the Indian American Friendship Council in Washington, D.C., on July 28, U.S. Representative Benjamin Gilman, chairman of the House International Relations Committee, and Democratic minority leader Richard Gephardt described themselves as "mystified" by the administration's double standard toward "totalitarian China" and "democratic India." They accused the administration of pandering to Beijing, overlooking its nuclear proliferation activities with Pakistan, while penalizing New Delhi for its nuclear tests. Gilman noted, "India is located in a tough neighborhood," with Burma to its east, ruled by a military junta; "authoritarian Pakistan" to its west; and Tibet to the north, "occupied by totalitarian China."

Senator Daniel Patrick Moynihan, who had spent time in Delhi as the U.S. ambassador to India, was always consistent and clear-visioned about our country. He had already advised President Clinton that India, like China, must be allowed to join the NPT and CTBT as a "nuclear power." He noted that "the political leadership in India as much as said they were going to begin testing. There is a tendency at the State Department to say, 'Gee, the CIA never told us.'"

Nevertheless, we knew that economic sanctions would follow; they were absorbed when imposed, and all needed steps were taken. An unsavory aspect of the economic sanctions was the restrictions placed on travel by our scientists, who were thus needlessly prevented from interacting with their American counterparts.[1] India's bilateral lenders, including

1. The U.S. administration canceled the visas of seven Indian scientists working in the United States and indicated that it was reviewing the status of another seventy-five scientists living there, despite warnings by senior U.S. scientists that restrictions on the free exchange of scientific information would be a dangerous precedent. In November, the Department of Energy followed suit, blacklisting and imposing sanctions on sixty-three scientific establishments, including agricultural and medical institutions. In addition, the Department of Commerce blacklisted 240 public and private firms and their subsidiaries.

Japan and Germany, were persuaded not to give us loans. Washington also worked on multilateral agencies such as the Asian Development Bank, the World Bank, and the International Monetary Fund to suspend all loans and grants to India. In consequence, the World Bank alone withheld loans totaling around $3 billion, all for the development of the country's infrastructure. Opinion in India saw in this a lack of evenhandedness on the part of the Clinton administration, which allowed $5.5 billion in IMF funds to go to an admittedly economically beleaguered Pakistan in November 1998, while simultaneously blocking similar funding for India. This was seen as yet another illustration of American bias. Assistant Secretary of State Rick Inderfurth justified this "additional flexibility" toward Pakistan on the grounds of a different interpretation of U.S. laws. I often wondered whether the United States was becoming increasingly riled by the knowledge that these sanctions were going to have no significant impact on India. In any event, sanctions can work only if citizens of that country are affected in their pockets, if essentials of daily use are rendered too costly or too scarce. Governments can then ride such sanctions, for if there is no pressure from the citizens, sanctions become merely an ineffective political statement. This the United States perhaps did not appreciate. In any event, there was, by then, a huge proliferation of sanctions being imposed by the world's lone superpower, thus devaluing even their political message. At that point, the United States had some fifty to ninety countries under its sanctions regime. Some commentators in India remarked acidly that Pakistan had been "let off the hook" and India "punished," and that this should "not be acceptable to any government in India, least of all to the Vajpayee government." I did not entirely share this view: an economically crippled Pakistan would be an additional worry for India, not a help.

For all these and several other reasons, the first mission of managing the international post-Pokhran fallout obviously had to be with the United States. Its was the preeminent global voice; the United States was the premier power, the "hyperpower" in Hubert Védrine's words, though this term often irritated the State Department. Besides, the United States was so clearly in the forefront of this entire "disapproval" campaign against India that unless it altered its stance, others would not do so, either. But it was not "approval" of the tests that I was seeking; I found the very notion unwarranted and patronizing. What I was searching for was an intellectual understanding, an acceptance of India's underlying rationale for Pokhran II. Nor was there any kind of deal or quid pro quo;

none was sought, none offered. What I sought—and I often shared this objective with Deputy Secretary of State Strobe Talbott, a man blessed with outstanding intellectual ability, transparent integrity, and an incredible ability to see the other person's point of view—was a "harmonization of positions between the United States and India, as they evolved through a harmonization of respective views." This was obviously a task of immense complexity, particularly because the views expressed by them were so divergent. It was not as if India, totally unrealistically, were seeking to get the United States to alter its position. Clearly that could not be; equally, the idea that India would abandon or resile from its own stated positions was also a nonstarter. Despite all this, if it was still "harmonization" that I worked for, then it could be achieved only through a degree of mutual acceptance, an accommodation of some components of the other's position. This involved moving from a position of rigid immovability to "flexion" (as in advanced equitation), but that too could be accomplished only in areas that were not of overriding national interest. There was another, unstated factor in my mind. Unquestionably, the ultimate factor relating to national security that would give India some muscle was its economy. India's economic development could not advance if relations with the United States continued to be so adversarial; we had to cooperate, to work together. To my mind, that was—and remains—a national security imperative for India. Thus we needed first to engage with the United States. But before that could happen, a practical issue had to be resolved: Did the U.S. even want to engage with India?

A cautious sounding was made by the MEA, through our already beleaguered mission in Washington. Here we were very ably manned by one of India's most senior civil servants. Ambassador Naresh Chandra, an appointee of the P. V. Narasimha Rao government (1991–96), was not a career diplomat, but he was an admirable choice. His deceptively mild exterior, combined with a circumlocutory but always civil style of making the sharpest of retorts—a characteristic both of Avadh, his home region, and of courtly Rajasthan, where he started his career in the Indian Administrative Service—is an attribute that professional diplomats simply cannot acquire through training alone. I found Naresh Chandra's presence in Washington reassuring. The United States responded without delay: yes, they would accept a visit by me; it would be hosted at the appropriate level—an aspect that the protocol-bound ministry had insisted upon, but which was never an issue for me personally. I sought the substance, not just a ceremonial form. Thus, when some futile and empty criticism was voiced back home about my interacting at a level other than what protocol demanded, I dismissed it as irrelevant and petty.

Hang-ups of History

To my mind, the core of the challenge, for both the United States and India, lay not so much in the technicalities of the nonproliferation debate as in the lingering reminders of the past, in those obstinate and deep shadows of the Cold War years that simply would not go away—not for India, and not for the U.S., either. With the collapse of the Soviet Union, the United States had global primacy over the entire range of the national power spectrum: military, industrial, economic, scientific, technological, and even cultural. A decade earlier, through diplomacy, it had achieved a long-sought goal—the disintegration of the other superpower. In his State of the Nation address on April 25, 2005, President Vladimir Putin called this disintegration "the biggest geopolitical catastrophe of the century" and declared it disastrous for Russia, but for America it was a great victory. In the succeeding period, therefore, the United States adopted the basics of the diplomatic style that had served its purpose so well: of enforcing its will; of dominating the situation, either singly or by forming or forcing into existence a coalition of countries.

In such a unique position of primacy, never before experienced by humankind, one great anxiety remains for the United States: its own security, and this despite its total and unquestioned supremacy in all spheres, including the military. Its ultimate national goal, however, is more than just supremacy: the U.S. aspires to the untouchable safety of inviolability. In addition to terrorism, the principal factor underlying this continuing anxiety of the U.S. is the capability, whether real or potential, of any country outside the P-5 to develop a nuclear or ballistic missile. All five members of the P-5 now accept American primacy—even China and France, which can sometimes be difficult. Those five nations are now the "haves," and the lean and hungry looks of the "have-nots" trouble them equally. The challenge to the United States' agenda of primacy lies first and foremost in being able to prevent, and then to minimize, the consequences of this possible "globalization of force," the lack of acceptance by other countries of this Washington-enforced status quo. Plus, there is the threat posed by emergent non-state actors who confront the U.S., as well countries such as India, through an unassailable power: that of suicide. They challenge not just America's but all established theories of power, of state sovereignties, and of the existing monopoly of the state over weapons of mass destruction. "A democracy," if that be the word, "of destructive forces" is now in existence, and this "nihilistic democracy" is dedicated to the total destruction of the existing (bourgeois) democracies and world order. It has made its presence felt by posing questions for which there are no answers. How can you defeat something that is not defeated by death? It was in this scenario that I was to engage with the United States.

But this was not the sum total of the baggage I carried. India, too, lived with so many remnants of the past, burdens that interfered with its vision, its clarity of judgment. History and its many humiliations, the weight of so many centuries of servitude, has imparted to India such an acute sense of hearing that it often hears insults where none are intended. In diplomatic discourse and conduct, therefore, India has tended to carry many chips on its shoulder, almost always moralistic, needlessly arrogant, and argumentative, an attitude it mistakenly views as an assertion of national pride. India did not then, and still does not, accept that there can be no compensation for the many injustices of history. The world is preoccupied with today; it addresses the uncertainties of tomorrow as best it can—not for it the real or imaginary errors and injustices of the centuries of yesterdays. Yet in India, this mentality has remained, a prejudice handed down with two roots. The first is from Jawaharlal Nehru and his anglicized condescension—in the words of his nephew B. K. Nehru, he "looked down somewhat arrogantly on the 'loudness' of American money."[2] This personal whim influenced policy—as it does always and everywhere—and resulted in needlessly arrogant and abrasive posturing by subsequent generations of India's foreign policy managers. The other was, again, so obviously a continuing policy prejudice, this time toward the United States—its policies and postures; its alliances both regional and global; its tilts and military assistance programs—almost always to India's detriment, and causing grave harm to our bilateral relations. After the Second World War, the American policy of containment effectively amounted to a containment of India, too; such has certainly been the case since 1952. As a leading nonaligned country, India became suspect in American eyes, through that simple "You are either with us or against us" formulation. Support for Pakistan brought no stability, because the foundation of U.S. policy in South Asia became simplistic: "parity between India and Pakistan." This policy of being an "offshore balancer" in South Asia by always tilting toward Pakistan resulted in giving that country an artificial and untenable support base. It cut both ways: when the American support was there,

2. B. K. Nehru, *Nice Guys Finish Second* (New Delhi: Viking, 1997), pp. 238, 366.

it destabilized the region by becoming essentially anti-India; and when it was not there, Pakistan would flounder and go into a downward spiral of internal turmoil. This policy of promoting an artificial and unsustainable parity has continued to contribute to instability in South Asia. The United States must bear some responsibility for conflicts in the region.

All these issues weigh heavily on the minds of Indian citizens, as well as the makers and implementers of policy. For example, India has found it more difficult to forget the forays of the USS *Enterprise* in the Bay of Bengal in 1971 than, say, even the Chinese invasion of 1962. Why? Entirely because of expectations on the part of the United States, its society, and the democratic nature of its nationhood. And also because at the root of this psychological selectivity lies the indelible imprint of so many past humiliations inflicted by Western imperialism, of the agony of servitude, of the layered silt of subjugation, loot, and societal trials, over the course of so many centuries. But this attitude is not only an Indian oddity; it is very widely shared, which is why a considerable psychological barrier still exists to negotiations, to close treaty or other relationships with the Western powers. Russia benefits from this because of its Eurasian geographical spread and the past policies of the Soviet Union as the "champion and protector" of the "Third World." "Champion," "protector," of the "Third World"? In a sense, such attitudes and words demonstrate precisely that "deafness of the West," which grates on the eastern ear with its offensiveness. The replacement of "Third" by the somewhat better-sounding "developing"—as a synonym for "underdeveloped," "retarded," or "deficient" in some essential sense?—is a belated and insufficient amendment.

The psychological scars of imperial servitude are so pervasive that they often impede rational negotiations and cause offense to be taken where none is meant, not even in the naturally heavy-footed manners of the West. China, Egypt, and India are, I think, classic examples of the psychologically scarred victims of history. Japan carries the scars deep within the folds of its national memory, layering them with overabundant material gains. But the scars are still there, and any incautious removal of those deliberately arranged layers of willful amnesia immediately rankles Japan's sense of national pride. China, harboring memories of the insulting treaties of the nineteenth century, now expressly demands "equality," and the gross materialism of the West provides that instantly, for the West has always been acquiescent to the demands of those with money. This conveys a message to others, perhaps mistaken, of what works with the West. A deep-rooted sense of history, of cultural and civilizational longevity, inspires (not just influences) the thinking of countries such as Egypt and India.[3] Pride and the public face are so important as to become an essential diplomatic quotient. Outer trappings are often as important as, if not more so than, the inner core of mutual understandings and agreements. That is why India is always so quick to react to observations, be they real or imaginary, intended or otherwise, because these acute sensitivities date back to well before Independence.

I could cite several examples, but one alone ought to suffice. In 1993, a diplomatic crisis arose during a background briefing for journalists when the new American assistant secretary for South Asia, Robin Lynn Raphel, noted in reply to a question that the United States did not recognize the 1947 document by which the late maharajah had ceded Jammu and Kashmir to India "as meaning that Kashmir is forevermore an integral part of India." Indian reaction was instantaneous and naturally vitriolic. This sentiment became so strong that Kenneth C. Brill, acting ambassador in Delhi, felt it necessary to answer the charges with a statement in a prominent newspaper. This feeling was then greatly accentuated when President Clinton, in February 1994, expressed concern at "the abuse of human rights [by the Indian Army] in Kashmir." A torrent of protest followed. There was a more topical source of Indian grievance—a sense that the Clinton administration, like all earlier administrations, was indifferent to India and was deliberately working to relegate India's international standing. In April 1993, Thomas Pickering, a senior American career diplomat, was transferred to Moscow after only a few months as ambassador in Delhi. His successor, former New York congressman Stephen Solarz, was then held up for more than a year, reportedly on account of background checks by the Federal Bureau of Investigation. By having no ambassador in Delhi for all those months, the United States was sending a message. India read it as indifference. But perhaps it was not just a sign; perhaps India did indeed rank low in American estimation in 1993–94.

In April 1994, Deputy Secretary of State Strobe Talbott was assigned to do some troubleshooting, to signal that the Clinton administration was not intentionally neglecting the region. Talbott invited Prime Minister P. V. Narasimha Rao to Washington, and requested approval of a senior diplomat, Under Secretary of Defense Frank Wisner, as ambassador to India. "Talbott's manner was exemplary: He said just the right things."[4] That was the first

3. This thought has been detailed very effectively by Raymond Cohen in *Negotiating across Cultures: International Communication in an Interdependent World* (Washington, D.C.: United States Institute of Peace, 1997), pp. 48–49.
4. Ibid.

time I had come across Strobe Talbott's name in the Indian context, a situation in which he was "engaging India." I remarked upon the restrained quality of his intervention. I did not, of course, know him at that point. I *did* know of the sensational coup he had scored earlier with his English translation of Nikita Khrushchev's memoirs. (Many years later, Strobe and I met in London for one of our rounds of talks. When he came to the hotel where I was staying, he revealed that it was the same hotel where, in a "converted maid's room," he had labored in secret for more than forty-eight hours, preparing a précis of those memoirs.)

Carrying my thoughts, I left for the United States, with no illusions about the enormity of the difficulties that lay ahead—or, for that matter, about what lay behind at home: opinionated views, prejudice, sheer hostility, and a propensity to remain imprisoned in the past, as against shedding the irrelevancies of inherited thought and adopting the kind of pragmatic realism that would enable us to meet today's challenges. That was my task: "to meld together contrasting opinions into a single, generally accepted viewpoint," to paraphrase a felicitous phrase of Kissinger's. India's added domestic baggage, and that of the United States, too, often hindered efforts. Such would perhaps not be the case if the two countries were not committed democracies, each with a demanding citizenry, an active and questioning opposition, an overactive and irreverent press, and that vast uncharted and mercurial ocean called "public opinion." It is perilous to conduct foreign policy in the full glare of public scrutiny, but that often is unavoidable. When it comes to delivering results, however, to getting things done in the subtle realm of international affairs, constant public scrutiny—almost always accompanied by ceaselessly critical comment—is not the most suitable accompaniment. I was fully aware of all this, of course, but not of the many pitfalls that lay ahead. I found, and painfully, that the road had many potholes, that the questioning would go to the extent of doubting my very bona fides, of searching constantly for my "true" motives. This made my task all the more trying. The very first assumption made was that as the Indian interlocutor, I was somehow out to "sell the country," that I was "abandoning national interests"; or, still more colorfully, that I was a CIA agent or was fast on the way to becoming one! At first I found such insinuations deeply wounding and sought to rebut each and every one. Then their sheer excessiveness converted them into absurd irrelevancies, and finally into comments worthy only of ridicule; amusement, perhaps occasionally, but no more. Yet all this is still very much a reality, and it will continue to exist so long as the entrapment of the past remains. Why does this tendency manifest itself in the case of the United States so much more than in the case of the United Kingdom, France, or Germany? The Indian public continues to hold Russia in high esteem despite its having been transformed almost beyond recognition. A partial explanation lies in the evolution of relations between India and the United States since 1947. Yet if any harmonization of positions was to be achieved, we first needed to free ourselves of this residue of the past. Such residue existed in America, too, ancient cobwebs in the corridors of decision-making systems.

Of central relevance to us was the Clinton administration's attitude. At a joint news conference with President Clinton in Washington on May 19, 1994, Prime Minister Narasimha Rao said: "The president and I agreed that we have an unprecedented opportunity to free India-US bilateral relations from the distortions induced by the Cold War, to look for areas of converging interest in the changed international situation, and work together for our mutual benefit." As subsequent events proved, however, the United States was less than willing to discard its Cold War prism, not showing any enhanced sensitivity to India's security and economic interests, certainly not with any discernible regard for "mutual benefit." Washington perhaps did not realize at the time that a restructuring of bilateral relations was necessary for both sides. As a result, when another Indian prime minister, Atal Bihari Vajpayee, went to the United States four years later, he had to repeat the theme of "mutual respect, shared values, and congruence of interests." In his address to the Asia Society in New York on September 28, 1998, he went even further: "Indo-US ties based on equality and mutuality of interests are going to be the mainstay of tomorrow's stable, democratic world order." At the same time, Prime Minister Vajpayee identified, accurately and concisely, what was wrong with the relationship:

> We in India believe that Indo-US relations, restructured on an equal footing, configure the key element in the architecture of tomorrow's democratised world order. However, I must confess to being baffled by the unsatisfactory current state of relations between our two countries. . . . We are the two largest democracies in the world, and have similar political cultures, a free press and the rule of law. We both have a tradition of private enterprise and free markets. . . . Above all, I see no conflict of interests between the two countries in the foreseeable future. And yet all of us here would agree that the full potential of our relationship has not been realised in the last 50 years. . . . I have been trying to analyse the

reasons and I think I can at least indicate where the shoe pinches us. First and foremost, it is American reluctance to accept us as a responsible member of the international community.

Whether it is regional arrangements dealing with Afghanistan, where we have vital security and other interests; cooperative arrangements in the Asia-Pacific region, where we have a positive, moderating and stabilising role to play; global organisations like the UN Security Council or the discriminatory Non-Proliferation Treaty: in all of these the United States does not appreciate and accommodate India's interests and concerns.

Secondly, we have been subjected to technology denials virtually from the time of our Independence. Our own export control regimes are extremely stringent and there has been no leakage of equipment or technology from India. Despite this, we find the US unwilling to accommodate us in terms of technology transfers.

Similarly, on South Asian issues where our supreme national interests are involved, we encounter policy approaches from America that go contrary to our basic irreducible security needs.

An even more serious case of incomprehension in India are the public statements made by American leaders where our sensitivities are involved. The statement issued on South Asia during President Clinton's visit to China, and American attempts at putting pressure on Russia to end its defence and scientific cooperation with India, are two prime examples of recent vintage.[5]
For democratic governments like ours, which desire closer understanding with the USA, it becomes extremely difficult to move forward in the face of such public declaration.

Separated by the Hyphen

The first Clinton administration (1993–97) had made a virtue of seeing India through Pakistan-tinted glasses. In 1993, Robin Raphel had called the Shimla Agreement, signed between India and Pakistan in 1972, just after the Bangladesh War, "ineffectual." She had further said that Pakistani complicity in the armed insurrection in Kashmir was "no excuse

5. During his visit to China in June 1998, President Clinton had asked his Chinese counterpart, Jiang Zemin, to "share the global responsibility" by maintaining peace and security in Asia in general and preventing nuclear and missile proliferation in South Asia in particular, following nuclear tests by India and Pakistan in May 1998.

for human rights abuses in the Kashmir Valley." In January 1996, Clinton signed into law a congressional bill—the Brown Amendment—granting Pakistan a one-time waiver on the Pressler Amendment and allowing the sale of $370 million worth of U.S. military equipment to Pakistan, even though the Pakistanis had received M-11 missiles and 5,000 "ring magnets," used to refine bomb-grade uranium, from China. This was part of a continuing pattern. Secretary of Defense William Perry signed a defense agreement with India in Delhi in January 1995. However, to put India and Pakistan on parity, he signed a similar agreement with Pakistan immediately following his visit to India. He also renewed a joint consultation group on defense cooperation that had been dormant since 1990. In June 1995, in an address to the Asia Society, Under Secretary of Defense for Policy Walter Slocombe said that it was imperative for the United States to "maintain a balance between India and Pakistan," and that any "deepened security relationship" with India should not affect the "traditional close cooperation between the U.S. and Pakistan." This external "balancing" of India continued. Raphel explained the growth of terrorism in Kashmir as an outcome of "India's maladministration in the Valley." Even so, Under Secretary of State Thomas Pickering, who led the American delegation during the first Indo-American strategic dialogue in 1997, insisted that the two countries had "identical views . . . terrorism in any form is reprehensible." He then added, "Both of us are committed to work together to enhance our capacity to fight terrorism, whether they are sponsored from the moon or from any other corner." During this dialogue, it was agreed that India and the United States would mobilize global opinion for the signing of a "Comprehensive Convention on Terrorism" at Geneva. There was a much wider canvas that Pickering conceptualized when talking of a strategic dialogue between India and the United States. He held that "what is important is the entire gamut of Indo-US ties. We are focused more on . . . regional and global issues, . . . how best we can cooperate in confronting them. At the same time . . . strategic dialogue should not be misconstrued in narrow military terms. For us, India is an important country, because of its democracy, because of its economic potentials and because of its position in the post Cold War world."[6] The resumption of the strategic dialogue was a positive development. But unlike India,

---

6. M. L. Sondhi and Prakash Nanda, *Vajpayee's Foreign Policy: Daring the Irreversible* (New Delhi: Har-Anand Publications, 1999), pp. 77–78. It has been suggested that India-U.S. relations might have improved much sooner had it not been for India's nuclear tests. In 1997, Madeleine Albright took the initiative to launch a "strategic dialogue" with India. But when she visited India, her trip ended abruptly when she had to rush to Geneva for discussions with European leaders on the Iraq crisis.

which thought that the dialogue would cover, as Pickering had put it, "the entire gamut" so that the relationship did not become hostage to any one specific issue, the United States continued to view relations as markedly "nuclear-centric." Washington did talk of the need to improve the relationship, but made it clear that everything would fall into place only after India abandoned its intentions to become a nuclear power.

That aside, the Clinton administration did not view India as a power on its own; it always saw us in the context of South Asia, thereby bringing Pakistan into the picture. Pickering, for instance, was not convinced by Prime Minister I. K. Gujral that India's claim on a permanent membership in the Security Council was based on objective and nondiscriminatory global criteria.[7] For him, India could obtain membership only if the "regional countries" wanted it to be "their representative." This was a curious thesis, advocating some totally untenable propositions about "regional representation" based on "consent" of the region. The Clinton administration did concede Pakistan's role in promoting terrorism in Kashmir, but it remained fixated upon "Kashmir as a potential flashpoint," arguing for its resolution but always impliedly to the satisfaction of Pakistan, and preferably with American help. It had also resumed "limited" economic and military aid to Pakistan in the wake of the Brown Amendment in 1995. This self-induced diplomatic astigmatism has prevented the United States from accepting the reality in South Asia; it first adopted and then persisted with a façade of indifference to Pakistan's nuclear and missile development programs, all of which were assisted by China and North Korea. When Pakistan test-fired its Ghauri missile in April 1998, the Clinton administration's response was so mild as to be almost inaudible. It was odd yet typical that even as it commenced a strategic dialogue with India, the Clinton administration also imposed, in 1997, curbs on exports to five leading Indian civilian scientific organizations, including the Bhabha Atomic Research Centre, Bharat Electronics, and Indian Rare Earths, on the ground that they produced dual-technology items. These curbs were actually imposed when an Indian minister of state for external affairs, Salim Sherwani, was on a visit to the United States to urge it to refrain from precisely that step. An immediate consequence of these curbs was a virtual repudiation of the Memorandum of Understanding for science and technology, which had been signed by the Reagan administration in 1984.

There was another worry, born of dissonance between America's words and its actions. Notwithstanding its loudly proclaimed commitments to

7. Ibid.

democracy—no doubt sincerely meant—the United States has always found itself far more comfortable with dictatorships, military rulers, and "manageable regimes" than with oddly questioning countries such as India, by nature given to abstract disputations, to never-ending shastrarth, to spouting mystifying notions like "maya" and "nonpermanence" and "nonduality."[8] This explained, at least in part, the ease with which the United States had always taken Pakistan under its wing, as its ally in the various contests that a superpower must apparently always engage in, all obviously for causes dear to the United States, though not necessarily—in fact, seldom—in Pakistan's long-term interests. This was pointedly so in the present context. Having continuously, year after year, looked away as Pakistan went on a missile and nuclear weapons production binge, the United States was finally being forced to actually do something, but what that "something" was to be, even the U.S. was not clear about. Thus the Americans and the British, in particular, actually continued to blame India for Pakistan's nuclear weapons tests! This often led to almost humorous observations from American commentators: "the ultimate responsibility is India's . . . even for Pakistan's actions." My task was to also address such prejudices, to correct them to the extent that I could, and to remove from the American mind this continuing addiction to a hyphenated (India-Pakistan) South Asia policy.

The other hyphenation, less stated but always seriously resented, was Sino-Indian. American policy and approaches to China have always intrigued me. With the exception of the Nixon-Kissinger period, I have consistently failed to grasp what it is that the United States actually wants. The United States and China have clearly had a confusing love-hate relationship, which by 1998 was already heavily overlayered by commerce, with the balance of advantage unevenly weighted in China's favor. The United States is not going to jeopardize its commercial interests— that has always been a part of American morality—and neither, for that matter, would post-1998 China. That much is clear. Of course, China, too, could damage itself, and were it ever to do so—though it has too much pragmatism to do so willingly—then it would cause grave harm to the American economy, too. This knowledge adds to the confusion at the China desk in the U.S. State Department. What troubled me then were more direct matters: pronouncements made by President Clinton during

---

8. Shastrarth: a religious debate invoking ancient Hindu traditions and scriptures. Maya: the "Great Illusion"; the obscuring of spiritual reality by the physical world. Nonduality (also advait, nondualism, monism): the view that there is only reality; "the individual and the Brahma (creator) are one."

his official visit to China in late June and early July of 1998. His remark that China must share its "global responsibility" in arresting nuclear and missile proliferation in Asia was highly offensive to India. It prompted the Vajpayee government to issue a sharply critical statement. India characterized President Clinton's remarks and his subsequent joint statement with President Jiang Zemin as an attempt to "carve out a supervisory role for themselves in this part of the world," as "hegemonistic," and as a demonstration of the "mentality of a bygone era."[9] From the Indian perspective, it was strange that Washington should want Beijing to "facilitate" peace and stability in South Asia. This completely overlooked the fact that China was part of the problem. It had taken from Pakistan about 2,600 square kilometers of the Jammu and Kashmir territory in the 1960s. Besides, it was in occupation of more than 15,000 square miles of the Aksai Chin. China's links with Pakistan's nuclear and missile programs had attracted America's own concerns. It was baffling, therefore, to observe the seriousness with which Clinton wanted to move ahead with his plan to "administer" Asia with Chinese help. It was noted by commentators in India that Clinton's stated reasons for befriending China were not applied to India. He regarded China as important for its "nuclear weapons and capacity to control nuclear proliferation," its "huge markets and massive population." Was the Clinton administration deliberately snubbing India, despite assertions about its commitment to democracy, free speech, human rights, and the like? There was an unintended message in all this—that despite China's having violated almost every U.S. nonproliferation law, the *application* of American laws was selective, as it has always been. Importantly, on both occasions it was the Clinton administration that had lifted sanctions when China pledged to stop its missile sales to Pakistan and to Iran. In fact, it was the State Department that had held in 1998 "that there is evidence to apply sanctions to China but the administration has not made any determination to do so."[10]

There was also a troubling thought that I carried, not just a thought, perhaps, but knowledge and some reflection, too, about this increasing militarization that the United States was so visibly demonstrating. Where would it all lead the United States, and the rest of Planet Earth? How did one marry democracy and militarization? And what effect would this have

---

9. Press release of June 27, 1998, by the government of India in response to the U.S.-China Joint Statement on South Asia.

10. Gary Milhollin, Director of the Wisconsin Project on Nuclear Arms Control, from testimony before the House Committees on International Relations and National Security, June 17, 1998.

on the responsibility that I bore? American assertions that democratic societies were peace-loving were not sustainable; such an empty claim could not be empirically established. Besides, the United States was itself constantly disproving it, for it was already a highly militarized society, and the brutalizing effects of this militarization were increasingly visible each time I visited an otherwise marvelously creative society. In the dying years of the Cold War, I shared the view of some American observers that the United States was being increasingly drawn toward "military power" as the compelling factor of reckoning. The original Wilsonian idealism of skepticism toward arms and armies that had dominated the early engagement of the world following World War I had slowly eroded. Liberals and conservatives, American politicians irrespective of affiliation, had become enamored of military might. To turn the concern inward: was India, too, demonstrating such a tendency? No, for India's was entirely a defensive initiative.

I need to insert a brief word here about prevailing American knowledge, opinion, and prejudices about the Bharatiya Janata Party, all unfortunately inherited and all at second hand. The U.S. administration's pursuit of a nuclear-centric policy toward India was such that even before the BJP-led NDA government had assumed office in March 1998, Washington had warned of dire consequences in case of implementation of the party's election promise to make India a nuclear weapons power. The American ambassador to India commented on the BJP manifesto soon after it was released in December 1997:

> If a government in India chooses to weaponise, declare India a nuclear weapon state and particularly if such a government were to test a nuclear weapon, I believe that would have very unsettling consequences in terms of India's relations in the neighbourhood and would be a great concern to my government. There would have consequences under the laws of my country on things we should do *vis-à-vis* India. I hope this would be carefully considered before any decision was taken to actually move down that road.[11]

Two aspects of these remarks surprised many. In the first instance, foreign envoys may and do express views on the declared policies of the governments

---

11. Ambassador Richard E. Celeste at an on-the-record Chennai breakfast meeting in early February 1998 with N. Ram, editor of *The Hindu*. Quoted in "The Risks of Nuclear Hawkishness," *Frontline* 15, no. 8 (April 11–24, 1998), http://www.hinduonnet.com/fline/fl1508/15080110.htm.

of their accredited countries, but not on statements of intent of political parties. Secondly, by doing so, was Ambassador Celeste seeking to influence Indian voters, advising them, as it were, to think before opting for the BJP? This was an unusual and serious deviation. A spokesman for the Ministry of External Affairs noted, "It was improper and inadvisable on the part of foreign envoys to comment on the election manifestos of our political parties, particularly when we are in the midst of our elections."[12] It was quite another thing that the BJP-led NDA emerged the victor in these elections.

The Road to the Village

The United States' approach, attitudes, and policies toward India changed, but cautiously. For the Americans, this engagement with India was an exercise at removing obstacles in the path of a universal subscription to the NPT and the CTBT; that was their stated and accepted national objective then. With the nuclear tests of May 11 and 13, 1998, India had become the principal obstacle preventing the U.S. from reaching that objective, and this was a national security issue for them, as the obverse was for India. Besides, the U.S. could not very well "remove" this obstacle called India. Could it then impose its will? It could certainly try by withholding its favors, as it had already done, and it could bring pressure on India, as had always been assessed by us, and as the P-5 and G-8 resolutions demonstrated. Would these stands have been taken if the U.S. had expressly not wanted them? I highly doubt it. It is with this kind of "double bind," their own and others', that the U.S. worked to change India's policy.

There was, however, one great fault line here: even America lacked the ability to remold the globe entirely according to its own design, as a tool only of U.S. interests. But for the United States, it was certainly worth a try, for there already was fairly widespread opposition to the tests. Besides, any "failure" of the venture would not bring in its wake a permanent stigma of incapacity or defeat for the U.S.

For me, on the other hand, a failure to convey India's viewpoint effectively, to defuse the present tension, to falter in carrying conviction with the rest of the international community, was not an option. I had only one try, no more, and any mistakes would be irreversible. I had to succeed, and in the public eye. There was just no scope to fail; that would amount to failing India, to a further belittling of India. That simply could not happen, and there was no way that India's national interests, prestige, or standing could conceivably be remolded by others.

---

12. Sondhi and Nanda, *Vajpayee's Foreign Policy,* p. 79.

These were the intellectual, historical, and diplomatic assets (and liabilities) with which I left for that land which Christopher Columbus had found when he was actually on his journey to discover India.

An Indian in Search of America

The overriding thought that accompanied me to New York in June 1998 was not of any great anxiety. I was convinced that India's stand was fundamentally just. I was fully aware of the difficulties that lay ahead, but that was no deterrent, for what I sought was an opportunity to engage fairly with the international community, and I carried a conviction that India could not fail. The events of May 11 and 13 had naturally preceded me to the United States; and for some time now, they had dominated the international media's attention. I had been interviewed in India by international agencies, and various correspondents had sought to meet me, though I did often wonder whether it was an attempt to elicit my views or to find fault, and thereafter condemn and castigate India for what it had done—to create an international atmosphere of hopelessness and doom about India's future. This did not impress me, nor did it affect me.

An international climate of disapproval had already been created, largely at the initiative of the United States. On June 3, President Clinton, accompanied by Secretary of State Albright, had given voice to the United States' policy in the rather incongruously pacific setting of the Rose Garden at the White House. The president had said:

> The nuclear tests by India and Pakistan stand in stark contrast to the progress the world has made over the past several years in reducing stockpiles and containing the spread of nuclear weapons. It is also contrary to the ideals of nonviolent democratic freedom and independence at the heart of Gandhi's struggle to end colonialism on the Indian subcontinent. India and Pakistan are great nations with boundless potential, but developing weapons of mass destruction is self-defeating, wasteful, and dangerous. It will make their people poorer and less secure. The international community must now come together to move them through a diverse course and to avoid a dangerous arms race in Asia.

I was a bit weary of this avalanche of homilies, and wary as well of too many correspondents trying too hard to trip me, even prior to my visit to determine the outcome of it. The only way to attend to the situation was to speak selectively to some of them, not the "sound bite" seekers, but rather those who had a desire to assess India's view. Foreign policy expert George Perkovich, who subsequently published the authoritative *India's Nuclear Bomb: The Impact on Global Proliferation,* spoke to me at some length over the telephone. Soon after the tests, Prime Minister Vajpayee had clearly enunciated that India would be observing a unilateral moratorium on any further testing, and also that we were ready to talk about the CTBT. I did share with Perkovich, who specialized in this subject, that it would be counterproductive to attempt to hustle India:

> We need to talk to the Americans first. We have concerns that must be addressed. The United States, in its pique, seems to want us to sign first and talk later. . . . If you hold a gun to [my] head and say, "Sign on the dotted line!" then it makes things very difficult. India has a long history of colonial domination. It's only fifty years free from it. Now, fifty years down the line, we are not prepared to accept another form of colonialism. If you say first I must crawl—India must crawl before we can talk with you—then it reminds us of Amritsar.[13]

On June 4, the foreign ministers of the P-5, meeting in Geneva, issued a joint communiqué in which they "condemned the tests, expressed their deep concern about the danger to peace and stability in the region, and pledged to cooperate closely and make urgent efforts to prevent a nuclear and missiles race in the subcontinent." The ministers exhorted India and Pakistan to "stop all further testing," to "refrain from weaponisation or deployment of nuclear weapons, from the testing or deployment of missiles capable of delivering nuclear weapons, and from any further production of fissile material for nuclear weapons."[14] Not content with all of this, they also advised India that "it should halt all provocative statements, refrain from any military movement that could be construed as threatening and increase transparency in actions." Exhortations followed about subscribing to the CTBT "immediately and unconditionally," and about participating "in a positive spirit" in the Conference on Disarmament for a fissile material cutoff convention. It was only later that I learned that

---

13. Amritsar is an ancient city in the state of Punjab in northern India where, in an infamous incident in 1919, General Reginald Dyer, a British commander, ordered Indians to crawl past the place where two Englishwomen were having an argument. General Dyer gained further notoriety when he ordered troops in Amritsar to open fire with machine guns on an assembly of unarmed Indians.
14. Paragraphs 1 and 2 of the P-5 Joint Communiqué, Geneva, June 4, 1998.

this statement was actually a result of the joint craftsmanship of Secretary of State Albright and Bob Einhorn, the U.S. official I later worked with and came to admire for his principled commitment to the cause of non-proliferation and for his unflustered negotiating skills. No doubt China used this meeting of the P-5 to sharpen the statement, making it more pointedly anti-India and demanding of India a variety of commitments that were impossible to fulfill. Hot on the trail of the P-5 joint communiqué, which was to "become the template for Washington's dealings with India for the next two years,"[15] came Security Council Resolution 1172 on June 6. The critical part of Resolution 1172 was the text that asked for an immediate cessation of nuclear weapons development and for India (as well as Pakistan) to join the NPT as a "non-nuclear-weapons state." There was also an unambiguous call upon India to "go back" on all that it had done, to roll back that program. This resolution went into some gratuitous references to "root causes," mentioning the Indian state of Jammu and Kashmir in this context.

A week later, on June 12, the P-5 and the Security Council having already armed themselves with all the diplomatic weapons that they sought, the G-8 entered the scene and adopted its own ministerial communiqué. It reiterated the formulations that the two earlier resolutions had adopted. There was one noteworthy addition, however: an exhortation to "discourage terrorist activity and any support for it." This was unusual, for it was one of the first times there had been even a mention of what I considered to be a greater and a very much more imminent danger facing the world than any nuclear standoff. This G-8 communiqué also cautioned that the tests would undermine "the region's attractiveness to both foreign and domestic investment, damaging business confidence and the prospects for economic growth." (As I write this, I cannot help reflecting on the inaccuracy of those forewarnings. Despite all those cautions, India is today experiencing the second-highest growth rate in the world! And Pakistan is the beneficiary of munificent handouts, courtesy of the U.S.)

This was certainly not the most encouraging of backgrounds against which to be flying to the United States, but the key to attending to the problems lay with America, so that was where I had to start. I reached New York on June 6, ostensibly to represent India in the UN General Assembly, which was holding a special meeting on narcotics. New York was a demanding but exhilarating experience. It made the adrenaline run, for I had chosen to do several television interviews and talk to a number of

15. Talbott, *Engaging India,* p. 76.

think tanks, with the conviction that the more I was able to communicate India's views directly to the people of the United States, the better I could convey our position. An unstated, often unrecognized difficulty lay in the very nature of this enterprise, principally for two reasons: First, India had already been projected prominently as a violator of international commitments, laws, or treaties. This representation was totally false. And second, over the years, particularly in the United States, an atmosphere had been created that vilified those that breached the barriers of nuclear apartheid, because, or so the Americans implied, this was "their" preserve, and anyone who breached it would have to account for it. I did not agree, because I did not believe that the world could be so apportioned. This was the simple—or not so simple—message that I had to communicate even before I could undertake any formal engagements with the U.S. administration.

On June 12, 1998, I reached Washington eager to formally initiate a dialogue. Ambassador Naresh Chandra received me at the airport, and protocol officers whisked me rapidly to downtown Washington. Ambassador Chandra then briefed me on the atmosphere, the expectations in the State Department, and the personalities I would be dealing with. I could courteously continue to pay sufficient attention to his briefing for only so long. I wanted to be by myself, with my thoughts and not with briefing papers—an attitude that then, and on all subsequent such diplomatic assignments, troubled the professionals in the Ministry of External Affairs. I had declined all invitations for that evening, so when the embassy team left, I was free to do what I chose. I watched the evening descend onto the Potomac, a warm summer evening, luminous and calm. Joggers chased health along the banks of the river, and rowers sketched lines on its pewter-hued waters. The joyous sound of children laughing as they cycled in abandon floated up to the room; the evening light deepened. I was filled with the stillness of that gathering twilight, a calm reassurance about what I had to do, about what I knew I would do.

I woke up very early on the morning of the 13th, as is my habit, and yet again I watched life along the banks of the Potomac, where early morning rowers were already practicing. Later that morning I drove to the State Department with Ambassador Chandra and Alok Prasad of the Ministry of External Affairs. We were ushered in with the usual protocol and courtesy. I was met at the door of the elevator and taken to Strobe Talbott's offices, where he greeted me affably. Shortly thereafter, I was escorted into the inner office. It had the comforting disorder of a postgraduate student's room, with books, jogging shoes, family photographs, and other such memorabilia giving it an informal, lived-in feel. With charming American informality, Strobe invited me to make myself at home. We were soon on first-name terms. I had already been introduced to some of the other members of the team: Inderfurth, Riedel, and Einhorn. Sandy Berger, the national security advisor, had also come in for a short introduction, but it was a one-to-one that Strobe was keen on, and I was not averse. The professionals accompanying me were not as enthusiastic, for they were not entirely confident about what I might do or do wrong or commit India to. This is a natural reserve that all professionals have, for they work on the rather protective theory that those who reach ministerial office are in fact interlopers, and thus should be prevented from doing anything beyond the purely ceremonial, and, if pushed, then the minimum possible. This attitude did change, but it has taken time for the MEA to accept.

Strobe and I reached a conversational informality fairly quickly. I do not have to rely much on my diary notes of that period, for my recollections are still vivid. I soon shared with Strobe that I was not there to negotiate, either to give or to ask for anything. I was really there much more to engage in a dialogue. "We could," I said to Strobe, "go back over the years and carry out a detailed analysis and a damage audit of the past fifty years—the years that the rats ate away, those wasted years—and thereafter, once we have satisfied ourselves about that 'audit,' only then come to 'dialoguing' about present-day events. Alternatively, without abandoning our respectively basic and immutable national positions, we could endeavor to harmonize our views so that the first requirement—a restoration of confidence—is achieved, even if only in part. For this," I added, "we would need to first have some agreement on confidentiality; we would need to combine openness and accountability with essential confidentiality." Strobe agreed, adding that the United States principally wanted to address three areas—nonproliferation, India-Pakistan and associated issues, and the rectangle of the United States, China, Pakistan, and India.

This conversation, the first between Strobe and me, was not structured around any fixed agenda. It was more a mutual exploration of minds, approaches, and attitudes toward the tasks ahead. In sum, it was an assessment of the personality of the interlocutor, and of the brief he was carrying. Thus it did not have an adversarial air. Besides, Strobe made it clear early on that the United States was not set upon a course to "punish" anybody: "We are trying to limit what [has] happened to South Asia. . . . [The] tests, though dangerous, are not disastrous, but what happens next might be disastrous." I responded by briefly explaining India's stand, telling him that India viewed weaponization more as a contingency than as an immutable necessity: "It was not a question of arranging just a display. What India demonstrated in May cannot be rolled back." And because it was not just a display, I could not "foreswear weaponization," either. "But I assure you," I told Strobe, "we do not intend to reinvent the Cold War with all its archaic phraseology." I then spelled out the phrases, all irrelevant to the context in which we were speaking: "first strike," "second strike," all the way to "mutually assured destruction." India's parameters, I informed him, were and would be "no first use": "Our approach is one of responsibility; our pain is born of the use of phrases like 'India is an international pariah.'" I then added that this word "pariah" originated in my country, and those who used it in the English language did not know its exact connotations; thus "this casual use of it is doubly unfortunate."

I moved on to several troubling aspects of American policy, as, for example, in connection with China, and the fact that the United States continued to look at India through "the prism of the Cold War years." It was here that Bruce Riedel intervened to clarify that the United States had "no intention of setting up China as an umpire." I responded by saying I was glad, adding, "India is now changing, and extremely rapidly. Which is why the world must come to recognize a transformed India." At this point I used a colloquialism that subsequently became a kind of leitmotif for my entire dialogue with Strobe: "If you do not wish to go to the village, don't ask the way to it." The phrase "way to the village" then became a kind of shorthand, a code for the entire endeavor. But there was another thought, too, that I shared, not from the world of diplomacy, but rather more military in its origin. I told Strobe, "If we have to work together, as clearly we have to, then we shall also have to learn to accommodate the other. It is really quite like military companionship: if you have to share a tent, then you have to accommodate the other person's habits, methods, even idiosyncrasies." The day's concluding comment by Strobe was, "You greatly encourage [me] both by the high tone and the high standards that we have set for 'finding the way to the village.' There is only one way to restore confidence; it is through dialogue. Only that is how trust can come. . . . We know that India would not go down the path of certain avenues. . . . Let us therefore move with a sense of urgency but not haste." The meeting, originally scheduled to last an hour, had gone on instead for two and a half hours, most of it one-to-one. This meeting laid the foundation for our future dialogue. As I got up to leave, Strobe touchingly presented me with a book, which he had inscribed warmly and somewhat flatteringly: "To my new friend—at the highest place." We agreed to meet again, and soon.

As we got out of the State Department building and moved toward the car, both Ambassador Naresh Chandra and Alok Prasad, the joint secretary who handled the Americas desk in the ministry, warmly shook my hand and remarked on how I had gone into this meeting, as I did for all subsequent meetings, without a single paper, file, or folder in my hand. "We have moved, Sir," Ambassador Chandra said, "much faster and much farther than we thought we would." I had no illusions that the problems were in any sense over. But this, as I wrote in my diary then, "is the turning point, exactly the opening that I had sought to restore dialogue, trust, and confidence between India and the United States of America."

I was back in Delhi in the middle of June and eagerly followed the progress of President Clinton's trip to China. That visit had originally been intended to be undertaken along with visits to India and Pakistan, but it obviously was now to be a stand-alone. It was during this visit that the troubling joint statement was issued—a statement that could not have been more poorly drafted from our standpoint, an unbelievably Sino-centric pronouncement that caused gratuitous offense to Indian sensibilities. It nullified what progress there had been in moving Indo-American relations in the right direction. I failed to grasp how the U.S. could advise President Jiang to act as a kind of an umpire in South Asia. Nothing could have been more offensive to India. I informed Strobe soon after the statement was issued that this could have very dampening consequences, and that it was important, therefore, that some early corrective be applied by the United States. Although he was busy with his other travels and commitments, Strobe understood the urgency. We agreed to find an intersecting point in our respective itineraries and to meet as soon as we could. The choice of venue fell to that junction of international travel, Frankfurt. When we met there on July 9 and 10, 1998, the Beijing statement of Presidents Clinton and Jiang hung like a huge question mark over the entire dialogue. How could the United States possibly want to dictate terms to India first and then simultaneously advise Jiang Zemin to act as an "umpire" in South Asian affairs? Was this policy statement to later become a presidential directive? Or was this an attempt by the U.S. establishment to pay back the National Democratic Alliance government, more specifically Prime Minister Vajpayee and his foreign policy and security team, for the tests of May 11 and 13?

The fact that we met, even if near Frankfurt, and were still talking was in itself a message of reassurance. This meeting further deepened our understanding of each other's views, positions, and objectives. The United States, bound by the P-5 and G-8 resolutions and Security Council Resolution 1172, sought immediate and total subscription to its agenda. India remained equally clear in its mind, and at that juncture was principally seeking the establishment of a lasting dialogue with the potential for progression. But India would certainly not talk with a pistol held to its temple, and it was equally impossible for us to joyfully start adhering to the demands of the P-5 or the United States when all those diplomatic missiles were being fired at us. Unless this minimum was done, there was no way that India could move anywhere toward accommodating any aspect of the United States' agenda. This perhaps suggests that the discussions were extremely disagreeable. In fact, they were not. We did obviously disagree, but that was much more an interaction of our respective viewpoints than any combative "either-or" assertion.

Two Cultures of Talking

If I am not mistaken, it was at Frankfurt that Strobe and I had an interesting discussion on the negotiating styles of different countries. I told him what was obvious—that countries negotiated in accordance with the characteristics, traits, and styles of their cultures. Though a kind of attendant European/Western patina had come into existence—tables, chairs, photographers, note-takers—when it came to the substance, national traits took over. Strobe explained how he found the Indian style so very different from the Russian, for example. In the latter case, "extreme stands" were the rule for the starting position, with negotiations thereafter a trying test of endurance, the final position not revealed or shared, the adversary slowly whittled down. In contrast, he found in our dialogue a much greater directness and openness. Along with national characteristics there was the individual aspect, which I think more often provides the true catalyst of movement, certainly more than policy papers or diplomatic notes.

Trust between individual negotiators thus often becomes the foundation of a transformation between two countries: the Chou Enlai Kissinger relationship being an outstanding example, in contrast, say, to the failure of Nehru and Chou to achieve any trusting rapport. But these examples I did not share with Strobe; what I did share were my views on how Indian and American styles differed. "Yours," I said, "is what I would call a 'checklist style' of diplomacy. You start in the morning, say, with your five or seven or however many points jotted on your memo pad, all as a checklist. And unless all of them have been scored out at the end of the day, there is no progress. India's approach, in contrast—or at least that certainly is how I approach my task—is to move from the general to the specific. If there is accord, agreement on the foundational basis, a general acceptance of the principles of it, then all else must, driven by its own inherent logic, follow. Settlement of the specifics will then be reached. But you, the United States, start with the specifics, and unless the entire checklist is agreed upon, nothing else is." These differences had consequences, as I was to experience later.

There was another by-product of the Frankfurt meeting. I do not recollect how it came up, but we did move on to Jammu and Kashmir. We were standing on the terrace of Strobe's suite, informally discussing the larger question of India-Pakistan relations, when this topic surfaced. I elucidated upon the history of the issue, how it was a tale of one error after another, from Partition, that inauspicious beginning; how Pakistan, starting as an aggressor, had slowly, over time, transformed itself into some kind of victim in Jammu and Kashmir; how repeatedly, over the years, first Nehru, then Shastri, and finally Indira Gandhi at Shimla had tried to settle the issue permanently. Obviously this could be done only on the basis of reexamining the Line of Control and its alignment. Subsequently, fragmented accounts of this discussion caused some excitement in the Indian media, though entirely unwarrantedly. All efforts at settling the matter, from Nehru onward, had been with a view to achieving lasting peace. Indeed, even if it is not directly connected with my post Pokhran II dialogue with Strobe Talbott, that part of India's history needs recounting. There are elements in it that cover almost the entire range of human experience.

After the tragedy of the 1962 war with China, Nehru made serious efforts at finding a solution to Jammu and Kashmir, partly because he desired a settlement, partly because he was under great pressure from the West. In a touching account, Y. D. Gundevia, India's foreign secretary in Nehru's final years, has shared with posterity the efforts made by a "fading, saddened and spent" Nehru. There was poignant heroism in those last efforts by the prime minister. The consequences of the October November 1962 conflict were manifold—economic shock, domestic uncertainty, and a sharp decline in Nehru's standing in India and abroad. In this milieu, against his own inclinations, Prime Minister Nehru accepted the advice of others and wrote to President Ayub Khan of Pakistan. Ayub's reply only rubbed salt into India's wounds: the general implied that India got what it deserved, ending by voicing his concern over an alleged arms buildup in India as a result of "Western arms aid." If it was accord with Pakistan that was sought, then this Nehru initiative did not even get off the ground. But an enfeebled India had to be kept under pressure and somehow nudged toward "making up with Pakistan." That was the price being sought by the United Kingdom and the United States for all the arms assistance that had been given to a wounded India; mere "cash payment for those weapons would simply not do." Besides, had not Nehru, at a conference of Indian ambassadors at Bürgenstock, Switzerland, in 1953, mentioned that he had suggested to the Pakistani prime minister that a settlement process be initiated on the basis of practical territorial readjustment of the Pakistan-occupied areas of Jammu and Kashmir? But by 1962, "Nehru's approach to this problem had become mostly theoretical, almost metaphysical, not at all empirical."[16]

"Fourteen years of a Ceasefire Line . . . could this not be a chance for some mutual understanding?" That was how the quest had begun, as it always has. Ayub, with a nudge from the West, "had also hinted to G. Parthasarathi, our then high commissioner, it was about time that India and Pakistan made some effort to arrive at a solution of their differences." Duncan Sandys, the British secretary of state for Commonwealth relations, was a regular visitor to the subcontinent in those days and explicitly stated that "his main objective in coming to India was to see whether, in the existing fluid situation, some steps could be taken towards solving the Kashmir problem." As Gundevia explains, "Unscrambled, [this] boiled down to the proposal of first 'minister level' talks on Kashmir, and then a 'summit between Nehru and Ayub,' with US and UK brokering the 'minister level' talks." It was this initiative that resulted in the communiqué of November 29, 1962, about renewed efforts to "resolve outstanding differences on Kashmir and other related matters through talks to be conducted initially at the ministerial level." India's priorities then included the "troubling matter of infiltration from East Bengal into Assam and West Bengal; and the continuing issue of evacuee property." These, too, were to be taken up. As for Jammu and Kashmir, Gundevia, then part of the negotiating team, has written that India was prepared to "voluntarily give up sovereignty over parts of its territory to Pakistan, so that there could be a 'reasonable new boundary line, acceptable to Pakistan,' thereby reaching an amicable settlement on everything, including Kashmir." All this resulted

16. Quotations in this and the following paragraphs from Gundevia, *Outside the Archives*, pp. 236, 240–379.

in ministerial-level talks, with Sardar Swaran Singh leading the Indian delegation. There were six rounds of talks spread over six months, moving from Rawalpindi to Delhi, Karachi to Calcutta. On the eve of the first round, soon after the Indian delegation had reached Rawalpindi, a broadcast from Karachi announced a "joint communiqué" issued simultaneously from Peking and Karachi. It concerned the signing of a border agreement between China and Pakistan, "which gave away a good chunk of the northeastern areas of the Indian state of Jammu and Kashmir to China." "The two parties are highly satisfied," Pakistan radio had then announced. Nevertheless, India kept the talks afloat. Should they have? To this question, as to so many others, history has as yet to provide an answer.

Zulfikar Ali Bhutto, leading the Pakistani delegation, had an approach that he shared with Gundevia: "You are a defeated nation, don't you see?" The talks went on after this—in India, then in Karachi; one round in Calcutta, yet another in Karachi; and the final breakdown came in the sixth round in Delhi, in May 1963. It was the third round—in Karachi, in February 1963—that shows how far Nehru had already gone in wanting to placate Pakistan. The Indian delegation had gone to Karachi with four maps. The first depicted the stand of "minimum concessions," the fourth that of the "maximum." But Bhutto wanted the whole, plus a great deal else. India, in turn, offered a "new International boundary with 1,500 square miles more to be given away to Pakistan. Still not satisfied, Bhutto wanted this territory to be up to Kathua, on the Jammu Kashmir-Himachal border; all that as part of Jammu and Kashmir." There was no settlement, of course; how could there be on such a basis? In the meantime, pressure from the United States and the United Kingdom persisted: "China might make trouble again in April 1963," they hinted. "Therefore, it was in the interest of India to keep Pakistan quiet—come to terms with Pakistan, then deal effectively with China." This outside interference made negotiations much more difficult because, as Gundevia writes, "the US and UK were insisting that India should not hang on to the whole of the Valley, but were at the same time telling Pakistan 'that they should not ask for the whole of the Valley.' This confused India and made Pakistan obdurate." After all, part of the Valley "could mean one-eighth of the Valley or even seven-eighths of the Valley," though Pakistan had "actually asked for the whole" of it, according to Gundevia.

There had also been an attempt, once again, to open up the Indus River Waters Treaty. Then, "Forty-eight hours before the next round [that was to ensue in Karachi]," says Gundevia, "our 'western' friends introduced another idea to Bhutto: they termed it 'Kashmir—elements of settlement.'" From "something" in the Valley, it was now finally "a substantial position" in the Valley. Further, there was to be a due recognition of the "defence needs of both countries." Whose defense against whom? The question was treated as rhetorical. Pakistan wanted the Chenab watershed, thus ending the Indus Water Treaty. In short, these "Western elements" wanted "everything that Pakistan had so far demanded; everything that we [India] had explained we could never yield." In these discussions in Karachi, "Bhutto had pressed his claim on the Chenab watershed and would not agree to the new International Line that Sardar Swaran Singh offered. As expected, Bhutto contended now that the 'Valley was indivisible,' and that they must have the whole of it. When the obvious issue of the defence of Ladakh, if the Valley was to be given away, came up, Bhutto's reply was: 'Why do you want to defend Ladakh at all? Don't defend Ladakh.' There could be some temporary arrangement in regard to the Valley and Ladakh if trouble ever took place with China." The last round was in Delhi on May 14, 1963. Here the talks finally broke down. Following the Bangladesh War, it was with this very same Bhutto that Indira Gandhi "negotiated a new settlement" about the Line of Control, from which he resiled almost as soon as he returned to Pakistan.

Nehru had tried one final time, through Sheikh Mohammad Abdullah. After a long "Nehru-imposed incarceration," the sheikh, the most popular politician in Kashmir, was released unconditionally. He came to Delhi, not at all embittered, had long discussions with Nehru, and thereafter went to Pakistan as a kind of an emissary. Tragically, nothing came of this. Even while Sheikh Abdullah was in Pakistan, on May 27, 1964, Nehru died. Earlier in the year, there had been yet another effort. After Nehru had fallen seriously ill in Bhubaneshwar and had been brought back to Delhi, on January 12, 1964, Lord Louis Mountbatten was among his first visitors. Nehru slowly recovered and made his first appearance in his South Block office, perhaps a day or two before Republic Day, January 26. In almost his first conversation with his Foreign Office aides M. J. Desai and Y. D. Gundevia, Nehru shared that Mountbatten had spoken to him at some length about Pakistan. "I must settle with Pakistan," Nehru had said; and "he could not leave this legacy behind." It is not clear whose legacy Mountbatten was more worried about—his own or Nehru's. To pursue this matter, Desai and Gundevia had a "private session lasting an hour with Lord Mountbatten." He was of the opinion that "the prime minister's health being what it was, a resolution of the conflict with Pakistan was most urgent. The partition that [Mountbatten] had brought about, had left only Kashmir undecided, which had created a major conflict, and so—'Kashmir must be solved,' whereafter repeatedly he urged 'Something just had to be done.'" On being asked as to what that "something" or "solution" could be, Mountbatten refused to go into any details: "I am quite out of touch with things. It is not for me to suggest anything. All I can say is that something has to be done. You can't be at loggerheads like this with Pakistan." Ayub, he said, was a soldier, and it might be easier to deal with him than with any other Pakistan politician.[17] It was explained to him that talks with Ayub and his spokesman, Zulfikar Ali Bhutto, had been a "total disappointment." The six rounds of talks were summarized, India's basic formula for modifying the Ceasefire Line "in favor of Pakistan" was clarified, and the recognition of such a new line as the international boundary was explained, as was the fact that "India had been prepared to give away another 1,500 square miles of territory to Pakistan." Nothing came of any of this, as "Pakistan had wanted India to give them the whole of the Valley, plus, Pakistan wanted to open up the entire Indus Waters Treaty signed by the two in 1960." "Lord Mountbatten wouldn't mind," Desai later briefed Nehru, "if you settled on Jammu and gave away the rest of Kashmir to Ayub and surrendered Ladakh to the Chinese."

It was not that I shared all this detail with Strobe; of course I didn't. But I did inform him of the talks of 1962–63, and later, how many times and how often India had gone out of its way to resolve the matter, only to be thwarted, primarily because Jammu and Kashmir was not the issue, not the cause; it was only a symptom. This nuance, unfortunately, I have not been able to convey convincingly to any of my several interlocutors from the West. It was not just Strobe whom I failed to reach. I did have a patient and courteous listener in him, but I did not gain his understanding because the overlayering of views on this subject was too settled.

Down to the Nitty-Gritty

Within ten days of Frankfurt, Strobe and I met in Delhi. This was a far more substantial meeting. If Frankfurt had been impromptu, intended primarily to prevent any adverse fallout from the Clinton-Jiang statement, Delhi was a planned, fully prepared effort by the Americans. Strobe's delegation came strengthened by the presence of the vice-chairman of their

---

17. Since the creation of Pakistan, the U.S., the UK, and most of the West have persistently advocated the cause of democracy in their public pronouncements, but whenever they have engaged with India on the subject of Pakistan, they have strongly urged us to accept whichever soldier was then at the helm of affairs as the "best option." This has been the unvarying refrain since the days of F. M. Ayub Khan.

Joint Chiefs of Staff, General Joseph Ralston. It was also the first time in a long time that a full American delegation had come to Delhi. On this occasion, Strobe for the first time spelled out in full his government's "benchmarks," as he termed them. He had had rather an unnerving journey in Ralston's special aircraft, which had flown nonstop from Washington to Delhi. A scheduled midair refueling somewhere over the Mediterranean had had to be abandoned because the two planes involved had suddenly encountered unexpected turbulence. Only a timely response by the pilots prevented calamity.

But the American side was not so shaken by this experience as to ease their pressure on India. I used the facilities of Delhi's majestic Hyderabad House for this round of the dialogue, and here Strobe enunciated the "benchmarks," explicitly stating what the United States wanted from India. Were India to demonstrate some "success" in this regard, to the satisfaction of the United States and the White House, then other relief from sanctions could follow. As stated in the benchmarks, the U.S. expected India to subscribe to the CTBT, and to make some suitable announcement in this regard during Prime Minister Vajpayee's visit to the UN General Assembly in September 1998. Also, India, working with the United States and "cooperating fully" with it at the Conference on Disarmament, should assist in the negotiation for a treaty on a permanent ban on fissile material production for nuclear weapons. The third benchmark—an innovative phrase, used, if I recollect correctly, for the first time—was termed "strategic restraint." Ostensibly this meant placing a limit of sorts on the development of missiles and missile technology, but neither that nor the provisions of the Missile Technology Control Regime were ever cited. The phraseology was ingenious "diplomatese" for a coverall provision; in reality, the United States was addressing its concern that India might move into the bracket of those nations with intercontinental ballistic missile capability. And that, it surmised, would directly intrude into the realm of American security concerns. This "strategic restraint" was such a catchall phrase that it could, and would if ever conceded—and as interpreted by the United States—result in India's options being severely emasculated. It would amount to the very antithesis of the "strategic autonomy" I had spoken of, and which India, through the tests of May 11 and 13, had reached out to acquire. Strobe's demands on export controls were not really needed. As I presented it to him, "India's export control record is far better than that of some of the P-5." The final "benchmark" was the settlement of the issue of Jammu and Kashmir.

I tried to understand as best I could the underlying rationale of the United States' position on all this, the timing of their putting forward these proposals, and the unstated but implicit hint that these benchmarks were a list of "dos and don'ts" for India to abide by as a condition for improving relations with the United States. These were to be the measure of our fidelity to nonproliferation. Clearly this was totally unacceptable. As I put across my viewpoint, it was becoming increasingly apparent to the U.S. team that they had perhaps expected too much too soon, and that such an approach would overload the system. India had a certain position on the CTBT, and we were going to move purposefully in that direction—but at our own pace. The prime minister had already stated that we were not going to conduct more nuclear tests. This was a self-imposed restraint amounting to a moratorium. The government had announced its "no first use" doctrine, enabling it to adopt a "credible minimum deterrent" policy. I explained that in no way were we trying to reinvent the Cold War, and we therefore had no use whatsoever for the phraseology of those dead years. Besides, the manner in which the CTBT had been pushed through by the Clinton administration, particularly Article XIV, had, in the Indian public mind, given this initiative the appearance of being an American device, of deliberately discriminating against India. India opposed the introduction of this particular article on several grounds: its approach toward nuclear disarmament, its perception of a potential threat from the existence of nuclear weapons, its strategic circumstances, and above all the unanimous rejection by the Indian Parliament of what was seen as an unequal, dangerous, and coercive treaty. "In the process, the CTBT has got demonized in my country," I told Strobe, and pointed out that the treaty carried both security implications and high political sensitivity. How, therefore, could India agree to concepts such as "strategic restraint" or abandoning forever its own future and technological developments? For what was being sought was not simply a "restraint" on the development of ballistic missiles; there was an implicit capping of India's nuclear capabilities, a rejection, in effect, even of "credible minimum deterrent." Who was to assess that needed "minimum credibility" but India? Someday soon, I had said to Strobe, a voluntary restraint will come about on further production of fissile material, but how could we assent to a cap being placed on India's technological developments, the future of our capacity to invent, to innovate, to use this great national asset of our nation's entrepreneurial and intellectual talent? All this I attempted to convey to Strobe.

But we had moved, both the United States and India. At least we were meeting and talking, which in itself was more progress than we had ever achieved before. This carried the needed reassurance that India was not out to destroy the rest of the world, that we were ready to sit down and reason—not, obviously, to negotiate away our national interests, but certainly to share our concerns, and to accommodate such global concerns as we could. During his stay in Delhi, Strobe gave a letter to Prime Minister Vajpayee from President Clinton. This was when he called on the prime minister and informed him of the progress made in the talks: "There is now a clearer understanding of each other's concerns and certain steps in the direction of addressing those concerns are contemplated. However, ground remains to be covered." We agreed that another round of talks should be held in the second half of August in Washington. The dialogue had by now been defined; the phase of generalities, mutual goodwill, desire for closer relations, and other such preliminaries was over. Though there was now greater mutual confidence, concretizing that general feeling into action was the demanding challenge. But at least we did not have to start from the first letter of the alphabet.[18]

It was against this backdrop that we met in Washington. I went there in a somber and reflective mood. A childhood friend of mine, now at a terminal stage of cancer, had chosen to spend his final days not back at his home in Jodhpur, not with his kin, but instead in my house in Delhi. He had told everyone in his family that he wanted to spend his last few days looking at the greenery from the verandah of my house. He knew he was going. He was beginning to lose his speech and the strength in his limbs. But his mind was clear, and he was blessed, for he was not in pain. After a few days, we could no longer even wheelchair him to the verandah. I was loath to leave him in this state, and yet I had to. When I told him that I would be leaving for Washington and would see him upon my return, he smiled and signaled assent. When I inquired whether there was anything I could get him from America, that cornucopia of material pleasures, he hoarsely expressed his wish for a particular kind of ham radio set. He had always been known for his great booming laughter, but now he could barely manage a smile as he asked for it. I did my best to get it to him before I left. The radio arrived, and when it was in his hands, he was filled with true delight—but by then

---

18. Whereas Strobe had taken the path of constructive engagement with India on this issue of nuclear proliferation, the nonproliferation advocates took a much harder stance. For example, on hearing a rumor that India had demanded U.S. support in its bid for a permanent seat on the Security Council as a quid pro quo for signing the CTBT, a State Department spokesman described that as a "fantasy" and said there was no way that India could "bomb its way" into such realms.

My paternal great-grandfather, Rawal
Moolrajji, with an unknown companion,
ca. 1880. Notice the fine black powder
rifle, and the belt holding the necessities:
powder and cap.

Two generations of maternal grandparents
in Khuri: my maternal great-grandfather,
Maheshdasji, and his son, Mool Singhji.

My paternal grandfather, Rawal Zorawar Singhji, in his townhouse in Jodhpur. His scabbard has a leather covering with no adornment of any kind. Similarly lacking in ostentation is the simple black belt over his straight, practical cummerbund of white cotton.

Thakur Mool Singhji, my maternal grandfather—"Nana" in our dialect and across the whole of South Asia.

Jaswanth's jadhi at Anandpur, Temawas, Rajasthan   Anthony Harrison 10-3-03

A watercolor sketch of my hut in my village. This is where I live when I am home. This sketch
was a gift from a man named Anthony Harrison, a visitor to the famous animal fair. We have
never met, but when he learned that I live here, he left this watercolor for me.

My paternal grandfather, Rawal Zorawar Singhji, on his favorite horse, a bay named Panch Kalyan, which literally means "five auspicious, beneficial attributes."

Above: A marriage party (rather a ragged lot—or is it rugged?) from Jasol, probably ca. the 1920s, with my paternal grandfather, Rawal Zorawar Singhji, in the middle. My two uncles, still children at the time, stand self-consciously on his left; the eldest—the heir, later to be Rawal Amar Singhji—poses elegantly with a slim swagger stick.

Below: A representative photograph of my clansmen, the Rathores, ca. 1890. Presumably they are shown here as part of a wedding party. I received this photograph through the courtesy and generosity of my friend David Campbell, who bought it at an auction, then graciously presented it to me when he visited India.

Above: The swearing-in ceremony of Shri A. B. Vajpayee as prime minister on October 13, 1999, in the forecourt of Rashtrapati Bhawan, the President's House.

Below: Soldiers scaled the gates of Pakistan Television in Islamabad after the announcement that the government had been dismissed. They also seized control of the key installations, closed down the country's main airports, and surrounded the residence of Prime Minister Nawaz Sharif.

A candid shot of Prime Minister Vajpayee and me. This unusual image was taken by a photographer for the Press Trust of India and thereafter was apparently misplaced. It was a welcome surprise when the chairman of PTI, Mr. Razdan, later presented it to me. I asked Mr. Vajpayee to autograph it, which he did with characteristic generosity.

Above: Some key scientists. In front, at the far left, is Colonel Abdul Kalam (with silver hair and glasses). Colonel R. Chidambaram stands next to him, holding a file. Standing behind Chidambaram is Anil Kakodkar (wearing glasses). At the far right, with the dashing tilt to his "jungle hat," is Colonel K. Santhanam.

Below: Prime Minister Vajpayee on a visit to Pokhran, May 20, 1998. He is seated second from left. To his right is Abdul Kalam; to his left are Defense Minister George Fernandes and R. Chidambaram. Standing third from right is S. K. Sikka, who led the Thermonuclear Weapon Development team for Operation Shakti. All are wearing Rajasthani turbans that had been presented to them.

Images from Kargil

Tiger Hill.

Enemy sangars (breastworks) at Shivling.

"Weapon maintenance" by flashlight.

Awesome weight carried in this terrain.

"Boulders" that were surmounted.

Another view of sangars constructed by the intruders.

Not a blade of grass: barren peaks with no cover.

Out in the open, exposed to the elements.

Formidable ridgelines with cliff-like approaches.

The capture of Point 5220 prevented the enemy from observing Turtuk.

Zulu Top.

Rocket launchers had to be frequently employed to destroy enemy sangars.

Above: With Prime Minister Zhu Rongji in Beijing, China, March 26, 2002.

Below: With Foreign Minister Tang Jiaxuan in Beijing, China, March 29, 2002.

Above: With President Pervez Musharraf of Pakistan at Rashtrapati Bhawan, July 14, 2001.

Below: Prime Minister Vajpayee receiving President Hamid Karzai of Afghanistan on the latter's first state visit to India, at Rashtrapati Bhawan, February 27, 2002.

Above: With His Majesty King Birendra Bikram Shah during a four-day visit to Nepal, September 10, 1999.

Below: With Prime Minister Begum Sheikh Hasina of Bangladesh in Calcutta during her three-day visit to West Bengal, January 27, 1999.

Departing Bagram for the swearing-in ceremony of Hamid Karzai in Kabul, Afghanistan, December 22, 2001. This helicopter, my hosts proudly informed me, had been the personal helicopter of the late Ahmed Shah Masood.

Addressing the UN General Assembly, August 8, 2000. I am wearing a turban, as is customary in West Rajasthan when in mourning.

With Pope John Paul II at Hyderabad House during his visit to India,
November 4, 1999.

Above: With Deputy Secretary of State Strobe Talbott at Hyderabad House in New Delhi, July 21, 1998.

Below: With President Vladimir Putin at the Kremlin in Moscow, May 14, 1999.

Above: With Prime Minister Tony Blair at 10 Downing Street, London, January 11, 2000.

Below: Shaking hands with Ariel Sharon during a visit to Israel, July 3, 2000.

Above: Receiving a memento from Yasser Arafat, chairman of the Palestine Liberation Organization and president of the Palestine National Authority, during a four-day visit to Israel and the Palestinian territories, June 30, 2000.

Below: With Mohammed Khatami, president of the Islamic Republic of Iran, in Tehran, May 24, 2000.

Above: With President George W. Bush at the White House, Washington, D.C., October 1, 2001.

Below: With President Jacques Chirac at the Elysée Palace, Paris, during a two-day visit to France, May 27, 1999.

With President Bill Clinton in Agra, March 22, 2000.

To Jaswant ..
Our effort made a difference — great meetings —
and this photo — Wow — What a setting —   With Admiration and Affection —
Madeleine

With Secretary of State Madeleine Albright in Agra during President Clinton's visit, posing with the Taj Mahal in the background, March 22, 2000. The inscription on the photograph reads: "Our efforts made a difference—great meetings—and this photo—Wow—What a setting—with admiration and affection."

R. K. Laxman. First published in *The Times of India*.

R. K. Laxman. First published in *The Times of India*.

R. K. Laxman. First published in *The Times of India*.

Courtesy of *The Hindustan Times*.

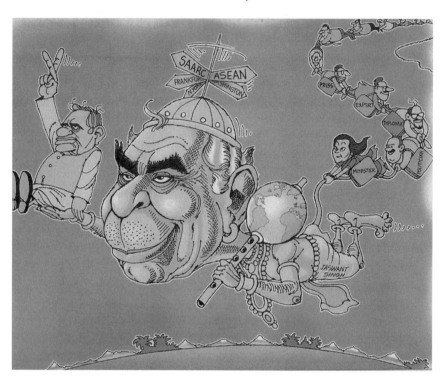

High-Flying Emissary: While Prime Minister Atal Behari Vajpayee keeps his fingers crossed, his special envoy Jaswant Singh is doing all the talking on India's nuclear issue. Of all the politicians and officials assigned the same task, it is the suave and articulate Singh who has saved the day for India around the globe.

he no longer had the strength to even lift it comfortably. "What am I going all over the world for when one of my oldest and dearest friends lies dying of cancer in my house?" This thought played in my mind like a metronome.

On Sunday, August 25, 1998, I reached Washington for the fourth round. As usual, I had woken up very early that morning. It was nearing the end of August, and the Potomac lay shrouded in a predawn haze, sleepy streetlights creating the illusion of a Whistler painting. Gradually the day lit up, and reality took over. Strobe had said that he would come to collect me for dinner that evening; we were to eat at his house. He came as promised, in a classic Mercedes convertible sports car, a rather stylish blue model, if I remember correctly. This was a touch of great friendliness on his part, a gesture he really did not have to make. We drove to his house and sat for a bit in the backyard before moving indoors to the sitting room. The conversation was free-flowing. I spoke at some length on 1947, on how the subcontinent, over the century, had seen many cataclysmic events arrive and flow over the land and its people, eventually to be absorbed by the resilience and the patience of its culture and civilization. I also shared my view that the West continued to demonstrate an absence of understanding of Islam. I cautioned Strobe that the challenges and dangers from terrorism that India had been confronting for decades now would surely— though I hoped very much that I was wrong—visit the United States, too. This was not a warning of any kind; it was only the sharing of an apprehension, to a friend and to a friendly country.

At supper we were joined by National Security Advisor Sandy Berger. Strobe told him that the two of us had been discussing Afghanistan, and I continued for a bit on the same theme. Sandy, however, was very preoccupied; he was immersed almost fully in the concerns of the White House. Thus he was in no mood for Afghanistan. That could wait, he told me somewhat brusquely; what he wanted to hear from me was what India was going to do about the CTBT. I was momentarily taken aback by the abruptness of the question, and by Sandy's tone, too. I had not really anticipated that this was going to be a "working dinner," so I was caught somewhat on the wrong foot. Sandy then said something about a letter that Prime Minister Vajpayee had sent, and how it would be difficult for him to present it to the president. The tone of his remarks placed me in a dilemma. How was I to react? How could I deliberately and knowingly enter into any disputation with my host's guest, let alone aggressively and combatively assert my views? There was no way I could respond in kind, for I was a guest at the home of a fine couple, and a caring lady. Also, there was just no way that

I could make visible my reaction, which was of anger. I later realized that Sandy Berger, as the custodian of the president's agenda, was but discharging his responsibilities diligently and with great dedication.

I lay awake for a long time that night, struggling between jet lag and the time differences, between the evening just spent at Strobe's home and thoughts about my friend who was slowly sinking back in Delhi. But I did learn a very valuable lesson about the negotiating ethos and attitude between different cultures. This difference often requires almost a different language of discourse, even if the medium of communication still be English. For the United States, this was a period of some domestic political pressure—on August 17, President Clinton had appeared before the grand jury investigating a domestic scandal—but I had no interest in that. I did sense that the U.S. administration badly wanted a break, some relief from this daily badgering by the press. Could that break come from India's surrender to the CTBT?

We had a formal meeting at the State Department the next day, a repeat of all that we had gone over earlier. Thereafter I left for New York, where I wrote in my diary, for my friend back in Delhi had gone into a coma and then died, silently but painlessly:

> Do I tire of travel? No, for they must not cease; in movement alone lies the future, in that is life, certainly not in stolid immovability. . . . Thomas Nigel, writing in the *TLS,* says: "Each of our inner lives is such a jungle of thoughts, feelings, fantasies and impulses that civilisation would be impossible if we expressed them all, or if we could all read each other's minds . . . in public encounters." . . . This NY, its skyline, the roads and the lamp-lit dusks, the police sirens, the crowds, the shopfronts; to be in this metropolis of all metropolises, and to be so cocooned, imprisoned really by time and events.

On August 29, speaking at the annual convention of the Indian American Forum for Political Education, Strobe had indicated that any lifting of sanctions would have to be contingent on a positive outcome of the talks. But there was a dramatic turnaround in the position held by Senator Jesse Helms, chairman of the Foreign Relations Committee. It is difficult to judge what caused it, though it is flattering to think that my meeting him contributed to his change of mind. The same senator who, immediately following India's tests, had said that he would "never support a lifting of the Glenn Amendment sanctions on India unless they abandon all nuclear ambitions" changed his views dramatically following my visit, softened his previous position, talked of supporting the repeal of sanctions, and pledged to help put United States India relations back on track.[19] The senator appreciated Delhi's perceptions of a security threat and its need to test nuclear devices so that it could have the needed "strategic autonomy." I caught up briefly with Strobe on September 3 at New York's Kennedy Airport. We agreed to meet later in the month, the date depending on the convenience of travel for both, and we left the venue undecided. Changes were now taking place within the United States; there were some internal difficulties, combined with the fact that President Clinton's second term was beginning to move toward a close. The Democratic administration was thus eager to find a satisfactory conclusion to its foreign policy initiatives.

The Light Turns Amber

Toward the beginning of November, Strobe called me on the telephone. He used our fairly lengthy conversation to both consult and inform me about certain developments. He said that President Clinton would now be moving toward exercising his executive authority for a waiver of sanctions. But before that, he would set in motion a process of serious exchanges with key figures in the United States Congress. All this, Strobe said, was born of the president's appraisal of the initiative that India had already taken and his "highest appreciation" of the prime minister's various steps, as well as Prime Minister Vajpayee's speech to the General Assembly, at which he had said:

> India, having harmonised its national imperatives and security obligations and desirous of continuing to cooperate with the international community, is now engaged in discussions with key interlocutors on a range of issues, including the CTBT. We are prepared to bring these discussions to a successful conclusion, so that the entry into force of the CTBT is not delayed beyond September 1999. . . . These tests [of May 1998] do not signal a dilution of India's commitment to the pursuit of global nuclear disarmament. Accordingly, after concluding this limited testing programme, India announced a voluntary moratorium on further

19. The 1994 Nuclear Proliferation Prevention Act, more commonly known as the Glenn Amendment, prohibits the U.S. from providing financial assistance to a non-nuclear-weapons state that tests a nuclear device. President Clinton imposed Glenn Amendment sanctions against us on May 13, two days after our first test at Pokhran.

underground nuclear test explosions. We conveyed our willing-ness to move towards a *de jure* formalisation of this obligation. In announcing a moratorium, India has already accepted the basic obligation of the CTBT.

Strobe said that as soon as consultations were completed with key con-gressional figures—essentially, with Clinton's political constituency—the president would announce a selective waiver of sanctions. Ambassador Celeste, who took part in the conference call, was required to fill in the details in consultation with Rick Inderfurth, who was also on the line from Washington. Though there was no time frame, it all was to be done at the "earliest possible." I asked whether certain multilateral develop-ment banks could be allowed to transfer funds, because the state of Gujarat had suffered a major cyclone earlier in the summer. Strobe also informed me that an exception was being made, and an IMF program was being recommended to "bail out, hopefully, a collapsing Pakistan." In addi-tion, November 19 was agreed upon as the date for our next meeting, in Rome.

In early November, President Clinton partially lifted the sanctions. That enabled American companies to conduct business in India (and also Pakistan) and gave those companies access to assistance and risk insur-ance from the United States Export-Import Bank, the Overseas Private Investment Corporation, and the Trade and Development Agency. Additionally, the ban on the International Military Education and Training program was lifted. This decision also repealed some parts of the 1985 Pressler Amendment against Pakistan, in effect enabling Pakistan to receive American economic and military assistance once again. In addition, the administration pledged not to oppose IMF credit to Pakistan, which had sought a bailout loan of between $1 and $5 billion. Sanctions contin-ued, of course, on the sale of high technology, including dual technology and military equipment. On November 8, while welcoming the partial relaxation of the ban, Prime Minister Vajpayee charged Washington with making a "discriminatory decision" when it singled out Pakistan for IMF loans but excluded India. On behalf of the State Department, Inderfurth rejected this charge, explaining that the decision was a one-time emer-gency plan because Pakistan's economy was on the brink of disaster. But before the partial removal of the ban, there was another event of some sig-nificance—a speech by Strobe that further clarified the American position. He told his audience at the Brookings Institution in Washington that his speech was a response to an article I had written for *Foreign Affairs.*[20] He said, "The tests in May have increased tensions, highlighted the consequences of misunderstanding and miscalculation, and posed a serious challenge to the viability of the global non-proliferation regime. That means we have no choice but to adjust the focus of our diplomacy accordingly, even while our long-term objectives and interests remain intact." He then outlined the principles that had guided the American team in this dialogue:

> First, we remain committed to the common position of the P-5, G-8, and South Asia Task Force, notably including on the long-range goal of universal adherence to the Nuclear Non-Proliferation Treaty. We do not and will not concede, even by implication, that India and Pakistan have established themselves as nuclear-weapons states under the NPT. Unless and until they disavow nuclear weapons and accept safeguards on all their nuclear activities, they will continue to forfeit the full recognition and benefits that accrue to members in good standing of the NPT. . . . This is a crucial and immutable guideline for our policy, not least because otherwise we would break faith with the states that foreswore a capability they could have acquired—and we would inadvertently provide an incentive for any country to blast its way into the ranks of the nuclear-weapons states.

I left Delhi for Rome on the morning of November 17. It was a long and tedious flight, taking nine and a half hours to reach Paris, where I hurriedly switched to an Alitalia plane. It was on such occasions that I greatly envied my better-equipped "colleagues in the trade," such as Madeleine Albright. After she demitted office as secretary of state, I once asked her what she missed most. Albright replied with her usual combination of wit and wisdom: "Oh, two things, Jaswant. The adrenaline run of challenging events, and my 'home in the air.' I had an aircraft totally at my disposal, to go where I wanted, when I wanted, to do what I wanted, and to live in, too. I sorely miss that now." Bereft of such luxury, my team and I were greeted by a mild southern evening upon our arrival in Rome. The contrast with the colder blasts of the more northern transit points in Europe was marked. To refresh my senses, I made an early morning visit to the Vatican, and to the

---

20. Jaswant Singh, "Against Nuclear Apartheid," *Foreign Affairs* 77, no. 5 (September–October 1998): 41–52.

Sistine Chapel. Its magnificence was truly overwhelming. It is impossible to absorb such riches for too long. I had to cut the visit short.

The round of discussions that followed brought me down to earth. Strobe forced the pace and sought to "adhere to a game plan based on a time frame." Till then, there had been no deadlines, no time frame for agreements or their implementation. Strobe spelled out what he called the "Big Package Approach." He said that the United States would uphold India's strategy, and that America's objectives and its nonproliferation role had been subserved. This was based on the tone and content of the relationship we had built, and because, he most generously added, of "your graciousness and understanding and inherently gentlemanly sense of fair play." He emphasized that India would not be pressured, and it was understood in the United States that India would not do anything under duress. I added a caution that we could not expect remarkable progress every time we met, that there would be times when we would have to pause, take stock, and reassess the whole situation. We issued a joint statement after the Rome round, and though it might have been somewhat anodyne, it still was "joint." And there was more in this joint statement than in any previous Indo-American statement.

In January 1999, Strobe came on a return visit to India, again with a large team. This was the eighth round; along with the plenary, expert-level discussions were also held, and there were several restricted sessions between Strobe, General Ralston, and me. We were delighted to provide General Ralston with an opportunity to hold separate consultations with senior military officials, on a variety of issues, including resumption of bilateral military cooperation in select areas. The restricted sessions that I had with Strobe were more open in approach, and so, I believe, more productive. To illustrate, I offer a single example, based on my notes, for which reason the words may not be exactly those that were used, but the thoughts and contents are accurate. We were discussing the generalities of the dialogue when Strobe, with some justification, said that he would not accept "cherry- picking and a selectivity of approach, your accepting what you prefer now, leaving the rest for later."

"What does it matter, Strobe; all cherries have to ripen and be picked or rot on the branch, or perhaps on the ground—some now, others later."

"But there has to be a time frame within which we deliver, you and me."

"Yes, true enough, but this time frame is not of today's making; we are the inheritors of our respective ends of it. How, then, can the 'frame' of it be the same?"

A short silence followed. Then I added: "It will be a great pity if we consign the future of India-U.S. relations to permanent uncertainty by not harmonizing our vision. Besides, I am not playing some devious end game of chess by engaging in the questionable tactics of *sitzfleisch*.[21] Also, do not push for putting a limit on India's capabilities; that binds my country's future."

After a bit, Strobe responded, "Jaswant, you continue to strive for a high level of sincerity, and always through generality."

The joint statement, issued on January 31, 1999, conveyed the essence of the talks:

> Both delegations are satisfied with the outcome of the talks. As with earlier meetings, the security perspectives of the two sides were further elaborated and clarified and proposals for harmonizing these perspectives were explored. The delegations believe progress was made in several of the subjects under discussion and remain committed to achieving more progress in the weeks ahead.
>
> In this regard, a work plan for the next steps in the U.S.-Indian dialogue was agreed. U.S. and Indian expert-level teams will meet in March [1999] for follow-up talks on export controls. The U.S. and Indian delegations at the Conference on Disarmament in Geneva will endeavor to consult frequently on the status of negotiations on a Fissile Material Cut-off Treaty (FMCT) and the possibility of other multilateral initiatives. Finally, Mr. Talbott and Mr. Singh will remain in close contact. While these contacts continue, both sides will endeavor to create a positive atmosphere for advancing their relations. A ninth round of the dialogue is envisioned towards the middle of the year, the dates and venue to be determined in consultation between the two capitals.
>
> The two delegations recognize that the length of the time devoted to these talks is unprecedented in U.S.-Indian relations. It is the view of both delegations that this is time well spent, laying the foundation for a new, broad-based relationship that has eluded the United States and India in the past, which both sides are determined to achieve in the future.

---

21. *Sitzfleisch*, literally "sitting meat," is an expressive Yiddish word that denotes the ability to sit patiently for as long as it takes to get the job done. In reference to a poker or chess match, it signifies the ability to maintain one's focus and continue making good plays throughout the course of a long game, and thereby to wait out one's opponent.

During this visit to Delhi, Strobe spoke at the India International Centre. The United States and India, he said, "should be natural partners, but all too often in history, circumstances and incompatibilities of perspective seemed to have kept us from being so. This is a reality. But this is not necessarily a permanent one or an immutable one." In an interview with *India Today*, Strobe underscored the progress made at the talks: "I will tell you that we have in this round made some real though not conclusive progress on several of the issues. I think the remaining work to be done could, with imagination and political will, be accomplished in a matter of months." He hinted that the remaining sanctions might be lifted soon: "We are prepared to reach a mode of understanding with each other that would allow us to put sanctions behind us."

We met briefly in the third week of May in Moscow, where I was on a bilateral visit and Strobe was on a different mission, managing United States Russia relations. One evening, I was standing outside the *dacha* where I was lodged when I saw a familiar figure in sneakers, jogging around the track. It was Strobe. We met subsequently, a brief meeting, unplanned and inevitably inconclusive.

By the time summer ended, much had happened. October 1999 was filled with events of historic dimensions. It was a post-Kargil month, and it was also the month when, following an early election, the BJP-led NDA was reelected. There were two other developments of note during that month. Prime Minister Vajpayee was sworn into office on October 13. A day earlier, in Pakistan, Nawaz Sharif had been unseated in a coup, arrested, and placed in military custody. General Pervez Musharraf, the principal architect of Pakistani adventurism in Kargil just months earlier, was now the head of state. (General Musharraf resents the use of the term "coup" for the ousting that put him in control. He prefers to call it a "counter-coup.") In another part of the world, again on October 13, the United States Senate rejected the CTBT. Although the Democratic administration had signed the treaty in 1996, the Republican Party and the Senate Republican leadership had not been in favor of it. Despite the administration's request for action on the CTBT, Helms and Republican majority leader Trent Lott not only opposed it, but also refused to bring it to the Senate floor for either further hearings or debate. In early September, Democratic senator Byron Dorgan warned the Republican leadership that he would "object to other routine business of the Senate" until they brought the treaty to a floor debate. In a surprise move, Senator Lott announced that he would take up the CTBT and schedule a vote on it after twelve hours of debate on October 13. Accordingly, the treaty was voted on and defeated by the Senate, by a vote of forty-eight to fifty-one, far short of the sixty-seven required for a two-thirds approval. This was a crippling defeat for the CTBT. President Clinton had badly wanted it to be ratified, not only to promote nonproliferation, but also so that it would be a part of his presidential legacy. This Senate vote was like a pressure release valve for India, too; suddenly the sting from U.S. efforts was gone.

The year drew to a close with Kandahar. Drained and emotionally exhausted by the challenge of the hijack, I met with Strobe again, for the ninth time, in London on January 18 and 19, 2000. The atmosphere had changed beyond recognition. This was a post-Kargil, post-Kandahar phase; we were relating to one other in a very different manner. It was not adversarial at all anymore; we were much more candid, much more trusting. And as often happens—reinforcing the truism that "Anything that can go wrong will go wrong"—it was in London that an unfortunate and unnecessary misunderstanding occurred. As our final session drew to a close, we withdrew to a corner for a few moments to piece together the wording of a concise press statement. Alok Prasad and Rakesh Sood of the Indian Foreign Service had worked on a "non-paper" to which they were keen to draw the attention of Inderfurth and Einhorn. It suggested steps that included an end to all remaining sanctions by international financial institutions. When the paper was shown to Strobe, it evoked uncharacteristic anger. We left things at that, and let the joint statement at the end of the talks say it all:

> They [Strobe and Jaswant] discussed issues related to disarmament and non-proliferation and focused, in particular, on the Comprehensive Test Ban Treaty (CTBT), the Fissile Material Cut-off Treaty (FMCT), control over exports of sensitive products and technologies, and issues related to defense posture. These four issues have been the subject of ongoing discussion between the two delegations.
>
> Both sides agree on the importance of these issues and the need to make tangible progress. The two sides also agreed that the purpose of the talks is to lay the foundation of a broad-based forward looking relationship between the United States and India. . . . They expressed the hope that a visit of the president of the United States to India in the coming year would provide the occasion to significantly improve mutual understanding and

cooperation. . . . To that end, the two sides agreed to intensify their contacts at all levels in the months ahead.

It was at this London meeting that India and the United States agreed to form a Joint Working Group on Counterterrorism. The talks were still concentrated on security and nuclear nonproliferation, but the focus on terrorism had also been pushed to the front, particularly after Kandahar. It was one of the aims of this Joint Working Group to ensure that the perpetrators of the hijack were brought to justice, and early.[22] But at the same time, the establishment of this group was not a consequence of the hijack alone; it was more a placing on the table of what both sides accepted as an international menace. The question of the CTBT and other aspects of nonproliferation remained, but new importance was also being accorded to events between India and Pakistan that had occurred in 1999. I was queried by the BBC as to what I considered to be a "proper environment for dialogue with Pakistan." I had no difficulty in responding that that would require Pakistan to abjure violence—to recognizably demonstrate that it would give up and stop all cross-border terrorism, currently encouraged by the state of Pakistan and agencies of that state. What was being waged against India was not a proxy war, I said—it was a clandestine war.

Strobe wanted to know more about the Kandahar incident. The most I could say was that it was a "nearly impossible hijack to negotiate. . . . in Kandahar we did not have even a toehold." I then shared a few thoughts about the American role before, during, and after the hijack. Strobe personally had been most supportive. It was also in London that we discussed President Clinton's decision to visit India. Strobe reassured me that the visit "was not related to any progress on NPT."

An interpretation, or rather a controversy, that persists even now in some quarters is that during this dialogue with the U.S., India came close to "signing the CTBT," and also that I was the "principal architect" of moving India in this direction. Of course, signing the CTBT had been a principal U.S. requirement, but it was the U.S. Senate that had derailed this on October 13, 1999. Thereafter, the U.S. administration lost whatever moral pressure they earlier could put on India. If, occasionally during the dialogue and in discussing the issue of adhering to the CTBT, recourse was taken to deflective ambiguity, that can hardly be characterized as adherence.

---

22. It is a matter of some lasting disappointment to me personally that this commitment to bring them to justice "early" went unfulfilled, principally on account of a shift in U.S. priorities for the region.

Clinton Arrives, and a Relationship Is Transformed

Indo-American relations were completely transformed when President Clinton visited India in March 2000. This presidential visit may have done more to change the relationship between our two countries than any other single event of recent times. During Kargil, for the first time in the India-Pakistan context, the United States had come out clearly on the side of facts. President Clinton's statement that the United States would not mediate to resolve the issue of Kashmir—"Only you [Pakistan] and India can do that through dialogue"—was a pleasantly novel experience for us. He had also stood clearly against violence propagated from across the border, dismissing the idea of a plebiscite in Jammu and Kashmir. As he told an audience in Pakistan, where he stopped over for a few hours following his visit to India, "this era does not reward people who struggle to redraw borders in blood. . . . There is no military solution to Kashmir. International sympathy, support, and intervention cannot be won by provoking a bigger, bloodier conflict."

By this time, the Indian economy had also begun to demonstrate its strength, its autarkic nature having been transformed by Prime Minister Vajpayee's policies of opening up trade and investment. The enhanced role and visibility of the nonresident Indian community and its numerous successes in America also made a very important contribution to our relationship with the U.S. The popular mood was ripe for a quantum leap, and President Clinton's visit effected precisely that. He came when India's mood toward the United States was fully attuned and accommodating. He said and did all the right things, sure in the knowledge that he would find a receptive audience, by touching the right chords, by describing the relationship between our two countries as having the elasticity of Indian classical music because it required the players to improvise.

President Clinton reached Delhi on March 19, accompanied by his daughter, Chelsea, and an entourage of sixty-three officials and more than a hundred journalists. After a ceremonial welcome at Rashtrapati Bhawan and a visit to the Gandhi Memorial, Clinton's official dialogue with Prime Minister Vajpayee took place. The meeting went on for an hour and a half. On nonproliferation, Clinton was firm but not offensive. Although he acknowledged that India had "the right to determine its own security needs," he wanted India to steer clear of an arms race or further nuclear testing. Vajpayee responded by reassuring his guest that "India's policy was no threat to the US, [and that] India was not keen on a war with

Pakistan or on an arms race." The talks ended with a ten-minute discussion between the two leaders, without any aides. Later they issued a joint "vision" statement setting out their "resolve to create a closer and cumulatively new relationship" between the two countries. They agreed to be "partners in peace, with a common interest in and complementary responsibility for ensuring regional and international security," promising to "work together for strategic stability in Asia and beyond."

In his address to a joint sitting of both houses of Parliament, Clinton urged India and the United States to "respectfully listen to each other." Ironically, he was conveying that which India had so often complained that the United States never did! Clinton accepted that India would not choose "a course of action simply because others wish it to do so." When he said, "You will believe what I say and understand better that America very much wants you to succeed" and that the United States wanted "India to be strong; to be secure; to be united; to be a force for a safer, more prosperous, more democratic world," he was saying what Indian parliamentarians believed in but still wanted to hear from an American president. When he concluded his eloquent address with such memorable phrases, President Clinton was applauded by the members of Parliament, a response from my hard-headed political compatriots, of all parties, that I, in my entire political career, had never seen accorded to a visiting head of state. This was Bill Clinton's own achievement; the response was what an immeasurably generous India would always give to a visitor who approached it with understanding and a spirit of respect for its soul.

Prime Minister Vajpayee was equally eloquent and riveting. And when he concluded, most imaginatively, most movingly, it was a befitting response:

> Mr. President, your visit marks the beginning of a new voyage in the new century by two countries which have all the potential to become natural allies. . . . We can do no better than to recall to ourselves the stirring words of the great American poet Walt Whitman. Noting that a "Passage to India" is always "Passage to more than India," Whitman, in his long and admiring poem on India, called upon our two peoples to:
>> Sail forth—steer for the deep waters only,
>> Reckless O soul, exploring, I with thee, and thou with me,
>> For we are bound where no mariner has not yet dared to go.

Mr. William Jefferson Clinton, I conclude by extending, on behalf of the people of India, my best wishes to you and to the people of your great country. I do hope your visit to India will be a memorable one.

It was.

In a press statement, the prime minister put the new relationship in perspective, calling it "a durable, politically constructive and economically productive partnership between the world's two largest democracies."

> President Clinton and I have just signed a vision statement. The statement outlines the contours of and defines the agenda of our partnership in the twenty-first century. We both agreed that our commitment to the principles and practice of democracy constitutes the bedrock of our relations and for our cooperative efforts internationally for peace, prosperity and democratic freedom. . . . We have also concluded agreements and understandings on the establishment of very wide-ranging dialogue architecture.

On the issues that Strobe and I had struggled over, Prime Minister Vajpayee added:

> President Clinton and I had a frank discussion on the issues of disarmament and non-proliferation of weapons of mass destruction. The dialogue which is in progress between our two countries on these issues has enhanced mutual understanding of our respective concerns. I've explained to President Clinton the reasons that compel us to maintain a minimum nuclear deterrent. I have reiterated our firm commitment not to conduct further nuclear explosive tests, not to engage in a nuclear arms race, and not to be the first to use nuclear weapons against any country.

Soon after Clinton had reached India, on March 20, there was a terrorist attack in Jammu. Thirty-five Sikhs were killed in the village of Chati-Singhpura in Anantnag District. The prime minister said, "The brutal massacre of thirty-five Sikhs in Jammu and Kashmir . . . is further evidence of the ethnic cleansing that has been underway for a decade, and is part of a pattern that we have experienced earlier. . . . This attempt at cloaking ethnic terrorism in the guise of jihad carries no conviction. We and the international community reject the notion that jihad can be a part of any civilised country's foreign policy."

A number of agreements were signed; and of course there was the obligatory visit to Agra, where Madeleine Albright and I signed an agreement. She had requested to do so at that indescribably romantic and beautiful place and wanted to be photographed with me there, with the Taj Mahal behind us. As the president's Gulfstream aircraft took off for Jaipur, clouds began to gather, and it rained, as if in celebration. The remainder of Clinton's visit was unofficial, and included a leisurely trip to the Ranthambore wildlife sanctuary. Even the tigers obliged, sauntering onto the trail that the president was being driven on. Clinton's visit coincided with the spring festival of Holi, and in the tradition of that "Festival of Colors," he was regaled by the inhabitants of a Rajasthani village and covered in colored powder. Bombay then followed, from where, on March 25, he left for Pakistan. He traveled in a decoy plane, guarding against any threat from terrorists linked to Osama bin Laden. In his five-hour stopover, he held talks with President Musharraf and told him that he should return Pakistan to democracy, forcefully stating that the United States had irrefutable evidence of involvement by Pakistan's ISI Agency in supporting terrorist groups such as the Harkatul-Ansar in Jammu and Kashmir. Addressing the people of Pakistan over television and radio, Clinton warned that the "endless, costly campaign in Kashmir only sets Pakistan back [from] economic development [and] the American people don't want to see tensions rise and suffering increase. We want to be a force for peace, but we cannot force peace. [The] Lahore meeting is the right road to peace for Pakistan and India and for the resolution of the problem in Kashmir." These or similar thoughts India had never heard from the United States, let alone from its president.

Postscript: An American president's visit is not without its pathos and its bathos, and sometimes the two do collide. On March 21, President Clinton left for a day's visit to Dhaka, but without the obligatory tuxedo; his valet had forgotten to put it on board. Great anxiety seized the officials of the Ministry of External Affairs when it was learned that an aircraft from the flight squad was returning. I was informed of this in hushed tones and even advised to keep the prime minister briefed. Later, I wondered what treatment was handed out to the hapless valet!

Just Short of the Village

Following President Clinton's visit, Prime Minister Vajpayee undertook a return visit to Washington between September 13 and 17, 2000. His address to a joint session of both houses of Congress is worth repeating:

> Many of you here in the Congress have in recent hearings recognized a stark fact: no region is a greater source of terrorism than our neighborhood. Indeed, in our neighborhood—in this, the twenty-first century—religious war has not just been fashioned into, it has been proclaimed to be, an instrument of state policy. Distance offers no insulation. It should not cause complacence. You know and I know, such evil cannot succeed. But even in failing, it could inflict untold suffering. That is why the United States and India have begun to deepen their cooperation for combating terrorism. We must redouble these efforts.

Prime Minister Vajpayee's visit was, for me personally, greatly satisfying. He was suffering acutely at the time because of a knee ailment. Surgery had been recommended, but he had deferred it so that he could complete this mission. It was an act of courage and stoicism, for he withstood the pressure and demands of a state visit, and given the weight of his years, he demonstrated exemplary fortitude. As President Clinton himself put it, the visit was "a great success; it rounds off our efforts to take a different turn in our relationship." The theme that underlined Prime Minister Vajpayee's visit was a "further deepening and widening of Indo-U.S. relations, as between two equals." There was scarcely a discordant note. It was this visit that laid the foundation of Indo-American military cooperation. The endeavor that had begun with Pokhran II had borne fruit. On September 17, President Clinton and First Lady Hillary Clinton hosted a state banquet on the South Lawn of the White House in honor of the Indian prime minister. More than 700 guests of diverse backgrounds attended. It was the largest banquet ever held by the Clinton administration. By then, Strobe knew and I knew that the venture on which we had started would remain unfinished. We had set out on our journey looking for "a way to the village." We had found the way, I was sure, but we did not have the time to conclude the journey and reach the village. That task was yet to be completed.

Elections followed in the United States, and the Democrats lost the White House. I had not had the benefit of meeting anyone who had served in the most recent Republican administrations (1980–92) except for George Schultz, secretary of state in the Reagan years and an elder statesman in the Republican hierarchy. In September 2000, at a lunch in San Francisco that Schultz kindly and thoughtfully arranged for me, I also met Condoleezza Rice. Somewhere in the distance, the village still beckoned.

10

The Republican Innings

The President Drops In

President George W. Bush was sworn in as the forty-third president of the United States on January 20, 2001. The inaugural was rather tense, accompanied by extensive security. The counting and recounting of the votes cast in Florida had generated a great deal of heat, and the new president's rivals were accusing him of "stealing" the election. Even so, there was a new man in the White House, and he was ready to get down to work. President Bush took little time in letting the world know that his foreign policy team would consist of General Colin Powell as secretary of state and Condoleezza Rice as national security advisor. Between the inaugural and the new foreign policy team reaching out to India, again, not much time was lost. This was in marked contrast to the previous presidency; India had waited in line, as it were, in Bill Clinton's first term. But during his second term, all that had changed.

This institutionalized dialogue and cooperation continued under the Bush administration. Even before the inaugural, on January 17, 2001, Secretary of State-Designate Colin Powell, during his confirmation hearings, emphasized to the Senate Foreign Relations Committee that he would review the situation with India and determine "whether this is the right time to move forward and remove the remaining sanctions that are in place." He noted that "India has to be a high priority for foreign policy activities of the U.S." I was at the time, and for some extremely challenging and rewarding months thereafter, simultaneously minister for both external affairs and defense. This was an experience to cherish, unique in Indian politics. Of immense value to me was this opportunity to do something for the armed forces, where, after all, I had started my public career. I had never imagined that I would ever be defense minister; more likely, I often remarked facetiously, "I would have been court-martialed had I remained in uniform!"

On March 20, 2001, a press release announced my upcoming visit to the United States in April. The month before, at the Annual Security Meeting in Munich in February, National Security Adviser Brajesh Mishra had met Donald Rumsfeld, the new U.S. secretary of defense. (There was an avoidable ruckus in Munich when Rumsfeld voiced the United States' plans for deployment of the National Missile Defense system. This unilateral announcement caused ruffled feathers.) I was clearly going to a very different Washington. There was the obvious enough political change, but also a change of atmosphere. President Bush had high approval ratings in the polls, and the nation felt that it was on the move. Whatever the electoral rhetoric, it was a sound economy that Bush had inherited, a secure country he had become the president of. For me this visit was a "get acquainted" effort. I was received by my counterpart, General Colin Powell, with military affability, an ease natural to the fraternity of the forces. There was no specific issue that needed to be addressed. I complimented him on the restraint with which the United States, particularly the State Department and he himself, had been able to defuse the tense moments following the loss of a Chinese Air Force pilot after his F-8 fighter jet had collided with a U.S. reconnaissance plane and crashed in the South China Sea. The American plane had sustained significant damage and was forced to land on the Chinese island of Hainan. Powell was a bit cautious in receiving my compliment, perhaps not quite sure what I really meant, though I had no hidden meaning. I called on Condoleezza Rice, too. Her office was much smaller than Colin Powell's. Indeed, the importance of the post of U.S. national security advisor has waxed and waned entirely on the strength of the occupant and his or her access to the president.

We had barely sat down to talk—it had been about ten minutes, I think—when I became the beneficiary of one of President Bush's drop-in visits. He walked in with disarming informality. After I was introduced, we sat down and exchanged some cursory views about India-U.S. relations. Missile defense was an issue of great interest to him at the time. I had my own views: "It would be much better to catch a missile in midair, if you could, even as it was heading for you, and destroy it, rather than the other options"—those "other options" consisting primarily of preemptive strikes on the adversary's missile silos, thus eliminating the possibility of the launch itself. But when do you launch? The United States pursued policies of "hair-trigger alert," of "launch on warning." That warning could be anything from hard intelligence to a flight of geese caught by the protective radar cover—as indeed had happened earlier. There could be serious errors in such warning-based launches. But the ability to intercept a missile that is headed for you and to destroy it right there in midair is infinitely better.

True, this is a very complex technology requiring great accuracy, and that can be an inhibiting factor. Also, the Patriot missiles used against the Iraqi Scuds in 1991 in the First Gulf War—aged, lumbering, unpredictable missiles of Soviet origin—had not been a shining success, either. Congress was then in session, and President Bush had to leave, or, as he said, he would "not be very popular with the First Lady." "So far so good," I thought, "a good beginning with the Republicans." Later, when I shared with the press that the president had dropped by during my meeting with Rice, there was a scramble for the headlines. I also referred to the short discussion we had had on missile defense. This generated a fierce and, I thought, totally unwarranted debate on what until then had been but a half-digested idea.

President Bush addressed the National Defense University in Washington on May 1, 2001. There he defined the policy platform for his government. He included a pertinent reference to missile defense:

> Several months ago, I asked Secretary of Defense Rumsfeld to examine all available technologies and basing modes for effective missile defenses that could protect the United States, our deployed forces, our friends, and our allies. The secretary has explored a number of complementary and innovative approaches. He has identified near-term options that could allow us to deploy an initial capability against limited threats. In some cases, we can draw on already established technologies that might involve land-based and sea-based capabilities to intercept missiles in mid-course or after they reenter the atmosphere. We also recognize the substantial advantages of intercepting missiles early in their flight, especially in the boost phase. The preliminary work has produced some promising options for advanced sensors and interceptors that may provide this capability. If based at sea or on aircraft, such approaches could provide limited, but effective, defenses. We have more work to do to determine the final form the defenses might take. We will explore all these options further. We recognize the technological difficulties we face, and we look forward to the challenge. Our nation will assign the best people to this critical task. I've made it clear from the very beginning that I would consult closely on the important subject with our friends and allies who are also threatened by missiles and weapons of mass destruction. . . .
>
> I'm announcing the dispatch of high-level representatives to allied capitals in Europe, Asia, Australia, and Canada to discuss

our common responsibility to create a new framework for security and stability that reflects the world of today. These will be real consultations. We are not presenting our friends and allies with unilateral decisions already made. We look forward to hearing their views, the views of our friends, and to take them into account.

The following day, Delhi reacted through a press release:

> The minister of external affairs had a telephonic conversation this afternoon with US national security adviser, Dr Condoleezza Rice . . . as part of an information and consultation process with India, among other countries, about a major policy statement that President Bush was . . . to make through a speech at the National Defence University. This is a far-reaching statement of US national security policy by the Bush administration [seeking] to transform the strategic parameters on which the Cold War security architecture was built.

The statement welcomed the announcement of unilateral reductions of nuclear forces by the United States, as well as movement away from the "hair-trigger alerts" otherwise associated with nuclear orthodoxies.

I chose the ministry's statement to affirm a strategic and technological inevitability in stepping away from a world held hostage to the doctrine of MAD (Mutually Assured Destruction) and toward a more cooperative, defensive transition, underpinned by a "de-alert of nuclear forces." This was an idea ahead of its time, but I wanted to place the subject of "de-alert" on the table. It was and remains an initiative worth examining. In consultations with "friends and allies," Rice conveyed President Bush's decision to send his personal special emissary, Deputy Secretary of State Richard Armitage, to Delhi. "He will consult with you," she said, "and discuss a new framework for security and stability that reflects the world of today." Armitage, who had assumed Strobe's former post, made a one-day visit to Delhi on May 11. He was carrying a letter from President Bush for Prime Minister Vajpayee, accepting an invitation to visit India. In this letter, Bush also conveyed his intention to work closely with Vajpayee "to promote common interests in Asia and beyond," since Vajpayee's government welcomed the American proposals "as a departure from the norms of the Cold War" and "based upon consultation and cooperation rather than confrontation."

Armitage elaborated that the American proposals did, in fact, outline a "New Strategic Framework that comprised four elements—non-proliferation; counter-proliferation; missile defense; and a reduction in the United States' strategic nuclear arsenal." He then explained the rationale for all of them and emphasized that missile defense was only one parameter of a much larger framework. To us, this was a very welcome development on a number of counts, and certainly a departure from past norms, when consultation and cooperation were an exception to the then prevalent climate of confrontation. I did underscore the importance of not unilaterally abrogating the ABM Treaty—the Treaty on the Limitation of Anti-Ballistic Missile Systems, signed between the United States and the Soviet Union in 1972—or similar international commitments. I conveyed India's expectations about enhancing regional and international stability and security. The American intention of a reduction in and de-alerting of nuclear weapons was greatly welcomed; we viewed it as a step in the direction of winding down the nuclear arms race. I did, however, share a concern about managing the transition from this current regime of "launch on warning" and "hair-trigger alerts" to a cooperative "New Strategic Framework." Inevitably, this would present a challenge to the will and commitment of the international community. Was not India's approach of no first use, non-use against non-nuclear-weapons states, and "de-alert" therefore a reliable mechanism for moving toward a new global security order? Never mind Armitage's answer; this consultation was in itself a far cry from those early months just after another May 11, in the summer of 1998. It had been only three years! Clearly, things were moving rapidly now between the United States and India. The foundation laid earlier was firm, and the new Republican policy frame enabled rapid progress.

Atavists in Our Backyard

Meanwhile, events were developing in India's immediate neighborhood, in Pakistan and in Afghanistan, where the situation continued to deteriorate. The struggle with the Taliban oscillated between Kabul and the Shomali Plains, between the Panjshir Valley and the deep north. One day, the news would be that the Taliban had reached the Amu Darya (the Oxus River), that Mazar-e-Sharif had fallen. The next day, it would change hands again. But that was the nature of conflict in Afghanistan: it is not a land much given to pitched battles. Toward the end of May, at our invitation, arrived Ahmad Shah Massood, leader of the Northern Alliance, the "Lion of Panjshir." He spent four days in Delhi. This had to be a closely guarded visit, as any number of terrorist groups from Afghanistan and Pakistan were vying to assassinate him. I was glad I had a chance to meet with him at leisure. It enabled me to understand how he, as commander of an essentially Tajik force somewhat grandly dubbed the "Afghan Army," was meeting the challenge of the Taliban, who were armed and being assisted by Pakistan. How was he managing the rigorous demands of that fluctuating war, of uncertain supplies, and of keeping the Panjshir Valley fed and looked after? Massood had an easy manner, a presence that he was fully aware of and which he used to advantage. He had gained renown as much inside Afghanistan as internationally with his stand against the occupying Soviet troops, and thereafter the Taliban, for they too represented foreign subjugation. In the process, he came to epitomize the spirit of freedom of Afghanistan. That was why he was accepted by the entire Northern Alliance as leader even though he was a Tajik in a Pashtun-dominated area.

I had lengthy talks with him, at which we discussed the movement of forces, the form of warfare, the terrain, logistics, and supplies. We examined the Tirich-Mir Pass, close to the border with Pakistan-Occupied Kashmir. Massood and I discussed whether a threat or an attack on the Panjshir Valley could occur through this pass, thus catching his forces from the rear. He explained, at some length and with logic, why this was not a militarily sustainable venture. Because the opening was so narrow, only a small patrol—maybe five to seven strong—could go over that pass into Tajik-dominated Panjshir, and they would be risking their lives in the process. "Were they to stupidly do so, there is only one fate they would meet," he said. Massood also shared with me what he knew about the hijack in 1999 of flight IC-814. I was astonished at his knowledge of details, but not when he said that he knew who the hijackers were and where they were at that moment: "They all are in Pakistan now, because it was a Taliban-assisted hijack." Upon the conclusion of the visit, we had Massood escorted back to Afghanistan by a circuitous route, not flying over Pakistan. I did not know then that I would not meet him again.

Massood fell victim to a suicide attack at Khoja Baha-ud-din (also spelled Khwaja Baha-ud-din) on September 9, 2001, just two days before 9/11. The timing was ominous. It is believed that Osama bin Laden ordered this assassination so as to ensure that he would have the grateful Taliban's protection after the attack on America. Massood was assassinated by two Moroccan Arabs claiming to be journalists from Belgium. Akbar Khaleeli, the Afghan ambassador in Delhi, was visiting Massood in the Panjshir and sitting next to him when the assassination was carried out. Khaleeli had a providential escape, but Massood suffered fatal injuries. As an eyewitness, Khaleeli asserts that the bomb was hidden in the video camera; the two killers had been in Massood's area for approximately three weeks, studying, assessing, and reconnoitering before they struck. Khaleeli further recalls that when he noticed the video camera focusing on Ahmed Shah Massood's chest, he asked the assassins "whether they were planning to photograph their bellies." One of the "photographers" died in this "suicide photography" attack; the other was shot while trying to escape. Their passports turned out to be stolen, and on October 16, 2003, the French secret service disclosed that the camera they used had also been stolen, from Grenoble, France, in December 2000. Through determined tracking, this investigative agency was able to determine the identity of the original owner. The French secret service then traced the route that the camera had taken from Grenoble to Massood's final moments.[1] Pakistan played a role in that camera's travels!

India's cooperation with the Northern Alliance is largely a story yet to be told. A more complete narration of it will have to wait. Our cooperation occurred over several years, encountering many difficulties and passing through difficult phases, but it was consistent and covered many areas. Of great use to the Northern Alliance, particularly to Ahmad Shah Massood and his force, was the hospital we established, staffed, and operated at Farkhor, on the Afghanistan-Tajikistan border. It was there that he was flown after the attack, although given the nature of his injuries (some shrapnel had pierced his heart), he must have died almost instantly. I do derive some satisfaction from knowing that the helicopter in which Massood always flew was the one that later flew me from Bagram to Kabul to witness the realization of Massood's great dream: the inauguration in December 2002 of Hamid Karzai as the president of a new, post-USSR, post-Taliban, independent Afghanistan.

On the afternoon of September 11, 2001, I was sitting in my office when Raghavan, who then helped me with my work, rushed in, anxiety written all over his face. "Sir, a terrible tragedy seems to have occurred," he said. "An airplane has collided with the World Trade Center in New York." There is little point now in recounting the entire chain of events. That attack did not cripple the United States, as its perpetrators had hoped;

---

1. Some details not in my own knowledge are from http://en.wikipedia.org/wiki/Ahmed_Shah_Massoud; Jon Lee Anderson, "A Lion's Death," *The New Yorker,* October 1, 2001; and Jon Lee Anderson, "The Assassins," ibid., June 10, 2002.

instead it awakened the might of that nation to the global menace of radical Islam. It was a day to throw protocol aside. As an immediate gesture of support, I telephoned the American ambassador, Robert Blackwill, and said, "I would be very happy if I could be of any use in this hour of trial for the U.S. The people and the government of India share the pain of your country." Later that evening, after a special meeting of the Cabinet Committee on Security, the press was informed that "the Cabinet Committee on Security has expressed its great horror at this crime that has been perpetrated and has offered its deepest condolences and sympathy to the people, government, and the president of the United States of America. We have already initiated action for providing all necessary [and] additional security and safeguards required for the US Embassy and consulates in India. Terrorism is a crime against humanity, and India is committed to fight it, and we shall." Prime Minister Vajpayee called President Bush on the evening of September 16 and had a fairly lengthy conversation with him. Both leaders agreed that the dialogue already established between the two countries required that they keep each other informed about terrorist organizations. Accordingly, National Security Adviser Brajesh Mishra was deputed for the purpose.

Toward the end of September, Prime Minister Vajpayee traveled to the United Nations for the General Assembly's annual meeting. In that period, the Security Council adopted a resolution on international terrorism. It was prompted by the Twin Towers attack, of course, but it included in its ambit so much more, so much of what had happened in India, so many of our concerns. Our reaction acknowledged this: "UN Security Council Resolution 1373, of 28 September 2001, signals the global nature of international terrorism and the need for comprehensive international cooperation in combating it." This resolution called upon all states to "prevent and suppress" any financing of terrorist acts; to prohibit their nationals from making any "resources or services available" to those who had a hand in terrorist acts; to place curbs on those who "finance, plan, support or commit terrorist acts; and to prevent terrorists from using their territories for terrorist acts against other states or citizens." The resolution provided a template for collective action against terrorism; for India, it could not have come sooner.

On October 2, a day after the Security Council adopted Resolution 1373, I met Colin Powell again. It was an altogether different kind of meeting, for now I could reaffirm our stand against terrorism as from one victim to another. On that first visit after 9/11, I wanted particularly to go to the Pentagon. I had been moved by the knowledge that Donald Rumsfeld, who was in the Pentagon when the attack came, had chosen, as soon as the alarm was over, to rush to the damaged portion of the building to assist the injured. That is why I wanted to go to the Pentagon, and to meet Rumsfeld. In the aftermath of 9/11, relations between our two countries became even better. The Bush administration lifted the remaining economic sanctions, and when an attack was to be launched against al-Qaeda and the Taliban in Afghanistan, India volunteered its cooperation. On October 7, the United States–led attack on Afghanistan began. Beforehand, President Bush had telephoned Prime Minister Vajpayee and informed him of all the essential details. As expected, the targeting was selective, minimizing as much as possible the impact of the operations on the civilian population. India, with its long tradition of warm and friendly ties with the people of Afghanistan, welcomed President Bush's statement of October 7 reiterating that "the current focus on Afghanistan is part of a broader battle against terrorism." India's position on the global character of terrorism and the need for concerted worldwide action against terrorism everywhere was well known.

By now, events were moving fast. Within a week of the attack on Afghanistan, Colin Powell came to India. In Delhi he expressed what he had not said earlier: that the United States and India were united against terrorism, "and that includes terrorism directed at India." He said that the U.S. and India were "natural allies," standing "shoulder to shoulder." The three issues that dominated discussions—and were, significantly, of mutual concern—were terrorism, the debate on missile defense, and nonproliferation along with nuclear missiles and intercontinental ballistic missiles (ICBMs). With respect to the first point, terrorism, India affirmed that 9/11 "was an assault on freedom, on civilization, on democracy." The United States finally recognized that India's stand against terrorism had not originated with September 11 but dated from much earlier, and that India had never been equivocal in this battle. Powell also made it clear that one of President Bush's priorities was to transform the U.S.-India relationship and move it to a higher plane. The secretary of state outlined the contours and content of American policy: "I want to make it clear that our focus in Afghanistan now is eradicating the al-Qaeda network, to end the terrorist use of Afghanistan as a safe haven, to stop the invasion of Afghanistan that has taken place as a result of the presence of al-Qaeda. We will achieve that goal." A hiccup had occurred during Powell's visit to the region—whether intentionally or otherwise, I do not know.

In Pakistan, just before he arrived in India, he had referred to Kashmir as "a central issue." Inevitably, the remark was strongly criticized in India. "We certainly do not agree with this premise," the Ministry of External Affairs spokesperson promptly reacted. "There should be no confusion between cause and effect. The present situation in Jammu and Kashmir is a consequence of state-sponsored terrorism, and not its cause."

Powell was obviously embarrassed. In response to a question at his press conference in Delhi, he attempted a fairly verbose clarification:

> I didn't say "a central." If you look at it carefully, I said "central" in the sense that I believe it is an important issue, and to suggest that it isn't wouldn't have been accurate. But it is more important to look at the rest of my statement where I said that we should move forward on the basis of dialogue, on the basis of efforts to reduce tension, to avoid violence, and with respect to human rights. I think that is a sound statement. The issue of Kashmir is one that has to be resolved between India and Pakistan. The United States is a friend of both of those nations. To the extent that [the two] find our efforts helpful in some way or the other, we will be willing to be helpful.

He also attempted to put "missile defense" into perspective. There were questions raised about whether this program would incite China to expand its nuclear arsenal, in turn pushing India and then Pakistan into an arms race in South Asia. This Powell dismissed easily:

> No, I don't agree with that assessment. I think the kind of missile defense that we are planning . . . is very limited. I think once people come to understand the kind of reductions we are going to make in our strategic offensive weapons—significant reductions, to much, much lower numbers—and when people have a chance to get a look-in, come to understand the nature of our limited missile defense, I don't think either Russia or China will find it destabilizing with respect to their deterrent forces. In my conversations, both here and in Islamabad, I heard from both sides about this issue. I took the opportunity of my meeting with the prime minister to describe the president's strategic framework concept and to thank the Indians for their understanding of the importance of missile defense. I get the sense that both nations under-

stand the nature of these weapons and the importance of constraining their developments so that they serve as deterrents, and do not move from a strategy of deterrence to any other kind of strategy. So there is no reason for an arms race to develop based on what the United States is planning.

That visit left me with plenty of food for thought. Naturally, with so much conflict in the vicinity of both India and Pakistan and with American troops now physically present in Pakistan, there were concerns about a growing relationship between a democratic United States and military Pakistan. What would this do to India's relationship with the United States? How might it affect India's approach to Pakistan? Also, how could our neighbor combat terrorism in Afghanistan while simultaneously promoting it in Jammu and Kashmir? These were and remain complex challenges, more so in their cumulative effect on India. Finding an answer was India's responsibility, I knew. We would find no accommodation from the United States on this, for after 9/11, the Americans were completely preoccupied with their own concerns.

At the beginning of November 2001, I demitted the office of minister of defense, which I had been holding simultaneously with my position in external affairs. George Fernandes, in whose place I had been temporarily entrusted with this charge, was back in office, and his very first visitor, in a happy coincidence, was Donald Rumsfeld. This was yet another indication of the evolving strategic relationship between the two countries. This round was dominated by Afghanistan, Pakistan, and terrorism. It was an opportunity for the Pentagon and the Ministry of Defence to engage directly on these issues. On November 5, an invitation was extended by President Bush to Prime Minister Vajpayee for an official working visit between November 7 and 9. At a meeting during that visit, President Bush emphasized India's "fantastic ability to grow, because her greatest export is intelligence and brainpower." He also talked about lifting the sanctions against India so as to enable it to combat terrorism: "There needs to be a commitment by all of us to do more than just talk. It's to achieve certain objectives, to cut off the finances, to put diplomatic pressure on the terrorists . . . stand firm in the face of terror." The agenda was growing. Cyber-terrorism, civilian space cooperation, and energy were already emerging as bilateral issues.

Meanwhile, the need in Afghanistan was for the urgent establishment of political order and for provision of relief to the refugees, but differences were already discernible in an understanding of the nature of the challenge posed by Afghanistan, or of the conflict itself in that country, for the United States. "This is a different kind of war," said President Bush. "It's a war that matches high-technology weapons with people on horseback. It's a war in which the enemy thinks they can hide in caves and we'll forget about them. It is a war that's going to take a deliberate, systematic effort to achieve our objectives. And our nation has not only got the patience to achieve that objective, we've got the determination to achieve the objective. And we will achieve it."

All of this was timely and extremely relevant, because the Northern Alliance had by then defeated the Taliban, and the regime in Kabul had changed hands yet again as the Northern Alliance forces streamed into that ancient and historic capital. The date was November 15, 2001.

Yet again my schedule required that I complete a round of my own meetings and consultations. Therefore, on Monday I met with National Security Advisor Condoleezza Rice in her White House office. For the second time, President Bush dropped in, and more than half of the roughly seventy-five minutes of the meeting that I had with the national security advisor were spent discussing various aspects of the current situation, including Afghanistan, with President Bush.

But by then the latest potentially destructive event had already occurred, prevented by only a miraculous set of circumstances. This was the attack on the Jammu and Kashmir Assembly on October 1, 2001. The incident outraged Prime Minister Vajpayee and all of us, as well as the rest of the country. This export of terrorism to India by America's newly rediscovered ally Pakistan was clearly going to pose problems for us, because the Pakistani military regime was very much a part of the problem—and up to that point it had not played any part at all in the solution. It was necessary that I emphasize this, and as candidly as I could, I did convey it to both President Bush and his national security advisor. To us, I insisted and made clear, no fight against terrorism could be unidirectional or even unidimensional. It was a global fight, which is why it was necessary for me to assert that while the United States was understandably focused on al-Qaeda, Bin Laden, and the Taliban, the vast number of other terrorist organizations that had been spawned by or cloned from the original were still in operation, severely testing India's patience and "inflicting upon innocent citizens of my country deliberate and defiant acts of terrorist violence." Thus I stressed to both President Bush and Condoleezza Rice that "the responsibility for dealing with terrorism in India has to rest with India. We have been fighting it for the past several decades, and we will continue to do so. How can, or why should, anyone protect India against this menace if we do not protect ourselves? That is why Pakistan turning itself over to terrorist groups like the Taliban is a matter of continuing concern to us." Soon after my return, on December 13, 2001, while I was working in my office at the Parliament, it was attacked by a group of terrorists. (See chapter 8.) This was another "first time ever"—a terrorist attack on India's Parliament.

Condemnations of this heinous crime flashed across the globe. Messages began to arrive from presidents and prime ministers, heads of state and heads of government. The United States, too, aware of how important nuances and phrasing had become in those terrorism-infected circumstances, called the assault "an act of terrorism." But Pakistan had a problem: the government there found it difficult to accept even that which was so explicit, so clearly visible to all. Their first reactions were baffling and nonchalant. Although it was public knowledge that one of the attacking terrorists had called Karachi on his cell phone minutes before entering Parliament, General Musharraf chose to react by asking why Pakistan would have undertaken such a risky endeavor. Besides, he wondered, "what kind of terrorists are they if all of them go and get killed?" That was a reasonable enough query on the general's part, if you think about it, but it was also rather limitedly military.

What, then, was the aim of these two attacks? The first, on October 1, 2001, was carried out against the state legislature of Jammu and Kashmir, where just minutes before, Chief Minister Farooq Abdullah had fortuitously walked out of the premises; and the second, on December 13, 2001, was targeted against the Parliament. Was the intention to cripple and eliminate first the political leadership of Jammu and Kashmir, and then the rest of the country? If the goal was not to eliminate that leadership, then it was certainly to inflict grievous injury, both physically and morally. Pakistan later announced that "the excuse that there was a terrorist attack on Parliament, for which we have no evidence, should not have been met with this brinkmanship, this response of moving forces to the border and creating a climate of possible war between two countries with nuclear potential. This is brinkmanship at its worst."

Yes, the Army had been mobilized in the meantime, for if this was the sum of what General Musharraf's government had assessed and had to say, then India was seriously concerned. The nation was outraged: "We have been tolerant for too long; enough is enough; there is a limit to what Pakistan can get away with, or what we should always have to put up with" became the widely held and expressed sentiment in the country. The Parliament, too, seethed with anger. The premises, the very sanctity, of this great and venerable symbol of the country's democracy, the seat of its sovereignty, had been violated through a flagrant terrorist attack; the Parliament's purity had been sullied by an invasion of violence. For the first time ever, gunfire and the booming explosions of grenades were heard in these great and historic halls. There was death in the air and bloodshed and corpses on the ground in this temple of our democracy. It is impossible to fully convey the unprecedented horror of it, or the cold fury with which even the most placid were then seized. The outraged government ordered a troop mobilization, and a nearly year-long standoff between India and Pakistan followed.

The War That Wasn't

There are aspects of this standoff that merit clarification, and also a better understanding, because the specter of a "nuclear war" was then raised, primarily by the U.S. and the UK. I found this reaction odd, and completely unnecessary. Why deliberately cause a scare by raising alarms about the possibility of a nuclear conflict, or by suggesting that the troop mobilization signified some kind of uncontrollable autonomy? It was incomprehensible that anyone would try to ascribe a nuclear dimension to the situation. That was so totally not in India's cards that when the alarm was first sounded, I heard in it a kind of Western posturing, an echo of a long-forgotten imperial past. It was, of course, very much a sovereign decision of the United States and the United Kingdom, and as there were several thousand Americans and Britons then living and working in India and Pakistan, their safety was doubtless a matter of concern for their respective governments. But to issue advisories urging their citizens to "leave India," to ask those who intended to visit India not to do so, and to continuously harp on the possibility of a conflict that could "go nuclear" was to grossly overstate the case. In my opinion, it was tantamount to scaremongering.

I have never been able to fathom the reason for this scare, nor why the United States took the lead in the matter. Tellingly, however, almost no other country followed suit; they were unmoved by the Anglo-American alarms. Was it a larger ploy? Was it a warning of some kind, particularly to Pakistan, which was engaged as a U.S. ally in the war in Afghanistan, to back off, to not get carried away and exploit American preoccupation with Kabul by running wild in Jammu and Kashmir or elsewhere? It seemed an unlikely reason for creating such a scare in Pakistan about an Indian nuclear attack, for that could have led to the exact opposite of what was intended. Pakistan's antennae would have jangled even more with alarm. Was it, on the other hand, a warning to India not to become provoked, not to compromise the American effort in Afghanistan, not to push Pakistan too hard? This reasoning, too, did not fully impress, for India had always exercised great restraint. It was discomfiting nevertheless, and not at all agreeable to have this artificial scare created, and then for India to be inundated with gratuitous "guidance and counseling." This we clearly had no need of. The Americans had evidently assessed the situation in accordance with their own historical experience, particularly of the Cold War. To the U.S., therefore, as to the UK, India had a fledgling nuclear weapons program; it could not possibly have the maturity needed to handle these awesome instruments of global destruction. "Only we in the U.S. and the UK know how to . . ."

I found this attitude offensively patronizing, and also patently wrong. The United States was the only country in the world that had used nuclear weapons in war, in anger against civilian targets. "They really ought not to now counsel restraint," I thought, when perhaps it would have been much more direct to stick to the line that Secretary of State Powell constantly used with me: "Jaswant, please do not do anything that will deflect attention from our main effort in Afghanistan." The nuclear alarm was possibly a by-product of this line of thinking. With the exception of Kargil, the United States had never fully understood or accepted that terrorist activity in Jammu and Kashmir was merely another face of the same malevolent evil they were fighting in Afghanistan. Besides, at first I only apprehended, but then later better understood, that Pakistan, an ally upon whom the U.S. had initially leaned heavily to get it to fall in line, had now become a "driver of policy." This deprived the United States of an autonomous policy for the region. "You cannot do anything in Afghanistan without our support and help," Pak generals clamored constantly into the ears of their U.S. counterparts. The U.S. and the UK thereafter willingly diluted the scope of their options. In consequence, they suffered significant losses with respect to their own primacy of position and role. Besides, the principal coercive measure available to the U.S. had already been reduced to the economic; and this, too, became so blunted with time that to "turn off the tap" would actually have resulted in turning off the tap of U.S. options, too. U.S. policy for the region had thus reached a dead end, or so it appeared to us in Delhi in 2002.

There was, however, another reason for the fears that the U.S. and UK were voicing. This was almost entirely a consequence of their own inac-

tion, or of continuous failure, decade after decade, to address gross violations of the NPT as Pakistan developed its nuclear arsenal. The Americans
had chosen not even to see these violations; for example, knowing full well
what A. Q. Khan was doing, the U.S. elected to keep quiet. Thereafter,
Pakistan's command and control of its own nuclear organizations evolved
haphazardly; it broke down somewhat during the country's Talibanized,
extremist-dominated period, which then gave rise to a virtual free-for-all.
A. Q. Khan's "Khan Research Laboratories"—the country's main facility for the development and testing of nuclear weapons—was established
then; it is separate from and independent of the Pakistan Atomic Energy
Commission, and instead reports directly to the Prime Minister's Office.
After May 1998, Nawaz Sharif attempted a reorganization, trying to assert
at least some degree of authority. Thus in 2000, the Pakistan Strategic
Plans Division was born, which theoretically is meant to oversee the country's entire nuclear program, but in reality is a combat organization.

Delhi, in the meantime, continued as it has always done—casual, laidback, chaotic. There were no blackouts, no concerns about nuclear bombs
or even about war, something that the city had already experienced twice—
during the 1965 and 1971 wars between India and Pakistan. Pakistan had
made halfhearted attempts to lob a bomb or two at the Indian capital, but
nothing more had happened. Not surprisingly, therefore, in 2001–2002,
movies played to full audiences, citizens enjoyed evening shopping outings, consumer spending suggested a robust economy, buses ran as usual,
and children went to school—albeit as reluctantly as they have always
done. Life continued even after the advisories had been issued by London
and Washington, and after some British and American citizens had left
India to casual media coverage. This minor trickle caused no worries; India
continued to go its own way, at its own pace, and with no nuclear fears in
its mind or its heart. This was not an attitude born of ignorance of conflict or of an absence of fear of death or destruction. India has known such
things only too well, and for too long.

As American troops made progress against the Taliban and al-Qaeda
in Afghanistan, they came across additional information. For example,
there were some drawings recovered in the al-Qaeda camps that, although
almost indecipherable, were viewed suspiciously as potential blueprints
for weapons, possibly nuclear. It was common knowledge by then that
at least two Pakistani nuclear scientists had been working with a charity
associated with the Taliban in Afghanistan. These two were detained, and
"at least one of them" confessed to having met Osama bin Laden, who, the

whole world knew, was encouraging Pakistan to develop a nuclear arsenal so as to "terrorize the enemy," as Osama himself had stated—with admirable directness, I would say. All this deeply troubled the U.S. India might or might not be a "nuclear fledgling," but the U.S. was certainly "new on the ground," and not fully familiar with it, either. This ground India had lived with, with all its attendant extras; for decades upon end we had confronted and contained it, even as the West had deliberately looked the other way.

If there was any basis for this scaremongering on the part of the United States and the United Kingdom, it was the substantial knowledge that had been in their possession since the late 1980s. The late president of Pakistan, Zia-ul-Haq, had explicitly leaked information and implied that "were India to cross a certain undefined line of success in military operations, then 'nuclear retaliation' from Pakistan will follow," and this specter now haunted the West. The incident in question had occurred during "Exercise Brasstacks," a major Indian military training maneuver conducted in the Rajasthan desert near the Pakistani border in 1986–87, in response to which Pakistani troops had been mobilized and deployed along the border. General Zia had then secretly flown to Delhi to meet the late Rajiv Gandhi and seek assurances, which were duly given. There had also been the Gates Mission, when the U.S. had responded to a totally false alarm by sending a special envoy to the region to defuse a nuclear crisis that did not exist. Capping all this were comments made in Pakistan along the lines of "Well, if we are to go down, then we will surely take India down with us. Let Pakistan be destroyed—OK! But, we will destroy India with us." I had treated such blood-curdling warnings as jejune and pointless, not worth paying much heed to, for India had no such intentions, and Pakistan's fears were totally groundless. I had on several occasions stated that for India, our nuclear deterrent was just that—a deterrent, not for fighting wars. The U.S. calculated that India could nevertheless make the "mistake" of achieving "unacceptable success" on the ground, on the strength of its "conventional forces" superiority; in which event Pakistan might take recourse to employing its "last resource," to do exactly what it had threatened. Theoretically this was not impossible, however remote it appeared at the time. This therefore was not "South Asia's First Nuclear Crisis," however much the West may delight in coining such phrases.

On January 12, 2002, General Musharraf made a lengthy speech to the nation, which was carried live on Pakistan's national television network. In it he departed from all earlier pronouncements and publicly denounced religious extremists. He pledged to reform madrasas in Pakistan, and also officially banned five jihadi groups, including Lashkar-e-Taiba and Jaish-e-Mohammad.[2] However, the refrain "Kashmir runs in our blood" continued, with the general reaffirming "moral, political, and diplomatic support" for the terrorists there. Yet, for the first time, he finally condemned the attack on India's Parliament, accepting it as a "terrorist act," and equating it with September 11. There was more: "No organization," he declared, "will be allowed to indulge in terrorism in the name of Kashmir." This was in marked contrast to his previous statements. I was still cautious, having been singed earlier, and having dealt over the years with the many incarnations of General Musharraf. Secretary of State Powell, meanwhile, kept calling to reiterate, "Please don't undermine our war in Afghanistan." The pressure had eased somewhat, but we continued to wait, for we wanted a confirmation of the trend.

On May 14, 2002, another terrorist attack took place. Three terrorists dressed as soldiers got off a public bus at Kaluchak, eight miles from Jammu, and rushed into an Army camp. They shot dead twenty-two people, all of whom were the wives and children of our soldiers, and by the time they too had been killed, the total death count was thirty-four. Another fifty or so had been wounded.

For the Army, this cold-blooded murder of women and children in their own camp was a direct provocation, a stain upon their honor. The troops boiled with revengeful anger and were (almost rebelliously) bent upon retaliation. To my mind, this attack at Kaluchak was pretty much the last straw, coming on the heels of the attack on our Parliament only five months earlier. Despite this, or perhaps because of the sharpness of this provocation, I counseled restraint. I had assessed that immediate retaliatory action would be strategically faulty; the region was already embroiled in a major conflict in Afghanistan. Militarily it would amount to falling into a classic trap: a deliberate provocation launched to intentionally invite a predictable retaliation, with both time and place thus being of the adversary's choice. The alternative to my views was compelling, and certainly had more appeal; there was a powerful sentiment that Pakistan could not be allowed to foster such repeated attacks. These two attacks, on the Parliament and in Kaluchak, constituted the principal setbacks

---

2. Lashkar-e-Taiba and Jaish-e-Mohammad are Islamic extremist groups that are based in Pakistan and conduct operations in Jammu and Kashmir. Lashkar-e-Toiba, formed in 1989, is the military wing of the Sunni religious organization Markaz-ud-Dawa-wal-Irshad. Its ultimate goal is to establish Islamic rule not just in Jammu and Kashmir but in all of India. Jaish-e-Mohammad was formed in early 2000 by Masood Azhar after he was released from prison in India. Its mission is to unite Kashmir with Pakistan.

to normalization. The government, caught in a nearly impossible situation, remained calm, continuing to counsel restraint. It was a very difficult time, painful even to recall. There is no doubt, however, that this restraint was yet another act of great courage and challenging statesmanship on the part of Prime Minister Vajpayee.

Finally, in September 2002, elections were held for the legislature of Jammu and Kashmir, one of the undeclared aims of the standoff. The elections were praiseworthy for their independence, fairness, and participation, and as a test of the functioning of India's democratic institutions, despite externally aided and abetted violence. What little excitement or violence there was came from across the LOC and was aimed at disrupting the elections. The citizens of Jammu and Kashmir stood firm and refused to be cowed into not exercising their franchise, or abdicating their right to be the guardians of their own political destiny. The National Conference, the ruling party in the state, lost the elections, and a new coalition came into existence. Although this was a domestic process, I found the election to be an extremely satisfying Foreign Office success, too.

In the meantime, the standoff against Pakistan continued. It was an example of coercive diplomacy, combining aggressive diplomatic action internationally with firm military positioning that had the potential to mete out punishment should recalcitrance persist. India, firm yet restrained, achieved what its government had set out to do. It was a complex and challenging task, as coercive diplomacy always is, for we had to get our message across to both the United States and Pakistan. The U.S., partnered with India in an alliance against terrorism, but also "employing" Pakistan in Afghanistan, could not be allowed to apply one criterion where their own interests were involved, and another whenever or wherever India confronted the same kind of challenge. Simultaneously, India had to continue to strive for peace with Pakistan through persuasion, not compulsion. We needed to transform the Pakistanis' mindset, to get them to abandon their path of perpetual and induced hostility toward India. They had adopted that stance early on, as an essential aspect of separate nationhood, fearing that they otherwise would lose the sharp edges, corners, and contours of their "separateness." Such neurosis and insecurity is born of the very act of Partition, which is why mutual hostility is inherent in the situations of both Pakistan and India. That is also why patience is of central importance here, a finely tuned sense of strategic restraint as a tool of military diplomacy; and even though coercive diplomacy may appear to be passive, particularly in the India-Pakistan context, it is a difficult policy to employ, yet is unquestionably the correct approach. Obviously, coercive diplomacy cannot succeed against the irrational, which message also had to be sent to the United States. The U.S. had to understand how seriously India took these direct assaults against the seats of its democratic authority—first on the Jammu and Kashmir assembly on October 1, 2001, then on our Parliament on December 13, 2001, then on Kaluchak on May 14, 2002—and so much else in the continuing narrative of that grim, grisly course.

I have an unshakable conviction: India must pursue its own path, its own destiny, not follow the West. Reflect on the post-9/11 United States and the India of a post-Kargil, post-Kandahar, post–December 13 challenge. Clearly, India has been reminded once again that it must have its own answers in this fight against terrorism. Experience has led the Americans into excessive and gross militarization. That is doubtless their own sovereign choice, but I do not think that is the answer—not for the United States, and certainly not for India. We have to go down our own path, undeterred, meeting whatever challenges face us, overcoming whatever form of terrorism confronts us—for India possesses absolutely unconquerable attributes. We have unmatched resilience, the ability to absorb shocks. We will go on, of that I am sure.

Our firm stand changed the atmosphere markedly in the India-Pakistan context, as well as the atmosphere in Jammu and Kashmir. This marked a point of departure from many fixities of policy for my country, and, as it turned out, for me personally as well.

Only a few months earlier, in July 2002, Prime Minister Vajpayee had suggested that I move to the Finance Ministry—a suggestion that was repeated by Deputy Prime Minister Advani. I was not particularly enthused at the prospect; in fact, I was hesitant. I felt that I needed more time in the Ministry of External Affairs to complete the work I had started. I consulted a close friend. In a sense, he made the decision for me. He said that in terms of action on the foreign policy and defense fronts, the past few years had been so packed, so eventful, so challenging, that the situation could not possibly go on forever. Therefore, he said, "Jaswant, move. In movement lies the answer. The next challenge is Finance; go there." I ruminated for a few days, then did what the prime minister had asked me to. But that is altogether a different account.

New Doctrines for Old

In the period after December 13, India experimented with coercive diplomacy. As it happened, the Americans were also in the season of foreign policy innovation. Significant initiatives were announced by President Bush, including what amounted to a doctrine of preemption, an emphasis on unilateral action, and impatience with the restraint of collective consultation at the United Nations. Though these measures were announced after I had left the Ministry of External Affairs for the Ministry of Finance, I still had a sort of residual responsibility, and a continuing interest. The release of President Bush's first National Security Strategy (NSS) report on September 20, 2002, marked a forceful statement of America's grand policy plans in the post-9/11 world. The report received praise as "a clear, farsighted, and impressive response" to the threats the United States faced, but it also attracted criticism as "a radical and troubling departure" from traditional American foreign policy.

Four pertinent issues covered in the Bush NSS generated particular debate. First, the report called for "preemptive military action" against hostile states and terrorist groups seeking to develop weapons of mass destruction (WMD). Second, it announced that the United States would not permit any other power to surpass its dominant military presence. Third, while the NSS expressed an obligation to engage in multilateral international cooperation, it said that the United States would "not hesitate to act alone, if necessary." Fourth, the report proclaimed the goal of spreading democracy and human rights, particularly in the "Muslim world." It justified the preemptive use of military force against terrorists or state sponsors of terrorism that attempted to gain or use WMD, calling these the "most serious threats which the United States faces": "As a matter of common sense and self-defense, America will act against such emerging threats before they are fully formed." It widened the meaning of preemption to encompass military action "even if uncertainty remains as to the time and place of the enemy's attack." Many argued that there was no legal or practical precedent for including preventive military action under the category of preemption, and this deviation needed to be further deliberated upon. The United States would be walking a fine line between preemption and prevention.

In 1945, the rules governing the use of force were internationally agreed upon and enshrined in the United Nations Charter. This use of force was limited to self-defense in an armed attack or military actions authorized by the Security Council. The Bush administration was now saying that the right to self-defense should include the right to use force against terrorist and rogue states *before* they had "fully formed," before the terrorists had struck or used nuclear weapons, or before dangerous technologies had

STATECRAFT IS A CRUEL BUSINESS

fallen into the wrong hands. In response to President Bush's NSS, which challenged the rulebook as it stood, a high-level UN panel was formed to review its implications. The resulting report, which was presented in December 2004, marked an important evolution in the eternal debate about whether and when to use force. It recognized that states had a right to defend themselves not only against actual threats, but also against those that were imminent. It also accepted that use of force would be appropriate in dealing with covert threats, including terrorism and proliferation, but only if this were mandated by the Security Council. The panel declined to accept the United States' assertion that states could act on their own in specific situations. That, the panel argued, would lead to anarchy.

However, this evolution failed to grasp the basic issue: that present-day threats bear no relation to those that were known at the time of the UN's founding. The assertion now is that it is not just what states do beyond their borders that constitutes an international concern, but also what they do within them—how they treat their citizens, and whether they encourage terrorists or develop WMD, for instance. If members of the United Nations insisted that states had a responsibility to protect their own citizens from any and all attacks, then, by that very reasoning, their territory could not be used to pose a threat to the security of others, whether through encouragement of terrorist activity or developing WMD or, for example, through allowing environmental hazards to spread. If and when some states failed to live up to such responsibilities, how should the international community respond? It takes time for all these early, soft weapons of diplomacy and economic pressure to take effect. There might be situations in which the only emergent, effective way to neutralize a threat would be "limited military action before these threats became imminent."

The problem with the American doctrine is an over-reliance on "preventive force." Its use is defined too narrowly—to deal with "terrorism and as a means of forcible regime change." The other problem was the insistence that individual states had a right to decide when "preventive force" was justified; certainly the United States did have this right, even though the threats addressed were global in scope and affected the security of many states. The decision to use force in such circumstances could hardly be one state's alone. To the question of who should decide, the Security Council remains the preferred vehicle for authorizing such an action, but the United States is impatient with the Council's methods and pace. It is instructive that before the First Gulf War in 1991, the Security Council had authorized the use of force beyond traditional peacekeeping operations on only two occasions—in Korea and in Congo. Since 1991, it has done so no fewer than seventeen times. In today's world, there has to be a role for preventive military force in addressing security challenges. This acknowledgment is the first step. The second is to agree on standards for this use. The third, then, is to codify these standards, and to grant authority to an efficiently functioning institutional mechanism. The Bush administration had taken the first step correctly, and, if you use the logic of the United States' own arguments, the second as well. It has patently erred at the third. That is why a clear need exists not to accept unilateralism as an alternative to the UN Security Council. Employing regional organizations or even new coalitions of democratic states to "legitimize the use of force" has already devalued the Security Council.

Another thing that currently eludes us in the realm of foreign policy is clarity about "idealism" and what sets it distinctly apart from "realism." Can both of these attributes be retained simultaneously in the conduct of policy? The reality of a world confronted with the complexities of ideology, religion, fundamentalism, and environmental disasters, all waiting to happen, has to be fully understood before the "ideal" of a peaceful, civilized world can be realized.[3]

The Future of Indo-Americana

In January 2004, India and the United States executed a document called the "Next Steps in Strategic Partnership" (NSSP). This joint statement had been planned while I was still in the Ministry of External Affairs; indeed, it had been the aim of the Vajpayee government since the 1998 tests, not just to establish a strategic partnership with the United States but to give it enough substance and muscle that the "natural allies" could achieve a functional partnership. Before Bush was elected, his principal foreign policy advisor, Condoleezza Rice, in an article in *Foreign Affairs,* had recognized India's rise as a regional power. On assuming office, Bush quickened the pace. This move was based on America's own strategic vision that India was an emerging global power, that by 2025 we would be one of the world's five largest economies. India would also be the world's most populous nation, with a "demographic dividend" of an enormous pool of highly educated young people. India embodied a vibrant, diverse society with individual freedom, rule of law, and a government mandated by a constitution to come to power through free and fair elections. President Bush

---

3. This same thought was, with great lucidity, voiced by Max M. Kampelman in "Bombs Away," an op-ed piece in the *New York Times* on April 24, 2006.

phrased it succinctly: "This century will see democratic India's arrival as a force in the world." It would be in America's national interest to empower this relationship with the world's largest democracy as the political and economic focus of the global system shifted, inevitably and inexorably, to Asia.

It was this realization that led to the agreement on the NSSP. Under its aegis, the two sides addressed the sale of civilian nuclear technology, joint space exploration, missile defense, and high-technology trade. Progress has since been made on these fronts, and mutual concerns about the reliability of commitments have been addressed. The recent decision to allow the sale of civilian nuclear technology to India is a consequent and crucial part of this rapprochement. On July 18, 2005, an agreement was signed in the presence of President Bush and Prime Minister Manmohan Singh as part of the NSSP. It sought to flesh out nuclear and space cooperation plus a variety of other agreements, obligations as reciprocal steps. The United States emphasized that although it did not regard India as a nuclear weapons state under the NPT, it would not deny India the benefits of the NPT. India was accepted as an "advanced, responsible nuclear state" that must be given assistance with its civilian nuclear program.

Multiple-level consultations were then held to meld our viewpoints into a mutual understanding. It was thus that on March 2, 2006, President Bush and Prime Minister Dr. Manmohan Singh announced that as a follow-up to the July 18, 2005, Washington Agreement between the U.S. and India on Nuclear Cooperation for Energy, yet another milestone had been reached: our two countries had successfully worked out a plan for the separation of India's nuclear plants. Plants to be used for power production will come under the inspection regime of the International Atomic Energy Agency; those used for processing weapons-grade fuel will remain free of such surveillance. In return for India's agreement to effect such a separation, the accord ensured that after due completion, the needed fuel for India's plants would not be disrupted.

The implications of this development are myriad, all substantial and all long-term. Principal among them are an implied acceptance of the essentials of Fissile Material Control, but without a formal international treaty (FMCT) on the subject. This agreement now legitimizes India's continuing nuclear program, not just bilaterally but internationally as well, albeit with clear curbs in place. In exchange for such an explicit recognition of its nuclear program, India must "voluntarily" give up some aspects of it. As a consequence, India's autonomy with respect to its nuclear policy, its stand,

and its functions are diluted. This compromise on our part is matched by the U.S., which agreed to abandon some of its own earlier asserted planks. India is not a nuclear weapons state; it has not subscribed to the Nuclear Non-Proliferation Treaty, and hence is not part of the Nuclear Supplier's Group, either. Of course, it has not been formally granted the benefits of any of these exclusive "clubs," yet there has been some movement forward, most of which has been satisfactory. For want of a better analogy, it would not be inaccurate to say that India has now been accepted as a "visiting member" of these bodies. But is that really the case?

This development is clearly not a giant step forward, either by India or by the U.S., but at least it is a step in the right direction. India and the U.S. will both have to guard against any regression of this evolving relationship. The logic of May 1998 asserted itself in bringing this about, and for me this is a matter of considerable satisfaction. I had sought a "harmonization" of views with Strobe, and only then some accord. That goal of harmonizing has not yet been fully reached, but one more step toward it has been taken. Many high and difficult passes still remain to be crossed, but India and the U.S. now display much greater accord, and even though our views are not yet fully consonant, enough has happened to keep us moving. The seed that we planted in May–June 1998 is now a young tree.

For me, this was like completing a circle. My mind went back to the period from May 11 to June 12, 1998, when I took that first step for India, to invite the United States to join us on this path of togetherness, of cooperation, of mutual recognition. It was a matter of great satisfaction, therefore, that in the course of only six years, this relationship was turned around by those early initiatives. No longer a "pariah state," India was now a country that the United States sought to cooperate with in nuclear energy, space, and weaponry. American analysts were now asserting that a "partnership" between India and the United States was vital for the latter's own geopolitical objectives, indeed as a measure of global good. It was important for India to be accommodated in the field of nuclear energy, in terms of access to space-related and dual-use high technology, so that its geopolitical profile is prominently projected, its rate of economic growth is enhanced, and its global reach is extended—so that these two great democracies can work together. I could not have predicted such an outcome on June 12, 1998, when I first stepped into Strobe Talbot's office in the State Department in Washington. I recollect often and vividly the great sense of satisfaction I experienced when I learned of this agreement of March 2, 2006. Of course, the BJP was out of government by then, having lost the 2004 election. But without that foundation of June 12, 1998, and all those early endeavors, this result would have been difficult to achieve. Yet it would be a great error to assume that the "village" that Strobe and I spoke of has now been reached, or the "house" built. Whether I am in government or not, the sound of the stonemason's hammer constantly striking that chisel, sculpting our many tomorrows, must continue to be heard; for the house has yet to be built, and we must not stop working on it.

11

Some Afterwords

Animal Spirit in the Economy

The Ministry of Finance having run into some rather rough weather was the main reason for my shift to North Block.

I had judged early in my tenure that one of my principal challenges in the ministry, and the task to be attended to first, was restoring national self-confidence. I wanted to revitalize people's faith in the economy, to free the productive capacities and the creative genius of India from quibbling bureaucratic tangles. It took some time to settle down, for the ways of my new ministry were very different. "All development projects," I had once said, "flow through the Finance Ministry. We spend endless weeks scouring their waters for small fish, and only then do we let these rivers of growth flow free again." Not only does the Finance Ministry regulate the country's economy, but it greatly influences and determines the financial functioning of the entire government. That is why I concluded early on that the first and most important reform needed was a change in mindset, not just of the bureaucracy but of the political community, too, of the very ethos of our governance. We had to relearn how to say "yes" easily, and in time. Without this central reform, all activity would either slow down or come to a halt. Our whimsical addiction to the "power of paper" had to be ended, or paralysis of action would set in. Our reliance on the "license raj" system, with its elaborate regulations and excessive red tape, made us prone to the obfuscation of bureaucracy.

The media in the early days of my stewardship of the Finance Ministry asked how I interpreted my new role and functions. On the spur of the moment, with no formal education in economic management—or in economics, for that matter—I responded that my job was "to put more money in the housewife's purse and more food in the stomachs of the poor." That impromptu remark, I realized later, was in reality the anchor around which the Finance Ministry must function. The key was growth. I had to work very hard to encourage the needed change in mindset across the entire ministry, to actively encourage more production. Such views had been heresy until as late as the early 1990s. Before that time, the Indian economy had lived and functioned under a highly centralized and excessively bureaucratic regime. Under the past dispensations, production targets were fixed by a government-controlled organization in Delhi. Once assigned, they could not be exceeded. Were any business or industrial unit to make the mistake of exceeding this fixed limit, of producing more than the licensed limit, a penalty would be imposed on that wayward defaulter. When I began to emphasize production, old arguments of insufficient demand emerged from dusty shelves. I offered an impromptu thesis that I believed in increased growth, hence greater supply, therefore more demand, and in consequence more money in circulation. As someone who was not an economist, I was greatly flattered when, some years later, the governor of the Reserve Bank, Y. V. Reddy, sent me a paper in which French economist Jean Baptiste Say had propounded the very same theory: "Supply creates its own demand."

On January 10, 2003, during a visit to Bombay (Mumbai) to address a meeting of one of our several trade and industry federations, I was walking with Governor Reddy down the stairs to the venue when I shared with him my fatigue at the tedium of having to repeatedly say the same thing week after week. "I want to do something different," I told him. Before assuming the governorship of the Reserve Bank, Reddy had served as India's executive director on the Board of the International Monetary Fund. With a lifetime's worth of experience in economic management, he displays an admirable mix of careful consideration and quick decision-making. "What do you want to do?" he questioned cautiously. "I want to instill our industrialists with an abundance of self-confidence," I replied, "to tell them: 'Go out, go and conquer the world; there is enough money. I will stand by you, support you, as will the Finance Ministry and the Reserve Bank of India and Governor Reddy.'" He stopped walking down the stairs—this was not a subject that could be dealt with so casually—reflected a bit, then asked, "No limits?" "Yes, no limits," I responded, "plus all possible help in borrowing, both here and abroad. I want to start a process of 'reverse economic imperialism'!" Governor Reddy did not smile, remaining silent for some time. He then spoke softly: "Sir, go ahead and make your announcement." I pressed for more. "But I want to give more to lay citizens, too. Why should we force them to become money smugglers by allocating meager amounts when they go abroad?" By then, Reddy had caught my mood, and he asked me for details. My response was direct: "Permissible amount to be raised to

$25,000 per visit, to be used however the citizen wants." He agreed, but with one caveat: "Not per visit, per annum, Sir." And thus, in a few short minutes, India's conservative foreign exchange policy was rewritten. I cite this not just as a case of unorthodox economic management, but as an example of developing in our country what John Maynard Keynes called "animal spirits": encouraging people to invest by generating optimism, raising morale, and building confidence in the enterprise that exists in every nation. That initiative, I now know, has contributed so meaningfully to India's investments abroad that they are now a source of global envy.

The Ministry of Finance simply cannot work on the basis that the creation of wealth is somehow a sin, whatever our past socialist indoctrinations and inheritance may be. There is an economic philosophy that I have always believed to be one of the cultural foundations of Indian society. This philosophy enjoins all of us to endeavor to the utmost, to achieve the maximum possible production of wealth, no matter what field of activity we are engaged in; that is our duty, our dharma. The next great obligation is to save. Thus, instinctively, from childhood, the idea of saving is implanted in every Indian's mind. Next comes "not to consume a grain more than is needed." In that sense, India does not have a consumer culture society, although a segment of it now increasingly demonstrates all the symptoms of rampant consumerism. Along with saving is also sharing, and acts of piety are treated as part of our dharmic obligations—be one a farmer, an artisan, or an industrialist. This was the native wisdom that I grew up with and sought to impart to the Finance Ministry. I succeeded— not totally, but substantially. The ministry did demonstrate a transformed spirit; it displayed much greater confidence, resulting in a higher growth rate all around, and a slew of reform measures then followed. The country achieved a GDP growth rate of 8.4 percent that year, and was back on the path of explosive development.

The Hope of India-nomics

Unquestionably, the number one challenge for India remains economic: a distributive spread of progress, consistent economic growth, enhanced spending power, and a markedly improved quality of life for all our citizens. Currently we have a window of opportunity, which Vijay Kelkar has characterized as the "grand demographic dividend," but for a limited period of about two or perhaps three decades.[1] During this period, India

---

1. "Grand demographic dividend" comes from Dr. Vijay Kelkar in his Gadgil Memorial Lecture of October 26, 2005, on the theme "India's Economic Future: Moving beyond State Capitalism."

must firmly and decisively move away from and beyond state capitalism. It should purposefully proceed toward an advanced national economy. It can do so only by accelerating institutional reform, including efficient privatization at the level of both the center and the state. We must modify the existing institutional framework to create a modern economy; that is where our economic future lies. In Kelkar's words, it is self-evident that "We need to fashion our own *sui generis* model of growth and development, so that we can move towards an advanced economy, always promoting inclusive growth; and thus gain the benefits of enhanced efficiency, greater equity and better governance under a liberal democracy." A routine, mechanical copying of American or British or Western policies and institutional mechanisms is not a viable option. That would be entirely the wrong path for India to follow.

Then there are areas such as urban infrastructure, where we have not even begun to address the issues. The crisis here is bigger than meets the eye, because contrary to popular perceptions, India is no longer primarily an agricultural economy. I am not advocating any neglect of agriculture; rather, it is necessary to upgrade our agricultural system, to pour capital into what is, after all, a way of life for us in India. But agricultural productivity and our income from agriculture must multiply: through improved methods of irrigation, wasteland reclamation, warehousing, marketing, infrastructural development, and free movement of produce within the country.

Overseer of Infrastructure

We in government had committed ourselves to an accelerated development of the country's physical and social infrastructure. Among a host of other programs was an ambitious project whereby every village with a population above 1,000 in the country, of a total of almost 640,000 villages, was to be connected by a passable road. There was also the Provision of Urban Amenities in Rural Areas (PURA) project, established to provide urban facilities in rural areas, including passable roads, electricity, water, and education. In the vernacular, "pura" also means "complete," and this was indeed the completion of a major responsibility.

Upon the strength of the experience gained from these projects, and also, of course, of the huge expressway project known as the Golden Quadrilateral, I came to the conclusion that for a proper and timely completion of infrastructure projects, it is essential to have an authorized body to serve as the "overseer of infrastructure." In our current federal structure there is no such body. The resulting gap is a need we must attend to.

According to Kelkar, "The government is the agent of the people, taking taxes and delivering public goods to the people in return." From that standpoint, the Indian state has been a rather poor agent; it collects little, and therefore delivers a pittance, and the public goods that are provided are of grossly inadequate quality. Yet it continues to ask a disproportionately high price of the people. That is why we need to tackle poverty directly. And unquestionably, the most effective anti-poverty program of all is a consistently high Gross Domestic Product (GDP). This has proven to be a vastly more effective method of reducing poverty than any other. High GDP growth will inevitably convert itself into a high level of what I call "GNC": "Gross National Contentment," which phrase I have often used in reference to the true index of growth, arguably to the horror of economists. But to abandon growth under the illusion that attaining equity should take precedence is to jettison both growth and equity, and to end up actually distributing poverty. That is why our eyes must be fixed firmly on the task of rapidly achieving a manifold increase in the per capita GDP. It will constitute our most powerful tool for transforming the lives of all, including our less fortunate citizens.

The real challenge is not in settling the debate about competing theories of poverty elimination. It is in finding practical ways to do so effectively and quickly. The goal of anti-poverty programs, according to Kelkar, is thus "to promote self-adjusting, self-targeting and self-liquidating programs," not endless debates or higher budgetary allocations. What counts is not what is allotted, but what is acted upon and delivered. Programs do not alleviate poverty; only delivery is capable of doing that. India's economic development is a vital requirement in this regard. It is so important that unless it is attended to purposefully, all growth indices of GDP and the like not only will be rendered null but actually will prove counterproductive. There absolutely must be an emphasis on GNC, or on the factor of inclusivity. The "India Shining" campaign was a challenge of economic management, a completely nonpartisan promotional effort to highlight the country's economic development to the outside world. Unfortunately, it was deliberately derailed by just this separation of non-inclusivity. How can increasing expectations be managed, fulfilled, and satisfied in India? This is part of the total politico-economic management of the country's reform agenda.

Politicians and civil servants need to recalibrate the "handed-down" mindset of "management of poverty," to another level of "an emerging economy of plenty" along with the needed imperatives to translate this "emerging" rapidly into a reality. The energy that has already been unleashed, and which today is transforming India through entrepreneurial zeal, needs to be mirrored by other facets, and across the entire cross-section of our society.

We certainly do not need more laws. We need more effective and more answerable governments. We do not need more regulations; quite the contrary, we need only a fraction of the regulations that we currently have, but a vastly larger canvas of individual freedoms and options. We need the Indian economy to be free of state control, not just of state capitalism. We need to move beyond governmental control as the organizing principle of our economy; progress will require individual enterprise and creativity. We have to first craft and then project the idea of "A New India"—as the flagship of a modern global economy. Economically, India is at the threshold of an age of unprecedented growth. The demographic dividend of a young India—those aged thirty and below—is an asset, but only for the next two or three decades. Like the arrow of time, this opportunity will fly, and then this door will close.

Some Reflections upon Our Times

It sometimes feels as if the century in which I grew up in Jasol and Khuri was hardly the twentieth. It was more like the nineteenth in its ambience, its priorities, and its pace, especially those early beginnings. What a great transition, what unbelievable change has occurred since, in this twentieth and now twenty-first century, and with what terrifying velocity. Merely an arithmetical counting of these decades will not do; they cannot account for such a total transformation of our "but one Earth."[2]

At the beginning of the twentieth century, India had begun to stir afresh. The aftershocks of the 1857 War of Independence, in which our soldiers had revolted against their British officers, had largely been absorbed. Even though Queen Victoria was dead by then, the power and prestige of the British Empire in India was at its pinnacle. And yet, just four and a half decades later, this great empire was sapped of its strength and authority, and it came to an end. The days of imperial glory were over. In that sense, India's Independence symbolized the great changes that came in the twentieth century. Empires vanished; monarchies tottered and sank through the trapdoors of history. It is humbling, and also revealing, to reflect on how rapidly and easily the great empires collapsed:

---

2. Struck by the thinking of political strategist P. N. Haksar, I have compressed an entire thought process and come up with the following "reflections upon our times."

the Ottoman, the Austro-Hungarian, the British, and the French, and of course the Soviet Empire, too—the heir of the mighty Orthodox Russian Empire. The great monarchies of Russia and of the East, the European crowns and the ancient Indian kingdoms, they have all been lost in the obscuring shadows of time.

A thought born earlier was adopted around the beginning of the twentieth century. It was a new and revolutionary way of thinking, claimed to have answers to the sufferings of all humankind, advocating equalization, a final leveling out. The German social philosopher Karl Marx, living in Paris and then in London, had propounded the pioneering concept of communism. For some seventy years, this was the rival philosophy to capitalism, and mankind was mesmerized by it. The "Great October Revolution" converted Russia to communism, but kept largely intact the physical spread and integrity of the Orthodox Russian Empire, which stretched from the borders of middle Europe to the shores of Japan, supposedly occupying "one-sixth of the world's surface." Yet, within the space of one human lifetime, this great theory emerged, dominated ruthlessly, and then collapsed—totally, in a single lifespan! When else in human history had this ever happened? A similar fate was suffered by fascism, communism's early contemporary. And what of the nihilists, who also emerged and then vanished? Or the anarchists? In early-twentieth-century Europe, were they not propounding, as serious political philosophy, ideas not dissimilar to those of today's terrorists?

Before the midway mark of the century, the world froze into glacially confrontational camps. It was a confrontation of ideologies, of systems, a rivalry that divided the First World from the Second World. And then a Third World emerged: shedding the weight of centuries of imperial occupation, India reawakened as the first Third World country, noncapitalist, noncommunist, and nonaligned. The twentieth century became the century of conflicts, of wars—the most violent and destructive ever experienced. The notion of "war" was reconceived in several new ways. "World war"—the entire world at war? "Total war"—finish, exterminate everything? Or "limited war"—perhaps only a few countries need to be eliminated under this rubric? And what, then, about the "Cold War"? The twentieth was undoubtedly the most violent of centuries, for it was then that we froze the world into sites of "mutually assured destruction." But how can "MAD" be characterized as cold? Populations, too, multiplied in this century, but they did so destructively, killing themselves and others of the species as never before. So many humans died on account of wars and revolutions, of governments killing their own citizens. In the twentieth century, an estimated 180 million human beings were killed at the hands—or by the bombs—of other humans. Of other species killed on Earth, I have no count.

Science and technology, and human beings, too, made startling progress. Within sixty-six years of that first uncertain flight by the Wright Brothers, Neil Armstrong had stepped onto the moon. Now, of course, we land spacecraft on Saturn's moons, and we destroy small comets and smaller asteroids with "earth shots." No longer does it seem strange to see the surface of Mars with our own eyes, or to collect dust from a distant comet and bring it back to Earth for analysis. Hubble has enabled us to look into the deepest depths of space, beyond our own solar system, to once-unimaginable distances, and then to peer into that soundless void of the "Other," that "shunya" nothingness that has existed from the time of the timeless, from that which was before the dawn of time, when there was neither time nor even a "before"!

> Yanmanasa na manute yenahur mano matam
> Tadeva Brahma tvam viddhi nedam yadidamupasate

> That which cannot be visualized by the mind; That by which the mind visualizes—so [they] say. Know That alone to be Brahman, not this, this which [people] worship.
> —Kenopanishad 1:6

India: Eternal, Internal

So how did India fare in the latter half of the twentieth century? After all, it had accepted the challenge of creating a viable and an efficiently functioning state—out of that paralyzing trauma of Partition. I do not think that it is possible to assess the history of a land and its people along the lines of a sublimated "profit and loss account," some kind of "balance sheet" of achievements and failures. So where are we now, six decades later? The whole of India is now a united and centralized state, perhaps excessively so, but still centralized for the first time in our history. We have a dynamic economy that continues to forge ahead, having shaken free from the governmental control that had kept our creativity shackled for so long. We have successfully (perhaps more than successfully) gone through fourteen parliamentary elections. With 671 million voters at last count, India's electorate challenges the combined populations of the United States (296 million) and Western Europe (457 million)!

The conduct of our elections is always a humbling experience, no matter how short of perfect they are in their execution. Six decades on, India continues to demonstrate that we have found an answer, in our own idiom and of our own kind, to the difficult question of how to ensure a peaceful and orderly succession in a democratic form of governance. Between 1989 and 2004, the decades that straddled the shift from the twentieth to the twenty-first century, India went through seven general elections and eight prime ministers, yet kept steadily rolling along, meeting every challenge along the way—natural, political, internal, and international. An observation could be made that such changes are a sign of democratic impermanence, instability, even immaturity. Yes, perhaps so. But there is an obverse, too: in this vast land of ours, home to more than a billion human beings, we are successfully finding answers to the challenges that confront us, in spite of the obstacles and difficulties, the psychologically debilitating dominance of a single political party for four decades, and of just one single family being projected on a screen of illusions. This, of course, India must shed, or it will slide into being a spider web of desecrating, and self-destroying, oligarchies.

What about failures? An absence of internal order and harmony is perhaps the principal shortcoming of the post-1947 experience. Discord in our systems, discontent among our citizens, cynical disbelief about our governance, and a lack of faith in the state's ability to deliver on its promises: these have emerged as telling debilities. We have failed, too, in attending adequately to literacy, to primary education, to the elimination of poverty, to minimum health needs, and to sustainable population growth, the latter of which has paradoxically bestowed upon India a "demographic dividend." There is insufficient commitment to the rule of law, at least to the principle of it, and our lawmakers themselves do not set the best example, either. When adherence to law is lax, and legal systems are immobilized through congestion, the sense of order in the land erodes. Consequently, governance is reduced to excessive and empty legalism; "government servants" display a most "un-servant-like" aggression, resulting in an expropriatory mindset toward the citizen and the state. This breeds corruption. Citizens then begin to, because they have to, "pay" for their rights; nothing works without recourse to a "suvidha shulka," a "convenience tax."[3]

---

3. Metaphor for a "bribe," a caustic comment in Hindi.

Little wonder, therefore, that criminals, otherwise punishable under law, often expropriate for their own use the very functioning of Indian democracy.

An outstanding characteristic of India has been the self-governance of the rural population through their inherent sense of social order. This is now invaded by uncertainty and tension born of several factors, principally the political dynamic that has become predominant in both rural and urban India. "Reservations," a form of affirmative action that was adopted at Independence to reserve economic, educational, and governmental opportunities for the less privileged castes and tribes so as to put them on the "fast track," were originally intended to be of limited duration. Instead they have exceeded their constitutionally mandated shelf life and become self-perpetuating, thus giving birth to new inequalities. Ironically, "caste" has not been effaced in the process. Instead, it has become further ingrained; new privileges and the newly privileged have emerged. They keep their valuable newfound separateness intact, for a loss of this specified caste identity will result in a loss of "reservations," and hence a loss of economic opportunities. In time, this kind of "social engineering"—more often prompted by prospects of beneficial electoral fallout than by a nobler quest such as greater egalitarianism in society or more equalism, or even the transfer of social privileges to those who have been denied it—becomes self-perpetuating, and therefore self-defeating. Attempting such social engineering through prescriptive laws does not work; a society's fundamentals are not reformed through legislative processes—that has to come from within the society itself, as a societal cleansing action. And this self-cleansing, self-reforming instinct is something that India has always had and has demonstrated, time and again, over the centuries; but this is a slow, evolutionary process, and we live in impatient times—of instant foods and rapid delivery.

The spread of democracy in the country has been one of the most remarkable developments of post-1952 India. Now, of course, combined with reservations and an evolution of the Panchayat (rural local bodies) system, a social revolution has occurred in the country. Why, then, have we seen the spread of discontent, of cynicism, of a "disconnect" between the citizen and the state?

Part of the answer, of course, lies in the style of governance and the nature of the state that has evolved; another part lies, perhaps, in a failure of the delivery mechanisms of the government. Yet another lies in the social separation that the competing divisions of a society create.

These, paradoxically, are brought about by electoral democracy. It is in this sense that "democracy" has divided Indian society, and along its narrowest folds; every social particularism is now electorally emphasized, for it is electorally exploitable. Some social scientists describe this process as akin to a political awakening; others do not characterize it so positively. But we do need to accept this reality and then reflect upon it.

India: External

Independent India, by and large, met the international challenges that confronted it from 1947 onward with an increasing sureness of touch. It absorbed most of the internal turmoil, too, but the single greatest deficiency that sadly remains is our unsettled land borders. Six decades after Independence, we still cannot claim that our relations with all of our neighbors are settled, harmonious, and mutually beneficial. This is a troubling failure; it shackles our flexibility and limits the freedom of our options. It has consequences internally, too, for this deficiency contributes to the generation of social tensions within the country, which in turn strongly influences the government's approach, demonstrating yet again the unbreakable linkages between the external and the internal. The other fetter that continues to trouble is our lingering memories of Partition. However, this traumatic event must not add endlessly to the baggage that all of us in South Asia already carry. We ought instead to be traveling extremely light, especially India, because we need to address the challenge of our size, of being larger than most of our neighbors put together. Obviously, India cannot reduce its size, but then its statecraft, too, must reflect that "largeness," if not greatness. Admittedly, this is a difficult demand, but it has to be addressed. Here our scorecard is not reassuring. Our neighborhood fears what it sees as India's "hegemonic" tendencies. We protest that we have no such design, but perhaps we ourselves are not entirely clear that the partitioning of this land created at least two central primacies: of size and of the cultural imprint of India. In whichever direction you go, the stamp of this Indian culture exists, in one form or another, perhaps becoming faint and indistinct with great distance, but still there. This is not the product of any design on India's part; it is our common legacy—part Islamic, part others, mostly Hindu.

All in all, 2006 was much more uncertain globally than was that post–Boxer Rebellion world of an earlier century—1906. What was the cause? Why have we seen this lack of certitude, especially after such millennial predictions as the coming of a "New World Order" and the "End of

History"? Is it because of a reemergence of "unilateralism"? Although this is not such a radically new "-ism"—both the "Age of Imperial Civilization" and the USSR exemplified it in their pursuit of national interests—it troubles the world precisely because the United States has now adopted it as a policy plank. The world does not trust the U.S. in this imperial garb, and the Americans are new to this challenge. Are they up to the demands that imperialism makes upon them? At first we wonder; then we worry at the reply that surfaces: no, not really, for they do not demonstrate the needed restraint, patience, and tolerance; they are too unilateral. The world is disturbed by such tendencies, even if not everyone voices that discomfort. Between the "idealistic aspirations of mankind, the reality of human nature, and the imperatives of national interests" lie many yawning chasms.[4] How do we bridge them so that India's national security interests are best served? Here, two additional thoughts ought to be taken into account. First, the strategic frontiers of a power do not always coincide with the geographical definition of its boundaries. This is a sufficiently well-established aspect of international relations; therefore, what holds for others holds for India as well. This takes us to the second point. As India's strategic frontiers lie where our vital national interests do, therefore, in the realm of strategy, compartmentalization into the purely diplomatic, economic, or military is unwise and ineffective. Civilizationally and regionally, India's sphere of influence has transcended the rather staid and narrow confines of "South Asia," much as China is now discomfited by being relegated to "East Asia." Challenge to any of the vital interests will call for a response. It is axiomatic, then, that unless India gives some definition to its vital national interests, it will fail to conceptualize its strategic frontiers, and will fail thereafter to respond quickly, appropriately, and adequately if those interests are ever threatened. Consequently, a violation of those interests could go unchecked, as has happened in the past. This will add to India's difficulties.

It is acceptable to take preventive action against threats to one's country, but the employment of offensive preemptive action in the name of "prevention," sometimes on the basis of questionable information and in circumvention of the existing international systems, places the world in a state of fearful uncertainty. In the United States, some espouse "national power" as the ultimate national goal, because they regard it as synonymous with the national interest. This is not an illogical way of thinking; there are many subscribers to this philosophy, and in other countries, too.

---

4. From Henry Kissinger, *Diplomacy* (New York: Simon and Schuster, 1994).

The more idealistic Wilsonian internationalists, who aspired to a different global arrangement of affairs, appear to be in retreat; perhaps inevitably, for in rejecting history and its many lessons, they sought to create a new world inspired only by idealism. The incompatibility of this idealism with the reality of today's world caused its early relegation as a motivating thought. This is important, for the world wants to know in what direction American policy is actually headed. Besides, as India has known for many centuries, "the essence of power is to know the limits on power," or as Henry Kissinger concluded in his book *Does America Need a Foreign Policy,* "America's ultimate challenge is to transform its power into moral consensus, promoting . . . values, not any imposition."

I look at our neighbor, the People's Republic of China, with a better understanding of how it first settled its international borders, simultaneously achieving order internally (though at the cost of very great human suffering), thereafter pragmatically opting for high economic growth, and only then launching itself on the world stage. We in India have followed a totally different route and therefore attained a different status. Over the years, China has perhaps been more adept than we have at grasping the essence of national power: that such "power" in itself becomes a nationally driving, motivational force. To let go of this force, and hence motivation, is to lose power. That is why China has rapidly transformed from an ideological into a modern, technocratic nation-state. There is another aspect of power: paradoxically, its attainment heightens insecurity, for what has been achieved has to be preserved, and constantly; otherwise it too will disappear. It is a historically established fact that a powerful nation—one of the "haves"—must, for its own preservation, in order to prevent any loss or diminution of its status or position, become an assertive and dominating country. It cannot be otherwise; the very nature of its power mandates that. This we must understand clearly in India, and notwithstanding the reality of this current assertiveness of the powerful, we must recognize that others will challenge and eventually break this monopoly. Power eventually declines, and the powerful of today will not be the powerful of tomorrow; that, too, is mandated by history.

Yet, these valid observations about "power" notwithstanding, we need to continue on the path of peace; we must not relent in our constant striving for tranquility, order, and settled borders in our neighborhood. This has to be one of our primary objectives, even as we acknowledge that peace is not an easy fruit to pluck, and it demands that we take risks. In seeking orderly relations with our neighbors—Pakistan or Bangladesh, Nepal or

Sri Lanka—we are not just trying to reach a destination; we are embarking on a permanent journey. It is a journey on which it is necessary for all of us to travel together along a road that will never be straight, and to "keep building, keep moving, keep growing," for "the sound of a stonemason's hammer and chisel must always be heard." Among the aspects that stand out in this extraordinary contrast between the approach and actions of neighbors such as Bhutan and Bangladesh, on a similar challenge that affects both countries, are the lawlessness and criminal activities of the United Liberation Front of Assam (ULFA). On the one hand, Bhutan is robustly combating the challenge, with the king himself taking the lead along with his crown prince in uniform. On the other, Bangladesh has given the ULFA shelter and support.

In 1971, at about the halfway mark of this journey of independent India, the Bangladesh freedom struggle took place. The two wings of Pakistan, East and West, engaged in violent confrontation, and a war between India and Pakistan followed as a consequence. I was no longer in uniform by then, having resigned my commission earlier. Inevitably, my views were sought in the mofussil town in which I then lived.[5] "What do you think about these operations? About the breakup of Pakistan? About the emergence of Bangladesh as a 'friendly' neighbor?" I was asked. Popular opinion at the time was almost unanimous in offering paeans for this achievement. I took a different view. I disagreed, and did so publicly. I held even then that in the long run, this development would not be to India's strategic advantage. We had achieved some success in Bangladesh only because the diplomatic, international, internal, civil, military, and economic cards had all been stacked in our favor. But they would not always remain so. I was criticized for saying that we should not rejoice prematurely because a sense of gratitude is not a binding vow of diplomatic fidelity between countries, or even the best of glue among neighbors. There was rejoicing over the creation of Bangladesh, and over the tricky matter of the release of some 93,000 Pakistani prisoners of war without, as the critics said, "any reciprocal gesture from the Pakistan side," or, as most wanted, a "final settlement of the Jammu and Kashmir issue." I disagreed with this policy sentiment as well. My reasoning went somewhat along these lines: Holding POWs indefinitely on Indian soil, especially Pakistani POWs, is not a tenable or sustainable act of statecraft. There are provisions for the handling of POWs and for what should be done upon a ceasefire or truce.

---

5. "Mofussil" refers to a suburban locality, away from a major city.

Perceptions have differed on the "liberation" of Bangladesh. Indians interpret the Bangladeshi denial of India's role in its independence as ingratitude, whereas Bangladeshis feel that because the liberation war has reduced the security threat to India (but has it really?), that is sufficient compensation—so how could we expect permanent gratitude? This mismatch of imagined or real expectations, imagined ingratitude, a basket of imagined and imaginary wrongs, further complicates the situation: "Never remind about a favor done; never forget about a favor received" often comes back to me, as a vignette of my long-past childhood.

The options for India were thus extremely limited. Those 93,000 POWs could not be used as a bargaining chip for any other quid pro quo. The lack of sustaining logic in the original idea of Pakistan had surfaced tellingly, and in a very short span of time; pronouncements such as "Muslims are a separate nation" could not stand up against the more assertive reality of "language is identity." At another level, it was a clash between two very different cultures—Bengali and Punjabi. With such innate differences dividing them, with India hostile and with this vital need for Pakistan to be constantly, perpetually antagonistic toward India—or else its own "different" identity will be imperiled—how could a nation separated by 1,600 kilometers and consumed by disorder and distrust be kept together, and by a confused leadership? At the time, we did not really need to do anything but stay quiet and let the inherent illogic take its course. Instead, we interfered, and now we wonder why all this has come about. Of course, India must not quibble with its neighbors, or engage in petty negotiations, a characteristic of small-time diplomacy. India must never bargain only to score some trivial point, as we tend to do at times. Kissinger has memorably described international relations as an "endless struggle of statesmen to rescue some permanence from the tenuousness of human foresight."[6]

An overwhelming factor in international relations today is the enormous and unquestioned power of the United States. It wields this power at times with finesse and subtlety, and at other times ham-fistedly, but always asserting the hegemony that it values so highly. Surely the United States must know, as indeed we must, that political hegemony is seldom partnered with intellectual hegemony; dominating the control of information is not the same as possessing all wisdom.

For India, the questions that dominate our relationship with the United States continue, sadly, to be defined by the yet undelineated territorial limits of nonproliferation, and also by the confused and confusing

---

6. Henry Kissinger, "Chou En-lai," *Time,* October 1, 1979.

relationship that the United States has almost always had with Pakistan. We need to abandon our attempt to pursue this subject with the U.S. to any satisfactory conclusion. We have to resolve it all ourselves. For India to act in accord with its sovereign freedom, problems with our neighbors *have* to be resolved and then put behind us. They restrict the scope of our global relationships—with the United States, with Pakistan, and with other countries as well. Needlessly, and so avoidably, the bank balance of our international goodwill is constantly being drawn down by our persistent carping about our relationship with Pakistan. The complexities of that relationship are unparalleled, and the expectations of our respective citizens are extremely high, and often paralyzingly biased. On the other hand, the "expectation gap" between our two governments is nearly unbridgeable at this time. Over and above that, any kind of "foreign presence" in the region adds to our confusion. The people in the street have a role to play, too, by adding to or even dictating policy when the very obverse is needed: it is the leadership that should be working to calm the street. Pakistan must—for everyone's sake—be at ease with itself, socially, politically, and economically. That is also good for our region, which is currently among the world's most unstable zones. What can India do to encourage and assist Pakistan in achieving this, without generating anxieties about hegemonic intentions? This is a challenging foreign policy question and goal, but it has to be seriously addressed.

The Tri-Junction of Collapsed Empires

India lies at the junction of three collapsed empires, all of which crumbled during the twentieth century: the Ottoman Empire in the early decades, the British Empire around mid-century, and the Soviet Empire toward that century's turn to the twenty-first. Every collapsing empire makes an initial attempt to regain its colonial territories or at least retain some degree of political and economic hold on the former colonies—unless, of course, the loss of power is so total that scarcely a trace of the original remains, in which case no diplomatic reconstructive surgery can help. This was the case with the Ottomans. As a young officer in the British Army, Archibald Wavell served on General (later Field Marshal) Edmund Allenby's staff in the Palestine Campaign. Later, Wavell was himself to attain the rank of field marshal, serving in World War II and then becoming India's second-to-last viceroy. He also authored a biography of Allenby, titled *Allenby: A Study in Greatness.* Commenting on the maze of international agreements and treaties that had brought the First World War to an end, Wavell wrote, "After the 'War to end War,' they seem to have been pretty successful in Paris at making a 'Peace to end Peace.'"[7] This is exactly what happened in the Middle East following the collapse of the Ottoman Empire and the end of World War I. The consequences of this collapse were as direct and immediate for India as they were for the war theater itself in the Middle East. For one, the present-day Middle East was born out of this conflict. It emerged from the spate of decisions made by the Allies.

For a truer understanding of this phenomenon, and its connection with India, two aspects must be viewed as central: one, that the principal object of the "Great Game" of the nineteenth century was undoubtedly India; and two, that this crafting of a post–Great War, post–Ottoman Empire Middle East/West Asia is also a consequence of that continuing "Great Game," but the objectives are different now. The collapse of the Ottomans led to the emergence of new "nations" in the Middle East. Their boundaries were drawn arbitrarily, and all this new crafting was done on the high tables of Europe, at which only the Europeans and the Americans were seated. The consequences of this geopolitical cartography, however, have been borne by the "Asiatics," including India. Countries such as Iraq and today's Jordan were invented by the British. With a few lines drawn across a map, they divided up an area that until then had been entirely and happily innocent of national boundaries. Just like that, Saudi Arabia was divided from Kuwait, and Kuwait from Iraq. Iraq, in reality, consists of three different ethno-religious groups, very difficult to coalesce into a single "nation." Here also was the geographical genesis of Israel. Christianity was then separated from Islam, by France in Syria and Lebanon, by Russia on the borders of Armenia and Soviet Azerbaijan. The seeds of all future turmoil and conflict in this region were sown in the debris of this collapsed empire, and all in the short span between 1914 and 1922. Another consequence of this carving up of geography into nations has gone relatively unrecognized. It was here that the method for a future carving up of India was devised, a precedent established. India, too, did not recognize the deep import of this collapse, not at the time, and perhaps not fully even now. Developments of any consequence in the Middle East will affect India, always and inevitably.

The political geography of our region underwent another radical change when the British Empire dissolved, and yet again when the Soviet Union

---

7. As quoted by David Fromkin in *"A Peace to End All Peace": The Fall of the Ottoman Empire and the Creation of the Modern Middle East* (New York: Avon Books, 1990), p. 5.

disintegrated. Geography, which so directly influences a nation's security, is also a determinant of foreign policy. When the British departed India, they left a vivisected land, a divided people, and a fractured national psyche. Out of the Soviet Union's collapse were reborn the Islamic republics of Central Asia, leading to a renewed Islamic assertiveness, principally in the South Caucasus. But these developments all had consequences for India, too; after all, had not our history been altered by the arrival many centuries ago of a visitor from Samarkand?[8]

The most immediate and significant consequence for us was the turmoil in Afghanistan; the Soviet invasion of that country; the reentry of the West and its covert forces into our region which they surmised, then had to follow, as an inevitability—it is all very telling that these foreign armies arrived on India's doorstep within three decades of Independence! How could all of this not have consequences? Circumstances, expediency, and the total primacy of American objectives then gave rise to a malevolent energy, which radiated outward, bringing disorder, extremism, terrorism, and decades of conflict. That was the Taliban, who now have resurfaced, and in Pakistan and Afghanistan, the very same region that they were driven out of in 2001. To use a formulation that has been attributed to an Australian diplomat, America must recognize that its power is omnipotent, but it must not behave as if it is. Or behave as if it is not powerful enough and abandon its responsibilities, even for events that are its own direct contribution to the world.

An arc of instability now lies around India. It stretches across Pakistan, Afghanistan, Iran, Iraq, and the Central Asian countries to a post-Sharon, post–Abu Mazem Israel and Palestine, where—with Fatah in decline, Hamas ascendant—there remains no road, no map, and no visible peace. Lebanon, in turn, following Rafik Hariri's assassination, the withdrawal of Syrian forces, and the ascendance of Hezbollah, and with the continuing presence of Palestinians, is the other slow-burning fuse. This is India's larger neighborhood in the north and the west. What happens here or, for example, in Sri Lanka or Southeast Asia directly influences the stability of our region. Currently, the principal forces that influence the situation in

---

8. That "visitor" was Zahiruddin Muhammad Babur, who in 1526 founded the Mughal Empire, one of the most important empires in Indian history. A scion of the dynasty that had reigned undisputed throughout eastern Iran and Central Asia since the time of Amir Temür (1336–1405), Babur inherited the throne in Samarkand at the age of twelve, but was later driven out of his homeland. He worked his way south through what is now Uzbekistan and Tajikistan, then crossed the mountains into Afghanistan, where he established a kingdom in Kabul. He later turned his attention to the Indian subcontinent, eventually capturing most of northern India.

our neighborhood are all extraregional. Imperialism of the colonial variety is gone, but its successor is alive and well, whether through the United States' presence in Pakistan, NATO in Afghanistan, or American entanglements in Iraq, Palestine, Lebanon, and now Iran. This is the new reality, and India does not, so far, influence it in any fashion. Yet what these forces do, or fail to do, creates more direct consequences for India than for any other country in the region. This is the great challenge to our statecraft and to our foreign policy—as indeed is the challenge of failing states in our neighborhood.

Iran, the home of an ancient civilization, has suffered ceaselessly since about the end of the First World War, caught between two jaws of a pincer: near-continuous Islamic revolutionary turmoil with the resultant misgovernance, and constant, unnatural external interest and interference in the country's affairs, born of an insatiable greed for control over its petroleum resources. Iran exemplifies the multiple failures of U.S. foreign policy (read also the West), and for each of those failures, our entire region pays the price. With the aim of curbing Iran, the U.S. at first built up Iraq and Saddam, then abruptly reversed course and sent Iraq spiraling downward into a vortex of sectarian violence, killings, and disorder. The direct beneficiary here is Iran, the very opposite of what the U.S. intended. Whether it is Hamas in Palestine or Hezbollah in Lebanon, it is Iran's larger interests that are being served and its influence enhanced. Even though the International Atomic Energy Agency and the U.S. had evidence before 1991 of violations of the NPT by members of the P-5, Pakistan, and A. Q. Khan, the greatest power on earth was content to sit silently by. Now, because of its role in causing regional destabilization, Iran has been added to the list. Were military action to follow someday in Iran, the consequences would be incalculably damaging. India's interests would be directly affected, the more so if we continue to treat confusion as policy. If India chooses to become an adjunct to U.S. national interests instead of committing to its own strategic autonomy, it will surely lose much of what it gained in May 1998.

In the sense in which President Putin expressed the thought, the breakup of the USSR has been a true diplomatic and strategic disaster, and not just for Russia, but globally as well. It has unsettled the entire region, creating a vacuum into which extraregional forces have scrambled. The vast expanse of Central Asia has historically been India's hinterland. This is a geopolitical reality, and its imperatives remain; the lessons of history are a constant reminder of the region's inseparable linkages with India. Notwithstanding the consequences of the Soviet collapse, India and Russia should maintain a relationship. It will obviously be an altered relationship, reformed and, where necessary, reformulated to meet the challenge of this altered reality, but it is of great significance to both countries. As Russia emerges from the trauma of the collapse of the USSR, as it shakes free and stretches itself—touching as it does three oceans, and with a spread of two continents—so India must also work to strengthen this traditional relationship, but in the idiom of today, and with today's priorities—not in continuance of the unidirectional dependency of yesteryear. Russia is reordering itself internally, and it will reorder itself externally, too. We need to factor this into our assessments and monitor its development closely.

For India, the defining year of 1998 also signaled the true end of the twentieth century, that departed age of colonies. In 2001, President Clinton, who had earlier derided India, now offered it the needed "bridge" to cross into the twenty-first century. In reality, this was a bridge to the entire West, to all that had earlier been denied to India through the entire half-century of Independence. India is now on the other side of that bridge, having crossed from one century to the other, to a different era of international equations. It is bound to have an altered role and status in international affairs. Chou Enlai once shared a Chinese proverb with Kissinger: "Do not burn the bridge that you have crossed." India also must heed that advice; in fact, we must build many more such bridges to the future, to the West and the East, to this entire world, so new and challenging.

Proliferation of a Problem

What the world faces in the realm of nonproliferation today is to a large extent the result of the actions and inactions of the United States and other members of the P-5. Now that Iraq has been pulled into the maelstrom of disorder, is it Iran's turn, under President Mahmoud Ahmedinejad, to be similarly arraigned? This raises a number of fundamental questions. Iran is a signatory to the NPT, so it has been clearly established that its nuclear program was not unknown to the International Atomic Energy Agency, to the United States, or to Russia, China, France, and the United Kingdom. It is also well known that since about November 2003, perhaps even earlier, Iran has been set on a course to develop enriched uranium—a program that had actually been going on covertly for eighteen years. However, 2005 was the critical year. That November, IAEA inspectors explicitly stated that they had found documents in Iran, dating to around 1987, that pertained to castings and machining uranium metal into hemispherical forms, a design that is used for nuclear weapons. It was also evident then that Pakistan, North Korea, and also Russia and China had contributed in some way to Iran's nuclear program, some more significantly than others. If action of some kind is now to be taken against Iran, how can the other defaulting states be exonerated—and only because they are on friendly terms with the United States? And why are the defaults of the U.S. regarded as non-events? It is in this context that we ask: "Where, therefore, is nonproliferation now headed?" Is it to be in accord only with the wishes or the will of America? That is exactly what was happening in the CTBT era. This is why India must stand apart a bit; we must stop to reflect, to engage in some deep introspection about where this debate is going. Admittedly, the entire global nuclear order is in a state of flux. But even in that state of flux, where does India stand? That is the principal nonproliferation question for us to address.

Strobe and I, as commissioned by our respective governments, had set out to find the way to that "village" of good relations between our two countries; and after that, we were to find the way to nonproliferation. This order of priorities was mine; for Strobe, nonproliferation came first. Along the way, I found that several signposts—arms control, nonproliferation, WMD—were already in place. I was disconcerted by this changing prioritization, not so much in our dialogue, which remained consistent in its purpose, as in the world's later priorities. If the entire global nuclear order is placed in a state of flux, how will we chart that final path? Is this search—a vital and very worthwhile search to arrive at a world without any WMD—nothing more than a chimera? Or has this issue been deliberately downgraded? If the answer to the latter question is yes, then by implication, the potential danger of a nexus between terrorism and WMD (nuclear, biological, or chemical) is also downgraded, and that by itself is suicidal policy. It is for such reasons that these often changing priorities, this absence of fixed objectives, render our task so much more complex and difficult. The U.S. policy that dominated until recently—"preemption," "prevention," and "regime change"—no longer holds good. Or does it? Is it now nonproliferation again, but by focusing on fissile material control, through an enforced shutdown of nuclear plants, a denial of the means to produce fissionable material? This is an altered signpost; it is workable, but all must then accept the direction, and go along together. There cannot be two routes—one for the "haves" and another for the "have-nots."

The United States and Russia today have a combined nuclear stockpile ranging from 1,700 to 2,200 "operationally deployed strategic warheads."

These are unlikely to ever be used in war, but their very nomenclature and potential pose many challenges, principally to the security of the existing material. For those countries that have continued technologically to advance their weaponry, instead of going down the route of controlling tests, the current alternative is control of the production of fissile material. This, however, raises a question: If production is controlled, as it should be, then why not de-alert the existing stockpile, too? Why not go in for a major "stock reduction," as the United States and the Soviet Union once did when they signed the Strategic Arms Reduction Treaty? What about sharing civilian use of nuclear energy? There is also a need for the next generation of verification and enforcement protocols, for all WMD, biological, chemical, and, of course, nuclear.

Finally, there cannot be meaningful arms control unless the vast proliferation of small arms is addressed at the same time. This is a totally neglected area, even though small arms are the weapons of choice for today's terrorists, and terrorism is so often a malignancy of the psyche. Why, then, multiply our difficulties by arming malignant minds?

The Postmodern Scourge

Terrorism will continue to challenge India, although its idiom and identity have altered since 9/11, and will change again. Nevertheless, it is a problem that we must face; it will not easily leave us alone, and we cannot run away from it. The awesome impact of violence—not feigned or cinematic but real, projected live, in front of so many eyes, with sickening frequency—is such that it deadens our sensibilities. At the same time, it reminds us of this persistent, obstinate disease. The power of television as a means of communication most tellingly brings home to our citizens a sense of their personal and collective vulnerability, and also outrage and anger. Every act of terrorism is a reminder, as well as a visually transferred trauma; with each event, terrorist violence demonstrates its destructive power. Terrorism in India—as an aspect of our current history, now virtually an ideology, a new tool of coercion in the conduct of internal and international relations—has redefined both intrastate and interstate dynamics. There are issues here that we have neither sufficiently grasped nor addressed. Whatever we have done has been ad hoc. That is a sure recipe for ultimate failure, because terrorism has dramatically redefined patience, persistence, violence, conflict, killing, even death; and all these redefinitions are topped by a rejection of all restraints on means. No Geneva Conventions, no Red Cross or Red

Crescent, no social restraints, no inhibitions about targeting the innocent, now exist. On the contrary, terrorists spread terror by focusing their attacks on the innocent.

India has known war, peace, and truce; India has lived with clandestine war, proxy war, state-sponsored terrorism, and cross-border terrorism. We have long known how terrorism redefines war itself; it has no concept of truce, and it has an altogether different concept of what constitutes peace. All the earlier causes of mankind's conflicts remain—territorial/boundary disputes; ideological disputes such as the Cold War; conquests or colonialism—which often employed retribution as a justifiable means for initiating violent conflict. But they are now relegated in hierarchy, for terrorism accepts no one standard; it redefines political geography, knowing no boundary; it is an ideology in itself; it conquers and colonizes the mind through terror. It has thus redrawn the contours of geopolitics. The Westphalian system and the concept of national sovereignty have been made obsolete, ironically, by the neoconservatives and the terrorists alike.[9] An act of terror is, of course, not unique to the world; assassination is as old as recorded history. What is qualitatively different is the new environment in which terrorism is advocated, not just as an acceptable ideology, but often as the only ideology. The primary victim of terrorism is civil society, the citizens' sense of order and certainties; fear of the random is replacing the existing sense of order within societies. Thus, at the same time that peace has become a casualty of terrorism, democracy is being rendered as one of the "walking wounded." Individual liberty and free thought follow close behind, again because terrorism converts the strengths of freedom and democracy into major weaknesses. Terrorism exploits technology first, then communications, and it employs the resultant exposure using the "oxygen of publicity," as Margaret Thatcher once so aptly put it. Thus terrorism is effective only as a weapon of aggression, for it works only through intimidation, and intimidation works when it is employed against societies that have a free and open media, an ingrained and nonnegotiable right to freedom of expression. Second, terrorism is still able to exploit the confidentiality of our modern financial and banking systems. Third, the spread of terrorism is facilitated by the free movement of capital and, to a large extent, of persons within and between countries. These characteristics of freedom, which are vulnerable to terrorist assault, are the very building blocks of

---

9. The Peace of Westphalia refers to the series of treaties that ended the Thirty Years' War. It marked the beginning of the modern system of nation-states (or "Westphalian states").

a democratic society. It is ironic that what are considered to be the most cherished strengths of democracy are exploited as its weakest tactical links in the face of terrorism.

Our existing concepts and applications of power—both "hard," as in compelling, and "soft," as in persuasive—are no longer as relevant because terrorism questions both. Indeed, it questions all established hierarchies of power. It rejects the traditional norms of international order, for in its ideological terminology, there is no "balance of power," no "spheres of influence," nor even a "coalition of forces." Its aim is to establish the hegemony of terror. Obviously, therefore, it rejects all established boundaries, treaties, limitations, and norms—geographic or moral. Despite these anarchic attributes, terrorism is employed by some as an instrument of state policy. The ultimate perils of adopting this method are, at least in the early stages, discounted on the anvil of convenience, because this weapon of terrorism is a low-cost option, even if only in the short term.

While an individual can declare war on a nation, I have often questioned how a nation can declare war on an individual, for the objective reality is that terrorist organizations are like cellular structures, nothing like the beehives of the similarly motivated, which are dependent on one great "Queen Bee." Terrorism is much more akin to a tissue, a "system," a "qaeda," if you prefer; each cell—the unit of which is, in a sense, self-contained—can reproduce itself in identical forms. As it feeds on anarchy, it could theoretically exist for some period of time without a leader. To the extent that we look only for terrorist figureheads, we limit our understanding, and therefore our capability to confront this different challenge. The central task is to deny terrorism soil in which it can find root, and thereafter to deprive it of the kinds of nutrients and protective mechanisms that enable it to thrive. We are not dealing with a rational situation in which the risk of instability, arising from the existing order being upset, deters the adversary. That is terrorism's principal purpose—to upset the existing. An act of terror is not a negotiating instrument; it is a statement, a declaration made through an assault. After all, a terrorist, or a terrorist impulse, does not interpret politics in the same terms that democracies do; it aspires to dominate the existing political spectrum by coercion, by any means possible, and thus to redefine politics, too. Terror is both the means and an end. No discord or dichotomy exists here. To this, another aspect has to be added: small, unrepresentative groups acquire disproportionate power. Yet, precisely because they remain small, their power of destruction is far less responsive to traditional methods. That is also why, perversely, acts of terror so often take on the illusion of being the legitimate weapons of the "have-nots." All of this, when coupled with that "oxygen of publicity," gives terrorism and terrorists a degree of survivability. Unless the very roots, the system, the very "qaeda" of it is uprooted from the soil in which it was first permitted to grow, we will only tickle the snake, not crush it.

Torn between hegemonism and isolationism, since September 11 the United States has had its plank of isolationism snatched away, perhaps irretrievably. The very nature of terrorism makes coordination and interdependence between states vital. How else can the anarchic cry of global terror be confronted effectively? Thus the global change witnessed since 9/11 is profound and significant. Our soundest strategy consists of perseverance, of patience, of resolve and will, of reinvigorating the moral culture of the free world, and of being clear about the true nature of this scourge that the civilized world faces. Above all, the vital imperative of remaining "civilized" is to avoid becoming "terrorists" ourselves in order to fight terrorism. Our fight against the terrorists must not lead us to clone their methods: unseeing, uncaring, and totally unmindful of our civilizational and human norms.

"Defending India": Threats and Perceptions

If we are to defend India, we must start with an understanding of the debilitating consequences that were caused when our country was disarmed after 1857.[10] That disarming was an act of retribution, of revenge against all Indian males in what was then British India. It was not just the physical action of stripping Indian males of their weapons; it was a psychological wounding, a moral crippling of the county, and for the first time in memory. Until a consolidation of British power in India in 1858, all Indian males carried arms; it was de rigueur, for personal weapons were both a male adornment and a physical and psychological support. The *Ain-i-Akbari* speaks of four and a half million armed men available for military service in North India in the sixteenth century, and doubtless a similar number south of the Vindhyas, considering that the Vijayanagar Empire could field up to one million soldiers at a time.[11] When Guru Govind

---

10. In *Defending India* (Houndmills and New Delhi: Macmillan, 1999; New York: St. Martin's Press, 1999), I have attempted to comprehensively analyze the management of the security challenges faced by the country during its years of Independence.

11. The *Ain-i-Akbari* is a detailed treatise on the reign, administration, and times of the Mughal emperor Akbar (1556–1605), written by his learned courtier Abul Fazl. The Vindhya Range is a chain of hills that has historically divided the subcontinent into North India and South India. The Vijayanagar Empire was a large and powerful empire that dominated South India between the fourteenth and the seventeenth centuries.

Singh enjoined all Sikhs to carry a kirpan as a symbol of power and courage, he was reflecting the prevalent societal norm of his times. He urged the faithful to adhere to this norm, as an essential, and decreed that the kirpan was a symbol of faith. His aim was to psychologically arm the country, to enable the ordinary tillers of the land to stand strong, to arm themselves and stand up proudly against oppression. His was a fight against Islamic oppression, but the principle was the same. At a more personal level, long after I had resigned my commission and become an MP, whenever I bade my mother farewell to return to Delhi, she would unfailingly ask, "Are you carrying your shastra [personal weapon]?" (In the Army, incidentally, I never carried a personal weapon, not even during military operations; but that was my own eccentricity.) This query was not born of any worry; it was an assertion of the self-confidence and pride expressed through the carrying of personal arms. In what is today Uttar Pradesh, Bihar, Rajasthan, and Madhya Pradesh, the entire rural population was armed at the time; thus a substantial labor market existed, because of which there was no dearth of employment opportunities for would-be soldiers ("umeedvar" or "hopefuls," as they were called until recently). These recruits came from all strata of Indian society; caste was totally irrelevant, as it had always been, for there was no discrimination of any kind in the recruitment and treatment of soldiers. Today's examples of Maratha Light Infantry or Sikh Light Infantry are much later manifestations; indeed, this caste factor is a much more recent means of separating, this restricting of mobility. It is a historical fact that from the fourteenth to the eighteenth century, the status of "Rajput" was open and accessible to all soldiers; also, a "Hindu soldier" had multiple identities—for example, one in the service, another in transit, and a third in the village. Thus so dramatic a development as the disarming of a whole people, who for centuries had been used to carrying and wielding weapons, could not but have major consequences. The whole of British India, which would include most of today's Pakistan and Bangladesh, had been disarmed, but not that part of India which was *not* British, and did *not* fall into the category of the colonized. We had all learned from childhood how to wield weapons, how to carry them, and we continued to do so well into the 1960s, until arms licensing came to our parts, too.

The other great disarming was, sadly and totally unintentionally (it was in fact the very obverse of what he desired), carried out by Mahatma Gandhi, through his preaching a kind of pacifism and nonviolence as crucial to India's freedom struggle. This was converted into a tenet of personal conduct. Adherents of it were the volunteers, who willingly accepted a psychological disarming (along with the physical). As it happened, this attitude harmonized with the fundamentals of certain faiths, thus adding yet another element to a further decline in India's martial ethos, military expertise, and logic. To this, post-1947, was added a militarily illiterate and untrusting civilian control of the armed forces. As a result of the combined consequence of these two great disarmings, the whole psyche and approach to the defense of India was overturned. This was, of course, over and above the fact that as a nation, a civilization, we lack a sense of territory. Consequently, this responsibility of preserving Indian space and territory as inviolate suffered.

The point that I make has a direct link with India's strategic culture. It is a common error to assume that strategic thought is principally applied only in the realm of the military; the culture of strategy is not born in that crucible. It is a mix of many influences: civilization, culture, evolution, and the functioning of a civil society. It is a by-product of the political culture of a nation and its people; an extension of the functioning of a viable state, its understanding of and subscription to the concept of power—both the nature of that power and its application, and its limitations. Besides, power is not just military, but also diplomatic and economic, coercive or persuasive, of ideas and of thought, and also of example. And in all these ways, the power of a state can be used. But first, there has to be an understanding on the part of the political-military leadership of this "state power." That is where history and racial memory influence strategic thought and strategic culture, as does a sense of geography—the latter much more significantly, for it gives rise to a sense of territory.

When, therefore, we speak of "defending India," is it only a territorial protection of our geographically delineated borders—or is there a much larger and more holistic concern about the security of the nation, the state, its institutions? The Indian nation cannot be conquered. The Indian state, however, can be rendered a casualty, and not by military means alone. The defense of India thus involves a much wider canvas.

Let us move to specifics. As far as military threats are concerned, most of our threat assessment is based on the use of conventional weapons, with upgraded technologies, though not always in step with global advances. We structure our threat assessment on the premise of the "threat of use." But this very notion has been transformed. Threats could also arise from non-state actors, with the support or prompting of adversarial states. These threats could involve "conventional weapons" or WMD-related technologies or that threat to which there is no real answer: suicide. What, then, do we do? We must ask these questions of ourselves, for they are the security conundrums of today. Economic threats are relatively more subtle—attacks on internal energy resources, or on specific areas of the national economy, in consequence of not being able to meet the challenge of globalization or of the World Trade Organization. Unthinking extravagance in the use of global petroleum resources during the past eighty years or so, with an unbelievable "energy returned on energy invested" ratio of 30:1, has caused many irreparable wrongs. For one thing, oil as an energy source became an exploitative Western monopoly, and consequently a factor for conflict. Without doubt, this energy source gave great impetus to the industrial revolution, but it also provided the gasoline, oil, and lubricants for two world wars and all the other wars, too. It is this resource that has caused pollution and global warming, with some asserting that about 30 percent of our natural environment has been destroyed in this way alone. It has contributed to an enhancement of trade, and hence to globalization, but also to a simultaneous decline in our moral and spiritual values. The era of cheap oil is beginning to draw to a close. From here on out, we will witness a continuous and irreversible decline in the production of oil, but simultaneously a global increase in the demand for it, and thus inevitably an ascending curve in the cost of energy.

The barons of financial markets now talk of "super price spikes." What does this ominous-sounding "Americanese" mean? In brief, it means that we could well see spectacular leaps in the price per barrel of crude oil, on which, most tellingly, our existing global food security is dependent. As the supply of oil diminishes, and the need for food increases, and populations grow, with the capacity to obtain the needed energy input on the decline, new trouble spots will arise. Besides, the West will not always wield the key to the resources of West Asia and the Middle East, which is why we could well be in for a very rough ride in the decades ahead with regard to both global society and food security. It is also why our principal concerns today go beyond terrorism to include energy, water, and food. To this will now be added the consequences of human displacements, of unchecked (uncontrolled) migrations that further strain our energy, water, and food resources. The latter may occur in the area of agriculture—affecting conventional notions of food security—or in manufacturing. We could roam farther afield and address ourselves to challenges posed on our right to free movement of capital. There could be threats to the national economy that arise from damage done to a neighbor's environment, unintended or perhaps deliberately caused as an act of aggression. For example, what would happen if the great river systems of India were blocked or affected by water pollution or an engineered climate change? I have long held that the entire Himalayan mountain range complex is as climatologically vital as the rainforests of the Amazon. In their own fashion, these two—the Amazon forests and the Himalayas—are contributors to global weather patterns. If you radically alter the Amazon rainforest, its spread or its density, the consequences of that catastrophe will extend beyond South America to affect the world. Similarly, the ecology of the Himalayan range is also of vital importance, not just to India but to the entire world. Thus this is a national security issue, as, for that matter, is the threat posed to our economy and integrity and social homogeneity and public and electoral honesty by the unchecked movement of people across international borders.

Next, there are a whole variety of internal threats: ideological, religious, fundamentalist, political, or social, based on rising unemployment, or on real or imagined wrongs, as, for example, the Maoist strain of extremism that runs through the length of India like a troubled vein. That is, again, why any consideration of national security must incorporate the total range of national threats; all those structures, organizations, and agencies whose task is to collect, collate, and analyze threats must act to prevent, and where necessary minimize the impact of, any threat. The process by which these entities act—always in concert and in service of national requirements duly prioritized by the political leadership—becomes our tool against such threats. This is only the briefest of brief sketches of our responsibilities. "Defending India" is the totality of all this.

"The Rest Leave to the Gods" (Cicero)

I must stop here, though it is as difficult to decide where to end this narrative as it was to determine where and how to begin. Time stretches ahead, beyond human vision, its blind corners rendering our future "eyeless." The road ahead cannot all be predetermined; that in any event is largely beyond the ken of human will or ingenuity, and it is also why beyond a certain point, "a time to keep silence" arrives.[12]

That sunlit world of Jasol and Khuri, where in my childhood we still occasionally lit fires by coaxing sparks from a flint and stone, is now not just a remote and faraway memory; that world itself has gone. But without that beginning, there could not have arrived this "today," for this day

---

12. Patrick Leigh Fermor, *A Time to Keep Silence* (London: Queen Anne Press, 1953).

is not a consequence of any unstoppable calculus of time alone, not just an arithmetic of dates adding up to the present. This "today" of ours defines our world. In that seemingly faraway time of the "sunlit world," we were firmly on earth, fixed to the globe; today we reach out, yearning to hear the echoes of the primordial sound of time itself, of that very first act of creation about which we ask: What was there then, before that moment of creation? Was it shunya, that depthless silence of nothingness when even time had not arrived? So moving that in this inquiry, in our quests of today, I find an unaltering sameness with humankind's perennial quests: From where have I come? To where am I headed? What energy is behind it all? Or is this all merely a random play of events? Is this just another "Leela" or "Maya"?[13] Occasionally then I reread St Augustine's haunting lament and take solace: "My Lord! I do not even know what I do not know"—and that about sums it all up, does it not?

---

13. In Vedic philosophy, "Leela" or "Maya" connotes the illusionary stage of worldly existence.

Appendix 1.

Text of the United States Administration Statement Giving Details of the Sanctions on June 18, 1998

The United States imposed sanctions on India and Pakistan as a result of their nuclear tests in May. In imposing these sanctions we seek:

- to send a strong message to would-be nuclear testers;
- to have maximum influence on Indian and Pakistani behavior;
- to target the governments, rather than the people; and,
- to minimize the damage to other U.S. interests.

Our goals are that India and Pakistan:

- halt further nuclear testing;
- sign the Comprehensive Test Ban Treaty (CTBT) immediately and without conditions;
- not deploy or test missiles or nuclear weapons;
- cut off fissile material production for nuclear weapons;
- cooperate in Fissile Material Cut-off Treaty (FMCT) negotiations in Geneva;
- maintain and formalize restraints on sharing sensitive goods and technologies with other countries; and
- reduce bilateral tensions, including Kashmir.

Accordingly, the United States:

- Terminated or suspended foreign assistance under the Foreign Assistance Act, with exceptions provided by law (e.g., humanitarian assistance, food, or other agricultural commodities).
  - —$21 million in economic development assistance and housing guarantee authority for India terminated.
  - —$6 million greenhouse gas program in India suspended.
  - —Trade Development Agency will not consider new projects.
  - —Most assistance to Pakistan had already been prohibited.
- Terminated foreign military sales under the Arms Export Control Act, and revoked licenses for the commercial sale of any item on the U.S. munitions list.

—Suspended delivery of previously approved defense articles and services to India.

- Halted any new commitments of USG credits and credit guarantees by USG equities (EXIM, OPIC, CCC).

  —The administration will permit legislation to permit CCC credits for food and agricultural commodities.

  —OPIC had only recently reopened in Pakistan; however, India was one of OPIC's top five countries receiving an average of $300 million annually in OPIC support.

  —EXIM had only recently reopened in Pakistan with one expression of interest pending for $1.1 million; $500 million in pending financing in India will not go forward.

- Gained G-8 support to postpone consideration of non-basic human needs loans to India and Pakistan by the International Financial Institution (IFI) to bolster the effect of the Glenn amendment requirement that the U.S. oppose non-BHN IFI loans.

  —$1.71 billion in IFI lending postponed for India.

  —Although no IFI loans for Pakistan have been presented for board consideration, $25 million in IMF assistance has been postponed for failure to meet economic benchmarks.

- Will issue executive orders to prohibit U.S. banks from extending loans or credits to Governments of India and Pakistan.

- Will deny export of all dual use items controlled for nuclear or missile reasons. Will presume denial for all other dual use exports to entities involved in nuclear or missile programs.

  —will toughen existing controls for government military entities.

  —will continue denial of nuclear exports licensed by NRC or authorized by DOE; and

  —will continue to favorably consider on a case-by-case basis other transactions which do not support nuclear, missile, or inappropriate military activities.

Appendix 2.

Full Text of Sardar Vallabhbhai Patel's Letter to Jawaharlal Nehru on November 7, 1950

My dear Jawaharlal,

Ever since my return from Ahmedabad and after the cabinet meeting the same day, which I had to attend at practically 15 minutes' notice and for which I regret I was not able to read all the papers, I have been anxiously thinking over the problem of Tibet and I thought I should share with you what is passing through my mind.

I have carefully gone through the correspondence between the External Affairs Ministry and our ambassador in Peking and through him the Chinese government. I have tried to peruse this correspondence as favourably to our ambassador and the Chinese government as possible, but I regret to say that neither of them comes out well as a result of this study. The Chinese government has tried to delude us by professions of peaceful intention. My own feeling is that at a crucial period they managed to instill into our ambassador a false sense of confidence in their so-called desire to settle the Tibetan problem by peaceful means. There can be no doubt that during the period covered by this correspondence the Chinese must have been concentrating for an onslaught on Tibet. The final action of the Chinese, in my judgement, is little short of perfidy. The tragedy of it is that the Tibetans put faith in us; they chose to be guided by us; and we have been unable to get them out of the meshes of Chinese diplomacy or Chinese malevolence. From the latest position, it appears that we shall not be able to rescue the Dalai Lama. Our ambassador has been at great pains to find an explanation or justification for Chinese policy and actions.

As the External Affairs Ministry remarked in one of their telegrams, there was a lack of firmness and unnecessary apology in one or two representations that he made to the Chinese government on our behalf. It is impossible to imagine any sensible person believing in the so-called threat to China from Anglo-American machinations in Tibet. Therefore, if the Chinese put faith in this, they must have distrusted us so completely as to have taken us as tools or stooges of Anglo-American diplomacy or strategy. This feeling, if genuinely entertained by the Chinese in spite of your direct approaches to them, indicates that even though we regard ourselves as the friends of China, the Chinese do not regard us as their friends. With the communist mentality of 'whoever is not with them being against them', this is a significant pointer of which we have to take due note. During the last several months, outside the Russian camp, we have practically been alone in championing the cause of Chinese entry into UN and in securing from the Americans assurances on the question of Formosa. We have done everything we could to assuage Chinese feelings, to allay its apprehensions and to defend its legitimate claims in our discussions and correspondence with America and Britain and in the UN. In spite of this, China is not convinced about our disinterestedness; it continues to regard us with suspicion and the whole psychology is one, at least outwardly, of scepticism perhaps mixed with a little hostility. I doubt if we can go any further than we have done already to convince China of our good intentions, friendliness and goodwill. In Peking we have an ambassador who is eminently suitable for putting across the friendly point of view. Even he seems to have failed to convert the Chinese. Their last telegram to us is an act of gross discourtesy not only in the summary way it disposes of our protest against the entry of Chinese forces into Tibet but also in the wild insinuation that our attitude is determined by foreign influences. It looks as though it is not a friend speaking in that language but a potential enemy.

In the background of this, we have to consider what new situation now faces us as a result of the disappearance of Tibet, as we knew it, and the expansion of China almost up to our gates. Throughout history we have seldom been worried about our north-east frontier. The Himalayas have been regarded as an impenetrable barrier against any threat from the north. We had a friendly Tibet which gave us no trouble. The Chinese were divided. They had their own domestic problems and never bothered us about frontiers. In 1914, we entered into a convention with Tibet which was not endorsed by the Chinese. We seem to have regarded Tibetan autonomy as extending to independent treaty relationship. Presumably, all that we required was Chinese counter-signature. The Chinese interpretation of suzerainty seems to be different. We can, therefore, safely assume that very soon they will disown all the stipulations which Tibet has entered into with us in the past. That throws into the melting pot all frontier and commercial settlements with Tibet on which we have been functioning and acting during the last half a century. China is no longer divided. It is united and strong. All along the Himalayas, in the north and north-east, we have on our side of the frontier a population ethnologically and culturally not different from Tibetans and Mongoloids. The undefined state of the frontier and the existence on our side of a population with its affinities to the Tibetans or Chinese have all the elements of potential trouble between China and ourselves. Recent and bitter history also tells us that communism is no shield against imperialism and that the communists are as good or as bad imperialists as any other. Chinese ambitions in this respect not only cover the Himalayan slopes on our side but also include the important part of Assam. They have their ambitions in Burma also. Burma has the added difficulty that it has no McMahon Line round which to build up even the semblance of an agreement. Chinese irredentism and communist imperialism are different from the expansionism or imperialism of the western powers. The former has a cloak of ideology which makes it ten times more dangerous. In the guise of ideological expansion lie concealed racial, national or historical claims. The danger from the north and north-east, therefore, becomes both communist and imperialist. While our western and north-western threat to security is still as prominent as before, a new threat has developed from the north and north-east. Thus, for the first time, after centuries, India's defence has to concentrate itself on two fronts simultaneously. Our defence measures have so far been based on the calculations of superiority over Pakistan. In our calculations we shall now have to reckon with communist China in the north and in the north-east, a communist China which has definite ambitions and aims and which does not, in any way, seem friendly disposed towards us.

Let us also consider the political conditions on this potentially troublesome frontier. Our northern and north-eastern approaches consist of Nepal, Bhutan, Sikkim, Darjeeling and the tribal areas in Assam. From the point of view of communication, there are weak spots. Continuous defensive lines do not exist. There is almost an unlimited scope for infiltration. Police protection is limited to a very small number of passes. There, too, our outposts do not seem to be fully manned. The contact of these areas with us is by no means close and intimate. The people inhabiting these portions have no established loyalty or devotion to India. Even Darjeeling and Kalimpong areas are not free from pro-Mongoloid prejudices. During the last three years, we have not been able to make any appreciable approaches to the Nagas and other hill tribes in Assam. European missionaries and other visitors had been in touch with them, but their influence was in no way friendly to India or Indians. In Sikkim, there was political ferment some time ago. It is quite possible that discontent is smouldering there. Bhutan is comparatively quiet, but its affinity with Tibetans would be a handicap. Nepal has a weak oligarchic regime based almost entirely on force: it is in conflict with a turbulent element of the population as well as with enlightened ideas of the modern age. In these circumstances, to make people alive to the new danger or to make them defensively strong is a very difficult task indeed and that difficulty can be got over only by enlightened firmness, strength and a clear line of policy. I am sure the Chinese and their source of inspiration, Soviet Union, would not miss any opportunity of exploiting these weak spots, partly in support of their ideology and partly in support of their ambitions. In my judgement the situation is one which we cannot afford either to be complacent or to be vacillating. We must have a clear idea of what we wish to achieve and also of the methods by which we should achieve it. Any faltering or lack of decisiveness in formulating our objectives or in pursuing our policies to attain those objectives is bound to weaken us and increase the threats which are so evident.

Side by side with these external dangers, we shall now have to face serious internal problems as well. I have already asked Iengar to send to the External Affairs Ministry a copy of the Intelligence Bureau's appreciation of these matters. Hitherto, the Communist Party of India has found some difficulty in contacting communists abroad, or in getting supplies of arms, literature, etc., from them. They had to contend with the difficult Burmese and Pakistan frontiers on the east or with the long seaboard. They shall now have a comparatively easy means of access to Chinese communists and through them to other foreign communists. Infiltration of spies, fifth columnists and communists would now be easier. Instead of having to deal with isolated communist pockets in Telengana and Warangal we may have to deal with communist threats to our security along our northern and north-eastern frontiers, where, for supplies of arms and ammunition, they can safely depend on communist arsenals in China. The whole situation thus raises a number of problems on which we must come to an early decision so that we can, as I said earlier, formulate the objectives of our policy and decide the method by which those objectives are to be attained. It is also clear that the action will have to be fairly comprehensive, involving not only our defence strategy and state of preparations but also problem of internal security to deal with which we have not a moment to lose. We shall also have to deal with administrative and political problems in the weak spots along the frontier to which I have already referred.

It is of course, impossible to be exhaustive in setting out all these problems. I am, however, giving below some of the problems which, in my opinion, require early solution and round which we have to build our administrative or military policies and measures to implement them.

a) A military and intelligence appreciation of the Chinese threat to India both on the frontier and to internal security.

b) An examination of military position and such re-disposition of our forces as might be necessary, particularly with the idea of guarding important routes or areas which are likely to be the subject of dispute.

c) An appraisement of the strength of our forces and, if necessary, reconsideration of our retrenchment plans for the Army in the light of the new threat.

d) A long-term consideration of our defence needs. My own feeling is that, unless we assure our supplies of arms, ammunition and armour, we would be making our defence perpetually weak and we would not be able to stand up to the double threat of difficulties both from the west and north-west and north and north-east.

e) The question of China's entry into the UN. In view of the rebuff which China has given us and the method which it has followed in dealing with Tibet, I am doubtful whether we can advocate its claim any longer. There would probably be a threat in the UN virtually to outlaw China, in view of its active participation in the Korean war. We must determine our attitude on this question also.

f) The political and administrative steps which we should take to strengthen our northern and north-eastern frontier. This would include the whole of the border, i.e., Nepal, Bhutan, Sikkim, Darjeeling and the tribal territory in Assam.

g) Measures of internal security in the border areas as well as the states flanking those areas such as Uttar Pradesh, Bihar, Bengal and Assam.

h) Improvement of our communication, road, rail, air and wireless, in these areas and with the frontier outposts,

i) The future of our mission at Lhasa and the trade posts at Gyangtse and Yatung and the forces which we have in operation in Tibet to guard the trade routes.

j) The policy in regard to the McMahon Line.

These are some of the questions which occur to my mind. It is possible that a consideration of these matters may lead us into wider question of our relationship with China, Russia, America, Britain and Burma. This, however, would be of a general nature, though some might be basically very important, e.g., we might have to consider whether we should not enter into closer association with Burma in order to strengthen the latter in its dealings with China. I do not rule out the possibility that, before applying pressure on us, China might apply pressure on Burma. With Burma, the frontier is entirely undefined and the Chinese territorial claims are more substantial. In its present position, Burma might offer an easier problem to China, and therefore, might claim its first attention.

I suggest that we meet early to have a general discussion on these problems and decide on such steps as we might think to be immediately necessary and direct, quick examination of other problems with a view to taking early measures to deal with them.

Vallabhbhai Patel

Appendix 3.

Statement and Verbatim Record of Press Conference of Shri Jaswant Singh, External Affairs and Defence Minister, July 17, 2001, Agra

At the invitation of Prime Minister Shri Atal Bihari Vajpayee, the President of Pakistan H.E. General Pervez Musharraf visited India during 14–16 July, 2001.

In keeping with his abiding vision of good neighbourly relations between India and Pakistan, the Prime Minister had invited President General Pervez Musharraf to walk the high road of Peace and reconciliation. Our commitment to that noble objective, upon the attainment of which, rests the welfare of many, is not transitory. It is that commitment, which was demonstrated at Simla, in Lahore and recently during President General Pervez Musharraf's visit.

Significant Confidence Building Measures (CBMs) that were announced prior to President Musharraf's visit would be fully implemented on our part. It is our conviction that, when put in place, they will make an important contribution to our relations.

During his visit, the President of Pakistan had extensive discussions with our entire leadership. These included three rounds of one-on-one meetings with the Prime Minister and an hour-long farewell call prior to his departure yesterday night. There were also detailed discussions during delegation level talks. All these meetings were marked by cordiality and candour. They provided an invaluable opportunity to both sides to understand each other's view points, concerns and compulsions.

Our negotiations for an agreed text of a document were seriously pursued. There were long hours of discussions at official and political levels. During these negotiations India did not shy away from any issue. In keeping with the confidentiality, which is necessary for these negotiations, and the maintenance of which is essential for the future of bilateral relations themselves, it would not be proper to go into details. However, it needs asserting that during the negotiating process, India fully respected all established international norms. As a mature and responsible democracy, we negotiate to improve bilateral relations with our neighbours, not to indulge in public relations.

We are, of course, disappointed that the two sides could not arrive at an agreed text. It will not be a breach of confidentiality to clarify that this was on account of the difficulty in reconciling our basic approaches to bilateral relations. India is convinced that narrow, segmented or unifocal approaches, will simply not work. Our focus has to remain on the totality of relationship, our endeavour to build trust and confidence, and a mutually beneficial relationship even as we address and move forward on all outstanding issues, including Jammu & Kashmir: building upon the existing compacts of Simla and Lahore.

It was also made abundantly clear to the Pakistan side during the visit, that the promotion of cross-border terrorism and violence are unacceptable and must cease. Let there be no illusions on this score: India has the will and resolve to defeat all such challenges.

We will pick up the threads from the visit of the President of Pakistan. We will unceasingly endeavour to realise our vision of a relationship of peace, friendship and cooperation with Pakistan.

Glossary

auspicious Moli thread: An intertwined red and yellow thread, "Moli" is considered auspicious and is used for various rituals; it is also tied to the wrist as a bracelet for protection, good luck, etc.

Awadh or Oudh: The former name of what is now Lucknow (capital of the Indian state of Uttar Pradesh) and surrounding areas, then a prosperous kingdom; the name goes back to mythical days.

dharma: Principle of life, and so much more: duty, law, obligations, etc.

the Emergency: In 1975, Prime Minister Indira Gandhi declared a state of emergency in India, citing the threat of "internal disturbances." For a period of nineteen months, democracy was shelved, and governance was practiced outside all established norms. Thousands of opposition leaders and activists were arrested and imprisoned; democratic rights and civil liberties as provided for in the Constitution were suspended; the press was rigidly censored; and the Parliament was rendered virtually defunct.

Jasu: An affectionate diminutive of the name Jaswant.

kabbadi: A team sport popular in Nepal, Bangladesh, Sri Lanka, Japan, and Pakistan; it combines the characteristics of wrestling and rugby.

Kautilya: A minister under Chandragupta Maurya (r. 321–296 BC) who wrote the *Arthashastra,* a treatise on statecraft.

Lok Sabha: The Lower House of Parliament.

maharawal: A traditional term for a ruler in Dungarpur and Jaisalmer in Rajasthan, India.

Marwari: A language spoken in Rajasthan, as well as some parts of Gujarat and the adjoining areas in Sindh, Pakistan; closely related languages are Shekhawati, Mewari, and Mewathi.

maulana: A title used with a Muslim name to show respect, primarily to a learned scholar of Islam; sometimes also used sarcastically or jocularly.

privy purse: Annual income that the former ruling princes of the independent states of India received from the government of India in compensation for giving up their titles and joining the Union of India.

punditji: A learned man schooled in Indian scriptures.

quango: A nongovernmental organization that is financed by the government yet acts independently of it.

shunya: A unique concept in Sanatan that is very complex and extremely difficult to simplify. It means "nothingness." Related words are "anadi," which means having neither beginning nor end, and "anant," which means infinity, without an end.

tent pegging: An ancient equestrian sport that is especially popular in the Indian subcontinent. It originated with mounted soldiers charging into enemy camps at the crack of dawn, using the tips of their spears to remove the pegs that held the tents in place.

yagna or yajna: An ancient purification ceremony conducted by qualified priests in which offerings are made to a sacred fire.

Index

An authority on Indian foreign policy and national security, **Jaswant Singh** is among the most respected names in the country's public life, and in the world of diplomacy. Born in the desert districts of Rajasthan, he was commissioned in the Indian Army when barely nineteen. He served during two wars, 1962 and 1965, before resigning his commission to pursue a political career. He has served seven terms in India's Parliament and is currently the Leader of the Opposition in the Rajya Sabha, the Upper House of Parliament. He has been a visiting professor at Oxford University, an honorary professor at Warwick University, and a senior fellow at Harvard University. An ardent and lifelong bibliophile, an antiquarian, and a prolific writer, his personal library is among the most impressive in Delhi. Among his other pursuits are chess, golf, polo (he is Patron-in-Chief of the Indian Polo Association), and the promotion of Dingal, an ancient language of Rajasthan still extant, particularly in the arid regions of Marwar and his native Barmer. This is his seventh book.